LEGAL DEVELOPMENTS
IN CHINA:

MARKET ECONOMY AND LAW

Recommended Stockists

Australia
LBC Information Services Ltd
Sydney, Melbourne,
Brisbane, Perth

Canada
Carswell
Ontario

Hong Kong
Bloomsbury Books Ltd

Hong Kong Book Centre Ltd

Swindon Book Co. Ltd

Japan
Yushodo Fantas
Tokyo

Kokusai Shobo Ltd
Tokyo

Tokyo Publications
Tokyo

Malaysia/Singapore
Thomson Information (S.E. Asia)
Singapore

New Zealand
Brooker's Ltd
Wellington, Auckland

Thailand
Source One Ltd
Bangkok

UK & Europe
Sweet & Maxwell Ltd
London

USA
Carswell
Ontario, Canada

Professional Publications Services
New Jersey

Rest of World
Sweet & Maxwell Asia
Hong Kong

LEGAL DEVELOPMENTS IN CHINA:

MARKET ECONOMY AND LAW

Edited by

Professor Wang Guiguo, JSD, LL.M.
Director, Centre for Chinese and Comparative Law,
City University of Hong Kong

and

Professor Wei Zhenying, LL.B.
Dean, Department of Law, Peking University, Beijing

Published in collaboration with
Centre for Chinese and Comparative Law,
City University of Hong Kong

HONG KONG • SINGAPORE
SWEET & MAXWELL ASIA
1996

Published by
Sweet & Maxwell Asia
a division of
The Thomson Corporation (Hong Kong) Ltd
17/F Lyndhurst Tower, 1 Lyndhurst Terrace
Central, Hong Kong

First published 1996
Reprinted 1997

Affiliated Companies

AUSTRALIA
LBC Information Services
50 Waterloo Road, North Ryde,
NSW 2113

CANADA
Carswell
Corporate Plaza,
2075 Kennedy Road
Scarborough, Ontario M1T 3V4

NEW ZEALAND
Brooker's
PO Box 6343, Auckland

SINGAPORE / MALAYSIA
Thomson Information (S.E. Asia)
30 Prinsep Street, #05-02
LKN Prinsep House, Singapore 188647

UNITED KINGDOM
Sweet & Maxwell Ltd
100 Avenue Road, London NW3 3PF

Typeset by Best-set Typesetter Ltd.,
Hong Kong

Printed in China

A CIP catalogue record for this book is available from the British Library

ISBN 0 421 56890 9

All rights reserved. No part of this publication may be reproduced or
transmitted in any form or by any means, or stored in any retrieval system
of any nature without prior written permission, except for permitted fair
dealing under the Copyright, Designs and Patents Act 1988, or in
accordance with the terms of a licence issued by the Copyright Licensing
Agency in respect of photocopying and/or reprographic reproduction.
Application for permission for other use of copyright material including
permission to reproduce extracts in other published works shall be made to
the publishers. Full acknowledgment of the author, publisher and source
must be given.

© Sweet & Maxwell 1996

PREFACE

This volume is a result of the academic exchanges between the Law Faculty of the City University of Hong Kong and the Law Department of Peking University, China. The two Law Schools started the exchanges in 1991. Ever since, staff from both institutions have visited each other on a regular basis. The City University also sends a group of students to meet their counterparts from Peking University each year.

Starting in 1994, the two Law Schools decided to hold a bilateral academic conference yearly. The purpose of the conference was for staff from both Law Schools to exchange their academic achievements over the year so that a better understanding could be achieved between the people in Hong Kong and China. In order to benefit a wider group of people, each year we invite a small number of selected scholars from other institutions to participate in the conference. The conference venue alternates between Hong Kong and Beijing.

This volume includes papers delivered at the annual conference held in October 1995 in Hong Kong. These papers have been revised and selected since the conference. They cover most of the current legal issues in China and Hong Kong.

Needless to say, without the conference there might not have been this volume of the collective works of colleagues. In this regard, we wish to express our sincere gratitude to the conference organizers, Mr Wang Chenguang, Associate Head, and Dr Fu Hualing, Law Department, City University of Hong Kong and Professor Wu Zhipan, Associate Dean, Law Department, Peking University. Sweet & Maxwell participated in the organization of the conference without whose support the conference would not have been as successful. Our heartfelt thanks goes to Sweet & Maxwell, and in particular the members of the Hong Kong office, for their assistance and their far sightedness in this endeavour. Last, but certainly not least, we are most grateful to those colleagues who not only actively participated in the conference, but also allowed their works to be published in this volume.

Editors in Chief
Professor WANG Guiguo
Professor WEI Zhenying

CONTENTS

Preface   v

PART 1 — MODERNIZATION, MARKET ECONOMY AND LAW

The Developing Theory of Law and Market Economy in Contemporary China *(by Albert H.Y. Chen)*   3
    Introduction   3
    General Considerations   5
    Special Issues   9
    Conclusion   12
    Notes   15

Administrative Law and the Market Economy
(by Professor Jiang Mingan)   21
    Introduction   21
    The Nature and History of Administrative Law   22
    Administrative Law and the Market Economy   22
    Functions of Administrative Law   23
    Conclusion   26

From Mixed to Market Economy — Constitutional Experience in India *(by Professor Mahendra P. Singh)*   27
    Notes   35
    Appendix — The Constitution of India   36

vii

PART 2 — COMPANY LAW: HONG KONG AND CHINA

Proposals for a New Corporate Rescue Procedure in
Hong Kong (by Professor Edward L.G. Tyler)   51
    Corporate Failure Generally   51
    Current Position on Company Rescue   53
    Companies Ordinance (Cap 32) Section 166   55
    The Alternatives or Additions to Section 166   57
    Insolvency Law Reform in Hong Kong   57
    Characteristics of a Good Rescue Procedure   58
    The Sub-Committee's Recommendations   60
    The Carrot and the Stick   65
    Notes   68

Expanding Shareholder Control in Hong Kong
(by Philip Lawton)   70
    General Background   70
    The Enhancement of Shareholder Value   72
    Corporate Control and the Family Business   74
    Corporate Democracy and Shareholder Consent   79
    The Role of the Institutional Shareholder   80
    Ownership Concentration and Management Remuneration in
      Hong Kong   87
    The Market for Corporate Control   90
    The Case for Independent Directors   92
    Conclusion   96
    Notes   99

The Securities and Futures Commission and Securities
Regulation in Hong Kong (by Judith O'Hare)   108
    Introduction   108
    Development of a Securities Market in Hong Kong   109
    Origins of Security Regulation in the Modern Financial Market   114
    Market Reform and the Securities and Futures Commission (SFC)   117
    Current Role of the SFC and Recent Developments   121
    Conclusions   124
    Notes   126

Piercing the Company Veil and Regulation of Companies in China (*by Zhang Xianchu*)   129
  The Background and the Major Types of Abuses   129
  The Current Legal Framework against Abuses of Incorporation   131
  The Judicial Practice on Piercing Company Veil Actions   134
  The Urgency of Introducing the Doctrine into China   138
  Notes   140

Contemporary Market Economy and Mathematical Jurisprudence (*by Professor Liu Ruifu*)   144
  Mathematical Economy and the Law   144
  Characteristics of Mathematical Jurisprudence   148
  Field and Mission of Mathematical Jurisprudence   154
  Branch, Structure and Future of Mathematical Jurisprudence   166

PART 3 — BANKING AND CONTRACT

The Market Economy and Freedom of Contract — Issues Relating to the Unification of China's Contract Legislation (*by Professor Wei Zhenying*)   171
  Introduction   171
  The Development of the Principle of Freedom of Contract   172
  China's Market Economy and the Implementation of Freedom of Contract   175
  Issues Relating to Freedom and Restriction of Contract in China's Uniform Contract Law   178
  Notes   185

The Relationship between Commercial Banking Law and the Regulations of the PRC on Management of Foreign Funded Financial Institutions (*by Professor Wu Zhipan*)   186
  Origin and Development of the Legal Environment for Foreign Banks   187
  Special Characteristics of the Legal Environment for Foreign Banks   189
  Special Requirements for Foreign Financial Institutes   190

Special Licence Procedures 191
Special Scope of Business 192
Special Rules for Business Control 194
The Commercial Banking Law Applied to Foreign Banks 198
Effects of Different Legal Environments 202
Conclusion 204

A Step away from the Market? The Autonomy of Negotiable Instruments and the New Negotiable Instruments Law of the PRC

(by Professor Derek Roebuck and Wong Wai-Ip) 205
Background 205
Chinese and Common Law Ideologies 206
Planned Economies and Market Economies 207
The Need for Autonomy 209
Bills of Exchange 210
The York Airconditioning Case 211
The New Chinese Law 212
Documentary Letters of Credit 213
Conclusion 213
Notes 214

The Role of the Central Bank of China

(by Dr D.K. Srivastava and Wang Chenguang) 217
Introduction 217
The Role of the PBC in the Planned Economy 218
The Organization and Structure of the PBC 219
Formulation and Implementation of the Monetary Policy 220
Issuance of Renminbi (RMB) and Management of its Circulation 221
The Establishment of the Financial Institutions and the
    Supervision and Management of their Operation 221
The Supervision of Financial Markets 223
Reserve Funds 226
Re-discount 227
Interest Rates 228
Loans 229
Accounts for Financial Institutions and Clearing Services 230
Conclusion 231
Notes 231

Reconceptualizing China's Contract Law —
The Problem of Interpretation of Contract (*by Ling Bing*)   235
    The Relevance of the Problem   236
    The Civil Law Approach   237
    The Common Law Approach   238
    The CISG Approach   238
    The Draft Articles on Interpretation of Contract in the Uniform
      Contract Law   239
    Conclusion   241
    Notes   242

PART 4 — THE ROLE OF GOVERNMENT IN MARKET ECONOMY

A Comparative Study on the Act of State Doctrine —
With Special Reference to the Hong Kong Court of
Final Appeal (*by Professor Wang Guiguo*)   249
    Acts of State under the Common Law   251
    Acts of State under Civil Law   265
    The Chinese Position   271
    Synthesis of the Act of State Doctrine   276
    Acts of State and the Basic Law of Hong Kong   282
    Conclusion   284
    Notes   285

The Function of Legal Evasion in China's Economic
Reform — From a Socio-Legal Perspective (*by Dr Zhu Suli*)   294
    Issues   294
    A Case of Private Settlement   296
    Folk Law   296
    Reasons for Private Settlement   297
    The Role of State Law   298
    Final Analysis   299
    Notes   301

**Recent Developments in Consumer Production —
an Update** (*by Henry W.L.Chen and Stephen Foo*)   303
    Development of Consumer Movement in Hong Kong   303
    Formulation of a Set of Consumer Legislation in Hong Kong   305
    "Dealing as a Consumer'   305
    The Control of Exemption Clauses Ordinance (the "CECO')   306
    The Supply of Services(Implied Terms) Ordinance (the "SOSITO')   310
    The Unconscionable Contracts Ordinance (the "UCO')   310
    The Consumer Goods Safety Ordinance (the "CGSO')   312
    The Sale of Goods (Amendments) Ordinance 1994   313
    The Consumer Council   314
    The Consumer Legal Action Fund   315
    Pre-sale of Land in Hong Kong and China   315
    Advertisement and Sale of Properties Located in China   316
    Conclusion   317
    Notes   317

PART 5 — CORRUPTION, MARKET REFORM AND CRIMINAL JUSTICE

**Perfecting China's Legal System to Fight Crimes of
Bribery** (*by Professor Chu Huaizhi*)   325
    Definition of Concepts   325
    Factors Involved in Corruption and Bribery   326
    Developing a Legal System to Combat Bribery   328
    Notes   335

The Present and Future of Criminal Defence in China
(*by Dr Fu Hualing*)   336
    Introduction   336
    The Role of Defence Lawyers in China   337
    The Rights of Defence Lawyers   339
    The Reform   345
    Conclusion   348
    Notes   348
    References   350

**The Present Situation of Corruption in China and
Anti-corruption Countermeasures** (by Zhang Xiaoqin)   352
    The Present Situation of Corruption and Its Characteristics   352
    The Present Anti-corruption Counter-measures and Thoughts   354

PART 6 — ENVIRONMENTAL AND CONSUMER PROTECTION

Protecting Consumers' Rights to Information
(by Zhang Shouwen)   361
    Introduction   361
    The Consumer Right to Information   361
    The Importance of Protecting Consumer Rights to Information   362
    Legal Protection of the Consumer Right to Information   365
    Notes   369

**Environmental Tort and Civil Remedies — Problems in
Environmental Legislation** (by Professor Jin Ruilin)   371
    Introduction   371
    Characteristics of Environmental Tort   372
    Attribution — From Liability for Negligence to Liability Without
      Fault   373
    Continental Law   376
    The Causal Link Construction and the Shift of the Burden of
      Proof   377
    Civil Remedies in Environmental Tort   379
    Civil Remedies for Environmental Tort in China   383
    Notes   384

**Will the Balance Between Economic Development and
Environmental Protection be Tipped to the Latter? —
An Examination of the 1995 Amendments to the Law
of the PRC on Prevention and Control of Atmospheric
Pollution** (by Lin Feng)   386
    Introduction   386
    Current Status of China's Air Pollution   388
    Examination of the 1987 Air Pollution Law   389

Analysis and Comparison of the EPB Proposals with the 1995
    Amendments   393
Conclusion   402
Notes   403

**Common Law, Common Sense and the Environment in
Hong Kong** *(by Bryan Bachner)*   407
    Evolution of the Common Law in Hong Kong   408
    The Common Law and the Environment   413
    Problems with the Application of the Common Law of
        Environmental Protection   421
    Conclusion   423
    Notes   424

PART 1

MODERNIZATION, MARKET ECONOMY AND LAW

THE DEVELOPING THEORY OF LAW AND MARKET ECONOMY IN CONTEMPORARY CHINA

Albert H.Y. Chen

Reader in Law
University of Hong Kong

Albert Chen, *LL. B. University of Hong Kong, LL.M. (Harvard University), is a solicitor qualified in Hong Kong. He has taught at the University of Hong Kong since 1984 and is currently a reader in law. He has written five books and over 40 articles in English and Chinese in the areas of Hong Kong law, Chinese law and legal theory.*

Introduction

China's economic reforms[1] in the Dengist era started with the household contract responsibility production system in the country-side in the late 1970s. 1984 saw the beginnings of major economic institutional re-structuring in the urban areas, the declared objective being to develop a "planned commodity economy". The concept of the "socialist commodity economy", officially enunciated in 1988, marked the intended deepening of industrial reform, but this was held back temporarily after 1989. Determined to achieve a breakthrough in the midst of conservative opposition to his whole economic reform project, Deng Xiaoping undertook his now-famous trip to southern China in spring 1992, and boldly rehabilitated the hitherto forbidden idea of the market economy, declaring that socialism does not equal the planned economy, nor is the market economy intrinsically or necessarily capitalist. Thus the term "the socialist market economy" was born, and the new but powerful idea that the overall objective of China's economic reform in the next few decades would be the estab-lishment of a socialist market economy was quickly written into the Constitution of the Chinese Communist Party in late 1992, and into the Constitution of the People's Republic of China itself in early 1993.

The slogans "the market economy is a legal-system economy" (*fazhi jingji*)[2] or "the market economy is a rule-of-law economy" (*fazhi jingji*) have the same the *pinyin* romanization, but it should be noted that the Chinese character for *zhi* in the second expression means "rule", whereas the character for *zhi* in the previous expression means "system".[3] The slogans soon entered the daily vocabulary of officials and scholars alike.[4] It was stressed that the development of a sound legal system is a necessary condition for the success of the project of building a socialist market economy in China. Mr Qiao Shi, chairman of the Standing Committee of the National People's Congress and the most senior government leader in charge of legislative affairs, made the following points repeatedly in official speeches and press interviews since 1993:[5]

(a) The five-year period beginning from 1993 would be the crucial period for China's transition to the socialist market economy.

(b) The task would not be an easy one, as there exists no successful precedent elsewhere of a successful transition from the planned economy to the socialist market economy.

(c) The development of the socialist market economy is inseparable from "legal system construction". Law has a "guidance" function in relation to social and economic development. In particular, law is needed for the purpose of guiding, regulating, safeguarding and controlling the development of the socialist market economy. In this type of economy, law has a more significant role to play than in the centralized planned economy, which is largely managed by administrative means.

(d) During the term of office of the current Standing Committee of the 8th National People's Congress, the first-priority task that it has set for itself is to bring into existence the legislative framework required for the operation of a socialist market economy.

(e) In developing the Chinese law relating to the socialist market economy, China may boldly learn and borrow from the legislative experience of the economically advanced nations of the west, and appropriate legal provisions may even be "transplanted" therefrom, because such experience belongs to the common heritage of human civilization, and the globalization of economic activities requires Chinese law on trade and investment to be compatible with foreign and international practice.[6]

This, then, is the official view on law and the socialist market economy. The purpose of this article is to consider the views expressed by Chinese scholars since 1992 on the same issue, and to evaluate the fruits of their research on this issue. It is hoped that this will facilitate the development of a more general theory of law and the market, and at the same time contribute to our understanding of the major concerns of those involved in developing Chinese law in the rapidly changing circumstances of the late twentieth century.

General Considerations

The concept of the market economy is relatively new in China. Unlike the case in the west, where spontaneous developments towards market capitalism occurred long before a theory of the market was consciously formulated, in contemporary China the establishment of a socialist market economy has now become the declared objective of deliberate efforts on the part of the State. It is therefore necessary, before we consider the developing theory of law and the market economy, to clarify what exactly is the concept of the socialist market economy as understood by contemporary Chinese legal theorists.

Some of these thinkers rely on the works of Marx and Engels in enunciating their concept of the market economy. As the term the "commodity economy" is more often used in these classical works, some Chinese authors define the market economy in terms of the commodity economy. For example, it is said that the market economy is a "highly developed commodity economy",[7] or an "institutionalized and high-level commodity economy".[8] Several writers referred to the "law of value", which appears in Marxist writings, as one of the fundamental principles underlying the market economy.[9] One scholar understood the market in terms of two sets of relationships (as discussed in the works of Marx and Engels): (a) relationships between use value and exchange value, between commodity and money, and between buyers and sellers; and (b) relationships between producers and consumers.[10]

As regards the nature and essential characteristics of the market economy, many scholars[11] expressed the following understanding. The exchange of commodities is the core of the market phenomenon, and the market is the totality of exchange relationships. Unlike the case in the planned economy, economic decision-making in the market economy is highly decentralized. A countless number of subjects or actors enter into market transactions with one another, and market transactions are co-ordinated by price signals, the laws of supply and demand and market competition. Unlike the case in the planned economy where producers and other actors simply obey the commands of superior authority, actors in the market economy have the freedom and autonomy to make decisions for themselves,[12] and the driving force behind the system is not the obligation to obey (as in the planned economy) or considerations of moral righteousness (as in China's Confucian tradition which elevates righteousness and disdains profit) but the profit motive of the individual actors, that is, their self-interest.[13] The operation of the "invisible hand" of the market will be, however, such that the pursuit of self-interest on the part of various actors in the market will contribute to the common interest of society at large.[14] This is because the market is the best mechanism to ensure an optimum allocation of resources in the economy, achieving both productive and allocative efficiency in the use of the scarce resources of society.[15]

The model of the market transaction is one entered into by parties with equal legal status and having the freedom to choose what transactions to enter into. Thus many Chinese writers glorify the market as being the embodiment of freedom, autonomy, equality and democracy.[16] One leading thinker goes as far as saying that whereas the planned economy represses the human being's dignity, freedom and rights as a subject, the market economy liberates the human subject and enables the human being to be a true master of himself/herself.[17]

Although scholars generally write about the market economy in a very positive tone, some do point out that the operation of market forces is spontaneous and "blind" (in the sense that they have no regard to issues of social justice or human suffering),[18] and some draw attention to the phenomena of market failures.[19] State intervention is seen as desirable in both types of situations. The State has an important role to play in the "macro-control" (hongguan tiaokong) of the market economy. As regards the "socialist" element in the socialist market economy, it is pointed out that this refers to the predominant role of that part of the economy covered by public ownership[20] and operated according to the principle of "to each according to his work".[21] It is argued that the socialist market economy will thus be able to give effect to both the values of efficiency and of fairness.[22] According to the latest theory of socialism adopted at the Chinese Communist Party's 14th Congress in 1992, economic efficiency is part of socialism, since the essence of socialism has now been defined as the development of productivity, the elimination of exploitation, the overcoming of social polarization, and, ultimately, the common prosperity of all, and the major "contradiction" currently facing China is seen as that between the material needs of the people and the relatively low productive capacity of the economy.[23]

It is instructive to contrast Chinese scholars' current conception of the market economy with their present views of: (a) the pre-industrial "natural economy" (ziran jingji); and (b) the planned economy, which according to the formerly orthodox view is the cornerstone and self-evident embodiment of socialism. Their portrait of the "natural economy" is one marked by rank, status, hierarchy, relationships of personal dependence, and the direct subordination of the individual to others or to social organizations.[24] The planned economy is negatively

6

depicted as characterized by the over-expansion of executive power unchecked by any effective rule of law (so that there is in effect the rule of man or rule by the will of officials), the over-concentration of power, and bureaucratic privileges.[25] The system is described as wasteful[26] and lacking in vitality, as productive units simply obey superior orders passively and are not allowed any room for self-initiative, autonomy and creativity.[27] One senior legal philosopher even points out that such passive compliance with and execution of production commands is akin to that of slaves' obedience to their masters. He also writes that the planned economy by its very nature weakens any checks and controls on executive power for the purpose of safeguarding people's rights, and requires the over-subordination of the interests of individuals or social units to those of the State or "the whole people".[28]

The implications for legal theory of the transition from the planned economy to the socialist market economy are understood by many Chinese scholars in terms of the Marxian conception of the relationship between the economic base and the social superstructure. Thus it is pointed out that according to historical materialism, legal theory reflects and serves the economic base of society; in the new era of economic reform and construction of the socialist market economy, the old legal theory of the era of the planned economy should be discarded.[29] The orthodox paradigm in post-1949 Chinese legal thought has been the idea of law as an expression of the "will of the ruling class" and as an instrument for the "dictatorship of the proletariat" in the socialist state. Quoting Deng Xiaoping's statement that the essence of socialism is the liberation and development of economic productivity with a view to achieving common prosperity for all ultimately, Chinese scholars now emphasize the function of law in promoting productive efficiency and economic development, and in providing useful rules regulating the multifarious relationships that exist in the developing market economy.[30] The value of economic efficiency is particularly stressed, sometimes even to the extent of stating that it deserves to have priority over moral ideas of fairness or justice.[31]

The transition from the planned economy to the socialist market economy is seen by many contemporary Chinese legal philosophers as a transition from the rule of man to the rule of law, from the supremacy of power to the supremacy of law, from status to contract, and from the priority of power to the priority of rights.[32] As mentioned in the introduction to this essay, the saying is now fashionable that the market economy is a legal-system economy or rule-of-law economy. It is believed that the dependence of the market on the law, or the intrinsic connection between the market and the law, is much stronger than the case of the planned economy and the law. In the planned economy, the actions of economic actors are mainly governed by administrative commands. In the market economy, economic actors enjoy the freedom to decide their courses of action, and the law provides the rules of the game on the basis of which the interplay of various actors occur.[33] It is pointed out that without such rules, the result could only be chaos.[34]

The existence of clear, stable and general rules of law is seen to be a necessary condition for the smooth operation of a market economy.[35] Unlike other forms of economy such as the "natural economy" or the planned economy, the market economy has a particularly great need for the use of abstract and uniform legal rules as a primary means of regulation and co-ordination.[36] In particular, the complex property relationships that arise in a market economy need to be defined and regulated by complex legal rules.[37] The law of contract provides the background norms in accordance with which negotiations are conducted and transactions entered into, without which the transaction costs of many dealings would be so high as to render them unfeasible.[38] Unlike in the planned economy, where productive units do not (at least in theory) have individual interests to pursue and disputes among them are resolved administratively,[39] the market economy consists of plural self-interested actors[40] whose conflicts are resolved by the judicial machinery on the basis of legal rules.[41]

Some Chinese writers refer to the historical experience and legal theory of the western world in attempting to elucidate the relationship between law and the market economy. Thus it has been argued that western experience demonstrates that the connection between legal development and the market economy is no historical accident but is intrinsic; a well-developed market economy is impossible in the absence of a well-developed legal system.[42] The works of Joseph Needham and Ray Huang on comparative Chinese and western history have been cited in support of the thesis that the absence of the rise of capitalism in traditional China is closely connected to the lack of a sound and elaborate legal and judicial system, while the development of the English legal system and the establishment of its constitutional monarchy provided favourable conditions for trade, industry and capital accumulation.[43] Tian Jiyun, a senior government minister, solemnly declared that the experience of the economically advanced nations shows that countries which have well-developed legal systems also have a well-functioning social and economic order, and are able to achieve fast economic development and success in international competition in the economic arena.[44] One leading scholar wrote about the relevance for China of Weber's theory of formally rational law and the importance for economic activities of precise, systematic and consistent legal rules whose operation is logical, autonomous and predictable.[45] Another scholar cited the works of Buchanan and Coase in arguing that legal protection of rights lowers transaction costs and promotes economic efficiency.[46] Other writers have also relied on

Coase in pointing out that the manner of a system's initial delineation of lawful rights has an important effect on its economic efficiency, different rights-structures have different degrees of efficiency, and rights may be regarded as an essential factor of production.[47]

As regards the actual characteristics of the law in a socialist market economy, the following aspects have been highlighted:[48] the freedom, autonomy and equality of economic actors (called the "subjects in the market" (shichang zhuti)); the freedom of contract; protection of property rights; the priority of rights over duties; the priority of rule over administrative discretion; the priority of empowering norms over prohibitory norms; the promotion of fair competition; the construction of a nationwide market governed by uniform rules of contract and corporate law equally applicable to state and private enterprises; appropriate provisions for social security, social justice and state intervention in the market; private law as the basis of public law, and private rights as the basis of public rights. Some of these themes will be elaborated below.

Special Issues

Freedom, Equality, Contract and the Market

One of the most striking features of the developing literature produced by legal philosophers in contemporary China is their affirmation of the values of freedom, autonomy and equality that they believe are embodied in the market economy[49] but hitherto denied and suppressed by the planned economy, their celebration of Maine's thesis of the move "from status to contract",[50] and their exaltation of the principle of the autonomy of the will of private parties (in the continental civil law tradition)[51] and the concept of freedom of contract.[52] In making these points, the writings of Marx and Maine have been referred to, and the heritage discussed of Roman jurisprudence and of the legal trends initiated by the making of the French Civil Code in 1804.

Marx has pointed out that social evolution in modern times involves a transition from a state of personal dependence of man on other men to a state of man's dependence on material things and the consequent acquisition of independence of others. Contemporary Chinese thinkers[53] now reflect on this insight and argue that this transition represents a liberation of the human being as a subject. In the new state of affairs, that is, the market economy, individuals have become autonomous subjects, and they enter into exchange relationships with one another as subjects of equal legal status, exercising their free will.

Maine's thesis of the move from status to contract is apparently

9

even more often quoted in the contemporary literature produced by Chinese legal philosophers[54] than the views of Marx himself. The Chinese writers unanimously understand this move as a kind of historical progress. In particular, they read into the idea of the contract the whole story of modernization, freedom, autonomy, equality — in short, the collection of the aspirations of humankind in modernity. In a sense, the philosophy of law and the market in contemporary China is largely a philosophy of the contract in modern society and modern law.

Several highly influential legal thinkers[55] in China today write that modern society is a "contract society", and that the contract is the legal prototype of the market. Contractual relationships are described as the most fundamental kind of legal relationships in modern society, and the market economy is one in which economic relations are contractualized. The freedom of contract is said to be the basis of modern economic life, as well as an essential ingredient of the "spirit of modern law".[56] One writer wrote of the contract as the paradigmatic concept and the soul of the law in the market economy.[57] One of the most respected and senior jurists wrote that freedom of contract constitutes the core of the principle of the autonomy of the will of private parties, and the latter principle is in turn the soul of and a golden thread running through the whole of modern private law.[58] In a sense, the contract is the law, because the parties create for themselves legally valid and enforceable rights and obligations by means of the contract.[59] The contract is thus at once the embodiment of the law and of the free will of equal and autonomous subjects.[60] This vision has, therefore, integrated into itself all the important concepts and values of contract, freedom, autonomy, equality, law and modernity.

Right-Based Jurisprudence and the Market

Since the late 1980s, there has been a thriving debate among Chinese legal philosophers regarding whether law and jurisprudence is ultimately rights-based, duties-based, or should give equal priority to both the concepts of rights and duties.[61] The official promotion of the idea of the socialist market economy since 1992 has given new vitality to this existing debate. The general trend seems to be that those who previously advocated rights discourse have been able to use the theory of the socialist market economy to strengthen their position, while their original opponents have not been able to find theoretical reinforcement from the new concept of the socialist market economy.

Advocates of the priority of rights argue that whereas the planned economy is characterized by the priority of power (of superior administrative authority) and of duties (of economic units to whom commands are issued and who are duty-bound to perform according to the

10

State's economic plan),[62] the market economy is a rights-based economy (*quanli jingji*) (which can also be translated as an economy of rights).[63] Many of these scholars[64] refer to Marx's conception of the exchange of commodities as the essence of the market. It is then pointed out that a prerequisite to exchange is the existence and recognition of the rights of the parties who are entering into the exchange, such as ownership or property rights over or the right to dispose of commodities. The rights of the subjects-actors in the market are thus the constituent atoms of the market economy. These rights[65] also include rights to autonomy in conducting one's own business affairs, freedom from state interference, and to equality of status with other subjects-actors in the market.

One leading philosopher writes that the transition from the planned economy to the market economy may be understood as the restoration to subjects-actors of their rights and freedoms which were originally subsumed within state power.[66] Another argues that the priority of rights is one of the ingredients of the "spirit of modern law".[67] It has also been pointed out that the priority of rights forms the basis of the fundamental principle of the autonomy of the will of parties in private law,[68] and that jurisprudence is a science of rights.[69] Rights are understood by many writers as interest-based or as the legal expression of interests;[70] and the priority of rights means that duties are secondary in the sense that they are no more than means for securing and realizing rights.[71]

The Fundamental Status of Private Law and Private Rights

The transition from the planned economy to the socialist market economy has also been interpreted by leading Chinese jurists as a shift from the priority of public law to the priority of private law,[72] as well as a change in the nature of public law itself. It has been pointed out that the traditional legal culture of imperial China privileged public law, particularly criminal law, and is state-centred.[73] This tradition was then reinforced by the socialist planned economy, and by the influence of Soviet legal theory which tended to conceive all law as public law (since property relationships were largely administrative relationships in a planned economy), and denied any independent status to private law.[74] The market is seen as a powerful force challenging and re-making this whole tradition.

The market economy is, according to contemporary Chinese thinkers,[75] governed by private law, the foundation of which is the principle of the autonomy of the will of private parties, the security (and some writers[76] even use the terms "inviolability" and "sacredness") of private rights, and the paradigm of the contract. In their perception, the underlying values in private law are freedom, autonomy and equality.[77]

11

They then theorise that the public law of a market society should be inspired by, modelled on and serve purposes similar to its private law.[78] In particular, the state in a market society may be understood in terms of the social contract theory;[79] public law and executive power should serve the private rights of subjects-actors in the market[80] (and one leading legal philosopher[81] summarizes these rights in terms of life, liberty and property), which are seen as constituting the basis of citizenship rights and as the prototype of public law rights;[82] public law should promote the values of freedom, autonomy and equality.

The market economy and the rise of private law are also welcomed as a boost to the rule of law, constitutionalism,[83] democracy[84] and human rights[85] in the political and public law arena. It is said that the market's "contract culture",[86] "civil law culture"[87] and the "spirit of private law"[88] will contribute significantly to the development of the rule of law and democracy in China.[89] Some thinkers[90] make use of the Marxist conceptions of the economic substructure and the social superstructure, and point out that the market economy needs a rule of law (in the private law sense), and the rule of law in the economic sense both requires and promotes the socialist Rechtstaat. Others[91] argue that a market economy will only thrive under favourable social and political conditions, and these include public law protection of human rights such as liberty of the person, freedom of thought, speech, press and information, freedom of choice of occupation, freedom to migrate, freedom of association, freedom of business operation and freedom to go on strike.

Conclusion

After the Second World War, theories of law and development were developed in the west, particularly in the USA, in the context of the provision of foreign aid to Third World countries for the purpose of promoting their economic development.[92] Scholars interested in comparative law and social theory also developed theoretical models of the different roles of law in planned and market economies.[93] The Chinese jurisprudential thinking in the 1990s on law and the economic system transition from plan to market may be viewed as a contribution to these existing fields of socio-legal, jurisprudential and law-related interdisciplinary studies at a macro-level.

This article has set out what may be called the "mainstream" view among contemporary Chinese thinkers on the major issues of legal theory relevant to the development of the socialist market economy. It should be noted, however, that a minority of scholars have — to varying extents — distanced themselves from such mainstream view.

For example, some have expressed doubts about whether the market economy should be described as a "legal-system economy" or "rule-of-law economy".[94] Some are sceptical about the mainstream view that the enactment of appropriate legislation will usher in the era of the socialist market economy, pointing out that the relationship between law and social change is complex, the behavioural norms and legal culture that people have become accustomed to for a long time are slow to change, and even in the west the legal systems that support and facilitate the operation of the market economy have taken centuries to mature.[95]

It has also been pointed out that the mainstream research paradigm is largely a construction of an idealized model of what the law ought to be in an ideal socialist market economy, ignoring the actual role played by law in contemporary China, and neglecting the reality that China's present economic system is still far from being a market economy,[96] and that the nature of the process of developing a market economy in China is very different from that in the Western experience. One important point of difference, for example, is that in the west the bourgeoisie and civil society were the main driving forces behind marketization and corresponding legal change, whereas in late twentieth century China the State has been the dominant actor in the move towards the market economy.[97] Whereas in the west many legal institutions were already in place when economic development began to leap forward, a noteworthy fact in the Chinese case is that nearly all the major steps in the post-1978 economic reform were initiated by policy instruments issued by the Party and the State rather than by duly enacted law; indeed, many innovations in economic institutions and practices were, from a strictly legal point of view, in violation of the law as it stood at the time.[98]

These reflections form a useful balancing and supplementary perspective in relation to the mainstream view, but they have not challenged the core of that view, which may be interpreted as a jurisprudential celebration of the market and condemnation of the planned economy. As has been described above in this paper, in the contemporary Chinese jurisprudential literature the market economy is almost invariably associated with the positive values of the rule of law, freedom, autonomy, equality, democracy, human rights and human flourishing, and the planned economy with arbitrary power, bureaucratic privilege, unquestioning obedience to commands of superiors, and lack of freedom, initiative and creativity. It is ironical that the writings of these Chinese thinkers, all extremely well-versed in the Marxian classics (and it should also be borne in mind that legal theory in post-1949 China has been "colonized" by the Marxist-Leninist orthodoxy much more thoroughly than the fields of substantive and procedural law), display no trace of the Marxist critique of the market, such as extreme commodification and endless accumulation, alienation, exploitation, and the plight of the proletariat that is produced by the system.

The best explanation for this otherwise strange phenomenon probably lies with the socio-political context in which these writings are produced. China is in a critical historical phase of transition, and many social, political, economic and ideological forces acting in different directions are at work. The future of the economic reform is still largely uncertain, with the question of privatization still largely untouched. The future of political reform is even more unknown. Yet faith in and commitment to the old system and ideology has disintegrated. For many intellectuals, marketization and democratization have become the conceptual paradigms with which they express their hope for China's future. The contemporary literature on law and the market may thus be interpreted as an expression of intellectuals' aspirations for a future China in which the modern humanistic values of freedom, autonomy, equality, human rights and democracy will be finally realized.

This does not necessarily mean that the literature is worthy of being read only as psychology or polemics, or that it is devoid of theoretical insight of objective significance to scholars' understanding of the relationship between law and the market. On the contrary, the literature has truly raised real issues of great importance, the resolution of which by further research in China and elsewhere may yield important insights for the legal and social theory of the next century. For example, should the emergence of the market economy as a product of social evolution be conceived, as in the case of the rule of law, as an "unqualified human good"?[99] What are the historical and logical connections, if any, between the rise of the market economy and the development of the rule of law and the Rechtstaat? Should the legal conception of the contract be understood as foundation of the law of the market society? Can the triumph of the discourse of rights in modernity be attributed to the triumph of the market? Is the market the socio-economic foundation of both private law and modern public law? To what extent has the development of modern public law been influenced by the longer tradition of private law traced back to ancient Rome? Should the principles and concepts of private law be understood as constituting the basis of modern public law? These are the kind of fundamental questions generated by the work of contemporary legal thinkers in China. They are questions formed and shaped by the unique experience of this generation of thinkers who face the challenges of China's move away from the socialist planned economy, yet they are also of universal significance for the whole of humankind in its jurisprudential reflections on the complex and perplexing relationships between the phenomena of the market, law, modernity and progress.

14

Notes

1 See generally Jan S. Prybyla, *Reform in China and Other Socialist Economies* (Washington, D.C.: AEI Press, 1990); Richard Baum, *Burying Mao: Chinese Politics in the Age of Deng Xiaoping* (Princeton: Princeton University Press, 1994). For a brief survey, see Ren Zhongping, "From the third plenary session of the 11th Central Committee of the CCP to the third plenary session of the 14th Central Committee", *Renmin ribao (People's Daily)*, December 22, 1993, reprinted in [1994] 2 *Xinhua wenzhai (New China Digest)* 23.

2 See, *e.g.* Ren Zhongping, *op. cit.*; Chen Yingge et al, "Forming the framework of the legal system of the socialist market economy in 5 years: an interview with Vice-Chairman Tian Jiyun", *Fazhi ribao (Legal System Daily)*, July 2, 1993, p.1, reprinted in [1993] 4 *Jingjifa (Economic Law)* 11; Yang Zixuan, "The establishment of a market economy and the development of economic law", *Guangming ribao*, June 6, 1993, p.3, reprinted in [1993] 3 *Jingjifa (Economic Law)* 25; Sun Guohua, "Socialist market economy and legal regulation" [1993] 1 *Faxuejia (Jurists' Review)* 4; Zheng Chengliang, "Law, contract and market" [1994] 11 *Xinhua wenzhai (New China Digest)* 20. For a critical perspective on this view, see Su Li, "Some reflections on market economy and legal culture" [1993] 4 *Beijing daxue xuebao: zhesheban (Journal of Peking University: section on philosophy and social science)* 8, reprinted in [1994] 1 *Jingji faxue (Science of Economic Law)* 33.

3 See, *e.g.* Liu Shengping et al, "Market economy and renewal and change in jurisprudence" [1993] 4 *Zhongguo faxue (Chinese Legal Science)* 3; Liu Han and Xia Yong, "New topics for jurisprudence" [1993] 1 *Faxue yanjiu (Studies in Law)* 3; Wang Baoshu, "The socialist market economy and research in civil and economic law" [1993] 3 *Zhongguo faxue (Chinese Legal Science)* 20; Wen Zhengbang, "The modern market economy as a Rule of Law economy" [1994] 1 *Faxue yanjiu (Studies in Law)* 25. For a critical perspective of this view, see Wang Chenguang, "The establishment of a market economy and the gradual perfection of its legal system" [1994] 2 *Faxue yanjiu (Studies in Law)* 3.

4 Apart from the works cited in nn.2 and 3, see also editorial, "Developing the discussion about market economy and legal construction'" [1993] 3 *Zhongguo faxue (Chinese Legal Science)* 11; Zhang Wenxian, "Three arguments about market economy and legal construction" [1993] 3 *Zhongguo faxue (Chinese Legal Science)* 12; Wang Chenguang et al, "Market economy and new legal issues (speeches at a seminar)" [1993] 3 *Faxuejia (Jurists' Review)* 46.

5 "Chairman Qiao Shi talks about speeding up law-making in economic law at the 1st session of the 8th National People's Congress Standing Committee (April 1, 1993)" [1993] 5 *Zhongguo shangye fazhi (Chinese Business Law)* 3, reprinted in [1993] 4 *Jingjifa (Economic Law)* 7; "Chairman Qiao Shi emphasizes law-making for the socialist market economy at the 2nd session of the 8th National People's Congress Standing Committee", *Renmin ribao (People's Daily)*, July 3, 1993, p.1, reprinted in [1993] 4 *Jingjifa (Economic Law)* 9; "To establish the legal framework of socialist market economy: interview with Qiao Shi" (1994) 1 *China Law Quarterly* (bilingual periodical published in Hong Kong) 8, Chinese version reprinted in [1995] 1 *Xinhua yuebao (Xinhua Monthly)* 24. See also Chen Yingge et al, *op. cit.* (n.2 above).

6 The importance of borrowing from foreign legal systems is also stressed in

scholarly writings in recent years. See, *e.g.* Project Group on "the legal system of the socialist market economy" of the Institute of Law, Chinese Academy of Social Science, "Theoretical reflections and practical suggestions on the construction of the legal system of a socialist market economy" [1993] 6 *Faxue yanjiu (Studies in Law)* 3 at pp.6, 17; Wang Baoshu, *op. cit.* (n.3 above) at p.22; Liu Shengping et al, *op. cit.* (n.3 above) at p.9; Guo Daohui, "Market economy and changes in legal theory and concepts of law: a review of the new theories in the jurisprudence of recent years" [1994] 2 *Faxue (Jurisprudence)* (Shanghai) 2 at p.5 (reprinted in [1994] 5 *Faxue (Science of Law)* (Renmin University) 7); Sun Guohua, *op. cit.* (n.2 above) at p.7; Ma Hong, "Speeding up the construction of the legal system of the socialist market economy" [1993] 2 *Zhongguo jingji tizhi gaige* 29, reprinted in [1993] 4 *Jingjifa (Economic Law)* 14, at p.16; Fang Shirong, "An inquiry into several issues relating to the compatibility between the legal system and the market economy" [1993] 2 *Zhongnan zhengfa xueyuan xuebao (Journal of the Central-Southern Institute of Law and Politics)* 1 at p.3 (reprinted in [1993] 7 *Faxue (Science of Law)* (Renmin University) 20); Wang Chenguang et al, *op. cit.* (n.4 above) at p.51 (Zhang Qi's speech).

7 Liu Shengping et al, *op. cit.* (n.3 above) at p.8.

8 Ma Hong, "Market economy and law" [1993] 1 *Caijing yanjiu (Studies in Finance and Economy)* (Shanghai) 11 at p.12, reprinted in [1993] 1 *Jingjifa (Economic Law)* 16.

9 Zhao Zhenjiang, "Legal constructions for the socialist market economy" [1993] 4 *Beijing daxue xuebao: zhesheban (Journal of Peking University: section on philosophy and social science)* 1 at p.4, reprinted in [1994] 1 *Jingji faxue (Science of Economic Law)* 26; Jiang Ping, "Reflections on the perfection of the legal system of the market economy" [1993] 1 *Zhongguo faxue (Chinese Legal Science)* 7 at p.11; Yin Zhongqing, "A preliminary investigation of the framework of the legal system of a socialist market economy" [1993] 6 *Faxue yanjiu (Studies in Law)* 26.

10 Guo Fuqing, "The construction of the legal system of a socialist market economy" [1993] 4 *Falü kexue (Law Science)* 19, reprinted in [1993] 11 *Faxue (Science of Law)* (Renmin University) 23.

11 See, *e.g.* Zheng Chengliang, *op. cit.* (n.2 above); Project Group, *op. cit.* (n.6 above); Wang Baoshu, *op. cit.* (n.3 above).

12 Ma Hong, *op. cit.* (n.8 above) at p.17; Zhao Zhenjiang, *op. cit.* (n.9 above) at p.5; Guo Dauhui, "Principles and methods for constructing a legal system suitable for a market economy" [1994] 1 *Zhongguo faxue (Chinese Legal Science)* 35 at p.39; Guo Yuzhao, "Socialist market economy consciousness and legal construction" [1994] 3 *Faxue yanjiu (Studies in Law)* 19 at p.20.

13 Zhang Wenxian, "Market economy and the spirit of modern law" [1994] 6 *Zhongguo faxue (Chinese Legal Science)* 5 at pp.6, 9; Zhang Wenxian, "Reflections on macroeconomic control and its law and policy" [1994] 1 *Zhongwai faxue (Peking University Law Journal)* 1 at pp.1, 2, reprinted in [1994] 2 *Jingji faxue (Science of Economic Law)* 11; Gong Pixiang, "Socialist market economy and legal regulation" [1993] 1 *Falü kexue (Law Science)* 3 at p.7, reprinted in [1993] 2 *Faxue (Science of Law)* (Renmin University) 20.

14 Wang Chenguang et al, *op. cit.* (n.4 above) at p.55 (Wang Lei's speech); Zheng Chengliang, *op. cit.* (n.2 above) at p.23.

15 Zhang Wenxian, *op. cit.* (n.4 above) at p.18; Zhang Wenxian, "Reflections", *op. cit.* (n.13 above) at pp.1, 2; Zhang Wenxian, "Market economy", *op. cit.* (n.13 above) at p.8; Zhao Zhenjiang, *op. cit.* (n.9 above) at p.4; Ma Hong, *op. cit.* (n.8 above) at p.12; Shi Tang, "Market economy and legal modernization" [1993] 2 *Faxue (Jurisprudence)* (Shanghai) 1 at p.4, reprinted in [1993] 7 *Jingjifa (Economic Law)* 15.

[16] See "Freedom, Equality, Contract and the Market" below.
[17] Wang Chenguang et al, *op. cit.* (n.4 above) at p.48 (Du Gangjian's speech).
[18] Zhao Zhenjiang, *op. cit.* (n.9 above) at p.3; Guo Yuzhao, *op. cit.* (n.12 above) at p.20.
[19] Zhang Wenxian, "Reflections", *op. cit.* (n.13 above) at p.3.
[20] Guo Yuzhao, *op. cit.* (n.12 above) at p.20; Zhao Zhenjiang, *op. cit.* (n.9 above) at p.3; Zhang Wenxian, *op. cit.* (n.4 above) at p.15.
[21] Wen Zhengbang, *op. cit.* (n.3 above) at p.26; Zhao Zhenjiang, *op. cit.* (n.9 above) at p.7.
[22] See the works cited in n.21 above.
[23] Liu Han and Xia Yong, *op. cit.* (n.3 above) at p.10.
[24] Ma Hong, *op. cit.* (n.8 above) at pp.12–13, 15–16.
[25] Gong Pixiang, *op. cit.* (n.13 above) at p.5; Jiang Ping, *op. cit.* (n.9 above) at p.7; Lin Zhe, "Queries on the view that 'the market economy is a legal system economy'" [1994] 1 *Zhongguo faxue (Chinese Legal Science)* 68; Zhang Wenxian, "Market economy", *op. cit.* (n.13 above) at p.6.
[26] Zhang Wenxian, *op. cit.* (n.4 above) at p.18; Lin Zhe, *op. cit.* (n.25 above).
[27] Liu Shengping et al, *op. cit.* (n.3 above) at p.6; Zhang Wenxian, *op. cit.* (n.4 above) at pp.12–13; Zhang Wenxian, "Market economy", *op. cit.* (n.13 above) at p.9.
[28] Lu Yun, "Transition of legal model: a profound revolutionary change" [1994] 1 *Zhongguo faxue (Chinese Legal Science)* 27 at p.33.
[29] Project Group, *op. cit.* (n.6 above) at p.7.
[30] Wang Chenguang et al, *op. cit.* (n.4 above) at p.47; Sun Guohua, *op. cit.* (n.2 above) at pp.4–7; Liu Shengping et al, *op. cit.* (n.3 above) at pp.3–4; Guo Daohui, *op. cit.* (n.6 above) at p.5.
[31] Zhang Wenxian, "Market economy", *op. cit.* (n.13 above) at p.5; Liu Shengping et al, *op. cit.* (n.3 above) at pp.3–4; Guo Daohui, *op. cit.* (n.6 above) at p.5; Lin Zhe, "Rights-orientation as the necessary requirement of the development of a market economy" [1992] 6 *Faxue yanjiu (Studies in Law)* 23.
[32] Lu Yun, *op. cit.* (n.28 above) at p.28; Guo Daohui, *op. cit.* (n.6 above) at p.2; Gong Pixiang, *op. cit.* (n.13 above) at pp.3, 9; Wen Zhengbang, *op. cit.* (n.3 above) at pp.25–27.
[33] Wang He, "Confirming the legal status in China of the new socialist market economy" [1993] 3 *Jingji wenti tansuo (Inquiries into Economic Problems)* (Kunming) 1, reprinted in [1993] 3 *Jingjifa (Economic Law)* 38 (see particularly p.39); Ma Hong, *op. cit.* (n.6 above) at p.29; Yu Zhongmin, "The orientation of the market economy: rules first, then market" [1993] 3 *Zhongguo faxue (Chinese Legal Science)* 28; Liu Shengping et al, *op. cit.* (n.3 above) at p.6; Dong Ansheng, "A socialist market economy is a Rule of Law economy" [1993] 1 *Faxuejia (Jurists' Review)* 8; Zhang Wenxian, *op. cit.* (n.4 above) at p.13; Project Group, *op. cit.* (n.6 above) at p.3; Zheng Chengliang, *op. cit.* (n.2 above) at p.20.
[34] Liu Han and Xia Yong, *op. cit.* (n.3 above) at p.7.
[35] Wen Zhengbang, *op. cit.* (n.3 above) at p.25; Guo Daohui et al, "Market economy and legal modernization (speeches at a seminar)" [1992] 6 *Faxue yanjiu (Studies in Law)* 1 at p.5 (Liu Han's speech).
[36] Ma Hong, *op. cit.* (n.8 above) at pp.11, 12.
[37] *Ibid.* at p.12.
[38] Gu Peidong, "Reflections on several issues relating to China's market economy and legal constructions" [1994] 1 *Faxue yanjiu (Studies in Law)* 19.
[39] Zhang Wenxian, *op. cit.* (n.4 above) at pp.12–13.
[40] Gao Hongjun et al, "A summary of the international symposium on 'The

Rule of Law and social and economic development'" [1992] 1 *Faxue yanjiu (Studies in Law)* 85.

41 Zhang Wenxian, *op. cit.* (n.4 above) at p.13.

42 Fang Jiamin, "An inquiry into the legal system of a socialist market economy" [1994] 1 *Tianjin shangxueyuan xuebao (Tianjin Business School Journal)* 35 at pp.36–37, reprinted in [1994] 3 *Jingji faxue (Science of Economic Law)* 22.

43 Guo Daohui et al, *op. cit.* (n.35 above) at p.4 (He Weifang's speech).

44 Chen Yingge et al, *op. cit.* (n.2 above).

45 Su Li, *op. cit.* (n.2 above) at pp.8–9.

46 Guo Fuqing, *op. cit.* (n.10 above) at p.19.

47 Zhang Wenxian, "Market economy", *op. cit.* (n.13 above) at p.10; Gong Pixiang, *op. cit.* (n.13 above) at p.7.

48 Project Group, *op. cit.* (n.6 above); Liu Han and Xia Yong, *op. cit.* (n.3 above); Jiang Ping, *op. cit.* (n.9 above); Jiang Ping, "Market economy, legal mechanism and legal ideas" (1993) 2 *Zhongguo shehui kexue jikan (Chinese Social Sciences Quarterly)* 15. See also the works cited in "Special Issues" below in this chapter.

49 See generally Jiang Ping, *op. cit.* (n.9 above) at pp.7, 12; Jiang Ping, *op. cit.* (n.48 above) at pp.16–17; Lu Yun, *op. cit.* (n.28 above) at pp.32–33; Guo Daohui, *op. cit.* (n.12 above) at p.39; Guo Daohui, *op. cit.* (n.6 above) at pp.3–4; Liu Han and Xia Yong, *op. cit.* (n.3 above) at p.7; Ma Hong, *op. cit.* (n.8 above) at p.17; Guo Daohui et al, *op. cit.* (n.35 above) at p.4 (He Weifang's speech); Wang Chenguang et al, *op. cit.* (n.4 above) at pp.48 (Du Gangjian's speech), 51 (Zhang Qi's speech); Shi Tang, *op. cit.* (n.15 above) at p.4; Guo Yuzhao, *op. cit.* (n.12 above) at p.20.

50 See n.54 below.

51 See n.58 below.

52 See nn.55–60 below.

53 Gong Pixiang, *op. cit.* (n.13 above) at pp.3–4; Zhang Wenxian, "Market economy", *op. cit.* (n.13 above) at pp.7–8.

54 Jiang Ping, *op. cit.* (n.9 above) at p.12; Jiang Ping, *op. cit.* (n.48 above) at pp.16–17; Zhang Wenxian, "Market economy", *op. cit.* (n.13 above) at pp.7–8; Wen Zhengbang, *op. cit.* (n.3 above) at p.25; Liu Shengping et al, *op. cit.* (n.3 above) at p.8; Lu Yun, *op. cit.* (n.28 above) at p.33; Guo Daohui, *op. cit.* (n.6 above) at p.5; Guo Yuzhao, *op. cit.* (n.12 above) at p.20.

55 Zheng Chengliang, *op. cit.* (n.2 above) at p.21; Project Group, *op. cit.* (n.6 above) at p.4; Zhang Wenxian, "Market economy", *op. cit.* (n.13 above) at p.8; Lu Yun, *op. cit.* (n.28 above) at pp.32–33; Wen Zhengbang, *op. cit.* (n.3 above) at p.25.

56 Zhang Wenxian, "Market economy", *op. cit.* (n.13 above) at p.5.

57 Zheng Chengliang, *op. cit.* (n.2 above) at p.22.

58 Jiang Ping and Zhang Lihong, "Market economy and autonomy of will" [1993] 6 *Faxue yanjiu (Studies in Law)* 20; Guo Daohui et al, *op. cit.* (n.35 above) at p.3 (Liang Huixing's speech).

59 Jiang Ping and Zhang Lihong, *op. cit.* (n.58 above) at p.24.

60 Gong Pixiang, *op. cit.* (n.13 above) at p.4.

61 See generally Albert H.Y. Chen, "Developing theories of rights and human rights in China", in Raymond Wacks (ed.), *Hong Kong, China and 1997: Essays in Legal Theory* (Hong Kong: Hong Kong University Press, 1993) chapter 5.

62 Guo Daohui, *op. cit.* (n.6 above) at p.3; Liu Shengping et al, *op. cit.* (n.3 above) at p.9; Sun Guohua, *op. cit.* (n.2 above) at p.7; Jiang Ping, *op. cit.* (n.48 above) at p.15.

63 Liu Shengping et al, *op. cit.* (n.3 above) at p.9; Wang He, *op. cit.* (n.33 above)

at p.3; Yu Meisun, "The new economic system necessitates a new legal system", *Jingji cankao bao (Economic Reference News)*, February 21, 1993, p.4, reprinted in [1993] 2 *Jingjifa (Economic Law)* 34; Wen Zhengbang, *op. cit.* (n.3 above) at p.25; Jiang Ping and Zhang Lihong, *op. cit.* (n.58 above) at pp.21–22; Jiang Ping, *op. cit.* (n.9 above) at p.7.

64 Lin Zhe, *op. cit.* (n.31 above) at pp.24–25; Zhang Wenxian, "Market economy", *op. cit.* (n.13 above) at p.6; Ma Hong, *op. cit.* (n.8 above) at pp.16–17; Gong Pixiang, *op. cit.* (n.13 above) at p.6; Guo Fuqing, *op. cit.* (n.10 above) at p.22.
65 Guo Daohui, *op. cit.* (n.12 above) at p.39; Wang Chenguang, *op. cit.* (n.3 above) at p.8.
66 Jiang Ping and Zhang Lihong, *op. cit.* (n.58 above) at pp.21–22. See also Zheng Chengliang, *op. cit.* (n.2 above) at p.22.
67 Zhang Wenxian, "Market economy", *op. cit.* (n.13 above) at p.5. See also Wen Zhengbang, *op. cit.* (n.3 above).
68 Jiang Ping and Zhang Lihong, *op. cit.* (n.58 above) at pp.20–21.
69 *Ibid.* pp.21–22.
70 Loc. cit; Zhang Wenxian, "Market economy", *op. cit.* (n.13 above) at p.6; Ma Hong, *op. cit.* (n.8 above) at pp.16–17.
71 Lin Zhe, *op. cit.* (n.31 above); Chen, *op. cit.* (n.61 above).
72 Guo Daohui et al, *op. cit.* (n.35 above) at p.2 (Liang Huixing's speech).
73 *Loc. cit*; Sun Guohua, *op. cit.* (n.2 above) at p.7.
74 Ma Hong, *op. cit.* (n.8 above) at p.14; Project Group, *op. cit.* (n.6 above) at p.6; Guo Daohui et al, *op. cit.* (n.35 above) at p.2 (Liang Huixing's speech).
75 Guo Daohui, *op. cit.* (n.6 above) at p.4; Guo Daohui et al, *op. cit.* (n.35 above) at p.6 (Liu Junhai's speech).
76 Zheng Chengliang, *op. cit.* (n.2 above) at p.23; Guo Daohui et al, *op. cit.* (n.35 above) at p.2 (Liang Huixing's speech); Guo Daohui, *op. cit.* (n.6 above) at p.4; Liu Shengping et al, *op. cit.* (n.3 above) at p.5.
77 See n.49 above.
78 Liu Shengping et al, *op. cit.* (n.3 above) at p.5.
79 *Ibid.* p.8; Zhang Wenxian, "Market economy", *op. cit.* (n.13 above) at p.8.
80 Guo Daohui, *op. cit.* (n.6 above) at p.4; Guo Daohui et al, *op. cit.* (n.35 above) at p.2 (Liang Huixing's speech); Guo Daohui, *op. cit.* (n.12 above) at p.39.
81 Zhang Wenxian, "Market economy", *op. cit.* (n.13 above) at p.8.
82 Guo Daohui, *op. cit.* (n.6 above) at p.3; Zhang Wenxian, "Market economy", *op. cit.* (n.13 above) at p.7; Liu Shengping et al, *op. cit.* (n.3 above) at p.5.
83 Liu Han and Xia Yong, *op. cit.* (n.3 above) at p.7.
84 Liu Shengping et al, *op. cit.* (n.3 above) at p.9.
85 Guo Daohui et al, *op. cit.* (n.35 above) at p.3 (Liang Huixing's speech).
86 Liu Shengping et al, *op. cit.* (n.3 above) at p.8.
87 *Ibid.* p.5; Zheng Chengliang, *op. cit.* (n.2 above) at p.23.
88 Liu Shengping et al, *op. cit.* (n.3 above) at p.5.
89 Guo Daohui et al, *op. cit.* (n.35 above) at p.3 (Liang Huixing's speech).
90 Lu Yun, *op. cit.* (n.28 above) at p.29; Liu Han and Xia Yong, *op. cit.* (n.3 above) at p.9.
91 Wang Chenguang et al, *op. cit.* (n.4 above) at p.48 (Du Gangjian's speech); Guo Daohui, *op. cit.* (n.12 above) at p.39; Guo Daohui, *op. cit.* (n.6 above) at pp.2, 6.
92 For a detailed but critical review, see David M. Trubek and Marc Galanter, "Scholars in self-estrangement: some reflections on the crisis in law and development studies in the United States" [1974] *Wisconsin Law Review* 1062.
93 See, *e.g.* David M. Trubek, "Toward a social theory of law: an essay on the study of law and development" (1972) 82 *Yale Law Journal* 1.

[94] Su Li, *op. cit.* (n.2 above) at p.36; Wang Chenguang, *op. cit.* (n.3 above) at p.3; Lin Zhe, op cit. (n.25 above) at p.68.

[95] Shi Taifeng, "Market economy and legal development: reflections in sociology of law" [1993] 5 *Zhongwai faxue (Peking University Law Journal)* 18 at pp.22–23, reprinted in [1993] 11 *Faxue (Science of Law)* (Renmin University) 17; Su Li, *op. cit.* (n.2 above) at pp.35–36; Wang Chenguang et al, *op. cit.* (n.4 above) at pp.49–50 (Su Li's speech); Wang Chenguang, *op. cit.* (n.3 above) at pp.4, 8, 10.

[96] Shi Taifeng, *op. cit.* (n.95 above) at p.18; Wang Chenguaug, *op. cit.* (n.3 above) at p.3.

[97] Shi Taifeng, *op. cit.* (n.95 above) at pp.19–20; Wang Chenguang, *op. cit.* (n.3 above) at p.5; Guo Daohui, *op. cit.* (n.6 above) at p.3; Guo Yuzhao, *op. cit.* (n.12 above) at p.22.

[98] Ma Hong, *op. cit.* (n.8 above) at p.11.

[99] E.P. Thompson, *Whigs and Hunters: The Origin of the Black Act* (London, Penguin Books, 1977), p.266.

ADMINISTRATIVE LAW
AND THE MARKET ECONOMY

Professor Jiang Mingan

Administrative Law Section
Peking University

Professor Jiang Ming-an, *LL.B. (1981) Peking University, has been a lecturer (1982); associate professor (1990); Head of the Teaching and Research Section on Administrative Law (1991); Professor (1994) at Peking University; and deputy general secretary of the China Administrative Law Research Association. He is the author of several important textbooks and many articles on administrative law.*

Introduction

The development of administrative law in China has been closely related to the development of the market economy.

During the decades of planned economy, there was virtually no system of administrative law in China. Other branches of the law were also relatively undeveloped, but civil and criminal cases were still heard by the courts according to law and policy. In contrast, citizens had no recourse against unlawful administrative action and tort. The court didn't accept administrative cases, and there were no government agencies handling administrative review. Equally, there were no statutes regulating administrative action or examining administrative liability.

It was not until the 1980s when China switched to a market economy that administrative law really came into existence. New laws were introduced to regulate the actions of the administration and to normalize the organization of administrative agencies. Following this, principles and rules were laid down to define administrative powers and to challenge illegal administrative action and tort.

In the 1990s, China has established a basic framework for its administrative law. This includes the Administrative Litigation Law and the State Compensation Law (passed by the National People's Congress);

the Regulation on Administrative Reconsideration; the Administrative Supervision Act; and the Regulation on Concerning Public Functionaires (passed by the State Council). One of the most significant developments has been the establishment of a system whereby citizens will have the opportunity to pursue litigation against the government.

In less than 10 years, an almost completely new system of administrative law has been established in China — a process which has taken several decades or even nearly a century in other parts of the world. This recent and rapid development of administrative law is directly related to the rapid development of China's market economy.

The Nature and History of Administrative Law

In essence, administrative law is the law which regulates the relationship between the government and its citizens (individuals and organs) by means of controlling administrative power. In feudal times, when the monarch was the sovereign power and subject to no controls, it was impossible for administrative law to develop. Under liberal capitalism, when government interference in civil society was limited, no need for administrative law was felt, and the environment was not right for its true development.

It is only in the twentieth century that administrative law has really come into its own. The rapid technological and economic progress experienced in this century has produced tremendous wealth but also problems such as pollution, unfair competition, inflation, unemployment and violence. The only way to handle these problems has been to arm the government with sufficient power. As a result, the administrative state was born: the government became responsible for its citizens from cradle to grave.

Administrative agencies helped to control social problems and maintain social order, but also brought with them new problems, such as abuse of power, corruption and violation of private interests. Threatened by the potentially overwhelming power of the regulatory machinery that had been created, a whole new set of machinery was then created to keep it in check and maintain its efficiency. This regulatory machinery is commonly known as administrative law.

Administrative Law and the Market Economy

Administrative law establishes a set of rules to keep the exercise of government power in accordance with its statutory purpose and establishes fair procedures to safeguard citizens from its abuses.

The question is why administrative law developed so rapidly with the advent of the market economy and not under China's planned economy. This was not because government power was limited or because there was no abuse of this power, but because administrative law is also dependent on other social factors. Among these, independence and respect for the individual are crucial.

Under the planned economy, individuals were strictly attached to organizations which were in turn subordinate to the administration. Neither state enterprises and institutions nor collective enterprises enjoyed much autonomy. The relationship between government and society was one of command and obedience; it cannot be interpreted in terms of legal rights and duties. In addition, as most enterprises and institutions had no property, and citizens earned little, it was impossible for the public to challenge the government.

This situation changed radically when China switched to a market economy. Today, enterprises are becoming increasingly independent, and the private economy is taking on a significant role. Enterprises are being forced to compete on the open market and are keen to reduce levels of administrative interference. In addition, as individuals accumulate more wealth and economic power, they are finding the strength to confront the government.

As this independence grows, new laws are required to limit governmental power, but at the same time the government must play an essential role in regulating unfair competition, monopolies, illegal transactions and the growth in crime. In this context, China has been asking itself what the function of government should be, and how it should use its power to protect property. It has become obvious that the establishment of a system of administrative law is essential.

In China, the relationship between the market economy and administrative law is clear. The development of the market economy has fostered the development of administrative law, in turn administrative law has become an essential tool in regulating and protecting the market economy.

Functions of Administrative Law

Investing Government Power and Defining its Limits

For the market economy to prosper, both an active government and safeguards against excessive government intervention are required in order to maintain stability without affecting the dynamics of business. As a result, China is trying to institute organic law of administration, which is meant to:

(a) define the areas administrative agencies are entitled to operate in, and what measures they can take;
(b) clarify the duties of administrative agencies. Failure to provide services or take appropriate measures may result in litigation;
(c) determine the limits of administrative agencies. In line with the principle of legality, they do not have legal power over administrative acts outside their jurisdiction, and these may be nullifed on the ground of *ultra vires*. Technically speaking, administrative power means the capacity to administer and the obligation to do what is required without overstepping these boundaries.

Regulating the Exercise of Government Power

The healthy operation of the market economy depends to a large extent on containing government power. If the government is too powerful, the market will lose its vitality and China will end up back to a planned economy.

In order to maintain smooth market operation and protect enterprises from unreasonable interference it is not enough simply to limit government powers. Even where the power of government is clearly and reasonably defined, an abuse of executive power by government officials can easily result in market disruption and a loss of confidence. As a result, legislation on administrative procedures is being introduced in China to establish the fundamental principles and procedures relating to administrative action. This legislation will play an indispensable role in three major areas:

Maintaining Democracy and Preventing Arbitrary Use of Power

Although the heads of administrative organizations are ultimately responsible for the work of the organization, this work must be carried out in a democratic manner. For instance, interested parties should be given the chance to participate in the making of rules, regulations and policies; and those who will be adversely affected by administrative decisions should have the rights to be informed and to be heard.

Preventing Corruption

The principle methods for preventing corruption include maintaining public or open government; holding hearings; separating functions; instituting a rule prohibiting *ex parte* communications; and explaining decisions.

In public or open government, rules, regulations, policies and other documents must be made available to the public, and decisions taken should be made accessible to those affected, unless there is an explicit excluding clause in the statute.

Before an administrative agency reaches a decision concerning citizens' rights or interests, it is obliged to hold hearings for them to voice their complaints, opinions and suggestions; to receive evidence and relevant materials; to organize cross examinations if necessary; and to take every relevant factor into consideration.

Separation of functions helps to prevent the abuse of power by conferring closely related functions on different officials or units within an agency.

The rule prohibiting *ex parte* communications demands that the agency not be in contact with one party separately when the matter in question concerns two or more parties.

Finally, the agency is bound to explain its decisions or verdicts, and to give the legal sources, facts and reasons behind them, particularly where they will have adverse effects.

Protecting Citizens' Rights and Interests

There are a number of procedures related to decisions which aim to prevent administrative power from violating the interests of the governed parties. For example, giving notice before decisions, and conducting investigations, hearings, administrative and judicial reviews all help to protect the rights of individuals.

Improving Administrative Efficiency

This relates to the establishment of reasonable steps and time limits for administrative action. These procedural provisions are very important to the functioning of administrative law, and violation of them can be as disastrous as the violation of substantive rules.

Stipulating Government Liability and Legal Remedies

The vitality of the market economy depends on the competitive spirit of its participants, which in turn demands legal protection of their rights and freedom from interference, including government interference. This means that, in addition to the organic laws and legislation on administrative procedures previously mentioned, legislation providing for remedies for unlawful government actions is also a necessary part of the system.

Such legislation allows victims of administrative abuse to challenge the agency or officials and to claim compensation. A system for dealing with administrative complaints, litigation and compensation already exists in China. It is useful in:

(a) heightening individual confidence in the government and creating a sense of security and economic stability. This sense of security is essential to the prosperity of the market economy. If the government is not answerable for its actions and citizens or organizations have no recourse, their enthusiasm and creativity will be lost

(b) promoting legality in administration among government officials. Rule of law implies respect of human and legal rights and the interests of the governed parties. Through the mechanism of tort liability, officials learn to act according to law and to respect citizens' rights

(c) encouraging foreign investment. As foreign investors are directly interested in making profit, they are particularly concerned about the security of their investment. Adminstrative law and legislation on administrative remedies in particular are crucial in safeguarding person and property, and could be viewed as a part of investment law

(d) maintaining social justice and stability. Injustice, corruption and disaffection with administrative policy will always exist regardless of what laws are introduced. It is important for administrative law to provide an outlet for public complaints. When this is not allowed to happen, social stability can be threatened, and without stability, economic prosperity the goal of "wealth and strength" will not be achievable.

Conclusion

In conclusion, it is obvious that the development of administrative law and the market economy are closely connected. It is equally obvious that the further development of the system of administrative law is as crucial to the success of the market economy as the development of China's civil and commercial law, and, as such, it deserves equal emphasis.

FROM MIXED TO MARKET ECONOMY — CONSTITUTIONAL EXPERIENCE IN INDIA

Professor Mahendra P. Singh

Faculty of Law
University of Delhi

Professor Singh, *B.A., LL.B. (Agra), LL.M. (Columbia), LL.M., LL.D. (Lucknow), is the Dean and Head of the Faculty of Law at the University of Delhi. He is Professor of Public Law and Comparative Law. He has published several books and has taken visiting professorships at various overseas universities.*

A keen scholar of the constitutional developments in India, Granville Austin, has said:

"Two revolutions, the national and the social, had been running parallel in India since the end of the First World War. With Independence, the national revolution would be completed, but the social revolution must go on".[1]

Addressing the Constituent Assembly, Pandit Nehru, the then prime minister and architect of modern India, reminded:

"The first task of this Assembly is to free India through a new constitution, to feed the starving people, and to cloth the naked masses and to give every Indian the fullest opportunity to develop himself according to his capacity".[2]

Pandit Nehru was expressing a view shared by many others. A prominent member of the Assembly, K. Santhanam, envisaged three revolutions.

"The political revolution would end with independence. The social revolution meant to get [India] out of the medievalism based

27

on birth, religion, custom and community and reconstruct her social structure on modern foundations of law, individual merit and secular education. The third revolution was an economic one: the transition from primitive rural economy to scientific and planned agriculture and industry".[3]

The Assembly's task was to draft a constitution that would serve the ultimate goal of social revolution, of national renaissance. This was a task far more complicated than the simple drafting of the fundamental rights or the moral precepts of a preamble. What forms of political institutions would foster or at least permit a social revolution? What political institution, therefore, would help to establish the conditions in which social change would more easily take place? The major choice was more basic: to what political tradition, to the European or the Indian, should the Assembly look for a constitutional pattern? By which of these routes could India best arrive at the goal of social revolution.

The two alternatives before the Assembly were either to adopt a constitution in the Euro-American tradition that had become part of the Indian constitutional tradition during the British rule, or to look back to the indigenous Indian traditions of some sort of Panchayat system, as envisaged by Mahatma Gandhi. "In either case," Austin says, "the constitution must be democratic, there was to be no return to the Indian precedent of a despot with his *darbar*; nor would the Assembly have Europe's totalitarianism or the Soviet system".[4]

Gandhi's idea of a constitution for India — found in his writings starting with *Hind Swaraj* and continuing until after independence — was given a concrete shape by Shriman Narayana Agarwal in his *Gandhian Constitution for Free India*. It was based on bottom up democratic institutions, taking the village as the first unit creating a Panchayat for itself, which will create regional or provincial Panchayats; and the latter finally constituting a national Panchayat. Gandhi believed that the achievement of social justice must proceed from a character reformation of each individual: from the heart and mind of each Indian outward into society as a whole. The impetus for reform must not come downward from the government, and a reformed society would need no government to regulate or control it. Gandhians wanted as minimal a "state" as possible. "The state that governs best, governs least," they preached; "Keep government to the minimum, and what you must have, decentralize." A beneficial by-product of this minimal government would be to increase the individual's responsibility for his own welfare.

The Gandhian model was different from the Euro-American model, which provided for directly elected governments. The tendency in that model was towards centralization. Though these constitutions were products of laissez-faire thinking, they had come more and more to assume responsibility for the citizen's welfare, and the scope of modern government had been steadily widening, not decreasing. These constitutions were also not made with the aim of creating a single economy country.

The Assembly had to decide between these two alternatives. Ultimately, when Rau's draft constitution appeared (on which the Drafting Committee built its draft in 1948) it was based on the Euro-American model and not on the Gandhian. There was no mention in it of Panchayats. There were some protests against it, including one from the President of the Constitutional Assembly, Dr Rajendra Prasad. Many of the protests were more in terms of recognising the village as an important unit where large masses lived and which required immediate attention than in support of the Gandhian model. These demands, it was believed, could well be met administratively by creating greater administrative decentralization. Their emotional attachment to Panchayats was given expression in one of the Directive Principles of State Policy (Article 40) without, however, adopting the Gandhian Panchayat model in any form.

The reasons for this decision, as Glanville Austin has stated, were, firstly, that the congress had never been Gandhian; its members and leaders believed in social transformation through the instrument of the state, following perhaps the liberal democratic traditions that they had imbibed through their education and travel to western countries.

Secondly, they had a commitment to socialism. Although they ranged from Marxists through Gandhian socialists to conservative capitalists, each with his own definition of socialism, nearly everyone was Fabian and Laski-ite enough to believe that socialism is everyday politics for social regeneration, and that democratic constitutions are inseparably associated with the drive towards economic equality. Under Patel's influence, Nehru omitted the word "socialism" from the Objective Resolution and thus from the constitution. The Assembly wanted a democratic constitution with a socialist bias so as to allow the nation in the future to become as socialist as its citizens desired or as its needs demanded.

Thirdly, the conditions existing at the time of the making of the Constitution — partition of the country, communal strife and a hostile neighbour — reinforced the idea of strong centralized government even for socio-economic transformation with central planning, development of modern agricultural methods, transport, communications, heavy and light industry, electric power and technical advancement in general.

Finally, the Assembly's belief in adult suffrage. They firmly believed that adult suffrage not only at the village Panchayat level but in the formation of the national government directly would be the most powerful instrument of social transformation. Forming the national government indirectly through village Panchayats would have rather perpetuated the age-old caste and class distinctions in society. Adult sufferage would, however, have empowered the weakest and most underpriveleged to participate in the formation of the government and its policies. Experience of the working of the constitution has proved that the constituton makers were correct in their assessment.

On a fair assessment of the alternative models before the Constituent Assembly, as discussed, it is clear that nobody in the Assembly spoke for any kind of totalitarian regime even for a short while. The Gandhian model as well as the Euro-American model are based on the central position of the individual and the restricted, if not minimal, role of the state. In any case, the Euro-American model is a product and representative of liberalism which is the basis of free market economy. Adoption of this model by the Indian Constitution makers is no more than an addition to the liberal democratic traditions of constitution making. Accordingly, it creates institutions which are the products and promoters of that tradition. At the same time the constitution makers were fully aware of the glaring differences — particularly on the social and economic fronts — between the Euro-American and Indian societies. They clearly warned that the political democracy provided by the constitution would collapse unless the social and economic disparities and inequalities were removed from Indian society.

Criticism of the adoption of the Euro-American model of the Constitution did not come as much from the Gandhians as from the communist and socialist parties. Replying to their criticism, Dr Ambedkar, while moving the adoption of the constitution, said:

> "The Communist Party wants a constitution based upon the principle of the Dictatorship of the Proletariat. They condemn the Constitution because it is based upon parliamentary democracy. The socialists want two things. The first thing they want is that if they come in power, the constitution must give them the freedom to nationalize or socialize all private property without payment of compensation. The second thing that the socialists want is that the fundamental rights mentioned in the constitution must be absolute and without any limitations so that if their party were to come to power they would have the unfettered freedom not merely to criticize but also to overthrow the state".[5]

Although the constitution makers did not enshrine in the Constitution any particular economic policy — apart from creating liberal democratic institutions and laying down some broad goals in the Preamble, the Fundamental Rights and the Directive Principles of State Policy — the independence movement, particularly since the First World War, was guided by the principles of a social welfare state.

As early as 1925 in the Karachi Resolution it was resolved that major public services must be in the hands of the state. Later, after independence, in 1948, the decision was taken to have a mixed economy. This was vigorously pursued by regulating industry and trade. Wherever there was a conflict in implementing the principle of mixed economy, with the Constitution was amended. This process was continued until the doctrine of basic structure was expounded. The word "socialist", which the constitution makers had omitted, was introduced by the 42nd amendement in 1976. It was interpreted by the courts in different cases.

Until the end of Mrs Gandhi's first period in office in 1977 the concept of mixed economy and greater state control and regulation was pursued. With the coming of the Janata Party government at the centre in that year a rethinking had started. In a blueprint of the economic philosophy for the Janata Party, the then Deputy Prime Minister (later the Prime Minister for a shortwhile) Mr Charan Singh, who was always critical of too much state ownership and of the public sector, produced an alternative based on the Gandhian ideas of social and indigenous industry. That may not have brought any immediate change in India's economic policy, but it opened the gate for an alternative official level of thinking. Even though Mrs Gandhi was back in power in 1980, she never pursued her former policies of nationalization and state control with the same vigour as previously. After her assassination in 1984, her son Rajiv Gandhi preserved a visibly liberal economic policy that was pursued without any let up by two short term Janta Dal Governments of V.P. Singh and Chandra Shekhar. Not until 1991 when Narsimha Rao came to power with Manmohan Singh as Finance Minister did the government make a clear statement in regard to economic policy. Their declaration has come to be known as the New Economic Policy (NEP). Its package falls into four categories: budgetary, industrial, trading, and financial. These policies are interlinked to each other. The first lot of polices was announced in the budget for the year 1991–92 and the new industrial policy on the same day, *i.e.* July 25, 1991. Trade and financial policies were announced subsequently. To fill some of the gaps left in the NEP, new policy statements were being made, creating a lot of uncertainty even though the direction was clear. An important aspect of the NEP is that post-budgetary policies reveal much greater pressures from IMF-Bank sources and are being introduced in phases.

The main features of the new Industrial policy are:

(a) delicensing of all industries except those specified schedule;
(b) the removal of the MRTP Act restrictions on size and capacity creation;
(c) removal of restrictions on expansion, mergers, takeovers and appointments of directors;

31

(d) raising of foreign equity investments up to 51 per cent in 34 industries;

(e) automatic clearance of investments of both Indian and foreign companies under the new dispensation;

(f) abolition of approval for phased manufacturing programs to which was tied phased imports;

(g) removal of location restrictions outside the radius with one million or more of population;

(h) private participation to be allowed in some sectors covered so far in the core areas by the public sector, such as defence, atomic energy, minerals and mineral oils;

(i) removal of restrictions on and compulsory registration of broad-banding facilities;

(j) a limited exit policy of sick units through their revaluation by the Bureau of Industrial and Financial Reconstruction (BIFR) and disinvestment of up 20 per cent of the government equity in selected units in the public sector; and

(k) increase in the limits on investment in the small scale units to the level of one crore of rupees.

Apart from a massive downward revision of the rupee, the new trade policy comprises the following changes:

(a) automatic clearance for import of capital goods in cases where foreign exchange is earned back in foreign equity or in export earnings;

(b) removal of all restrictions on the import of capital goods up to two crores;

(c) foreign companies investing up to 51 per cent to be given encouragement to set up trading houses and to be treated at par with the Indian companies;

(d) reduction in export subsidies;

(e) liberalization of import of technology; and

(f) introduction of Exim scrips up to 30 per cent of the export earnings to be freely treated.

In the field of finance, a number of measures have been taken for liberalization that include:

(a) removal of restrictions on the interest rate structure, particularly on private sector debentures and bonds;

(b) allowing the private sector to have mutual funds to shore up the capital market;

(c) the Securities and Exchange Bureau of India (SEBI) to have full control over the stock exchanges;

(d) the scrapping of inconvertibility clause by 20 per cent of loans in excess of rupees 5 crores were converted into equities;

(e) the setting up of the Special Empowered Board (SEB) to negotiate with a specific type of large multinationals for direct foreign investment in selected areas to obtain sophisticated technologies;

(f) provision of rupees 700 crores towards strengthening the capital base of the banks and provision of rupees 1,500 crores for debt waiver scheme;

(g) assurance that the Government will not intervene in the interest rate structure of the market in the name of helping the priority sectors thus linking the cost of capital with capital worthiness; and

(h) tax on the interest rates earned from deposits followed by increase in lending rates, thus enhancing the whole interest and lending rates structure.

The budgetary changes include:

(a) a reduction of fiscal deficit;

(b) reduction in subsidies, particularly for exports, food and fertilizers;

(c) promise to reduce the non-plan expenditure which has now become almost 2.5 times that of the planned expenditure;

(d) reduction in the depreciation rate from 33.3 per cent to 25 per cent in order to reduce capital intensity;

(e) no let-up in external borrowings; and

(f) three schemes announced to mop up the black money.

The open declaration and adoption of the NEP was expedited by the failure of the Russian and East European communist economies and the rise of Reagan-Thatcher right wing liberalism. The prevalent paradigm of liberalism is composed of a four-fold political economy: maximum play of market forces by privatization; representative democracy; free trade, and welfare state. To this was added another component: the multi-polarization of the global economy with dollar, yen and mark as the three major currencies forced the major economic powers to compete fiercely but only within the context of a globalized economy. The dominant paradigm was thus extended from the nation-state to the global economy. Ideologically, all this was reduced to a free market rhetoric against the rhetoric of state planning.

Economists have their own reservations about the NEP into which we need not go. It has also been attacked by lawyers. For example, Professor Baxi says:

"Indeed, the kind of privatization ... currently being globally talked about will require thorough going revisions in the Constitution, as has occurred in some leading socialist societies. Ours, at

33

least explicitly since 1976, is a socialist democratic republic and in interpreting it, as well as laws under it, Indian Courts have to give as complete an effect as they can to the basic socialist structure of the Constitution. Without any amendment of the Preamble, it is not fully open to the proponents of 'privatization' to practise unbridled forms of it. Similarly, it is not open to advocate or practise 'privatization' without changing the text of Articles 38,39 or 43-A".[6]

Similarly, S.S. Singh and Suresh Mishra say:

"It may not be disputed by anyone, with a clear and unpreju-diced conscience, that the 'economic reforms', with their over-whelming ideology, involving 'disinvestment' in public enterprises, thining of labour force and torpedoing the existence of the welfare state all of which go against the ideals and spirit of socialism and thereby impinging on one of the basic features of the Constitution".[7]

In view of the fact that since the First World War, socialist thinking in India was predominant and pursued even after Independence and repeatedly incorporated into the Constitution through amendments, the doubts expressed about the constitutional legitimacy and validity of the NEP are not unfounded. The question is, however, whether the constitution really incorporates any particular economic policy so that the adoption of one or other policy on the part of the government of the day will be unconstitutional? We have noted above that the makers of the Constitution decried that they were incorporating any economic policy in the constitution. On the contrary they had to defend it. That implied that the constitution did not incorporate communist or social-ist economic principles but adopted the Euro-American model of lib-eral democratic constitutions. It is that model that the constitution has continued to represent even after successive amendments, includ-ing the introduction of the expression "socialist" in the Preamble. Of course the Preamble is the soul of the constitution and contains much of what may be described as the basic structure of the constitution. That does not mean that the basic structure is static and incapable of adjusting itself with the evolution and development in human think-ing and institutions. Justice Holmes had said about the American Constitution that it did not contain Herbert Spacer's statics.[8] The Constitution of India also does not have written into it the communist manifesto. Apart from the fact that it has never been authoritatively held or declared by any court or other authority that socialism is part of the basic structure of the Constitution, the word "socialist" is incapable of having any fixed and agreed meaning. Different people have defined it differently. The countries which have coined that word such as Germany, France and Britain are the foremost examples of free market economies.

Interestingly, the German Basic Law in article 20(1) declares that "The Federal Republic of Germany is a democratic and social federal state". This provision is an entrenched provision under article 79(3) and its amendment is not permitted. Even then we know what the economic policy and the structure of Germany is.

Similarly Article 2 of the French Constitution states that "France is an indivisible, lay, democratic and social Republic", yet we know what the French economic approach is.

The Indian courts have not gone far in interpreting the terms "social" or "socialist". Nor did those who introduced these words throw any light on its meaning. The presumption is that they left it to be interpreted in light of the future developments. Of course any such interpretation cannot ignore its core which is social welfare. So long as the NEP keeps social welfare to the forefront it cannot be condemned as in violation of the Preamble to the Constitution.

Article 19, Clause (6)(ii) and Article 305, which authorize state monopoly to the partial or full exclusion of the individual in any trade, business or industry, are optional enabling provisions and not compulsory obligations to be carried out in any and every situation. They also do not stand in the way of the NEP.

Coming to the directive principles of the state policy laid down in articles 38, 39, 43-A or any other of them, we do not find anything inconsistent with the NEP. They talk of social justice, elimination of inequalities, ownership and control of material resources for the common good and workers' participation in the management of industry. The NEP does nothing expressly or impliedly that goes against any of these directives. The only question is whether these directives will be better served by privatization or by nationalization. Our experience so far has proved that they have not been served by nationalization. Why should we then be prohibited from experimenting with the privatization that is the call of the day and which many economists sincerely believe is the only solution to social ills and injustice?

Notes

[1] Austin, G., *The Indian Constitution* 1966, p.26.
[2] Nehru, J.L., *Unity of India* 1938, p.11.
[3] Austin, *op. cit.*
[4] *Ibid.* at 28.
[5] Shiva Rao, B., *The Framing of India's Constitution — A Study* 1968, p.939.
[6] Baxi, U., "Constitutional perspectives on Privatization", *Main Stream*, July 6, 1991.

[7] Singh, S.S. and Suresh Mishra, "Public Law Issues in Privatization Process"(1994) 40 IJPA 396.
[8] *Lochner v. New York.*

Appendix

THE CONSTITUTION OF INDIA

PREAMBLE

WE, THE PEOPLE OF INDIA, having solemnly resolved to constitute India into a [1][SOVEREIGN SOCIALIST SECULAR DEMOCRATIC REPUBLIC] and to secure to all its citizens:

JUSTICE, social, economic and political;

LIBERTY of thought, expression, belief, faith and worship;

EQUALITY of status and of opportunity;

and to promote among them all

FRATERNITY assuring the dignity of the individual and the [unity and integrity of the Nation];

IN OUR CONSTITUENT ASSEMBLY this twenty-sixth day of November, 1949, do HEREBY ADOPT, ENACT AND GIVE TO OURSELVES THIS CONSTITUTION.

PART III

FUNDAMENTAL RIGHTS

General

12. *Definition.* — In this Part, unless the context otherwise requires, "the State" includes the Government and Parliament of India and the Government and the Legislature of each of the States and all local or other authorities within the territory of India or under the control of the Government of India.

13. *Laws inconsistent with or in derogation of the fundamental rights.* — (1) All laws in force in the territory of India immediately before the commencement of this Constitution, in so far as they are inconsistent with the provisions of this Part, shall, to the extent of such inconsistency, be void.

(2) The State shall not make any law which takes away or abridges the rights conferred by this Part and any law made in contravention of this clause shall, to the extent of the contravention, be void.

(3) In this article, unless the context otherwise requires, —

    (a) "law" includes any Ordinance, order, bye-law, rule, regulation, notification, custom or usage having in the territory of India the force of law;

    (b) "laws in force" includes laws passed or made by a Legislature or other competent authority in the territory of India before the commencement of this Constitution and not previously repealed, notwithstanding that any such law or any part thereof may not be then in operation either at all or in particular areas.

[(4) Nothing in this article shall apply to any amendment of this Constitution made under article 368.]

Right to Equality

14. *Equality before law.* — The State shall not deny to any person equality before the law or the equal protection of the laws within the territory of India.

15. *Prohibition of discrimination on grounds of religion, race, caste, sex or place of birth.* — (1) The State shall not discriminate against any citizen on grounds only of religion, race, caste, sex, place of birth or any of them.

(2) No citizen shall, on grounds only of religion, race, caste, sex, place of birth or any of them, be subject to any disability, liability, restriction or condition with regard to —
  (*a*) access to shops, public restaurants, hotels and places of public entertainment; or
  (*b*) the use of wells, tanks, bathing ghats, roads and places of public resort maintained wholly or partly out of State funds or dedicated to the use of the general public.

(3) Nothing in this article shall prevent the State from making any special provision for women and children.

[(4) Nothing in this article or in clause (2) of article 29 shall prevent the State from making any special provision for the advancement of any socially and educationally backward classes of citizens or for the Scheduled Castes and the Scheduled Tribes.]   [s. 298, G.I. Act]

16. *Equality of opportunity in matters of public employment* — (1) There shall be equality of opportunity for all citizens in matters relating to employment or appointment to any office under the State.

(2) No citizen shall, on grounds only of religion, race, caste, sex, descent, place of birth, residence or any of them, be ineligible for, or discriminated against in respect of, any employment of office under the State.

(3) Nothing in this article shall prevent Parliament from making any law prescribing, in regard to a class or classes of employment or appointment to an office [under the Government of, or any local or other authority within, a State or Union territory, any requirement as to residence within that State or Union territory] prior to such employment or appointment.

(4) Nothing in this article shall prevent the State from making any provision for the reservation of appointments or posts in favour of any backward class of citizens which, in the opinion of the State is not adequately represented in the services under the State.

(5) Nothing in this article shall affect the operation of any law which provides that the incumbent of an office in connection with the affairs of any religious or denominational institution or any member of the governing body thereof shall be a person professing a particular religion or belonging to a particular denomination.   [s. 275, 298, G.I. Act]

17. *Abolition of Untouchability.* — "Untouchability" is abolished and its practice in any form is forbidden. The enforcement of any disability arising out of "Untouchability" shall be an offence punishable in accordance with law.

18. *Abolition of titles.* — (1) No title, not being a military or academic distinction, shall be conferred by the State.

(2) No citizen of India shall accept any title from any foreign State.

(3) No person who is not a citizen of India shall, while he holds any office of profit or trust under the State, accept without the consent of the President any title from any foreign State.

(4) No person holding any office of profit or trust under the State shall, without the consent of the President, accept any present, emolument, or office of any kind from or under any foreign State.

Right to Freedom

19. *Protection of certain rights regarding freedom of speech, etc.* — (1) All citizens shall have the right —
  (a) to freedom of speech and expression;
  (b) to assemble peaceably and without arms;
  (c) to form associations or unions;
  (d) to move freely throughout the territory of India;
  (e) to reside and settle in any part of the territory of India; [and]
  (g) to practise any profession, or to carry on any occupation, trade or business.
[(2) Nothing in sub-clause (a) of clause (1) shall affect the operation of any existing law, or prevent the State from making any law, in so far as such law imposes reasonable restrictions on the exercise of the right conferred by the said sub-clause in the interests of [the sovereignty and integrity of India,] the security of the State, friendly relations with foreign States, public order, decency or morality, or in relation to contempt of court, defamation or incitement to an offence]
(3) Nothing in sub-clause (b) of the said clause shall affect the operation of any existing law in so far as it imposes, or prevent the State from making any law imposing, in the interests of [the sovereignty and integrity of India or] public order, reasonable restrictions on the exercise of the right conferred by the said sub-clause.
(4) Nothing in sub-clause (c) of the said clause shall affect the operation of any existing law in so far as it imposes, or prevent the State from making any law imposing, in the interests of [the sovereignty and integrity of India or] public order or morality, reasonable restrictions on the exercise of the right conferred by the said sub-clause.
(5) Nothing in [sub-clauses (d) and (e)] of the said clause shall affect the operation of any existing law in so far as it imposes, or prevent the State from making any law imposing, reasonable restrictions on the exercise of any of the rights conferred by the said sub-clauses either in the interests of the general public or for the protection of the interests of any Scheduled Tribe.
(6) Nothing in sub-clause (g) of the said clause shall affect the operation of any existing law in so far as it imposes, or prevent the State from making any law imposing, in the interests of the general public, reasonable restrictions on the exercise of the right conferred by the said sub-clause, and, in particular, [nothing in the said sub-clause shall affect the operation of any existing law in so far as it relates to, or prevent the State from making any law relating to, —
  (i) the professional or technical qualifications necessary for practising any profession or carrying on any occupation, trade or business, or
  (ii) the carrying on by the State or by a corporation owned or controlled by the State, of any trade, business, industry or service, whether to the exclusion, complete or partial, of citizens or otherwise].

20. *Protection in respect of conviction for offences.* — (1) No person shall be convicted of any offence except for violation of a law in force at the time of the commission of the act charged as an offence, not be subjected to a penalty greater than that which might have been inflicted under the law in force at the time of the commission of the offence.

(2) No person shall be prosecuted and punished for the same offence more than once.

(3) No person accused of any offence shall be compelled to be a witness against himself.

21. *Protection of life and personal liberty.* — No person shall be deprived of his life or personal liberty except according to procedure established by law.

22. *Protection against arrest and detention in certain cases.* — (1) No person who is arrested shall be detained in custody without being informed, as soon as may be, of the grounds for such arrest nor shall he be denied the right to consult, and to be defended by, a legal practitioner of his choice.

(2) Every person who is arrested and detained in custody shall be produced before the nearest magistrate within a period of twenty-four hours of such arrest excluding the time necessary for the journey from the place of arrest to the court of the magistrate and no such person shall be detained in custody beyond the said period without the authority of a magistrate.

(3) Nothing in clauses (1) and (2) shall apply —

(a) to any person who for the time being is an enemy alien; or

(b) to any person who is arrested or detained under any law providing for preventive detention.

(4) No law providing for preventive detention shall authorize the detention of a person for a longer period than three months unless —

(a) an Advisory Board consisting of persons who are, or have been, or are qualified to be appointed as, Judges of a High Court has reported before the expiration of the said period of three months that there is in its opinion sufficient cause for such detention:

Provided that nothing in this sub-clause shall authorize the detention of any person beyond the maximum period prescribed by any law made by Parliament under sub-clause (b) of clause (7); or

(b) such person is detained in accordance with the provisions of any law made by Parliament under sub-clauses (a) and (b) of clause (7).

(5) When any person is detained in pursuance of an order made under any law providing for preventive detention, the authority making the order shall, as soon as may be, communicate to such person the grounds on which the order has been made and shall afford him the earliest opportunity of making a representation against the order.

(6) Nothing in clause (5) shall require the authority making any such order as is referred to in that clause to disclose facts which such authority considers to be against the public interest to disclose.

(7) Parliament may be law prescribe —

(a) the circumstances under which, and the class or classes of cases in which, a person may be detained for a period longer than three months under any law providing for preventive detention without obtaining the opinion of an Advisory Board in accordance with the provisions of sub-clause (a) of clause (4);

(b) the maximum period for which any person may in any class or classes of cases be detained under any law providing for preventive detention; and

(c) the procedure to be followed by an Advisory Board in an inquiry under sub-clause (a) of clause (4).

Right against Exploitation

23. *Prohibition of traffic in human beings and forced labour.* — (1) Traffic in human beings and *begar* and other similar forms of forced labour are prohibited and any contravention of this provision shall be an offence punishable in accordance with law.

(2) Nothing in this article shall prevent the State from imposing compulsory service for public purposes, and in imposing such service the State shall not make any discrimination on grounds only of religion, race, caste or class or any of them.

24. *Prohibition of employment of children in factories, etc.* — No child below the age of fourteen years shall be employed to work in any factory or mine or engaged in any other hazardous employment.

Right to Freedom of Religion

25. *Freedom of conscience and free profession, practice and propagation of religion.* — (1) Subject to public order, morality and health and to the other provisions of this Part, all persons are equally entitled to freedom of conscience and the right freely to profess, practise and propagate religion.

(2) Nothing in this article shall affect the operation of any existing law or prevent the State from making any law —

   (a) regulating or restricting any economic, financial, political or other secular activity which may be associated with religious practice;
   (b) providing for social welfare and reform or the throwing open of Hindu religious institutions of a public character to all classes and sections of Hindus.

Explanation I. — The wearing and carrying of *kirpans* shall be deemed to be included in the profession of the Sikh religion.

Explanation II. — In sub-clause (b) of clause (2), the reference to Hindus shall be construed as including a reference to persons professing the Sikh, Jaina or Buddhist religion, and the reference to Hindu religious institutions shall be construed accordingly.

26. *Freedom to manage religious affairs.* — Subject to public order, morality and health, every religious denomination or any section thereof shall have the right —

   (a) to establish and maintain institutions for religious and charitable purposes;
   (b) to manage its own affairs in matters of religion;
   (c) to own and acquire movable and immovable property; and
   (d) to administer such property in accordance with law.

27. *Freedom as to payment of taxes for promotion of any particular religion.* — No person shall be compelled to pay any taxes, the proceeds of which are specifically appropriated in payment of expenses for the promotion or maintenance of any particular religion or religious denomination.

28. *Freedom as to attendance at religious instruction or religious worship in certain educational institutions.* — (1) No religious instruction shall be provided in any educational institution wholly maintained out of State funds.

(2) Nothing in clause (1) shall apply to an educational institution which is administered by the State but has been established under any endowment or trust which requires that religious instruction shall be imparted in such institution.

(3) No person attending any educational institution recognized by the State or receiving aid out of State funds shall be required to take part in any religious instruction that may be imparted in such institution or to attend any religious worship that may be conducted in such institution or in any premises attached

thereto unless such person or, if such person is a minor, his guardian has given his consent thereto.

Cultural and Educational Rights

29. *Protection of interests of minorities.* — (1) Any section of the citizens residing in the territory of India or any part thereof having a distinct language, script or culture of its own shall have the right to conserve the same.

(2) No citizen shall be denied admission into any educational institutions maintained by the State or receiving aid out of State funds on grounds only of religion, race, caste, language or any of them.

30. *Right of minorities to establish and administer educational institutions.* — (1) All minorities, whether based on religion or language, shall have the right to establish and administer educational institutions of their choice.

[(1A) In making any law providing for the compulsory acquisition of any property of an educational institution established and administered by a minority, referred to in clause (1), the State shall ensure that the amount fixed by or determined under such law for the acquisition of such property is such as would not restrict or abrogate the right guaranteed under that clause.]

(2) The State shall not, in granting aid to educational institutions, discriminate against any educational institution on the ground that it is under the management of a minority, whether based on religion or language.

31. [*Compulsory acquisition of property.*] *Rep. by the Constitution (Fortyfourth Amendment) Act, 1978, s. 6 (w.e.f. 20-6-1979).*

[Article 31, which appeared under the sub-title "Right to Property", before its repeal by the Const. (44th Am.) Act, 1978, stood as follows]:

'**31.** *Compulsory acquisition of property.* — (1) No person shall be deprived of his property save by authority of law.

[(2) No property shall be compulsorily acquired or requisitioned save for a public purpose and save by authority of a law which provides for acquisition or requisitioning of the property for an amount which may be fixed by such law or which may be determined in accordance with such principles and given in such manner as may be specified in such law; and no such law shall be called in question in any court on the ground that the amount so fixed or determined is not adequate or that the whole or any part of such amount is to be given otherwise than in cash;

Provided that in making any law providing for the compulsory acquisition of any property of an educational institution established and administered by a minority, referred to in clause (1) of article 30, the State shall ensure that the amount fixed or determined under such law for the acquisition of such property is such as would not restrict or abrogate the right guaranteed under that clause.]

[(2A) Where a law does not provide for the transfer of the ownership or right to possession of any property to the State or to a corporation owned or controlled by the State, it shall not be deemed to provide for the compulsory acquisition or requisitioning of property, notwithstanding that it deprives any person of his property.]

[(2B) Nothing in sub-clause (f) of clause (1) of article 19 shall affect any such law as is referred to in clause (2).]

41

(3) No such law as is referred to in clause (2) made by the Legislature of a State shall have effect unless such law, having been reserved for the consideration of the President, has received his assent.

(4) If any Bill pending at the commencement of this Constitution in the Legislature of a State has, after it has been passed by such Legislature, been reserved for the consideration of the President and has received his assent then, notwithstanding anything in this Constitution, the law so assented to shall not be called in question in any court on the ground that it contravenes the provisions of clause (2).

(5) Nothing in clause (2) shall affect —
   (a) the provisions of any existing law other than a law to which the provisions of clause (6) apply, or
   (b) the provisions of any law which the State may hereafter make —
      (i) for the purpose of imposing or levying any tax or penalty, or
      (ii) for the promotion of public health or the prevention of danger to life or property, or
      (iii) in pursuance of any agreement entered into between the Government of the Dominion of India or the Government of India and the Government of any other country, or otherwise, with respect to property declared by law to be evacuee property.

(6) Any law of the State enacted not more than eighteen months before the commencement of this Constitution may within three months from such commencement be submitted to the President for his certification; and thereupon, if the President by public notification so certifies, it shall not be called in question in any court on the ground that it contravenes the provisions of clause (2) of this article or has contravened the provisions of sub-section (2) of section 299 of the Government of India Act, 1935."   [s. 299, G.I. Act]
[*Saving of Certain Laws*]

[**31A.** *Saving of laws providing for acquisition of estates, etc.* —[(1) Notwithstanding anything contained in article 13, no law providing for —
   (a) the acquisition by the State of any estate or of any rights therein or the extinguishment or modification of any such rights, or
   (b) the taking over of the management of any property by the State for a limited period either in the public interest or in order to secure the proper management of the property, or
   (c) the amalgamation of two or more corporations either in the public interest or in order to secure the proper management of any of corporations, or
   (d) the extinguishment or modification of any rights of managing agents, secretaries and treasurers, managing directors, directors or managers of corporations, or of any voting rights of shareholders thereof, or
   (e) the extinguishment or modification of any rights accruing by virtue of any agreement, lease or licence for the purpose of searching for, or winning, any mineral or mineral oil, or the premature termination or cancellation of any such agreement, lease or licence,
shall be deemed to be void on the ground that it is inconsistent with, or takes away or abridges any of the rights conferred by ²⁸[article 14 or article 19]:

Provided that where such law is a law made by the Legislature of a State, the provisions of this article shall not apply thereto unless such law, having been reserved for the consideration of the President, has received his assent:

[Provided further that where any law makes any provision for the acquisition by the State of any estate and where any land comprised therein is held by a person under his personal cultivation, it shall not be lawful for the State to acquire any portion of such land as is within the ceiling limit applicable to him under any law for the time being in force or any building or structure standing thereon or appurtenant thereto, unless the law relating to the acquisition of such land, building or structure, provides for payment of compensation at a rate which shall not be less than the market value thereof.]

(2) In this article, —

[(a) the expression "estate" shall, in relation to any local area, have the same meaning as that expression or its local equivalent has in the existing law relating to land tenures in force in that area and shall also include —

(i) any *Jagir, inam or muafi* or other similar grant and in the States of [Tamil Nadu] and [Kerala,] any *janmam* right;

(ii) any land held under ryotwari settlement;

(iii) any land held or let for purposes of agriculture or for purposes ancillary thereto, including waste land, forest land, land for pasture or sites of buildings and other structures occupied by cultivators or land, agricultural labourers and village artisans;

(b) the expression "rights", in relation to an estate, shall include any rights vesting in a proprietor, sub-proprietor, under-proprietor, tenure-holder, [*raiyat, under-raiyat*] or other intermediary and any rights or privileges in respect of land revenue.]

[**31B.** *Validation of certain Acts and Regulations.* — Without prejudice to the generality of the provisions contained in article 31A, none of the Acts and Regulations specified in the Ninth Schedule nor any of the provisions thereof shall be deemed to be void, or ever to have become void, on the ground that such Act, Regulation or provision is inconsistent with, or takes away or abridges any of the rights conferred by, any provisions of this Part, and notwithstanding any judgment, decree or order of any court or tribunal to the contrary, each of the said Acts and Regulations shall, subject to the power of any competent Legislature to repeal or amend it, continue in force.]

31C. *Saving of laws giving effect to certain directive principles.* — Notwithstanding anything contained in article 13, no law giving effect to the policy of the State towards securing [all or any of the principles laid down in Part IV] shall be deemed to be void on the ground that it is inconsistent with, or takes away or abridges any of the rights conferred by [article 14 or article 19]; *and no law containing a declaration that it is for giving effect to such policy shall be called in question in any court on the ground that it does not give effect to such policy:*

Provided that where such law is made by the Legislature of a State, the provisions of this article shall not apply thereto unless such law, having been reserved for the consideration of the President, has received his assent.]

31D. [*Saving of laws in respect of anti-national activities.*] *Rep. by the Constitution (Forty-third Amendment) Act, 1977, s. 2 (w.e.f. 13-4-1978).*

Rights to Constitutional Remedies

32. *Remedies for enforcement of rights conferred by this Part.* — (1) The right to move the Supreme Court by appropriate proceedings for the enforcement of the rights conferred by this Part is guaranteed.

(2) The Supreme Court shall have power to issue directions or orders or writs, including writs in the nature of *habeas corpus, mandamus*, prohibition, *quo warranto* and *certiorari*, whichever may be appropriate, for the enforcement of any of the rights conferred by this Part.

43

(3) Without prejudice to the powers conferred on the Supreme Court by clauses (1) and (2), Parliament may by law empower any other court to exercise within the local limits of its jurisdiction all or any of the powers exercisable by the Supreme Court under clause (2).

(4) The right guaranteed by this article shall not be suspended except as otherwise provided for by this Constitution.

32A. [*Constitutional validity of State laws not to be considered in proceedings under article* 32.] *Rep. by the Constitution (Forty-third Amendment) Act,* 1977, s. 3 (w.e.f. 13-4-1978).

33. *Power of Parliament to modify the rights conferred by this Part in their application ect.* — Parliament may, by law, determine to what extent any of the rights conferred by this Part shall, in their application to, —
  (a) the members of the Armed Forces; or
  (b) the members of the Forces charged with the maintenance of public order, or
  (c) persons employed in any bureau or other organization established by the State for purposes of intelligence or counter intelligence; or
  (d) persons employed in, or in connection with, the telecommunication systems set up for the purposes of any Force, bureau or organization referred to in clauses (a) to (c), be restricted or abrogated so as to ensure the proper discharge of their duties and the maintenance of discipline among them.]

34. *Restriction on rights conferred by this Part while martial law is in force in any area* — Notwithstanding anything in the foregoing provisions of this Part, Parliament may by law indemnify any person in the service of the Union or of a State or any other person in respect of any act done by him in connection with the maintenance or restoration of order in any area within the territory of India where martial law was in force or validate any sentence passed, punishment inflicted, forfeiture ordered or other act done under martial law in such area.

35. *Legislation to give effect to the provisions of this Part* — Notwithstanding, anything in this Constitution, —
  (a) Parliament shall have, and the Legislature of a State shall not have power to make laws —
    (i) with respect to any of the matters which under clause (3) of article 16, clause (3) of article 32, article 33 and article 34 may be provided for by law made by Parliament; and
    (ii) for prescribing punishment for those acts which are declared to be offences under this Part;
and Parliament shall, as soon as may be after the commencement of this Constitution, make laws for prescribing punishment for the acts referred to in sub-clause (ii);
  (b) any law in force immediately before the commencement of this Constitution in the territory of India with respect to any of the matters referred to in sub-clause (i) of clause (a) or providing for punishment or any act referred to in sub-clause (ii) of that clause shall, subject to the terms thereof and to any adaptations and modifications that may be made therein under article 372, continue in force until altered or repealed or amended by Parliament.

Explanation — In this article, the expression "law in force" has the same meaning as in articie 372.

PART IV

DIRECTIVE PRINCIPLES OF STATE POLICY

36. *Definition.* — In this Part, unless the context otherwise requires: "the State" has the same meaning as in Part III.

37. *Application of the principles contained in this Part.* — The provisions contained in this Part shall not be enforceable by any court, but the principles therein laid down are nevertheless fundamental in the governance of the country and it shall be the duty of the State to apply these principles in making laws.

38. *State to secure a social order for the promotion of welfare of the people.* — [(1) The State shall strive to promote the welfare of the people by securing and protecting as effectively as it may a social order in which justice, social, economic and political, shall inform all the institutions of the national life.

[(2) The State shall, in particular, strive to minimize the inequalities in income, and endeavour to eliminate inequalities in status, facilities and opportunities, not only amongst individuals but also amongst groups of people residing in different areas or engaged in different vocations.]

39. *Certain principles of policy to be followed by the State.* — The State shall, in particular, direct its policy towards securing —
   (a) that the citizens, men and women equally, have the right to an adequate means of livelihood;
   (b) that the ownership and control of the material resources of the community are so distributed as best to subserve the common good;
   (c) that the operation of the economic system does not result in the concentration of wealth and means of production to the common detriment;
   (d) that there is equal pay for equal work for both men and women;
   (e) that the health and strength of workers, men and women, and the tender age of children are not abused and that citizens are not forced by economic necessity to enter avocations unsuited to their age or strength;
[(f) that children are given opportunities and facilities to develop in a healthy manner and in conditions of freedom and dignity and that childhood and youth are protected against exploitation and against moral and material abandonment.]

[**39A.** *Equal justice and free legal aid.* — The State shall secure that the operation of the legal system promotes justice, on a basis of equal opportunity, and shall, in particular, provide free legal aid, by suitable legislation or schemes or in any other way, to ensure that opportunities for securing justice are not denied to any citizen by reason of economic or other disabilities.]

40. *Organization of village panchayats.* — The State shall take steps to organize village panchayats and endow them with such powers and authority as may be necessary to enable them to function as units of self-government.

41. *Right to work, to education and to public assistance in certain cases.* — The State shall, within the limits of its economic capacity and development, make effective provision for securing the right to work, to education and to public assistance in cases of unemployment, old age, sickness and disablement, and in other cases of undeserved want.

42. *Provision for just and humane conditions of work and maternity relief.* — The State shall make provision for securing just and humane conditions of work and for maternity relief.

43. *Living wage, etc. for workers.* — The State shall endeavour to secure, by suitable legislation or economic organization or in any other way, to all workers, agricultural, industrial or otherwise, work, a living wage, conditions of work ensuring a decent standard of life and full enjoyment of leisure and social and cultural opportunities and, in particular, the State shall endeavour to promote cottage industries on an individual or co-operative basis in rural area.

[**43A.** *Participation of workers in management of industries,* — The State shall take steps, by suitable legislation or in any other way, to secure the participation of workers in the management of undertakings, establishments or other organizations engaged in any industry.]

44. *Uniform civil code for the citizens* — The State shall endeavour to secure for the citizens a uniform civil code throughout the territory of India.

45. *Provision for free and compulsory education for children.* — The State shall endeavour to provide, within a period of ten years from the commencement of this Constitution, for free and compulsory education for all children until they complete the age of fourteen years.

46. *Promotion of educational and economic interests of Scheduled Castes, Scheduled Tribes and other weaker sections.* — The State shall promote with special care the educational and economic interests of the weaker sections of the people, and, in particular, of the Scheduled Castes and the Scheduled Tribes, and shall protect them from social injustice and all forms of exploitation.

47. *Duty of the State to raise the level of nutrition and the standard of living and to improve public health.* — The State shall regard the raising of the level of nutrition and the standard of living of its people and the improvement of public health as among its primary duties and, in particular, the State shall endeavour to bring about prohibition of the consumption except for medicinal purposes of intoxicating drinks and of drugs which are injuries to health.

48. *Organization of agriculture and animal husbandry.* — The State shall endeavour to organize agriculture and animal husbandry on modern and scientific lines and shall, in particular, take steps for preserving and improving the breeds, and prohibiting the slaughter, of cows and calves and other milch and draught cattle.

[**48A.** *Protection and improvement of environment and safeguarding of forests and wild life.* — The State shall endeavour to protect and improve the environment and to safeguard the forests and wild life of the country.]

49. *Protection of monuments and places and objects of national importance.* — It shall be the obligation of the State to protect every monument or place or object of artistic or historic interest, [47][declared by or under law made by Parliament] to be of national importance, from spoliation, disfigurement, destruction, removal, disposal or export, as the case may be.

50. *Separation of judiciary from executive.* — The State shall take steps to separate the judiciary from the executive in the public services of the State.

51. *Promotion of international peace and security.* — The State shall endeavour to —

(a) promote international peace and security;
(b) maintain just and honourable relations between nations;
(c) foster respect for international law and treaty obligations in the dealings of organized peoples with one another; and
(d) encourage settlement of international disputes by arbitration.

[**PART IVA**

FUNDAMENTAL DUTIES

51A. *Fundamental duties.* — It shall be the duty of every citizen of India —
(a) to abide by the Constitution and respect its ideals and institutions, the National Flag and the National Anthem;
(b) to cherish and follow the noble ideals which inspired our national struggle for freedom;
(c) to uphold and protect the sovereignty, unity and integrity of India;
(d) to defend the country and render national service when called upon to do so;
(e) to promote harmony and the spirit of common brotherhood amongst all the people of India transcending religious, linguistic and regional or sectional diversities; to renounce practices derogatory to the dignity of women;
(f) to value and preserve the rich heritage of our composite culture;
(g) to protect and improve the natural environment including forests, lakes, rivers and wild life, and to have compassion for living creatures;
(h) to develop the scientific temper, humanism and the spirit of inquiry and reform;
(i) to safeguard public property and to abjure violence;
(j) to strive towards excellence in all spheres of individual and collective activity so that the nation constantly rises to higher levels of endeavour and achievement.]

PART 2

COMPANY LAW: HONG KONG AND CHINA

PROPOSALS FOR A NEW CORPORATE RESCUE PROCEDURE IN HONG KONG

Professor Edward L.G. Tyler

Department of Professional Legal Education
City University of Hong Kong

Professor Tyler *is the Head of the Department of Professional Legal Education at the City University of Hong Kong. He was formerly Professor and Head of the Department of Professional Legal Education at the University of Hong Kong. He is the chairman of the Law Reform Commission of Hong Kong Sub-Committee on Insolvency.*

Corporate Failure Generally

Businesses fail for a variety of reasons. John Argenti in *Corporate Collapse: The Causes and the Symptoms* (1976) included the following causes:

— management shortcomings;
— accountancy failings, *e.g.* lack of budgetary control;
— failure to respond to change;
— constraints, *e.g.* environmental, trade union;
— recession; and
— excessive gearing.

Hong Kong with its greater owner management with hands on approach, greater flexibility (Hong Kong the "flexible factory") and extended family support ought to, and does, show a lower rate of corporate failure than other jurisdictions (see the table below for Hong Kong rates). It seems, therefore, that only in the worst cases do companies go to the wall. The Law Reform Commission Sub-Committee on Insolvency (the Sub-Committee), in considering a new company rescue regime, asked itself whether Hong Kong needed a better system for restructuring companies than it has or whether it was better simply to allow companies to die and thereby encourage the development and growth of new businesses. The Sub-Committee was of the view that it was beyond dispute that there were valid reasons for seeking to save companies (see the Sub-Committee's Consultation Paper).[1] In the real world corporate failure does not necessarily result in a rational re-allocation of resources and whereas in past times of full employment the social consequences of corporate failure may not have had many social consequences the same is not necessarily true today.

As is apparent from the table below, the number of compulsory (court ordered) winding-up orders is a very small percentage of the number of new company registrations and a very small number against the overall number of companies on the register. In fact research has shown that during a period in the late 1980s Hong Kong liquidation figures were proportionately less than half those of the United Kingdom.[2] The likely reasons for this are the more Draconian debt enforcement procedures (both legal and extra-legal) available in Hong Kong, the flexibility of Hong Kong Chinese businesses, extended family financing and support and loss of "face" (shame), the latter still being a factor in Hong Kong. Whether these lower than usual rates of failure will continue in the new economic environment remains to be seen. The failure rates shown in the table indicate a higher failure rate than that indicated by the research of the late 1980s period and the latest figures show a disturbing increase.[3]

Also worth noting from the table is the dramatic drop in new company registration figures since the beginning of 1994. It is well known that many companies, even small companies, are incorporating offshore, but it is unlikely that the drop is matched by these offshore incorporations. The reality is that the Hong Kong economy is experi-

TABLE

Compulsory wind-up orders

1990/91	1991/92	1992/93	1993/94	1994/95	6 months (1.4.95 to 30.9.95)
306	355	327	433	429	209

Number of companies on the register at financial year end

1990/91	1991/92	1992/93	1993/94	1994/95	6 months (1.4.95 to 30.9.95)
272,883	316,096	373,406	429,070	457,994	467,794

Number of new companies registered during year

1990/91	1991/92	1992/93	1993/94	1994/95	6 months (1.4.95 to 30.9.95)
28,862	48,163	61,685	60,301	37,367	16,752

Compulsory winding-up orders as percentage of new company registrations

1990/91	1991/92	1992/93	1993/94	1994/95	6 months (1.4.95 to 30.9.95)
1.06	0.74	0.53	0.72	1.15	1.25

encing a prolonged downturn (unlike the temporary downturn during the Middle Eastern and Gulf Wars). This makes it all the more important to look to our liquidation law and rescue procedures.

Current Position on Company Rescue

Currently, where a company is in financial difficulty, there are three possibilities:

(a) a secured creditor might appoint a receiver; or
(b) any creditor might petition the Court to wind up the company; or
(c) the company might seek to enter into a scheme of arrangement with its creditors to save the company.

Each of these possibilities will be briefly discussed.

Receivership

Most security documentation expressly provides that on certain specified events (most of which indicate that the company is in financial difficulty) the creditor may appoint a receiver over the secured assets.[4] In the case of a company security document (usually called a debenture) there are likely to be fixed charges over the company's real estate, equitable charges over any future acquired real estate, fixed or floating charges over receivables and a floating charge over the company's stock in trade. In the absence of an express or statutorily implied power to appoint a receiver, a receiver can only be appointed by court order where the security is in jeopardy.

The effect of the appointment of a receiver, in Hong Kong usually an accountant, is that the receiver will take under his control the company's assets and business and determine the company's liabilities. The receiver has wide powers, including the power of sale.[5] Often receivership ends in the sale of the company or the sale of the company's business or parts of the business, then followed by the liquidation of the company. Sometimes a company can be saved, particularly where the downfall of the company is due to diversification. It may be possible to sell off the loss making businesses and keep an economic core business. Because receivers sometimes "save" companies in financial difficulties they have been called "company doctors" and in this sense in some cases receivership can result in a company rescue. The outcome of a receivership often turns on the attitude of the secured creditor who has appointed a receiver. In practice, a receiver is primarily concerned to look after the interests of the creditor who appointed the receiver, rather than all the creditors, but subject to an equitable duty, *e.g.* in the case of sale to obtain a proper market price for the asset being realized.[6]

Liquidation

A creditor may apply to the court under the Companies Ordinance (Cap 32) for an order that the company be wound up, *i.e.* put into liquidation.[7] A liquidator, usually the Official Receiver,[8] but sometimes an accountant, will be appointed to administer the company's estate and, where assets exceed liabilities, to pay a dividend. The appointment of a liquidator generally means the end of the company (very rarely is any rescue scheme put in place at this stage). It is for this reason that a liquidator is sometimes called a "company undertaker".

In most liquidations the secured creditors and the preferential creditors (of which the most important are the company's employees) may hope to be paid something. Most unsecured or general creditors will receive little or nothing.

The social and economic consequences of liquidation are substantial. Men and plant may lay idle. The ripple effect spreads out to suppliers, manufacturers, the family and the communities of the workers and beyond. These consequences do matter and more so today in Hong Kong than formerly. Some companies, not all, can be saved. This is where an effective company rescue scheme is important.

There is not much incentive for a secured creditor to agree to a rescue, unless the security is insufficient to discharge the loan but institutional investors — banks, etc.—may want to preserve a long term client or for other reasons agree to a rescue.

An unsecured creditor has a strong motive to agree to a rescue because such a creditor is unlikely to receive much, if anything. The administration of a liquidation often takes many years and then usually only a small dividend is paid. The *Consultation Paper* gives some figures. The average time for distribution is about five years and the average dividend is about 30 per cent. A successful rescue might produce more, quicker.

Scheme of Arrangement With Creditors

Hong Kong already has a sort of rescue procedure in section 166 of the Companies Ordinance (Cap 32) which provides for compromises and arrangements, which if approved by a majority in number representing three-quarters in value of the creditors and sanctioned by the court will bind all the creditors. Besides that section, if a rescue package is to be put together it requires 100 per cent creditor consent. If that is forthcoming a voluntary arrangement or deed of arrangement can be entered into, providing, *e.g.* for debt rescheduling or the issue of equity (shares) to the creditors in lieu of loan capital. Without 100 per cent approval any single creditor can run off to the court to petition to wind up the company.

We will now look at section 166.

Companies Ordinance (Cap 32) Section 166

The section falls within a part of the Ordinance entitled "Arrangements and Reconstructions" and is itself titled "Power to compromise with creditors and members".

Section 166 is very complicated.[9] There is a lot of court involvement. Application has to be made by those proposing the rescue scheme to the court for the court to call a meeting of creditors to consider the proposal. If that application is successful and the proposal is approved by the meeting, another application to the court to sanction the scheme, as approved by the meeting, is required. If that application is successful, and the scheme sanctioned by the court, the scheme comes into effect and binds all creditors. A majority in number representing three-quarters in value of the creditors voting either in person or by proxy is required to approve the scheme.

There is much detailed documentation required. Sometimes it looks more like a company prospectus. This involves lawyers and accountants and, therefore, is expensive. The whole process necessarily takes time. It is further complicated by the express recognition in the section of different classes of creditors and separate class meetings.[10]

But the most serious defect of section 166 is that there is no moratorium — no stay of proceedings by creditors, so any creditor can apply to the court to have the company wound up while the negotiations for a rescue scheme are ongoing.

Fortunately, so far Hong Kong has avoided the economic recession of much of the rest of the world. It has had some significant insolvencies in the past. In few of those cases was section 166 used.

There were a number of bank and public company insolvencies between 1983 and 1985. These followed a cooling of the economy as a result of the second oil crisis and of the Sino-British talks leading in 1984 to the Joint Declaration. The Carrian Group collapse was the most prominent of these and the ramifications of this affair still rumble on. The Da Da chain of department stores went into receivership and then liquidation, with the receiver saying that the company could have been saved from liquidation if it had been given time and patience by the banks and creditors.[11] The Associated Hotels Group was saved from liquidation in October 1985 by a scheme of arrangement under section 166. It took two and a half years to complete the rescue. The company is now known as Tian Teck Land and is listed on the Stock Exchange of Hong Kong.

The most dramatic rescues of this period were those of a number of shipping companies. There was a world-wide downturn in the shipping industry in the early 1980s exacerbated by the second oil crisis. Two of Hong Kong's major shipping groups, the Tung Group and the Wah Kwong Group, nearly went into liquidation. They were eventually saved by voluntary arrangements with 100 per cent shareholder approval. The Tung Group rescue took 16 months to put together. The Wah Kwong rescue took about 10 months. In neither case was section 166 used. If a moratorium had been available under that section it is very likely that it would have be used. As it was, in both the Tung and Wah Kwong cases "recalcitrant" creditors held out. In the Tung case there were government interests behind the scene: the Japanese Government, which would have been looked to for compensation by Japanese shipbuilders under export credit guarantees had the new ships ordered not been taken up, and the PRC Government which had shown an interest in saving the group.[12] Today Orient Overseas (International) Ltd, the holding company of the Tung family companies, is trading successfully. In 1994 it was voted best performer on the Hong Kong stock market with the price of its shares gaining 68.33 per cent over the year and its subsidiary Orient Overseas Container Line was one of the largest container shipping companies in the world.[13] Wah Kwong has gone on to be equally successful.

The reports in the business press about these various rescue schemes always pointed out the vulnerability of rescues in Hong Kong in the absence of any moratorium provision as in U.S. Chapter 11 or its equivalent in Japan and the United Kingdom. Nearly 10 years on we are a little bit closer to an alternative to section 166.

It should be mentioned in fairness to section 166 that it was used in the Bank of Credit and Commerce Hong Kong case, but this was a special situation because of government intervention and the large number of small depositors. The bank was in fact wound up and the scheme was used to get rid of the small depositors by making a full pay out to them. Since then other creditors have received dividends amounting to 83 per cent of their claims.[14]

The Alternatives or Additions to Section 166

If, as everyone agrees, section 166 is not very satisfactory, what are the alternatives? There are two main models: U.S. Bankruptcy Code Chapter 11 and United Kingdom administration order procedure, *i.e.* Insolvency Act Part II, 1986.

The U.S. Chapter 11 procedure has the following characteristics. It is debtor initiated and debtor managed, there is much court involvement and subsequent costs and delay, and the procedure is abused. There is a tendency for companies to run into Chapter 11 as protection from creditors and without any realistic proposals for restructuring.

The United Kingdom administration order procedure has the following characteristics. It is debtor initiated, the debtor is excluded from management, there is much court involvement and subsequent costs and delay. Both procedures involve a moratorium. Both have been subject to criticism, not only on the costs and delay aspects. Chapter 11 often leaves the existing management, which brought the company to its current situation, in control (the concept of the debtor in possession). The United Kingdom procedure has been criticized especially on grounds of costs and court involvement.[15]

Insolvency Law Reform in Hong Kong

In September 1990 the Attorney General and the Chief Justice of Hong Kong referred the topic of insolvency law to the Law Reform Commission of Hong Kong (LRC) for a thorough review of the law of insolvency — both individual and corporate. The LRC set up a sub-committee to carry out the research and preparatory work for this. The Sub-Committee divided its work into three stages:

(a) amendments to the Bankruptcy Ordinance, which dates from 1931 and is based on the English Bankruptcy Act 1914 (these were sought by the Official Receiver to make the process more efficient and cost effective);

(b) corporate rescue procedure as an alternative to the existing scheme of arrangement procedure under section 166 of the Companies Ordinance (this was introduced as a second stage of the review because of difficulties encountered in the existing procedures in the shipping group restructurings referred to above and fears for the need for an alternative procedure in the event of a downturn in the Hong Kong economy);

(c) amendments to liquidation procedure (the Companies Ordinance dates from 1932 and is based on the English Companies Act 1929) and certain topics common to both bankruptcy and liquidation and also transnational issues.

The LRC published its report on bankruptcy in May 1995. The legislation based on the report is expected in Summer 1996.[16]

The Sub-Committee published its *Consultation Paper on Corporate Rescue and Insolvent Trading* in June 1995 and the LRC's Report on these topics is expected to be published around June 1996. The Sub-Committee was in the happy position of coming late to the topics and thus was able to consider reforms in other jurisdictions. The Sub-Committee reviewed the rescue procedures under U.S. Bankruptcy Code Chapter 11 and the proposed new Chapter 10 for small businesses, the United Kingdom administration order, reforms in Australia in the Corporate Law Reform Act 1992 (creating a modified administration order procedure to replace the previous official management procedure),[17] the recent Singapore judicial management procedure (introduced by the Companies (Amendment) Act 1990 and based on the United Kingdom administration order),[18] amendments in Canada in the Bankruptcy and Insolvency Act 1992[19] and elsewhere.

The Sub-Committee sought to identify the characteristics of a good rescue procedure.

Characteristics of a Good Rescue Procedure

The Sub-Committee identified the following characteristics:

(a) The necessity for a moratorium, but not one too long nor too easily extended;

(b) court involvement to be kept as a last resort — to prevent delay and expense;

(c) an independent professional supervisor — not burdened with liabilities so as to be discouraged from taking on a job;

(d) the provision for proper management while the scheme was being considered — all directors not automatically excluded;

(e) realistically some preference for secured creditors could probably not be avoided;

(f) superpriority — to encourage bank creditors or others to fund the reorganization;

(g) simple procedures.

A moratorium is an essential requirement for any effective rescue scheme, but its length should not be so long as to make creditors unwilling parties. Good systems provide a short, *e.g.* 28 days or 30 days, initial period with the possibility of limited extensions. It will only be in the simplest cases that a scheme can be put together in such initial period. On the other hand where rescue is anticipated there will usually have been behind the scenes negotiations with creditors and the prospective administrator will have been brought in and will be reasonably familiar with the state of affairs of the company.

The courts should be kept out of the process as much as possible. One of the disadvantages of both the Chapter 11 and administration order procedure is the initial involvement of the courts. The Australian Administration Procedure only involves the court as a backstop. Court involvement leads to delays and expense. Courts require formal documentation and this tends to accumulate. The mere size and quantity of the documentation which had become the norm for the application to the court for an interim order (the moratorium) under the United Kingdom Insolvency Act 1986 lead to the judges issuing a practice statement[20] prohibiting excessive documentation.

Some expense cannot be avoided, especially if a qualified professional is to be the administrator of the process. What needs to be discouraged is the U.S. Chapter 11 situation where the very managers who have most likely brought the company to its current pass are allowed to remain in charge of management. In those jurisdictions that have a recognized insolvency practitioner regime such a practitioner is best suited to the task. She will be a professional with experience and accountable to a regulatory authority, and perhaps also to her professional body. This will give the necessary expertise and independence at a cost that can, if necessary, be subjected to scrutiny. The administrator must not be subjected to so many liabilities as to discourage persons taking up the position. Liability should be limited to contracts entered into by the administrator (and not those made prior to entering into office, unless expressly adopted and then only as to the future) with a priority right of indemnity against the assets of the company.

The administrator, usually an accountant or a lawyer, while hopefully having some management skills will have neither the management nor specialist business expertise to conduct the day to day affairs of the company. In this situation the administrator (just as the receiver/manager may do) may appoint some manager to attend to this. One of the disadvantages of the administration order, pursuant to which the administrator may remove and appoint directors, is that it usually results in the removal of the whole board of directors. A consequence of this is that the board is usually unwilling to initiate administration. Boards are usually neither wholly bad nor good.[21] What is wanted is a new environment in which greater use is made by administrators of the existing management, except for such as are clearly incapable.

The effect of any rescue procedure on secured creditors is a major consideration for any law reformer in Hong Kong. The sanctity of security has achieved almost a mystic quality. Few jurisdictions in introducing rescue procedures have dared to tamper with the sanctity of security and the priority rights of the secured creditor. Initially the Sub-Committee was minded to do so, but after being labelled "naive" by Professor Ziegel and Dr Gough (both of whom addressed the Sub-Committee) and being advised of the likely attitude of the banks and the knock-on effect (of more costly credit) by our bank colleague, it retreated.

Funds are needed to get the company through the rescue procedure. Existing creditors should be encouraged to fund the reorganization and there is a good argument that, in the liquidation, such funding should be given a superpriority, *i.e.* above the existing priority claims of preferred creditors under section 265 of the Companies Ordinance. Whether the superpriority should be limited to further funds put in by existing creditors or extended generally or in default of existing creditors being willing to provide further funds, is a matter of debate.

It is patently obvious that any rescue procedure needs simple procedures easily understood by business people and involving the courts as little as possible. Prescribed forms should be available for all the relevant stages of the process.

The Sub-Committee's Recommendations

With these characteristics in mind and after nearly two years' consideration (covering also the topic of insolvent trading) the Sub-Committee published its *Consultation Paper* with its proposals in June 1995. The *Consultation Paper* was distributed to various professional bodies and other interested organizations and persons for comments. Many comments were received, mostly supportive of the general principles. The Sub-Committee is currently considering the comments and amending its proposals.[22] These will go forward to the Law Reform Commission early in 1996 and a Report by the LRC based on the Sub-Committee's revised proposals should be published by mid-1996.[23] The Sub-Committee's paper includes a model bill. This should speed up the legislative drafting process. It is just possible that the Bill incorporating the proposals might get into the 1996–97 Legco session, *i.e.* October 1996 to June 1997.

The Sub-Committee has proposed a rescue procedure to be called "provisional supervision" and leading to a voluntary arrangement. The provisional supervision will be administered by a provisional supervisor, an accountant or solicitor, until a system of registered insolvency practitioners is established in Hong Kong.[24]

A moratorium will apply as soon as the resolution to go into provisional supervision and the provisional supervisor's consent to act have been filed at both the Supreme Court and the Companies Registry. The initial period of the moratorium is 30 days but may be extended to a maximum period of six months by the court or beyond that by the creditors' meeting. Immediately after appointment the provisional supervisor will have to start investigating the financial state of the company and, when this has been done, have to make a decision whether the purposes of a voluntary arrangement can be achieved. These purposes are set out in section 2 of the Model Bill as follows:

> "(1) (a) the avoidance of the winding up of the company;
> (b) the survival of the company, or the whole or any part of its undertaking as a going concern;
> (c) the satisfaction, in whole or in part, of the debts of the company.
>
> . . .
>
> (3) Without limiting the generality of the purposes . . . a company may make a proposal for a voluntary arrangement . . . for any one or more of the following purposes:
> (a) an extension of time for payment of its debts;
> (b) a composition in satisfaction of its debts;
> (c) the compromise of any claims against the company;
> (d) the variation or re-ordering of the rating for payment of its debts or any class of its debts;
> (e) the conversion of its debts in whole or in part into shares or other securities to be issued by the company;
> (f) any other scheme or arrangement in relation to the affairs of the company."

If the provisional supervisor considers that any one or these purposes can be achieved, then an arrangement plan will have to be prepared and when prepared put to a creditors' meeting for approval or rejection.

The easiest way to review the proposals is to walk through a typical case.

Sections 1–7 of Model Bill

X Company is facing financial difficulty, but is probably not yet technically insolvent, and its directors think it can trade out of its problems given time and perhaps some restructuring of the business.

Provisional supervision may be sought whether or not the company is insolvent (section 2(2)).

The directors discuss the matter with the company's major secured (those with mortgages or charges) and unsecured creditors. The creditors are sympathetic.

The directors also talk to the prospective provisional supervisor (Accountant A), who is familiar with the affairs of the company. He has been show some latest figures. He thinks that, on the information he has seen, the company might be saved, *i.e.* one or more of the purposes of a voluntary arrangement may be achievable and he is willing to be provisional supervisor if the directors decide to make a proposal for a voluntary arrangement and put the company into provisional supervision. They do so decide and so resolve at a board meeting. They also resolve to nominate Accountant A to be the provisional supervisor.[25] He consents in writing in the prescribed form. The copy of the board resolution and the consent of Accountant A are then filed at the Companies Registry and the Supreme Court Registry. The provisional supervision begins from the time of the last filing (section 7).

Sections 8–10 of Model Bill

The provisional supervisor (Accountant A) gives notice that Company X is in provisional supervision in the *Gazette* and local newspapers and probably will also call for notice of claims against the company.

From the moment of the last filing the moratorium applies. No action or other proceedings may be commenced or continued against the Company while the moratorium lasts (section 9). The moratorium lasts initially for 30 days (the initial moratorium period). In many cases the period will need to be extended.

In most cases whether or not a scheme can be achieved will depend on the attitude of the major secured creditors. Usually their views will have been canvassed before the directors make any decision about provisional supervision. A secured creditor with a floating charge over the whole or substantially the whole of the company's assets may elect not to participate in the supervision, whereupon the supervision ceases. Section 10 provides for the giving of notice to such a charge holder and such right of election. The Sub-Committee thought that there might be some psychological pressure on such a secured creditor to opt out. The alternative procedure was an opt in one. Some commentators on the *Consultation Paper* have a preference for the latter, saying that is inappropriate to start the process and then shortly afterwards cancel it.[26]

Fixed charge holders over particular assets will be subject to the supervision, but their rights are not prejudiced, though they may have to wait before they can exercise their rights. In an exceptional case a fixed charge holder might be able to be freed from the moratorium under the exemption procedure under section 19(8).

Sections 11–17 of Model Bill

The provisional supervisor's first task is to ascertain the financial state of the company (section 11). There is power to require relevant people to provide information (section 15).

The directors' powers are suspended during the supervision; if the provisional supervisor has confidence in particular directors, powers of the provisional supervisor can be delegated to them, specifically or generally (sections 12(3), (4)).

Having ascertained the financial state of the company the provisional supervisor has to make a decision whether the purposes of a voluntary arrangement are capable of being achieved. Application may be made to the court for an extension of time — a further 30 days (section 19(2)) ("the first court extension").[27]

If the provisional supervisor decides that the Company's position is hopeless, it will be necessary to call a meeting of creditors and report to them. The meeting will resolve to terminate the provisional supervision and wind up the company (section 17).

Sections 18–22 of Model Bill

If the provisional supervisor decides that the purposes of a voluntary arrangement can be achieved, the provisional supervisor will proceed to prepare an arrangement plan, *i.e.* reorganization plan (sections 17(3), 18).

If the provisional supervisor needs more time than the initial 30 days moratorium or a further 30 days first court extension of the moratorium, application must be made to the court for a subsequent court extension. Such extension will be for a specified period more or less than 30 days.[27] There is a maximum of six months from the beginning of the provisional supervision. After six months the moratorium and provisional supervision can only be extended by the decision of a creditors' meeting.

Having prepared a plan, the provisional supervisor calls a creditors' meeting to consider it (section 20). There is one class only of creditors. Admittedly this is simplistic, but it avoids complicating the procedure. Some commentators have said a single creditors' meeting is unacceptable. Others like the idea. To approve the plan there must be a majority in number and in excess of two-thirds in value of the creditors present in person or by proxy and voting. For other votes one half is substituted for two-thirds (sections 21(8), (9)). If the plan is approved the provisional supervision comes to an end and is superseded by the voluntary arrangement (sections 22(1), (2)).

If the creditors do not like the plan, the meeting may be adjourned

MORATORIUM PERIODS		
Type	Length	Source
Initial period	30 days subject to chargeholder's election not to participate.	s. 9(3) s. 10
Court extensions[28]	Max. 6 months from commencement of PS.	ss. 9(4), 19 s. 9(5)
First court extension	Up to 30 days. Conditions Opposition	s. 9(3) s. 19(4) s. 19(8)
Subsequent court extension	for as long as court thinks fit (subject to 6 months max). Conditions Opposition	s. 19(3) s. 19(5) s. 19(8)
Creditor extensions	Conditions/reports	s. 19(9) ss. 19(9), (13), (16)
Continuance of creditor extension		ss. 19(18), (19)
NON-APPLICATION OF MORATORIUM		
Excluded class(es) of creditors		ss. 9(7), 18(2)
Exempted creditor(s)	Significant financial hardship	ss. 9(8), 19(8)

SUPERPRIORITY (Section 26)

(1) Funds provided to the provisional supervisor or to the company by any creditor subject to the moratorium provisions herein during the provisional supervision period shall subject to section 28(2) have priority to the debts of all creditors whether preferential, secured, unsecured or otherwise, subject to the moratorium provisions for the purposes of any voluntary arrangement and for the purposes of any subsequent winding up of the company.

(2) The purpose of this provision is to provide working capital for the company during the provisional supervision period and the period of any voluntary arrangement. The priority shall apply only to funds provided for working capital for the company and such funds may not be used to discharge (in whole or in part) any liability of the company to the provider of the funds existing at the commencement of the provisional superivision period.

(3) For the purpose of this section the provision of funds includes (but is not limited to) advances of monies and the provision of credit by supplies of goods and services or the suspension of liability to pay by the suppliers of goods and services or lessors of property used by the company.

---

for further consideration of the plan. If the plan is ultimately rejected the company will be wound up (sections 20(7)(b), (8)).

Set out above is a table of the moratorium periods. Also indicated are the classes to which the moratorium does not apply. An excluded class of creditors is one excluded from the arrangement plan by arrangements between the provisional supervisor and that class. The provisional supervisor has power to compromise with a class. An example might be a secured minor creditor who is prepared to discharge a charge for a discount in order to get outside the moratorium delay. An exempted creditor is one who opposes a court extension of the initial moratorium and the court is satisfied that the extension could cause such creditor significant financial hardship. This might apply, for example, to a private lender or creditor who was in financial straits where delay in whole or partial repayment might lead to the bankruptcy of that person.

The Sub-Committee's proposals include superpriority for lending to the provisional supervisor as working capital (see above).

The Carrot and the Stick

The rescue scheme (provisional supervision) proposal is the carrot offering directors of failing companies an opportunity to seek a simple form of rescue rather than hang on until the situation gets worse and there is no alternative but liquidation. What is also needed is some stick to persuade directors to use the rescue procedure.

Fraudulent Trading

The current law is contained in section 275 of the Companies Ordinance (Cap 32), which makes a director found guilty of carrying on business to defraud creditors (fraudulent trading) criminally liable and also civilly liable to make good the loss to the creditors. The courts have construed this civil liability as involving, in effect, a criminal burden of proof. The section can rarely be used. There was one unreported case many years ago and a case involving the section is before the courts at the time of writing in a long trial following various earlier interlocutory applications, some of which have been reported (the Wheelock Marden litigation).

Insolvent Trading

The Sub-Committee has recommend, in addition to section 275, a new liability on directors for trading when their company is insolvent. This stick, hopefully, will encourage directors to go either into liquidation or provisional supervision sooner rather than later. Insolvent trading is based on a mixture of the insolvent trading provisions in the recent Australian amendments to their Corporations Law and the wrongful trading provisions of the United Kingdom Insolvency Act 1986. Insolvent trading will give rise to a civil remedy only, *i.e.* to compensate those creditors who suffer loss as a result of the insolvent trading. The criminal liability for fraudulent trading will remain. Only the liquidator can make an application to have someone made liable for insolvent trading. Persons who may be made liable are "responsible persons".

A responsible person is a person who is or has been a director or manager or other person involved in the management of the insolvent company at a time when any debt or debts were incurred and the company was insolvent at that time or there was no reasonable prospect of it avoiding becoming insolvent. (Note: it is the incurring of a debt or debts which is the triggering event. Note also the objective test as to the company being or becoming insolvent.)

In addition to being a responsible person it must also be proved that the responsible person at the time of the incurring of the debt or debts knew the company was insolvent, or ought to have known that the company was insolvent or would become so, or had reasonable grounds for suspecting that the company was insolvent or would become insolvent. (Note the subjective test as to knowledge and objective tests for the other criteria.) Then if, at that time, the responsible person failed to prevent the company from incurring such debt or debts, that person is guilty of insolvent trading. Suspecting or suspicion in this context means that the responsible person should be aware at that time that there are such grounds for so suspecting or a reasonable person in a like position in the company in the company's circumstances would be so aware.

The court has also to be satisfied that the debt was wholly or partially unsecured and the person to whom the debt is owed has suffered loss or damage because of the company's insolvency.

If there is a finding of insolvent trading the responsible person will be ordered to pay compensation to the person who has suffered such loss or damage equal to the loss or damage or such other sum as the court thinks fit.

Presumptions

The proposed new law would incorporate several presumptions.
Presumption of continuing insolvency — *i.e.* if it is proved that a company was insolvent at a particular time during the 12 months ending on the date of the commencement of winding up, there is a presumption that it was insolvent throughout the whole period between that time and the commencement of winding up. The burden is on responsible person to prove otherwise.
Presumption where failure to keep proper accounts — *i.e.* if a company contravenes Companies Ordinance s. 121 (failure to keep proper accounting records), it shall be presumed insolvent throughout the relevant, *i.e.* the 12 month, period. Technical contraventions are excluded. There is a defence if documents were destroyed and the responsible person was not concerned in or party thereto.
"Presumption" of insolvency — *i.e.* a company is insolvent for the purposes of the section if in the course of its business its assets are insufficient to discharge its debts or other liabilities in full as they fall due.

Defence

With the lesser burden of proof on the liquidator and the presumptions it is necessary to provide a defence where the responsible person has behaved reasonably. The defence is that, if the responsible person, after knowing that the company was insolvent etc., acting bona fide, took every step with a view to minimizing the potential loss to the company's creditors.

The test for these conditional criteria — "ought" to know or ascertain, or conclusions which "ought" to be reached, or steps taken those which "would" have been known, etc. — is that of a reasonably diligent person having *both* such general knowledge, etc. as may reasonably be expected of a person carrying out the functions that the responsible person was carrying out (objective test) *and* the general knowledge, etc. as that responsible person had (subjective test).

The onus of proving the defence is on the responsible person.

In determining whether a defence has been made out the court will have regard amongst other things to any action taken towards appointing a provisional supervisor; when that action was taken; and the results of that action.

As indicated above, comment to date on the Sub-Committee's proposals has been supportive in principle. It is likely, therefore, that any future legislation will be based on the proposals with some minor amendments.[31]

Notes

[1] Law Reform Commission Sub-Committee on Insolvency, *Consultation Paper or Company Rescue and Insolvent Trading* (June 1995), para. 1.18.
[2] Tyler, "Current Issues in Insolvency" in *Commercial Law* (1991), pp. 20–22.
[3] Noted in the *South China Morning Post* under the following sub-titles "Bankrupt population explosion" July 15, 1995, "Insolvency rate tipped to rise 30 percent" July 27, 1995.
[4] Section 50(1) of the Conveyancing and Property Ordinance (Cap 219) implies into any legal charge or equitable mortgage of land made by deed a power to appoint a receiver over that land and the income thereof when the mortgage money has become due.
[5] For the difference between a "receiver" and a "manager" see *Emsworth Ltd v. Howard William Burdett* [1978] HKLR 506. Most modern security documentation provides for the appointment of either or both.
[6] *China and South Sea Bank Ltd v. Tan Soon Gin* [1992] A.C. 536, P.C.; *Downsview Nominees Ltd v. First City Corp Ltd* [1993] A.C. 295, P.C.
[7] See Companies Ordinance (Cap 32) s. 177(1)(d) (on the ground that the company is unable to pay its debts) and s. 178 which deems the company to be unable to pay its debts where, *inter alia*, it fails to pay within three weeks after service of a statutory demand for payment.
[8] The Official Receiver plays a more important role in the insolvency process in Hong Kong than in most other jurisdictions. In fact there is comparatively little insolvency administration done by private accountants or lawyers. The Officer Receiver is generally the liquidator, save for a few large or complicated cases where the Official Receiver will not oppose the appointment of a suitably qualified private sector liquidator. See Annual Departmental Report of the Official Receiver's Office (1994–95), para. 3.7.
[9] The problems with the section are canvassed in some detail in the *Consultation Paper*, Chap. 1.

[10] See *Re Industrial Equity (Pacific) Ltd* [1991] 2 HKLR 614 for comment on the complexity of classes.

[11] "More opt for restructuring to stay afloat", the *South China Morning Post*, December 21, 1986.

[12] See (April 1987) *International Financial Law Review* 25.

[13] "Orient Overseas steams past the pack", the *South China Morning Post*, December 31, 1994.

[14] See Srivastava D.K., (1991) 1 Aus Jo. of Corp Law 170 for the background to the closure of the bank. See Annual Departmental Reports of the Official Receiver for the progress of the administration of the liquidation.

[15] See, *e.g. The Insolvency Act 1986: Review of Company Rescue Provisions* (1993), a Consultation Document of the Insolvency Service, London.

[16] Some of the issues arising out of aspects of the bankruptcy review can be found in Booth, (1993) 2 *International Insolvency Review* at 120–150.

[17] These reforms were based on the recommendations of the Australian Law Reform Commission's General Insolvency Enquiry (the Harmer Report). For an overview on the workings of the new procedure see M. Rose and L.J. Law (1995) 3 Insol. LJ 11.

[18] See Hicks [1987] 2 MLJ clxxxiii, cxciii.

[19] See, *e.g.* D.C. Tay, "Canadian Bankruptcy Reform: The Move from Liquidation to Rehabilitation" (1993) 2 International Insolvency Review at 44–65.

[20] (Administration Orders: Reports) [1994] 1 WLR 160.

[21] Like the people of Llareggub in Dylan Thomas' *Under Milk Wood*.

[22] Its Report was published in January 1996.

[23] The LRC is discussing the Sub-Committee's Report as this book goes to press. The final version of the proposals will go straight to the Legislation Draftsman (consultation already having taken place). Some modifications made as a result of the consultation and later by the LRC to the Sub-Committee's proposals are noted below.

[24] To ensure quality, practitioners eligible for appointment will need to be on a panel maintained by the Official Receiver. Fees will need to conform to a scheme controlled by the Official Receiver.

[25] To prevent directors abusing the process they will have to file an affidavit stating the background to their decision and their nominee.

[26] The LRC confirmed the opt out recommendation.

[27] The proposal for first and subsequent court extensions was changed after the consultation to court extension or extensions for any length of time subject to the maximum of six months.

[28] See n.27 for subsequent changes.

[29] This relates to the provisional supervisor's indemnity, which has a first priority.

[30] After the consultation the superpriority clause was amended to extend to other lenders where existing lenders were unwilling to lend.

[31] nn.24 and 30 above pick up some of the changes since this chapter was written.

EXPANDING SHAREHOLDER CONTROL IN HONG KONG

Philip Lawton

Faculty of Law
City University of Hong Kong

Philip Lawton *is an associate professor at City University of Hong Kong. Mr Lawton has experience as a legal academic, editor and consultant to large and small corporate businesses on a variety of legal and associated matters including corporate, revenue and intellectual property law.*

He has specialized and published in the United Kingdom and Hong Kong in revenue law, corporate law and the law of meetings. He is a regular speaker at professional and academic conferences in Hong Kong and overseas including Australia and the United Kingdom. Mr Lawton has focused in recent years on issues of corporate governance in the Asia Pacific region and is the author of Meetings in Hong Kong, Their Law and Practice.

General Background

In a recent article Harvard University Professor W.C. Kirby has emphasized that with its own organizational structures and values rooted in networks of family and regional ties, what may be called a "capitalism with Chinese characteristics" resisted the corporate structure even in the period of its most dynamic growth (the first half of the twentieth century)[1]. However leery of government, China's capitalists appeared even more suspicious of the public, finding the idea that they would be invited to share in one's business control and profits most disagreeable. As Li Chun writes, in explaining why the *Gongsilu* Law of 1904 was a *failure*:

"The idea that members of the public would be invited to join one's business and share in its control and profits was indeed repugnant. On the other hand, the notion that one's money be put into the pocket of some strangers for them to run a business was just as unthinkable."[2]

This comment goes to the root of two key structural issues now facing many Hong Kong family dominated listed companies.

The first is the issue of shareholder control and participation and the protection of minority shareholder interests. The second concerns the related issues of trust and delegation of decision making powers to professional managers. The latter raises questions concerning the separation of ownership and management control, often still a problem at the difficult "third generation" or in Wong Sui Lin's classification of the development of the Chinese family firm, the "disintegrative stage".[3] The professional manager or expert is as much a part of the Japanese Kieretsu structure or the European corporate scene as he is in the Anglo-American corporate model. In the Hong Kong context the strongest remnant of Confucian thought in modern Chinese behaviour is arguably in hierarchal authority and power.[4] Pye has analyzed the troublesome nature of power allocation in the context of China's "modernization" but his most insightful analysis in this respect is his comparison of the roles of Chinese and Japanese sons in understanding how the latter were better prepared to deal with modernization:

> "Probably the most profound difference between the socialization processes in China and Japan was that whereas in China the relations within the family were seen as the most important, Japanese training was more explicitly directed towards performance outside the family."[5]

The literature on Chinese family run companies in Hong Kong and elsewhere bears out this observation in relation to Chinese managers from two key perspectives, namely the inability of family run companies to delegate to and trust professional managers and also the common desire of the latter to set up their own businesses.[6] Yet even if there develops a greater willingness to appoint professional managers as in the Japanese and Anglo-American model this will only substitute one set of problems for another. In the "classic" Anglo-American Berle and Means type corporation there remains the problem of agency costs and the monitoring of managers with the concurrent issues of how to align the self interest of managers and shareholders.

A similar pattern to that in China is discernible in Hong Kong. Professor Tyler has emphasized that the use of the corporate form by Chinese businessmen in Hong Kong is largely a post Second World War phenomenon that has particular Chinese characteristics.[7] Indeed, Hong Kong Chinese businessmen resisted the territory's adoption of English partnership and corporate law to such an extent that the Chinese Partnership Ordinance 1911 was enacted to suit local business practice. Only after 1949 was the private registered company used to any great extent by the Hong Kong Chinese and only then after it was realized that the requirements of such a company (limits on the number of members, on the transfer of shares and a prohibition against offering shares to the public) made it an ideal vehicle for retaining family control. From just over 2,000 Hong Kong registered companies in 1949 their number has mushroomed to over 460,000 in 1995. In that year registered companies comprised over two thirds of the total number of registered businesses and there was one registered company for every 12.7 persons in the territory. The majority of Hong Kong's listed companies remain family dominated. This factor has had several implications for the HKSE attempts to reform the listing rules and improve standards of corporate governance and especially for expanding shareholder control.

This paper will explore the issue of expanding shareholder control but will first question the underlying assumption of the managerial revolution in the west and its application to the Chinese family firm in general.

The Enhancement of Shareholder Value

One of the underlying central themes of the Anglo-American model of corporate governance is the enhancement of shareholder value. In the nineteenth and for most of the twentieth centuries the United Kingdom model of corporate law was framed with the notion and assumption that the joint stock corporation, public in nature, was the norm. Exceptions were made throughout the legislation for the private company which became far more numerous. Hong Kong's current legislation, now under review,[8] is framed on the basis of this earlier and now largely discarded generation of corporate laws.

The view that corporations exist largely for the enhancement of firm or shareholder value is a narrow one but is embedded in the history of corporate law development in the Anglo-American model. As Romano has recently stated in the comparative corporate governance debate in the USA concerning the rolling back of U.S. laws restricting bank ownership of corporate stock or separating investment and commercial banking functions:

"But the rationale for such a policy reversal can not be readily found in the study of comparative institutions; it can be located more easily instead in our own corporate law tradition, namely, it is the policy most consonant with the competitive and enabling approach of U.S. corporate law, which, by permitting experimentation and innovation in the choice of institutions, tends to maximize firm value".[9]

It is respectfully submitted that this begs the question by assuming that firm and hence shareholder value is the ultimate goal. That view can be traced back to Adam Smith and the concept of the "invisible hand of the market".[10] In practice that is not the approach, in terms of general economic policy, pursued by many Asian countries, especially for example Japan and Korea whose preference is for the economics of Friedrich List.[11] Nor was it the approach followed by Britain or the USA during the period of their own development of an industrial base.[12] There is also a growing recognition in some quarters, particularly amongst some managerialists, that corporate businesses which survive and prosper are often "visionary" ones that, in the sense of achieving the corporate vision, put the organization first.[13] According to these writers, the figures often show that such "selfish" companies do far better for stockholders than the "economic" company of the textbook which puts shareholders first.[14] These managerialists question the approach of economic determinism in relation to the corporate lifecycle. Indeed this school of thought has asserted that companies that die in hostile situations are the ones where shareholders are the only stakeholders.[15]

A wider view is that corporate law is largely concerned with the organization of the production of wealth and the creation of economic strength which in turn relates to and directly raises the issue of how that wealth is distributed in society.[16] It is, in this regard, pertinent to note that the issue of directors' remuneration is embedded in such issues and not only those of agency costs for when, as in the U.S. context, executive pay might exceed that of the average worker by a factor in excess of 300 whilst in Japan that factor rarely exceeds 16,[17] it is difficult to deny that this clearly raises issues of a social and a political nature. This point has been made forcibly by Bogus in relation to the American context.[18]

Similarly, when factors such as pension funds for the benefit of workers are factored into the equation and it is noted that indirectly through such institutional investors workers collectively own a considerable portion of corporate America or corporate Britain other philosophical and political questions are raised. These include, as even some mangerialists have noted,[19] that since power follows property (a concept not only of Aristotle but also very Hong Kong Chinese[20]) the worker needs to be built into the decision making fabric of the corporation. This has been done in the West European model, particularly in Germany[21] and is reflected to some extent in the organization of the Japanese Kieretsu[22] and the recently enacted Chinese Corporation law.[23] In the Anglo-American and Hong Kong context the important issues remain largely centred around shareholder participation and control with the added dimension in Hong Kong of the family domination of many listed companies.

Corporate Control and the Family Business

The corporate control approach was conceptualized by Berle and Means under the notion of "a separation of ownership from management control in the modern corporation", which eventually centred around the question of who controls the business.[24] This idea put in its simplest form, crystallized into a scheme describing the modern corporation as result of a transition process from ownership control to management control. A typical example of this approach applied in relation to the dilution of family ownership and the domination of management control is the work of Herman. His survey of 200 non-financial American corporations in the mid-1970s found a definite deconcentration of family ownership as compared with the 1930s. Herman viewed the decline of family control as inevitable given: (a) the diffusion of corporate stock ownership as the business expands; (b) capital concentration through mergers and acquisitions; and (c) a deconcentration of holdings through diffusion of the founding family members themselves.[25] Nevertheless, some unique investigations of corporate data in America by Burch contradict this approach, finding a continuation of family control in American big business in the late 1960s.[26]

A broadly similar picture to that of Berle and Means was drawn for the United Kingdom by Florence in work carried out in the 1950s. That showed a dispersal of family shareholders.[27] Florence argued that the maximum size for a co-operating group of shareholders is twenty. His argument is the basis of the concept of control through a constellation of interests. The recent work of Gourvish and Wilson on the history of British brewing industry shows how, after incorporation in the late 1890s and early 1900s, many brewing companies operated much as they had done before, *i.e.* as family businesses, but many made the transition from a family based to a more professional top management in the period 1914–55. The introduction of trained brewers, company secretaries, lawyers and, later, accountants to brewing boards gave companies more of the skills necessary to the effective supervision of a modern business enterprise. This in turn helped to broaden the horizons of many family controlled brewers and to resolve the problem of succession in many an established family firm in the doldrums.[28] A similar pattern emerges in the history of the British textile industry.[29] In Hong Kong such a pattern is unusual. The development of interlocking directorships in the British brewing industries was also important.

74

Although these were essentially personal in character some of the arrangements indicated an informal understanding between the brewers concerned. These sometimes culminated in a formal merger but by 1955 there were definite signs of more formal, institutionalized interlocking agreements, and the development of hostile takeovers.[30] I will consider interlocking directorships below in the context of the introduction of independent non-executive directors in Hong Kong.

The work of Scott has pointed out that the managerialist thesis has increasingly departed from the original position taken by Berle and Means so that the terms "management control" and managerial "revolution" are inherently ambiguous.[31] There are also a number of models of control and voting power.[32] Scott's research on corporate control in Britain includes investigation into the control of the 250 largest financial and non-financial companies in Britain for the two years 1976 and 1988. He points out that during the period 1976–1988 families that had owned the whole of the share capital of their enterprise in the sample, had, by and large, been able to survive in control over the 12 years period. Those with less than complete ownership had fared less well. Among the 30 majority controlled non-financial campanies of 1970 that were less than wholly owned were 13 in which families or entrepreneurs were the controlling interest. The much depleted majority controlled non-financials of 1988 included just seven with personal controllers. Whether deliberately or otherwise, some families had failed to buy sufficient shares to retain their percentage holdings as their companies increased in size. Such enterprises passed from family majority control to minority control. In some cases control was exercised through a constellation of interests. There were also similarities within the financial sector. Merchant banks, for example, had grown in size and many controlling family holdings had, as a result, declined to minority levels or to become mere elements in a controlling constellation. Wholly owned family enterprises remained stronger. Scott concludes that the conventional sociological approach is correct to see Britain in an American context rather than as an European society. In his view the managerialist thesis *does not apply* to Britain and the USA but these two countries do show substantial similarities in their patterns of corporate control. He concludes that:

> "Any comparative account of corporate control must recognize that while there are certain uniformities of technology and business practice in all of the major capitalist economies there are equally important divergencies arising from specific historical experiences and differing cultural and legal systems. These national variations shape the constraints which operate on the actions and orientations of business leaders and result in the existence of a number of alternative patterns of capitalist development. The

pattern taken by impersonal possession in Britain, the USA, Australia, Canada and New Zealand is to be seen as the outcome of a specific convergence of national and international forces in the Anglo-American, English speaking world. In other parts of the world, and under the impact of other forces, different patterns of impersonal possession are apparent".[33]

An alternative approach to that of the managerialists, focusing on family structure and affiliation networks in Asia insists that the family business has a rationality of its own in the sense that, at least in the Asian context, it is not an early capitalist management form that will necessarily wither away in the midst of the advance of a modern joint-stock company system.[34] Hattori, for example, in examining the Chaebol in the Republic of Korea shows that as the economic scale of these groups increased the ownership control exercised by families tended to be further solidified.[35] Suehiro's research on financial conglomerates in Thailand describes how financial and insurance groups formed by coalitions of a number of families and their friends actually moved in a direction towards exclusive control by one particular family within the process of enterprise expansion.[36] A similar phenomenon is reported by Wong Sui Lin in his study of the textile industry in Hong Kong and is a key element of his model of the Chinese family firm particularly at the "emergent" and also to a lesser extent the "segmented" stages of development.[37] There has been in recent years a tendency amongst some listed companies in Hong Kong to follow a similar pattern by privatization.

More recently Suehiro has asserted that what is happening in the Thai "zaibatsu" today can not be explained by the conventional theory of the joint stock company, which states that as the scale of each group company grows and the sphere of enterprise expands, an evolution from family control to managerial control is bound to grow along with a corresponding dilution of shareholdings. He observes a clear intent on the part of the family business to maintain intact and even expand the family's enterprise and assets over a number of generations. He cites as reasons for their success in this endeavour, *inter alia*, successful diversification, as a result of polygamous families, a large pool of — often western educated — offspring and a greater willingness to employ professional managers from outside the family. The most telling point, as Suehiro emphasizes, is that many leading family businesses remain in the form of personal rather than corporate ownership and that both the domestic capital markets and the joint stock company form of business organization remain underdeveloped: "As of 1988, only 20 per cent of the top 250 corporations in Thailand had put their stock up for public sale. In addition increased stock activity resulting in possibility of widespread equity finance transactions has only occurred since 1987".[38] The extent to which this is changing, albeit through steadily growing family empires, is shown by examples such as the Charoen Pokphand conglomerate. That group's publicly traded companies include six in Bangkok, one each in Taipei and Shanghai, two in Jakarta and three in Hong Kong.[39]

In Hong Kong, as already mentioned, the corporate form has grown in popularity since 1949. Nevertheless, the company is often viewed as part of the family. The distinction between assets of the family and those of the company is not as clear cut as the western legal concept of the separate juristic person would require, a point made forcibly by Tricker and often commented upon by corporate regulators.[40] Redding has emphasized the classic problems of the third generation in many Hong Kong Chinese family dominated corporate businesses and the problematic introduction of external professional management.[41]

There is a tendency for family businesses to break up creating two or more smaller ones.[42] This often has a vigorous rejuvenating economic effect, much as management buyouts did in Britain during the 1980s.[43] Overall the evidence for larger corporate businesses successfully overcoming the third generation succession crisis by the introduction of professional management, as in the British brewing industry example cited earlier, is at best tendentious. The patterns of management are, however, changing as, owing to the massive expansion of the Hong Kong Tertiary system, more western style educated local graduates come onto the market and many return from education overseas.[44]

Control is often maintained by the family through the means of holding a significant number of shares, if not a controlling interest, on trust for the members of the family. These are often discretionary trusts and are usually based offshore for reasons, *inter alia*, of tax planning. A main purpose is to maintain family control of the company and to perhaps an equal or greater extent control over the family itself. The existence of these trusts is a factor in the continuance of family control from both perspectives, because according to some trust practitioners in Hong Kong, the fear of the possible third generation crisis is a key element in drafting the trust in the sense that the problem might challenge the family control of the business.[45] A similar phenomenon is observable in some family businesses in the United Kingdon.[46] The impact of such trusts and trustees on the governance of listed companies is worthy of further study.[47]

Another key element of family businesses is the preservation of the fortunes of the family. As Leach observes in the United Kingdom context: "Normally the stock market is not really the place for many family companies. There is a culture clash between the family wanting to maintain the wealth and outside shareholders wanting to grow the company as fast as possible".[48] This factor is recognized by Useem writing in the mould of the managerialist school which regards family business as the precursor or initial stage to the "managerial revolution". He views family capitalism as a series of kinship relations with the control and ownership of a business enterprise giving rise to a system consisting of business mergers via descent and marriage. According to Useem the overriding organizational principle of this system is upper-class coalition. The family is gentrified over the generations and apes the landed aristocracy assuming the character of an "anti industrial culture".[49] The independent work of Nakagawa on economic development and family enterprise management draws similar conclusions in relation to his observation on early starters such as the United Kingdom. In his view, family enterprises in these countries tended to fall to a level of activity that either emphasized real estate property as the most important form of family fortune, or became concerned with enterprises such as the professions, merchant banking, etc. that would build a material base for upholding the family's honour and social standing. Such a conservative pattern had a restrictive effect on economic development.[50]

Similarly in China, Confucian officials resolutely opposed the development of large concentrations of private wealth through commercial activities and the control of markets or towns. Unless it was for religious purposes or public relief measures any large scale private accumulation of wealth was automatically subject to state confiscation. This was often justified on the basis of the ruler's obligation to maintain harmony and frugality.[51] The result, as Whitley puts it was that:

> "Because long-term wealth accumulation derived from commercial activities had little legitimacy and was likely to encourage official depredations, merchants had every incentive to invest their capital in land and education and so concentrated on short-term gains which could be transformed into more prestigious and secure resources".[52]

Once outside of China the Chinese family business was largely freed from such restrictions.[53] Much of the existing research on developing economies strongly indicates that family businesses in these countries, especially in South East Asia, are the most active economic factors promoting industrialization. Suehiro observes a clear intent on the part of the Thai (often Chinese) family business to maintain intact and even expand the family's enterprise assets over a number of generations, *primarily through the drive to industrialize.*[54] A similar pattern may be noted in post-Second World War Hong Kong. Since 1979, however, with the opening up of China and the development of special economic zones such as Shenzhen and Zhuhai a huge proportion of Hong Kong's industry has migrated into China in the form of joint ventures with a variety of mainland partners.[55] Similarly mainland enterprises have been active in obtaining significant shareholdings in many important Hong Kong listed companies.[56] At present, the emerging pattern is opaque, but what is clear is that any notion that the Hong Kong listed company will follow or ought to follow a path similar to that in the Anglo American world from which, to date, it has drawn its corporate law model is at best misconceived, at worst harmful.

Corporate Democracy and Shareholder Consent

The argument that corporate performance may be improved by expanding the range of issues for which shareholder consent is required gained some credence as a method of limiting the ability of management to pursue non-profit maximizing goals. Several examples of this approach have been included in corporate legislation in recent years.[57] The underlying problem of shareholder passivity and sometimes gullibility remains. Similarly, shareholders may be all too willing to approve, for example, large remuneration packages as in the recent Sincere Co. example.[58] As one Australian High Court Judge put it:

> "... the approval of a general meeting of shareholders in a large public company may often be an illusory safeguard, since a great many shareholders are unable or unwilling to organize themselves as an effective voice ... Moreover, if the company concerned is making large profits, shareholders will often fail to perceive that in achieving these results, the executives are doing no more than performing their proper function and do not as a matter of course deserve huge rewards in recognition of their achievement."[59]

In Australia and the United Kingdom, as elsewhere, where large public corporations have experienced a degree of separation of ownership and control with a large number of members each owning a small percentage of shares, extending shareholder consent may serve little purpose. Consent procedures become a matter of formality due to the low information cost approach of voting with management, the use of proxy votes and the large number of abstentions. In the case of many of Hong Kong's listed companies, the general meeting is quite simply an additional formality, except that it does give minority shareholders the opportunity to be vociferous. Realistically, the "idea that shareholder democracy is a practicable concept or that it is a good solution to any problem, has been shown time and time again to be fallacious."[60]

Nevertheless, there have been examples of minority shareholders winning "meetings" battles in Hong Kong, albeit with the behind the scenes support of the regulatory bodies and the HKSE. The vociferous solicitor shareholder in the Evergo Holdings Ltd remuneration saga is one example.[61] Others include the extraordinary general meeting of Cavendish International in 1991, where a vocal crowd of minority shareholders foiled Mr Li Ka-shing's plan to privatize the company at a confrontational meeting; and the eventual defeat, by a vociferous minority, in 1992, of an attempted backdoor takeover and privatization of Chinese Estates by Evergo Holdings.[62] In Australia, shareholders' action groups have enhanced the ability of individual shareholders to institute proceedings against directors. The Australian Shareholders Association pushed for legislation to force directors to disclose related party transactions such as the controversial Quintex managerial fees and preferential loans to directors.[63] There are similar sporadic examples in the United Kingdom such as the rebellion against Sir Ralph Halpern's share option scheme at Burtons in 1987,[64] the removal of Satchi from the board of Satchi and Satchi is another recent example.[65] In Hong Kong, in September 1995, four members of the Kong family which founded the property developer firm Keng Fong Siu Kee Construction & Investment Co in 1964 were removed from the board by shareholders after certain unsatisfactory transactions were exposed following the appointment of two independent directors and a check on the firm's accounts.[66]

The Role of the Institutional Shareholder

The argument may be put that, with the growth of institutional shareholdings, in certain economies institutional control is a real possibility.[67] Whilst institutional investors spread their holdings in order to minimize risk and as a result very rarely own more than five per cent of an individual company's shares, their holding will usually be large enough to have a significant adverse effect on a share price if disposed of in the market.[68] To some extent, therefore, such investors have the power to play an active supervisory role. Where this is done, it is often on the informal level and fund managers have been known to boast that they have not attended an AGM for more than 15 years, having been given lots of other opportunities to meet the company's management to discuss its business performance.[69] In the United Kingdom the Institutional Shareholder's Committee has emphasized this aspect of "communication" in its statement on "The Responsibilities of Institutional Shareholders in the UK", emphasizing that formal methods of communication (reports, accounts and other explanatory circulars required by statute or the Stock Exchange) may not be sufficient to establish the type of direct relationship that enables directors and shareholders to obtain a deeper understanding of each others' aims and requirements. It goes on to encourage contact with companies, including contact at senior executive level on both sides.

"Such dialogue will enable shareholders to gain a better appreciation of the management's objectives, the problems confronting it and the quality of those involved, while also focusing the attention of management more sharply on the expectations and requirements of shareholders."[70]

The statement does reflect what often goes on in practice, at least in the United Kingdom,[71] as regards consultation, but the quality of that consultation and its contribution to effective supervision is highly limited for a number of reasons. Firstly, because of the needs of diversification and liquidity, institutions hold shares in too many companies to make monitoring practicable at anything more than a superficial level. This is often exacerbated by the relationship between investing institution and fund manager, which duplicates the problems of shareholder control of directors. The problem partly arises because of the difficulty of meaningful communication between trustees and fund managers,[72] and this creates a further problem of self-interest. It has been argued, as an agency problem, that "money managers are rationally apathetic because the expected gains from most ... governance issues are small, deferred, and received by investors, while the costs are potentially large, immediate and borne by money managers."[73]

The relatively small percentages of total outstanding shares held in any particular company also raises the question of whether institutional investors are capable of taking concerted action. The evidence that institutional shareholders fail to reach a consensus about how to vote in proxy battles in the USA and elsewhere demonstrates that historically they have not united to elect directors or reject policies that are principally designed to protect the personal interest of top executives or the controlling family. Let us examine some typical examples from the USA.

During a 1990 battle over the control of Lockheed Corporation, for example, CalPERS supported a dissident group, while the New York City Employment Retirement System (NYCERS) voted in favour of management. That same year, another battle was waged over a management sponsored proposal to increase retirement benefits for G.M. executives. Many were offended by the timing of the proposal: it was made just as CEO Roger B. Smith was retiring and increased his pension from U.S. $700,000 to U.S. $1.2 million a year. Although this type of decision is normally made by the board of directors, G.M. relented to considerable pressure brought by the UAW and a number of institutional investors and agreed to let stockholders vote on the matter. The Michigan State pension fund voted its 8.8 million shares of G.M. stock against the increases, but CalPERS voted for the proposal and management ultimately prevailed by an 83 per cent to 17 per cent margin.[74]

Secondly, whilst there is evidence of highly sophisticated groups, syndicates or rings comprising managers of large trusts involved in insider trading,[75] most institutional investors will be reluctant to receive price sensitive information that will curtail their capacity to deal. The Institutional Shareholders Committee guidelines quoted above, the laws against insider dealing[76] and the rules of the relevant stock exchange will militate against the acquisition of such information and, therefore, the effective supervision by institutional shareholders. The United Kingdom Institutional Shareholders' Committee's statement states that:

> "[W]here, exceptionally, there are compelling reasons for a board to consult institutional shareholders on issues which are price-sensitive, those shareholders may have to accept that such consultation would involve the receipt of confidences which will require that they suspend their ability to deal in the company's shares."[77]

It is also quite probable that public companies will not be disposed to release such information, not only because of Stock Exchange rules restricting the freedom to disclose information to a limited group,[78] but for reasons of confidentiality of a more general nature than that related to insider dealing legislation.

A leading investment manager has concluded that:

> "[A]ny conceivable increase in activity [by institutional investors] will not amount to a major new element of accountability in our system matching that of the bank-based economies, since share ownership unaccompanied by the additional involvement in providing finance and other services will never provide the depth of knowledge and commitment that arises with the combination of banking and proprietary interests".[79]

The most successful post-war corporate but bank based economies are arguably Japan and Germany whose systems, whilst different from each other, have two common elements. The first is that banks play a close and continuing monitoring role which sometimes is interventionist in nature when this is perceived to be necessary. Banks in both countries often have a stable long term interest in the companies in which they invest that is reinforced by the multifaceted character of the relationship between the parties as shareholder,[80] lender and, often in the case of Japan, customer.[81] The banks in these countries are much more able to exercise an active ownership role. In times of economic crisis they are more willing to nurse ailing corporations and turn them around, often by radically changing or adopting the nature of their businesses rather than sell or liquidate as in the Anglo-American system. They are also more likely to have more positive employee co-operation in doing do. The second element is securing long term commitment: employees, often a corporation's greatest resource, are either built into the decision making process, more particularly in Germany, or into the social fabric of an enterprise, as in Japan.[82] In the words of one recent *Economist* review of capitalism, the difference is between "proprietor" and "punter" capitalism.[83]

Institutional investors in the Anglo-American system tend to invest in *markets* rather than *the companies* in their portfolio, partly as a result of their much more limited relationship with those companies. Their holdings in companies are primarily viewed as investments, to be bought or sold according to investment criteria. As one commentator on the United Kingdom situation has noted, albeit during a year of worldwide stock market panic:

"There is plenty of evidence to confirm one in the view that the City is indeed becoming more short-termist in outlook. In the 70s, it was usual for a pension fund to hold an investment in a UK company for an average of 16 years. By 1981, according to figures from the very same Bank of England, that period had halved to eight years. In 1987, the average share was held for a mere two years. So over half a pension fund's portfolio is now turned over in just one year. Over half. How can managers possibly argue that they are investing for future generations when they are presented with starting figures like that? The insurance companies also now turn over half their portfolios each year, while the investment trusts manage a 90% turnover rate. Even that palls beside the unit trust groups which, in 1987, managed to achieve a record turnover rate of over 140%, churning their entire portfolios of UK shares every nine months!"[84]

This situation may simply reflect the fact that some institutional investors such as mutual funds and unit trusts (whose own investors can withdraw their funds on short notice) give a priority to liquidity. Exercising control is for these institutions, less acceptable if this results in their investment being less liquid.[85]

In Hong Kong, with its rather volatile market, the role of institutional investors in corporate governance is even less evident. The funds management industry in Hong Kong is unquestionably international both in terms of the origin of the funds authorized for distribution and also in terms of where the funds place their investment.[86] There is, as recent market activity would indicate, a great deal of investment in Hong Kong equities by funds based in North America, Europe and Australia and, although there is some anecdotal evidence of a long term commitment to the territory, there is little or no evidence of their role in corporate governance.[87]

One recent and more robust exception to this general rule is the threat of Regent Fund Management to wind up China Assets Holdings, a company in which it held a 10 per cent stake. According to the *South China Morning Post*, the Canadian controlled fund manager was critical of the company's slow progress in carrying out its investment strategy and unhappy at the way it was using its resources.[88] Less robust and probably more typical is the approach of the Templeton Group. The president of the Templeton Emerging Markets Fund, Dr Mark Mobius, has recently stated that the group is prepared to take a more activist role as an investor, although it did so reluctantly. He also stated that the group did not have the time to take an activist role in all the companies in which it had a stake. In those circumstances in which an activist role would be taken Templeton would avoid a confrontational approach and would use "friendly persuasion", occasionally holding discussions with regulatory authorities where necessary.[89] Within a few days Templeton was locked in a war of words over the privatization of a Dutch controlled listed company, East Asiatics, concerning the perceived unfair price of U.S $1.20 a share offered to the minority.[90]

In Australia, there has been relatively little study of the role of institutional investors. One recent survey points out that in Australia institutional investors hold only 36 per cent of the issued shares of listed companies compared to 50–60 per cent for the U.S., United Kingdom and Japan. That survey pointed to the overall passivity of Australian institutional investors, though did give some anecdotal evidence of increased activism both overseas and also in Australia.[91]

The United Kingdom Institutional Shareholders" Committee recommends that institutional investors should support boards of directors by a positive use of voting rights, unless they have good reasons for doing otherwise.[92] Reasons for voting against a motion should be made known to the board beforehand. Whilst there are relatively sporadic examples of institutional investors participating in ginger group activity to stimulate a portfolio company's management or intervene in companies,[93] their current use of voting rights is less than satisfactory and many institutional investors are clearly relatively inactive. In a recent CBI survey, it was discovered that more than half of the pension funds questioned never or only rarely voted.[94] Even if an institutional investor has access to sufficient information for monitoring purposes, it faces considerable problems in mounting a successful campaign against a management with which it is dissatisfied. The formation and maintained cohesion of a shareholder coalition with sufficient votes to threaten management's position is almost impossible in most Hong Kong listed companies and difficult elsewhere as the two CalPERS examples mentioned earlier show. With greater knowledge of and

familiarity with the company's affairs, directors are in a strong position to refute outside criticism. They often enjoy the unquestioning
loyalty of small shareholders and other institutional investors. Management may also to some extent manipulate the turnout at meetings.
Prudential Insurance plc v. Newman Industries Ltd[95] is an example of
the extremes that this manipulation may take.

As a general rule, where institutional investors do have a continuing business relationship with a company in which they have invested,
they are less likely to oppose management because of the fear of a
disruption to their relationship. This is reinforced by the possibility of
the flow of information available to them, which is often not made
available to smaller investors, being interrupted or stopped depending
upon the severity of the breakdown in the relationship. Overall, however, the evidence suggests that while institutional involvement at the
individual company level is increasingly frequent, it is sporadic in
nature and largely confined to the most obvious cases of mismanagement or misuse of position.[96]

Monks has argued that relational investing, in the U.S. context,
will only work if the right structure is put in place. Such a structure
would provide "rational activism", a capability for shareholders to
propose a value enhancing change to the management of "focused"
companies. This is accomplished through the alignment of the interests of owners and managers. The LENS Fund, established in 1992, was
created to provide such "rational activism". As a motivated shareholder with a large shareholding LENS is supposedly in a position to
direct attention to those areas where manager and owner attitudes are
not aligned, such as directors' compensation and dividends, and communicate effectively with other similarly placed shareholders and,
where necessary, secure approval for formal ownership action. He
continues:

> "Once the structure has been created, what is the agenda? Empow-
> ered shareholders should focus on the board of directors — its
> composition and its agenda. The job of effectively involved share-
> holders can be simply described as assuring that the board of
> directors does its job. This means making sure that the right
> people are on the board, that they are focusing on the right issues,
> and that they operate under a structure that enables them to ask
> the right questions and reach the right answers. This is the answer
> to the agency cost issue, the most effective way for the ownership
> to exercise the appropriate level of control."[97]

There remain arguments in favour of institutional involvement in
corporate governance at the macro level. The argument is put that
there are incentives for institutions to improve the corporate

governance system, for by ensuring that corporate governance arrangements are conducive to maximum efficiency, the holder of a widely diversified portfolio increases its returns by improving the performance of all the companies in its portfolio. This argument has been developed by Gilson and Krackman into the suggestion of a third means by which shareholders may exercise control between active participation in the organizations decision-making mechanisms on the one hand and simply selling shares when dissatisfied with performance on the other. It is suggested, therefore, that there is a middle way between "voice" and "exit". The process involves the appointment of a minority of genuinely independent directors to corporate boards. Such an approach, on a voluntary basis, was recommended in the Cadbury report, which was initially received in Hong Kong with an almost allergic reaction. In essence, Gilson and Krackman's proposal is that the effects of the separation of ownership and control can be overcome by inserting a block of expert and well informed monitors into the corporate organization at the highest level. They suggest that institutions might form some type of agency or clearing house to recruit suitable independent directors and nominate them for appointment to particular companies. Their election would be ensured by the routine use of the institutions' voting power.[98]

In the context of Hong Kong, the problem is not one of separation of ownership and control but more often that of the closely held family domination of public companies, which the family often regard and sometimes operate as private fiefdoms. Excess in this regard simply results in outside investors staying clear or simply selling their shares, and the increased threat of a stiffer regulatory regime has acted as an incentive for some of these companies to privatize.[99] If the proposal of independent directors were to be effective, it would first require a greater proportion of shares being made available to outside investors than is currently the case, for the minimum level of equities that are to be offered to the public on listing must be increased before such a proposal could work in Hong Kong. Parkinson points out that such a mechanism of internal monitoring and maintenance of managerial efficiency need not be tied exclusively to shareholders and the factors that encourage good performance will apply whether or not the independent directors are sponsored and financed by shareholders.[100] This becomes important in the context of a corporate model that focuses on a wider range of interests and stakeholders than those of the members. Some corporate theorists in the U.S., United Kingdom and Australia may be moving towards such a view, but in Hong Kong conservative self-interest still largely holds sway. All too often that self-interest is the interest of the founding family as perceived by the father-entrepreneur or his successors. I have commented earlier on the thrust of this, namely expanding family wealth through the medium of expansion of the corporate business.

Ownership Concentration and Management Remuneration in Hong Kong

The concentration of ownership has obvious consequences for management remuneration. Where shareholdings are diffuse, the shareholders do not have the capacity to monitor managers, so the latter may pay themselves excessive remuneration, for it is to be expected that there may be a positive correlation between the degree of discretion allowed to managers and the level of their remuneration. A U.S. study examined the ownership structure and the levels of remuneration of CEOs in 271 major U.S. industrial companies. This study found that CEO remuneration was less for those companies that had more concentrated ownership. Levels of management compensation are related, therefore, to the degree to which a firm is closely held because major shareholders have a meaningful economic incentive to engage in monitoring activities that reduce the residual loss portion of agency costs.[101] There may also be a significant relationship between ownership structure and the type of remuneration received by managers. The authors of another study examined the ownership structure and type of remuneration received by CEOs of 71 large U.S. manufacturing companies which were divided into two categories. The first category was shareholder controlled, defined as those companies where at least five per cent of the company's issued shares is in the hands of one individual or organization who is not involved in the management of the company. The second category, management controlled, was defined as those companies where no individual or organization controls five per cent or more of the issued shares. It was found that the type of ownership structure of a company is significantly related to the type of remuneration received by its CEO. In the case of a dominant shareholder, bonuses and long-term incentives adopted as part of the remuneration plan tended to ensure that the CEO's remuneration reflected the performance of the company. On the other hand, remuneration plans of management controlled companies were not designed well enough to maximize economic efficiency and profitability. This was because management controlled firms clearly designed compensation systems to avoid the vagaries of fluctuating performance and to take advantage of a more stable factor, size.[102]

In Hong Kong, however, management control of its remuneration results from quite opposite reasons. For many listed companies in Hong Kong the concentration of ownership in the hands of the controlling family produces a controlling shareholding exercised by the majority of the board. Managers can often directly or indirectly rely on the majority of votes in a general meeting and very few have actual service contracts with the company.[103] The choice of benefit from the company is influenced less by monitoring agency costs and more by the relative overall advantage of taking benefits in the form of remuneration (at the expense of minority shareholders) or dividends and in that decision factors such as taxation[104] may play a greater role (as it often does in the case of small private companies). The result is often similar to the management controlled companies in the second study mentioned above, but the reasons are as much influenced by other factors, sociological and behaviourial as they are due to any rational attempt to monitor agency costs.

To take this argument a stage further let us consider an example of a Hong Kong listed company where the founding family's shareholding is largely diluted. The Sincere company has made headlines over directors' remuneration previously.[105] The listed company has, *inter alia*, two major associated public companies as indicated below. The controlling Ma family holds *circa* six per cent of its shares — as far as can be determined from its annual reports and share register. The core group is knitted together through a series of interlocking shareholders and directorships as follows:

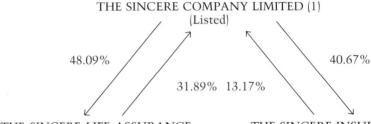

THE SINCERE COMPANY LIMITED (1)
(Listed)

48.09%   31.89% 13.17%   40.67%

THE SINCERE LIFE ASSURANCE ——→ THE SINCERE INSURANCE
COMPANY LIMITED (2)   36%   & INVESTMENT CO LTD (3)
(with over 1,000 shareholding) ←— — —   (with over 1,000 shareholding)
                              21.8%

According to the 1994/95 Annual Report, page 17, the Sincere directors' shareholding in this company represents 0.58% of its issued capital.	According to the 1994/95 Annual Report, page 17, the Sincere directors' shareholding in this company represents 0.37% of its issued capital.

Extracted from the 1994/95 Annual Reports, the directors of the above companies are:

1.	Walter K.W. Ma	2.	Walter K.W. Ma	3.	Walter K.W. Ma
	Philip K.H. Ma		Philip K.H. Ma		Philip K.H. Ma
	Selwyn Mar		Ma Siu Chung		Ma Siu Chung
	John K.K. Ma		Ma Hing Fong		Ma Hing Fong
	King Wing Ma		Ma Kin Loong		Ma Hing Yuk
	Eric K.K. Lo				Steve K.W. Ma

The family relationship of these directors is as follows:

Sincere Co (1)

Walter, Philip and King Wing Ma are all cousins (their fathers were brothers). Walter's grandmother and John Ma's grandmother were sisters. Eric Lo's maternal grandfather, Ma Woon Biu, was one of the earlier shareholders of Sincere as far back as 1909. His name could be found in Sincere's 75th Anniversary Issue.

Sincere Life (2)

Walter and Philip are cousins. Ma Hin Fong is their uncle. Ma Siu Cheung is uncle of John Ma. Ma Kin Loong is cousin of John Ma. The newly appointed director, Victor Ma, is the son of John Ma. John Ma is the chief manager of this company.

Sincere (1,2,3)

Walter, Philip, Steve and Ma Hing Yuk are all cousins. Of course, Philip and Steve are brothers. Mr Hing Fong is their uncle. Mr Siu Chung is the uncle of John Ma.

In conclusion, all of them are related to the families of Ma Ying Biu and Ma Wing Charm. The latter are brothers-in-law as their wives were sisters. The slightly odd man out is Eric Lo but his history can be traced back in the history of Sincere. The striking point, however, is the extent to which this family network dominates the boards of all three companies. Turning to the issue of directors' remuneration the following table of figures are extracted from the consolidated profit and loss account shown in the respective annual reports.

These figures indicate that directors' remuneration is far in excess of operating profit and arguably represent an erosion of the company's capital base. Remuneration also exceeds dividends, excluding bonus dividends. More shares representing a decreased asset base is hardly conducive to enhancing shareholder value. It would appear that subject

Executive Directors $millions							
	1990	*1991*	*1992*	*1993*	*1994*	*1995*	*Total*
Remuneration	16.60	14.26	19.36	44.39	35.27	22.29	152.17[A]
Operating Profit	39.91	44.22	47.66	61.20	66.29	(177.11)	82.17
Dividend	16.50	18.62	21.46*	22.81*	34.76	34.46	148.61

[A] Net off bonus repaid to the company
* Exclude bonus dividends

Combining the above figures over a six year period we arrive at the following ratios:

Remuneration / Operating Profit = 185%
Remuneration / Dividend = 102%

to the success of its development plans elsewhere such as in China a "controlling" family's wealth is being enhanced at the expense of the company and in particular non-family shareholders.

Another indicator of the degree of combination of ownership and control in many Hong Kong listed companies is the number of attempts to transfer wealth from smaller shareholders to the owning and controlling majority.[106] The classic example of such wealth transfer in Hong Kong is the privatization scheme effected by way of a scheme of arrangement and compulsory acquisition subsequent to general offers.[107] Although typically involving the surrender of shares for cash, this is not always the case and issues of shares for shares with a lower underlying asset value resulting in an expropriation of the minority (and wealth transfer) have also been attempted. The prevalence of the use of a scheme in order to dispossess the minority through forced sales has deeply concerned the SFC. Although schemes were not intended to be used in this manner, the closely held nature of listed companies in Hong Kong makes them convenient vehicles for privatization. There were 16 privatizations of public companies in 1991–92 and 24 in 1992–93.[108] As a result, the SFC has expressed the view that protection is necessary to avoid minority shareholder oppression and has recently circulated for comment proposals to increase the bargaining position of the minority.[109]

The Market for Corporate Control

It is true that there have been some spectacular and hard fought takeovers in the corporate history of Hong Kong. For example, towards the end of the 1970s some of the major British companies were taken over by Chinese businesses. The most prominent of these were the acquisition of the Hutchinson Group by Ka-Shing Li and the acquisition of the Wharf Company together with its associated businesses by Y.K. Pao. There were other significant acquisitions of traditional businesses.[110] They had the effect, *inter alia*, of dramatically changing the configuration of interlocking directorships a point to which I shall return when considering the introduction of independent non-executive directors. The participants in these takeover battles have sometimes played rough and with complete disregard for the Hong Kong code on takeovers and mergers. This has led one commentator to argue forcibly for giving the code legal status,[111] a threat which was echoed by the SFC in its consultative document on the reform of the code in 1990. Companies are sometimes taken over and inadequate management displaced, and this is regarded as a valuable effect of the takeover mechanism. The main significance claimed for the market for corporate control as an efficiency-inducing device is, however, that incumbent managements fear takeover and will strive to make the company efficient and its share price correspondingly high. Numerous criticisms of this claim have been made, and there are several reasons to doubt it. Empirical evidence does not always support the theory. Takeover threats only marginally and inconsistently influence management behaviour, as Buxbaum suggests.[112] As Fairburn and Kay have pointed out the market for control has peculiar features:

> "[I]f I produce a poor product, then I will gradually lose market share, and my competitors will gradually gain it. If I run a company badly, however, the market does not gradually transfer its management to someone else; it leaves me with the monopoly of corporate control until, at the consummation of a takeover bid it transfers it abruptly and completely."[113]

Fairburn and Kay argue that this feature of the market for corporate control necessitates detailed regulation of that market such as the takeover code to ensure a fair distribution of the take-over premium among the members and is an important reason why the market for corporate control is less efficient and effective than most other markets.

The efficiency of the market for control is called into question by surveys suggesting that inefficient companies are not regarded as favourable targets.[114] Furthermore, bidders are attracted to targets for a variety of reasons that are often unconnected with the potential for improving the target's management, such as diversification, access to new markets, economics of scale and empire building. A recent cause of many takeovers in Hong Kong has been the desire by mainland Chinese enterprises to obtain a backdoor listing on the Hong Kong stock exchange, which prompted the latter to tighten significantly its rules relating to such activity.[115]

Whilst the legal framework in Hong Kong is similar to the United Kingdom, where takeovers have been more frequent, the cultural and other structural factors are very different. Family control in Hong Kong is not unlike that in France, where over half of the largest 200 companies are family controlled and in France, Italy and the Netherlands companies frequently hold shares in each other for mutual protection.[116] The same applies in Japan, where takeovers are rare. Such factors make it difficult for an outsider to break in and obtain a controlling interest. This inhibits market activity for control. The large hongs in Hong Kong, whether British or Chinese controlled, have adopted complex interlocking shareholdings and directorships amongst the companies within the group they control which in turn inhibit takeover activity.[117] Though the potential threat of a takeover was one of the major reasons given for Jardine's recent announcement that it intends to delist,[118] overall the family control of many listed companies means that the market for corporate control does not, in

Hong Kong, act as a great incentive for managers to restrain their self-interest and optimize share values. Any takeover will be on terms acceptable to the controlling family.

The Case for Independent Directors

Non-executive directors (NEDs) are in general not involved in the actual running of a company's business and they, therefore, have the advantage, at least in theory, of being able to assess the company's performance, and that of management, from a neutral standpoint. Their presence on strategy, audit and compensation or remuneration committees ought, in theory, to give some objectivity to those committee determinations and the appointment of NEDs has been encouraged in the United Kingdom, Australia and, more recently, in Hong Kong.[119] In the UK, PRO NED's voluntary code of practice provides that one of the principal functions of NEDs is to ensure the "continuing effectiveness of the Executive Directors and Management" whilst a code put forward by the Institute of Directors requires them to "monitor executive performance against agreed objectives".

The Cadbury report recommended that audit committees consist exclusively of NEDs and remuneration committees should have a membership wholly or mainly composed of such directors.[120] There are certain conditions which need to be met if these proposals for the increased role of NEDs are to resolve the current impasse in corporate governance for NEDs. Problems have emerged of access to information and the use of informal channels upsetting the delicate relationship of trust and confidence that must exist between a managing director and his board. In one Hong Kong listed company non-executive directors are allowed to see relevant papers at the start of board meetings and have them taken away at the end.[121] According to Brudney:

> "[T]he institutionally generated disinclination to hold colleagues at arm's length is furthered by other psychological and social considerations. Besides pressure to follow the leader in the board-room along lines described in the learning on small group dynamics, other factors make independent directors particularly apt to view management's demands congenially. If they are not themselves corporate executives, independent directors tend, nevertheless, to share common business and professional backgrounds with, and to live in the same social and economic milieu as does, management."[122]

Tomasic and Bottomley point out that evidence in Australia confirms Brudney's last point.[123] In the context of Hong Kong this trend is even more marked given the cultural deference to authority and the concept of authority being tied to ownership. The *Economist* points out that "two-thirds of outside directors in America are themselves chief executives of other companies. They are therefore part of the same job market. Not surprisingly they are happy to see pay in that market go up".[124] Much the same applies elsewhere. A survey of the role of non-executive directors in United Kingdom listed companies, completed just before the publication of the Cadbury Report, found that strategic input to the company was seen to be a critical aspect of the role of the NED but there was a divergence of views as to what form this input should take. Chairmen and NEDs perceived that the role is to *contribute* to the development of strategy. The other board members, the institutional shareholders and the audit partners saw the role to be to *comment on* strategy formulated by the executive members of the board. This called for a clarification of the respective roles of board members. There was general agreement that NEDs were not as effective as they might be. Only amongst chairmen did a majority consider NEDs to be very effective, and this led the researchers to comment that some chairmen were showing a complacency with the status quo that no other audience (including NEDs) felt.[125]

All those surveyed[126] acknowledged that the selection and appointment of non-executive directors was not satisfactory. The reasons for this were that, in many cases, there was no written job/candidate profile and the chairman or CEO already had individuals in mind, using his own informal contacts and he eventually made the appointment. This was exacerbated by a lack of a written clarification of the non-executive role.

These factors clearly give rise to doubt about the effectiveness and independence of NEDs and obviously make more rigorous selection of candidates through nomination committees (or preferably some independent agency) and the use of more formal job descriptions desirable. The possible role of institutional shareholders in this respect has been noted.

It is most important that the NEDs be genuinely independent of management. Parkinson argues that this means that they must not be appointed by the executive directors, nor simply nominated by the executives and elected by the shareholders, given the likely outcome of such a procedure in the light of shareholder passivity. Some independent agency could play a useful role in this context. Careful consideration needs to be given to the relationship between the independent monitoring NEDs and the executive management. Since a major objective of internal monitoring is to prevent senior managers from exercizing unbridled control over the company and their own rewards, genuine accountability to some other body with ultimate power to remove them from office will provide a direct incentive to maximize their performance.[127] This structure would constitute a move towards a two tier board and, given the dedication to the unitary board of many of the players on the Anglo-American and Hong Kong corporate scene, this seems unlikely at the moment.

In Hong Kong, the Cadbury Report was initially regarded as meaningless in the local context. Leading businessmen and company secretaries especially doubted that its recommendations would work in Hong Kong because of the nature of closely held listed companies, and because the limited size of the Hong Kong business world produces a social and cultural nexus in which non-executive directors are closely related to the controlling shareholders or directors, and many of those involved in a particular business sector are known to each other. This nexus was said to "exaggerate the difficulty of finding a truly independent but suitably qualified non-executive director, other than those who may be considered competitors".[128] Given that there are also relatively few listed companies in Hong Kong where the controlling shareholding is not held by the family members of the board or companies they represent there was little likelihood of the Cadbury Code being accepted against the will of the management.

Nevertheless, in August 1993 the HKSE introduced a requirement into its listing rules that every board of directors of a listed issuer must include at least two independent NEDs, and set out guideline rules for ensuring their independence. There are transitional rules for companies admitted to listing on or before 1st August 1993. These required the appointment of at least one independent non-executive director by January 1, 1994 and a second by December 31, 1994.[129] Because of the difficulties or reluctance experienced in this regard the final deadline had to be extended to March 31, 1995.

The tests for assessing the independence of non-executive directors are expressed in the most general terms and are for guidance only. They are not regarded by the exchange as exhaustive.[130] These guidelines have remediable shortcomings which will mean that they will do little to ensure a large degree of independence. In particular, that having an existing role as a professional adviser to the company or to a connected person is allowed is to be regretted. As the PRO NED guidelines on remuneration committees emphasize, it is preferable that NEDs who receive fees as professional advisors to the company should not be involved in determining the remuneration of executives. Only NEDs for whom the fee for that particular appointment represents only a part of their total income, should form the committee.[131]

In the final analysis, however, the closely held character of many family controlled companies in Hong Kong will mean that independent directors are in effect appointed by the controlling management and it is only the possible broadening of the shareholder base over time which may change this situation. Any attempt to increase the regulation of listed companies is bound to meet with resistance at present.

Introducing non-executive directors with any real degree of independence is likely to be extremely difficult if not impossible.

Against this background, the HKSE took a very "softly, softly" approach, announcing that there would be no initial monitoring of the independence of NEDs appointed to listed companies as required under the listing rules mentioned above. After the first stage of the process officials of the exchange have admitted that they have no accurate figures on how many companies had complied and ruled out any positive search for non-complying companies. It was for the board of directors itself to take a view on independence. "Judging independence is not a science," said one official. "In fact, it is a bit of an elephant test — you know one when you see one." In response, the Institute of Directors in Hong Kong has warned that many companies have independent directors on paper but not in reality and that there is serious cause for concern.[132]

In fact, many listed companies had problems complying with the deadline.[133] This is not surprising. The work of Wong on interlocking directorships in Hong Kong demonstrates a distinctive interlocking behaviour in the nature of Chinese firms in Hong Kong. His research demonstrates that the ownership and control of the top 100 largest corporations in Hong Kong has actually become more concentrated and personalized in recent years and more of the boards were controlled by family members of the major shareholders. Many characteristics of the traditional small Chinese family firms were brought into large corporations which were once controlled by British owners and managements. Given the high degree of personalism in the management of Chinese family businesses, inter-corporate relationships became more personal and informal. According to Wong formal business networking ties, in the form of outside directors appointed to created corporate interlocks, is not a major ingredient in the Chinese business recipe. As Chinese business relationships are often based on personal trust it may well be regarded as an affront to the integrity of the businessmen concerned to force them to accept the western method of using outside directors to safeguard investment interests.

In this context of listed companies characterized by concentrated ownership relying on personalized trust and control, the emphasis is on the use of multiple executive directorships. This fosters an inward orientation based an inter-corporate relationships generally limited to the in group of businesses which are possessed of strong associations with each other based on ownership ties, family and other traditional linkages. According to Wong, therefore:

"The intense and personal commitment of executive directors to the family firms also means that it would be unlikely for other businesses to invite them to serve as non-executive directors. Their independence, in the context of the competitive environment of Hong Kong, would be questionable. In this situation, directorate linkages, if required at all, will be effected through outsiders who are not executives of either of the connected businesses. In consequence, executive and non-executive directors take up different roles in the Chinese businesses and this leads to a sharper differentiation in the roles of the strong and weak ties in the interlocking directorates."[134]

To introduce independent non-executive directors in this context with a view to their protecting outside investment interests emphasizing a "whistle blowing" role is to court disaster. In the case of the property developer King Fong Sin Kee Construction and Investment Co Ltd the chairman and managing director Chan Heng-fai was delighted with the role played by the independent directors: "Having two independent non-executive directors on the board is the best thing the stock exchange has done in the market"; but that case was an example of one side of the family betraying the trust placed in them by other elements of the family. In a case of the controlling family's interests versus those of outside investors such delight could easily turn into dismay, leading to a polarization of the board.[135]

Conclusion

This paper has examined the validity of the managerialist thesis in both the Anglo-American and Asian-Chinese family controlled business models and explored evidence that it is seriously flawed. The separation of ownership and management control is not as simple as managerialists and economic determinism portrays it to be; nor does the same approach apply to the "inevitable" dilution of shareholdings. As Roe has observed in the Anglo-American context this is as much due to reasons of politics and culture as it is to the "managerial revolution" and economic determinism.[136] The common thread of an urge to preserve family wealth manifests itself in a very different way in the overseas Chinese business model and results in different structures, including director and also shareholding interlocks as the Sincere Co Ltd example shows.

The reference at the beginning of this paper to the inherent dislike of public participation in family businesses, albeit listed ones, may be changing slowly. The same may be said for the delegation of decision making power to professional managers. The use of offshore discretionary trusts to hold all or the major part of the family's shareholding is designed as much for retaining control over it and the family as it is for tax planning and disclosure of interests reasons. Other realities, however, may gradually and inexorably be responsible for a broadening of the shareholder base.

China has a long history of official opposition to the development of large concentrations of private wealth[137] — a policy that may be applied in Hong Kong post-1997, if not already. PRC enterprises are now and increasingly acquiring major stakes in many of Hong Kong's family dominated listed companies. This may lead to broader share ownership in Hong Kong listed companies or, at least, control through a constellation of interests. The HKSE is also keen to broaden the retail shareholder base and the SFC is keen to see greater access to corporate information by them.

Nevertheless, there will remain basic problems under the current corporate structure which will militate against an effective shareholder voice in corporate governance. First, it is more efficient for shareholders, large and small alike, to devote their resources to investment strategies than to matters of corporate governance. Secondly, efforts to organize an effective coalition against a controlling family interest are difficult and expensive. Exit will prevail over voice.[138]

Two recent surveys of corporate governance aspects indicate that Hong Kong's listed companies pay little regard to investor concerns. The Price Waterhouse survey of Corporate Governance sampled 100 companies with a HKSE listing selected at random. The survey revealed that three quarters of the companies did not have a policy for dealing with investor complaints. Many of those companies, in answering the question relating to communication with investors, said that they do no need formal policies as they do no receive complaints from investors. According to the report this is probably a reflection of the extent to which the directors are controlling shareholders of Hong Kong listed companies.[139] A more thorough research project into the role of "The Company Secretary in Hong Kong's Listed Companies" by Tricker et al. came to similar conclusions. Instead of a telephone and questionnaire survey as used in the Price Waterhouse survey, Tricker's team used five sources to provide the data for their research. These were

(a) a literature survey;
(b) an initial round of interviews with "stakeholders" to establish key issues;
(c) a postal survey to all companies listed on the HKSE;
(d) questionnaires from company secretaries of China "H" share companies listed in Hong Kong;
(e) interviews with company secretaries of Hong Kong listed companies.[140]

Specific responses to a series of questions on the level of involvement of company secretaries included the following:

97

	Primary responsibility	Significant involvement	Neither	Work delegated to professional firms
Shareholder meetings Co-ordinate arrangements, prepare documentation, ensure correct procedures are followed	62%	30%	1%	7%
Shareholder registration and relations Maintain share register, carry out routine share registration work, handle shareholder relations	13%	13%	7%	67%
Share capital issues and restructuring Implement changes in the structure of the company's share and loan capital, devise, implement and administer share participation schemes[141]	32%	39%	14%	15%

This indicates that shareholder relations are given a low priority by the majority of listed companies in Hong Kong. Relational investing of the type advocated by Monks is, therefore, a non-starter without the apparatus for handling shareholder relations, for as indicated above 67 per cent of this work is delegated to external professional firms. It is, therefore, external to many companies' corporate governance structures and as such is relegated to the periphery of the boards' concerns. Without an appropriate structure, therefore, "voice" is excluded and when dissatisfaction is felt the tendency to "exit" is reinforced.

In the words of one commentator on the Anglo-American situation, "Waiting for institutional shareholders to finally sweep aside a century of stockholder passivity and replace it with vigorous and responsible ownership may be like waiting for Godot."[142] In Hong Kong that waiting will be even longer.

Notes

1 W.C. Kirby, "China Unincorporated: Company Law and Business Enterprise in Twentieth-Century China" (1995) 54 Journal of Asian Studies 43.

2 Chun, Li, "The Kung-SSu-lu of 1904 and the Modernization of Chinese Company Law" (1974) 10 Chengchi University Legal Review, at 171–221, continued (1974) 11 *ibid.* at 163–209.

3 S.L. Wong, "The Chinese Family Firm: a Model" (1985) 36 The British Journal of Sociology 58–69.

4 A.H. Yee, *A People Misruled: The Chinese Stepping Stone Syndrome* (1992), at 162.

5 L.W. Pye, *Asian Power and Politics: The Cultural Dimensions of Authority* (1985), at 74.

6 S.G. Redding, *The Spirit of Chinese Capitalism* (1990), at 157–169, 178; R.H. Silin, *Leadership and Values: The Organization of Large Scale Chinese Enterprises* (1976), S.L. Wong, "The Applicability of Asian Family Values to other Socio-Cultural Settings" in *In Search of an East Asian Development Model* (1988); S. Greenhalgh, "Families and Networks in Taiwan's Economic Development" in *Contending Approaches to the Political Economy of Taiwan* (1988); R. Whittey, *Business Systems in East Asia* (1994), at 62–69, 78–84, 202–205.

7 E.L.G. Tyler, "Does the complexity of Companies Legislation Impede Entrepreneurship? The Hong Kong experience" delivered at the Conference on Market Forces and the Law, Beijing University October 21–22, 1994.

8 The review is currently well under way and the review team has already issued draft discussion papers entitled *Hong Kong Companies Ordinance, Overview of the Hong Kong Companies Ordinance, Background to the Review* and *Review of the Hong Kong Companies Ordinance; Comparative Survey* in July 1995.

9 R. Romano, "A Cautionary Note on Drawing Lessons from Comparative Corporate Law" (1993) 102 *The Yale Law Journal* 2021 at 2023. See R.J. Gilson and M.J. Roe, "Understanding the Japanese Keiretsu. Overlaps Between Corporate Governance and Industrial Organization" (1993) 102 *The Yale Law Journal* 871–905.

10 Adam Smith, *An Inquiry into the Nature and Causes of the Wealth of Nations*; J. Fallows, *Looking at the Sun: The Rise of the New East Asian Economic and Political System* (1995), Chap. 4.

11 Friedrich List, *The Natural System of Political Economy* W.O. Henderson ed. (1983) at 42–3, 47; Friedrich List, *The National System of Political Economy* (1966), at 42, 43, 94–5, 172. See J. Fallows above.

12 Lazonick, *Business Organization and the Myth of the Market Economy* (1991).

13 J.C. Collins and J.I. Porras, *Built to Last: Successful Habits of Visionary Companies* (1994); Alfred D. Chandler Jr, "*Scale and Scope: The Dynamics of Industrial Capitalism* (1994); Stopford, *Rejuvinating the Mature Business* (1994); S. Caulkin, "The Pursuit of Immortality" (May 1995) *Management Today* May 36–40.

14 Collins and Porras above n.13 at 4. They compare 18 long-established, mainly U.S. "visionary companies" with a selection of "not-so-visionary" but by no means hopeless industry courterparts. They calculate that while $1 invested in a general stock-market fund in 1926, with all income and dividends reinvested, would now be worth $415 and the same amount invested in the comparison firms would have grown to $955, a "visionary

companies fund" would have produced a return of $6,356 — six times their rivals' and 15 times the market as a whole.

15 Stopford above n.13.

16 Weddeburn, "Trust, Corporation and the Worker" (1985) 25 *Osgood Hall Law Journal* 203.

17 *cf.* G.S. Crystal, *In Search of Excess: The Overcompensation of American Executives* (1992), at 206–207.

18 C.T. Bogus, "Excessive Executive Compensation and the Failure of Corporate Democracy" (1993) 41 *Buffalo Law Review* 1–83 at 20–25.

19 P.F. Drucker, *Managing in Turbulent Times* (1985), at 181–199; P.F. Drucker, *The Unseen Revolution: How Pension Fund Socialism Came to America* (1976); A. Blake, "Own as You Earn — An Unseen Revolution" (1983) 3 *Company Lawyer* 51–57; P. Nelson, "Own as You Earn: a Counter Revolution (1983) 3 *Company Lawyer* 257–261.

20 G.S. Redding, *The Spirit of Chinese Capitalism* (1990), at 155.

21 *cf.* T. Hadden, "Employee Participation — What Future for the German Model?" (1983) 3 *Company Lawyer* 250–257; T. Hadden, *Company Law and Capitalism* (3rd ed. 1995).

22 J. Charkham, *Keeping Good Company: A Study of Corporate Governance in Five Countries* (1994), Chap. 3.

23 *cf.* G.G. Wang and R. Tomasic, *China's Company Law: An Annotation* (1994), in particular articles 121, 122 and 124 at pp.108–109.

24 A.A. Berle and G.C. Means, *The Modern Corporation and Capitalist Property* (1947).

25 E.S. Herman, *Corporate Control, Corporate Power* (1981).

26 P.H. Burch, *The Managerial Revolution Reassessed: Family Control in America's Large Corporations* (1972).

27 P.S. Florence, *Ownership, Control and Success of Large Companies* (1961).

28 T.R. Gourvish and R.G. Wilson, *The British Brewing Industry 1830–1980* (1994), pp.389–390.

29 *cf.* D.C. Coleman, "Sir Thomas Paul Latham" in *Dictionary of Business Biography* (Jeremy and Shaw ed. 1985), pp.662–664.

30 Gourvish and Wilson above n.28 at 395.

31 J.P. Scott, "Corporate Control and Corporate Rule: Britain in an international perspective" (1990) 41 *British Journal of Sociology* 351 at 358; *cf.* Herman above n.25 at 19.

32 *ibid.* at 358–360; *cf.* J.P. Scott, *Capitalist Property and Financial Power* (1986), at 37–39.

33 Scott above n.31 at 371.

34 Yu Chungsun, *no Chainīzu: bōsōsuru kakyō, kakjin no keizairyoku* [Ethnic Chinese overseas: their expanding economic power] (Sekai ed. 1991); G.G. Hamilton, M. Orru and N.W. Biggart, "Enterprise Groups in East Asia: An Organizational Analysis" (1987) 161 *Shōken Keizai.*

35 T. Hattori, "Gendai Kankoku Kigyo no shoyu tokeiei" [Ownership and Management of Contempory Korean enterprises] (1984) 25 *Ajia Keizai* nos 5–6.

36 A. Suehiro, *Capital Accumulation in Thailand 1855–1985* (1984), at 251–265.

37 S.L. Wong, *Emigrant Entrepreneurs: Shanghai Industrialists in Hong Kong* (1988), at 146–159; S.L. Wong, "The Chinese Family Firm: A Model" (1985) 36 The *British Journal of Sociology* 58–76.

38 A. Suehiro, "Family Business Reassessed: Corporate Structure and Late Starting Industrialization in Thailand" (1993) 31 *The Developing Economies* 378–407 at 405.

[39] E.A. Gargon, "Chicken Feed Transforms Into Riches", *South China Morning Post* November 15, 1995; *cf.* E.A. Gurgan "When Family Empires Shape Asian Expansion", *International Herald Tribune*, November 16, 1995.

[40] R.I. Tricker, "Corporate Governance: A Ripple on the Cultural Reflection" in *Capitalism in Contrasting Cultures* (S.R. Clegg and S.G. Redding ed. 1990), at 208.

[41] G.S. Redding, above n.6 at 178.

[42] *ibid.*; *cf.* G.S. Redding, "To Grow Chinese Firms Must Look Beyond Family", *Asian Wall Street Journal* January 11, 1995 at 4. "You have to make a very important difference between the system itself and the individual firms within the system. You could have a very healthy economic system made up of firms which are churning over and living and dying relatively rapidly . . . Its like a jungle. Plants die but the jungle keeps going", M.W. Brauchli and D. Biers, "Overseas Chinese Reach Outside the Clan", *Asian Wall Street Journal* April 20, 1995; D. Biers and J. Mark, "Succession Battles Shake Asia's Family Businesses" *Asian Wall Street Journal* June 1, 1995.

[43] *cf. Divestment and Strategic Change* (J. Coyne and M. Wright ed. 1986) Chap. 3 and 6; P. Lawton, "Demergers: An Assessment" (1984) 5 *The Company Lawyer* 17. The success of management buyouts as a method of corporate divestment over the demergers of assets or subsidiaries to shareholders was in part due to the remarriage of ownership and management control.

[44] A western education, even a business one, does not guarantee that eastern cultural norms, even their nepotistic aspects are overcome, *cf.* S.L. Wong, above n.37 at 145; F. Trompenars, *Riding the Waves of Culture* (1993), at 139–148.

[45] Interviews with Hong Kong trust practitioners.

[46] P. Leach, *The Family Business* (1995). The Stoy figures, show that whilst 75 per cent of U.K. companies are family run, only 30 per cent of U.K. family businesses make it to the second generation and just 14 per cent to the third. *cf.* Beresford P, "The Independent Ones" (November 1995), *Director* 109–115 at 113.

[47] Contrast *Bartlett v. Barclays Bank Trust Co Ltd* [1980] Ch 575 with the Hong Kong case of *Standard Chartered Equitor Trustee HK Ltd v George Zee & Co Ltd* MP No 1248 of 1994 from the perspective of trustee interference with the affairs of the company whose shares they hold on trust for the founding family; *cf.* J. Brewer, "Balance of Power" (July 1995), *Company Secretary* Vol. 5 No. 7 at 30.

[48] Leach above n.46 at 25.

[49] M. Useem, *The Inner Circule: Large Corporations and the Rise of Businesses Political Activity in the US and UK* (1984).

[50] K. Nakagawa, *Hikaku Keieishi josetu* [An introduction to comparative business history] (1981) Tokyo, University of Tokyo Press at 261.

[51] R. Whitley, *Business Systems in East Asia* (1994), at 93.

[52] *ibid.* at 202–203.

[53] See generally K.B. Chan and C. Chiang, *Stepping Out: The Making of Chinese Entrepreneurs* (1994); L. Pan, *Sons of the Yellow Emperor* (1991); S.L. Wong, above n.37, V.F.S. Sit, R.D. Cremer and S.L. Wong, *Entrepreneurs and Enterprises in Macau* (1991), and sources quoted above at n.34.

[54] Suehiro, above n.38 at 386–387, 399–405. In Britain the government is easing tax burdens to encourage families to plough their wealth back into their businesses hoping that this may lead to a British *Mittelstand*, equivalent to the German medium-sized family company sector that is the engine of Germany's economic growth. *cf.* G. Rommel et al., (Partners in Mckinsey & Co Inc), *Simplicity Wins: How Germany's Mid-Sized Indus-*

trial Companies Succeed (1995). The latter appears to ignore the family aspect of these companies and the fact that the owner entrepreneurs in Mittelstand are often technicians and craftsman passionately dedicated to both their products and staff rather than "managers".

[55] A. Smart and J. Smart, "Personal Relations and Divergent Economies: A Case Study of Hong Kong Investment in China" (1991) 15 *International Journal of Urban and Regional Research* 216–33; *cf.* J. Child, *Management in China During the Age of Reform* (1994), Chap. 11–12.

[56] Compare the approach of the Swire and Jardines hongs to this development, see "The Noble Houses Look Forward" *The Economist* October 1, 1994, 75.

[57] For examples of these in the Hong Kong Context see P. Lawton, *"Meetings in Hong Kong: Their Law and Practice"* (1993) at pp.145–146. Note also s. 320 of the Companies Act 1985 which overrides waiver clauses in the articles and imposes a statutory version of the fiduciary principle in the case of "substantial property transactions". Apart from the value of the transaction needed for the section to bite (£100,000), the definition of "non cash assets" does not include the important category of management services, and so shareholder consent is not required in respect of directors" remuneration, either in the sense of payment for the performance of regular management duties or reward for "special services".

[58] Sincere Co.'s directors paid themselves a very large windfall bonus, greater than the company's net profit. The company's annual report revealed that approximately HK $114.75 million, including fees, salaries, bonuses and other perks, was granted to the directors in the year to February 28, 1993. The group reported a net profit of HK $46.66 million. Attributable profits the previous year amounted, however, to HK $1.12 billion largely due to a huge gain from the sale of the Sincere building in Central. A breakdown of fees, etc. showed that approximately HK $48 million was paid to the board, which comprises five executive and three non-executive directors. Of this sum, HK $44.39 million was shared among the five executive directors, four of whom are members of the controlling Ma family. Bonus payments to certain directors amounted to HK $66.6 million and had been charged as part of costs and expenses against the large gain from the property sale. Of bonuses paid to certain directors, HK $17.7 million had been capitalized as deferred expenditure which would be amortized over five years. Although not uncommon, such an accounting method may affect a company's profit and loss account. At the Sincere Co.'s AGM on August 3, 1993 shareholders approved a generous cash bonus, bonus shares and a dividend payment to themselves without raising any question relating to directors' remuneration. In the light of the large gain the previous year and the generous package for shareholders this is not surprising. Nevertheless, following adverse press coverage the directors repaid the special bonus of HK$66.68 million and commenced legal proceedings over some of the reports. As the very name of the company suggests, it had a good reputation to maintain, as did its directors. *cf. South China Morning Post* 4, 15 and August 4, 5 and 17, 1993.

[59] Mr Justice Dawson in an address delivered to the Second Business Lawyers Conference, April 10, 1989, Melbourne, at pp.4–5. This is cited in R. Tomasic and S. Bottomly, "Directing The Top 500: Corporate Governance and Accountability in Australian Companies" (1993), p. 25 and in Z. Adenwala, "Directors' Generous Remuneration to be or not to be paid" (1991) 3 *Bond Law Review* 25.

[60] L.S. Sealy, *Company Law and Commercial Reality* (1984), at 60. It was the view of the Jenkins Committee that "to say that it is useless to provide investors with further safeguards . . . which if provided they will not use is

a counsel of despair", Report of the Company Law Committee, Cmnd. 1749 (1962) at 39, para. 107.

[61] See *South China Morning Post* November 1, 1989, December 20, 1989 and April 15, 1993.

[62] P. Lawton, above n.57 at 150.

[63] R. Tomasic and S. Bottomley, *Directing the Top 500* at pp.150–151.

[64] See *Financial Times* July 21, 1987 reporting on this affair.

[65] See M. Vander Weyer, "The Power Behind the Putsch" (March 1995) *Management Today* at 40–44.

[66] N. Fung "Shareholders Vote Family out of Group" *South China Morning Post* September 29, 1995.

[67] A.F. Conrad, "Beyond Managerialism: Investor Capitalism" (1988) 22 U Mich J L Ref 117.

[68] R. Minns, *Pension Funds and British Capitalism: The Ownership and Control of Shareholdings* (1980), Chap. 2.

[69] S. Rose, *The Shareholder* (1989), at 163.

[70] Institutional Shareholders Committee "The Responsibilities of Institutional Shareholders in the UK", p.2.

[71] It has been reported that in 1988 more than 52 per cent of large United Kingdom companies had decisions influenced by institutional shareholders: Korn/Ferry International, *Board of Directors Study UK* (1989).

[72] Dobie, "Squandering the Potential of Annual Meetings", *The Independent*, June 10, 1991; Midgley, "How Much Control Do Shareholders Exercise?" (1974) *Lloyds Bank Review* 24; Tombs, "The Interrelationship Between Institutional Investors the Company in which they Invest and Company Management" in *Creative Tensions* (NAPF: 1990). In a recent CBI survey it was discovered that more than half the pension funds questioned never or only rarely voted: CBI, *Pension Fund Investment Management* (1988) at 64–6.

[73] J.C. Coffee, "Liquidity Versus Control: The Institutional Investor as Corporate Monitor" (1991) 91 Colum L. Rev. 1278 at 1328.

[74] C.T. Bogus, "Excessive Compensation and the Failure of Corporate Democracy", (1993) 41 *Buffalo Law Review* 3 at 43.

[75] J.M. Naylor, "The Use of Criminal Sanctions by UK and US Authorities for Insider Trading: How can the Two Systems Learn from Each Other" Part I (1990) II *Company Lawyer* 53 at 54.

[76] For example, Securities (Insider Dealing) Ordinance, s. 9.

[77] Above n.70.

[78] The Stock Exchange of Hong Kong Ltd, Rules Governing the Listing of Securities' Guidance Note 1, s. 6.

[79] R.E. Artus, (Group Chief Investment Manager of the Prudential Corporation plc) in *Creative Tensions*, above n.72, at 14.

[80] In Germany the banks' position as major shareholders in their own right is strengthened substantially by their ability to exercise the voting rights attached to bearer shares held by them on behalf of their customers. See generally F. Voge, *German Business After the Economic Miracle* (1973), Chapt. 2; E.J. Horn, *Management of Industrial Change in Germany* (1982), at 40–42; Coffee, above n.7 at 1302–1306; T. Baums, "Banks and Corporate Control in Germany" in *Corporate Control and Accountability* (1993), at 271–273; J. Charkham, "Corporate Governance and the Market for Control of Companies" (1989) Bank of England Panel Paper, No. 25 at pp.8-9 *cf.* J. Charkham, *Keeping Good Company: A Study of Corporate Governance in Five Countries* (1994), Chap. 2. For a warning against the temptation to use simple correlations in an analysis of the role of banks in german economic performance and corporate governance and a critical analysis of that role

see J. Edwards and Fischer, "Banks, Finance and Investment in Germany" (1994), at 6 *et seq.*

81 W.C. Kester, "*Japanese Takeovers*: The Global Contest for Corporate Control" (1991), at 58–60; R.J. Gilson and M.J. Roe, "Understanding the Japanese Kieretsu: Overlaps Between Corporate Governance and Industrial Organization", (1993) 102 *Yale Law Journal* 871 at 882; J. Charkham, *Keeping Good Company* (1994), at 12–18 and 109.

82 See generally E. Batstone and P.L. Davies, *Industrial Democracy. The European Experience* (1976); W.C. Kester, above n.81.

83 "A Survey of Capitalism: Punters or Proprietors" The Economist, May 5, 1990.

84 S. Rose, *The Shareholder*, at 183.

85 Coffee, above n.73 at 1317–28.

86 R.W. Nottle, "Regulation of the Funds Management Industry in Hong Kong" (1990) *Law Lectures for Practitioners* 113.

87 See "Scottish Fund Managers Take a Long Term View", *South China Morning Post* December 5, 1993.

88 *cf.* K. Wong, "Fear and Loathing of Global Funds in the Smaller Company Boardroom", *South China Morning Post* April 16, 95.

89 S. Kennedy, "Mobius Ready to Become Activist Investor", *South China Morning Post* November 15, 1995.

90 G. Hewitt, "Templeton in Battle Against Privatization" *South China Morning Post* November 18, 1995; G. Hewitt, "Minorities Reserve Level Playing Field" *ibid.*

91 I. Ramsay and M. Blair, "Ownership Concentration, Institutional Investment and Corporate Governance: An Empirical Investigation of 100 Australian Companies" (1993) *Melbourne University Law Review* 153 at 180.

92 *The Responsibilities of Institutional Shareholders* at 2–3. *cf.* P.L. Davies, "Institutional Investors in the United Kingdom" in *Contemporary Issues in Corporate Governance* (D.D. Prentice and P.R.J. Holland ed. 1993).

93 The CBI, *Pension Fund Investment Management* (1988) at 20; pp.64–66, notes that one in eight of the pension funds surveyed were aware that their managers had participated in at least one instance of "ginger group" activity in the previous five years intended to stimulate a portfolio company's management. L. Midgley *Companies and their Shareholders — The Uneasy Relationship* (1975) at 79–80 reports that an insurance company investment manager had told him that his company had intervened in companies 25 times over a period of 18 months.

94 CBI above n.93 at 64–66.

95 [1982] Ch 204, C.A. Only after they won a derivative action in the High Court did the majority of shareholders support the Prudential.

96 J.E. Parkinson, *Corporate Power and Responsibility* (1993) at 173 and 176–7.

97 R.A.G. Monks, "Relationship Investing" (1992) 2 *Corporate Governance* 59–76 at 72.

98 Gilson and Kraakman, "Reinventing the Outside Director. An Agenda for Institutional Investors", (1991) 43 Stan L. Rev. 863 at 870–1.

99 See generally Evans, "HK Should Embrace Governance Challenge", *South China Morning Post*, January 24, 1994.

100 Corporate Powers and Responsibility, *op. cit.*, at 176. For arguments against a government agency in such a role see Ramsay, I. "Directors and Officers Remuneration" (1993) JBL 351 at 370–2.

101 E.A. Dyl, "Corporate Control and Management Compensation: Evidence on the Agency Problem" (1988) 9 *Managerial and Decision Economics* 21.

102 L.R. Gamez-Mejia, H. Tasi and T. Hinkin, "Managerial Control, Perform-

ance and Executive Compensation" (1987) 30 *Academy of Management Journal* 51.

[103] A perusal of most annual reports of Hong Kong listed companies reveals a marked absence of directors' service contracts.

[104] Although in Hong Kong dividends are not usually subject to tax they are paid out of taxed profits. Profits tax is levied on companies at 17.5 per cent. Salaries Tax averages out at 15 per cent but salaries are tax deductible. There is "therefore" a marginal advantage in taking out salaries rather than dividends although the latter are tax free. Li Ka-Shing is exceptional; he receives HK$50,000 for his services as director but in 1993–4 received HK $610,000,000 in dividends. *cf.* G. Manuel, "Hutchinson Leads in Boardroom Payouts" *South China Morning Post* April 26, 1994.

[105] *cf. supra* n.58.

[106] S. Rasenstein and D.F. Rush, "The Stock Return Performance of Corporations that are Partially Owned by Other Corporations" (1990) 13 *Journal of Financial Economics* 39. This examines empirical evidence in the USA to the effect that a large shareholder may transfer wealth from other shareholders by co-opting management to engage in such activity, though the evidence suggests that this will generally be limited to situations where larger shareholders are able to control a company with less than 50% of the issued shares.

[107] Companies Ordinance ss. 166 and 168, Sched. 9.

[108] Registrar General, Annual Departmental Report 1992–3. For voluntary withdrawals and privatizations from the HKSE see HKSE annual Fact Books.

[109] See SFC Consultative Document, *Amendments to the Codes on Takeovers and Mergers and Share Repurchases in Relation to Schemes of Arrangement* (October 1992); E. Ko, "Industry Split on Privatization Proposals", (December 1992) *The Securities Journal*, p.4.

[110] G. Wong, "The Changing Pattern of Interlocking Directorate in Hong Kong — The Effects of the Rise of Chinese Big Business in the Period 1976–1986" paper presented at the conference The Last Half Century of the Chinese Overseas (1945–1994): Comparative Perspectives held at the University of Hong Kong, December 19–21, 1994 at 9–10; *cf.* D. Wilson, *Hong Kong* (1990) at 164. For a discussion of the sociological models of corporate power and interlocking directorships see J.P. Scott, "Theoretical Framework and Research Design" in *Networks of Corporate Power* (F.N. Stokman, R. Ziegler and J.P. Scott ed. 1985).

[111] A. Au, "Hong Kong Code on Takeovers and Mergers: Toothless Watchdog or Handmaiden of Equality" (1987) 17 HKLJ 24.

[112] R.M. Buxbaum, "Corporate Legitimacy, Economic Theory and Legal Doctrine" (1984) 45 Ohio State LJ 516 at 531.

[113] J.A. Fairburn and J.A. Kay, *Merger and Merger Policy* (1989) at 19.

[114] J.C. Coffee, "Regulating the Market for Corporate Control: A Critical Assessment of the Tender Offer's Role in Corporate Governance" (1984) 84 Colum L. Rev. 1145 at 1212.

[115] See generally E. Ko, "Clampdown on backdoor listings" (June 1993) *The Securities Journal* at 14. The owners of some of the companies targeted by mainland enterprises would welcome the reciprocal advantages such takeovers would allow in terms of doing business on the mainland.

[116] Coopers Lybrand, *Barriers to Takeovers in the European Community* (1989) at 22.

[117] M.K.H. Mok, K. Lam and I.Y.K. Cheung, "The Unique Structure of Stock Returns in Hong Kong", *The Securities Bulletin*, March 1989, at p.5; *cf.* G. Wong, above n.112.

[118] Jardine Matheson Holdings is the holding company of one of the territory's oldest hongs (over 140 years old) and has a relatively dispersed shareholding. The controlling Keswick family is estimated to hold *circa* seven per cent of the shares. The company feels vulnerable to a takeover. There was an alleged gentleman's agreement between the leading hongs not to mount a hostile takeover bid in recent years, which ends in 1995. The underlying reasons may be, however, political in the light of historical relations with China, see G. Hewitt, "Jardine and SFC on Collision Course", *South China Morning Post* March 24, 1994, *cf.* above n.56. For a case study of a similarly vulnerable company in a "greenmail" situation see R.I. Tricker, "International Corporate Governance: Text, Readings and Cases", The Hongkong and Shanghai Hotels Ltd (cases A, B, C and D) at 220–243. For an example of a company under dominant family control easily able to rebuff an unwanted takeover offer see C. Lee, "Family Rules out Nam Pei Hong Counter-bid" *South China Morning Post* October 18, 1994. A simple observation is that those much older companies which have listed, were founded by "westerners" and have a more dispersed shareholding are vulnerable to takeovers. Most Chinese family dominated companies are much younger with a dominant shareholding held by the family and are, therefore, much less vulnerable to hostile TOBs; *cf.* above n.50. For the percentage of the market capitalization controlled by the top ten families in HK as at March 31, 1988 see Redding, *The Spirit of Chinese Capitalism* at 152–3.

[119] In the U.K. these include the Bank of England, CBI and Stock Exchange and PRO NED; Australia has its own PRO NED Organization. In Hong Kong the Stock Exchange, SFC and Institute of Directors all support the appointment of independent directors to the boards of listed companies.

[120] Cadbury Committee Report, paras. 4.33–8 and 4.42.

[121] Fluendy, "Call for Action on Directors", *South China Morning Post*, October 18, 1994.

[122] V. Brudney, "The Independent Director — Heavenly City or Potemkin Village?" (1982) 95 *Harvard Law Review* 597 at 633.

[123] R. Tomasic and S. Bottomley, *Directing the Top 500* at 17.

[124] "Bosses Pay", *The Economist*, February 1, 1992 19 at 20.

[125] PRO NED, *Research into the Role of the Non-Executive Director* (July 1992).

[126] The audiences researched were: Chairmen, CEOs/MDs, NEDs, other directors, directors of subsidiary companies, investment directors of institutional shareholders and senior audit partners of firms of accountants.

[127] Parkinson, *Corporate Power and Responsibility*, at 147–8.

[128] Extract from a speech by Mr Merven Bowles, company secretary of John Swire and Sons (HK), at the 1992 Company Secretaries Conference reported in *Administrator*, December 1992, at 9.

[129] Hong Kong Listing Rules 3.10 and 3.15.

[130] *ibid.* Rule 3.11.

[131] PRO NED, *Guidelines for Remuneration Committees*, at 4.

[132] See "Independent Directors to Escape Stock Exchange Vetting", *South China Morning Post*, January 5, 1994.

[133] The deadline was extended to March 31, 1995. According to Mr Keniel Wong a director of the HKSE listing division, as at December 1, 1994 *circa* six listed companies had not appointed their first independent non-executive director, *i.e.* 11 months after the deadline, and almost 100 had not appointed their second independent non-executive director, *i.e.* with one month to go before the deadline for the second appointment. Speech given

at HKSA conference Advice to Directors and the Board — the Critical Issues, December 3, 1994.

[134] G. Wong, above n.116 at 23.

[135] *cf.* N. Fung, above n.66.

[136] M.J. Roe, *Strong Managers Weak Owners: The Political Roots of American Corporate Finance* (1994).

[137] See R. Whitley, above n.51 at 93.

[138] See J.E. Parkinson, "The Role of 'Exit' and 'Voice' in Corporate Governance" in *Corporate Governance and Corporate Control* (S. Shiekh and W. Rees ed. 1995).

[139] Price Waterhouse, *Corporate Governance*, January 1995 at 2, 23.

[140] R.I. Tricker, J. Leung and K. Lee, "The Company Secretary in Hong Kong's Listed Companies" (October 1995) HKICSA at 6–9.

[141] *ibid.* at 29.

[142] Bogus above n.74 at 46.

THE SECURITIES AND FUTURES COMMISSION AND SECURITIES REGULATION IN HONG KONG

Judith O'Hare

Faculty of Law
City University of Hong Kong

Judith O'Hare, *BEcLL B (Syd), is a lecturer at the City of University of Hong Kong and a solicitor of the Supreme Court of New South Wales and High Court of Australia.*

Introduction

The securities industry in Hong Kong has a long and interesting history based on its colonial origins, the cultural juxtaposition of "east meets west" and the operation of the market as a modern day version of the laissez-faire economy. In one relatively small city/state these forces, often contrary and operating in conflict, have been the impetus for and the means by which Hong Kong has emerged as an international economic heavy weight in the Asia-Pacific region.

The role of the primary securities regulator, the Securities and Futures Commission (SFC) and the role and, more importantly the operation of regulation in the securities industry generally, offers no better example of the dynamic forces at play in Hong Kong. The problems faced by Hong Kong in the establishment of a securities industry that is dynamic yet attractive to investors; domestic or international, individual and institutional alike, is similar to the many problems faced by other countries in similar emerging markets. The way in which Hong Kong has approached and dealt with these problems, in terms of the historical conflicts inherent in the market and idiosyncrasies within the market itself, is, however, unique.

This paper will endeavour to analyze the role of the SFC in the Hong Kong securities market and establish how the market and the SFC have come to terms with that role and the greater role played by regulation in the market generally. In this regard I will deal with three major issues:

(a) the historical development of regulation in the securities market;
(b) the blueprinted role established for regulation of the Hong Kong securities market and the SFC; and
(c) the changing and development nature of the SFC's role and its effectiveness in establishing the objectives of the market through regulation.

Development of a Securities Market in Hong Kong

Historical Origins of the Trading of Shares

The trading of shares has a history dating back almost to the colonization of Hong Kong itself.[1] Share trades were recorded as early as 1866. It was not until 1891, however, that a formal market was set up.[2] The Hong Kong Stock Exchange[3] ran a monopoly on the trading of public shares, and was virtually free from government interference. The stock market at this time did not play a major role in the raising of capital in the colony. The capital needs of the burgeoning colony were essentially provided by the banks.[4] Indeed the development of the Hong Kong economy had two clear divisions — the development of trade based on British interests and the development of trade based on local Chinese interests. The use of the corporate vehicle to conduct business was not widely accepted by the Chinese until after the Second World War.[5] The Chinese historically conducted business based on family connections. Capital needs for business expansion were generally found within the family or from banks. It represented the antipathy of the Chinese family business to admit strangers or relinquish control to outsiders. When the Chinese began to utilize the company structure for business it did not automatically lead to an increase in the number of listings. As the trend to list developed, enhanced by buoyant economic conditions, many of these companies retained their family identity, as Lawton notes, "most of the listed companies remain family dominated".[6]

The Hong Kong Stock Exchange was run as a monopoly on the trading of shares essentially for British interests. In an effort to break this monopoly, in December 1969 the Far East Stock Exchange was opened. Set up by local Chinese businessmen essentially for Chinese business interests, it broke with many of the traditions of the Hong

109

Kong Stock Exchange. Trading was in Cantonese and anyone with the right amount of cash could purchase a seat on this new exchange.[7]

The economic climate during this time was particularly sound. The new exchange was launched with great success. It encouraged other exchanges to be established including the Kam Ngan Stock Exchange in March 1971, and the Kowloon Stock Exchange in 1972. During this time there was little government intervention in the regulation of the securities market. As noted, the functions of the exchange as a source of capital raising were only beginning to take shape; company listings, and thereby share trading, was still at the periphery of the capital markets.

The revolution in the market took hold during 1969–73. Taking advantage of the "bull run", strong investor sentiment, easy listing procedures and the proliferation of exchanges, a flood of new companies lined up to be listed irrespective of "underlying assets or trading records".[8] The government was concerned at the escalation of activity in the market and legislative intervention was mooted as early as 1973. The Government's proposals lacked form and, although they had substance in individual instances, merely reflected the Financial Secretary's immediate concerns. For example, when it was realized that a fifth exchange was about to open in early 1973, legislation prohibiting the opening of further exchanges was rushed through the Legislative Council.

There was no formal policy for the development of regulation for the securities market. Hong Kong had always operated as an open market with little or no government intervention. "Government" in Hong Kong terms was really an extension of the British Foreign Office. There was little advance attention paid by the Government, in the form of the bureaucracy, to the needs of the economy. The Government was really more concerned with the day to day law and order issues and the development of British trade interests in the colony. Indeed government intervention usually only arose when industries experienced, for whatever reason, some kind of crisis (as illustrated by the intervention of the Government to regulate the banking industry in the late 1960s).[9] It became the accepted norm, and indeed the bulwark to later arguments against the regulation of the securities industry, that in all aspects of the economy Hong Kong "traditionally erred on the side of excessive laissez-faire".[10]

Initial Regulatory Framework

The early attempts to set up an effective regulatory structure in which securities trading would prosper and develop were doomed to fail. Regulation of the industry was to have little effect until both economic conditions *and* participant sentiment changed sufficiently to allow for acceptance and application of regulation in the market. In attempting to analyze the inadequacies of the early reforms and why they were doomed to fail it is necessary to understand the structures of those reforms.

The market crashed dramatically in March 1973. There followed five years in which a number of legislative enactments, carrying with them the initial regulatory structure of the securities market, were put into operation. A Securities Advisory Council and a Commissioner for Securities were appointed to oversee the application of the new legislation and promote a new regulatory framework. The legislative reforms included the enactment of the Securities Ordinance (which formally established the Securities Commission and the Office of the Commissioner) and the Protection of Investors Ordinance in February 1974.[11] Regulation in practice was first effected by the establishment of the Stock Exchanges Compensation Fund in August 1974, the introduction of a Takeover and Mergers Code in August 1975, the implementation of Stock Exchange Listing Rules in 1976 and the establishment of the Insider Trading Tribunal in 1977.[12]

The reforms effected a three tiered supervisory structure in the securities market. The Securities Commission was to advise the Financial Secretary on all matters relating to securities, apply the relevant ordinances, protect investors, ensure a fair market prevailed and supervise the stock exchanges. The Commissioner for Securities (a government appointed public servant) and his office were the administrative arm of the Commission. In this structure, the third tier was the role played by the exchanges. This required the exchanges to impose and then internally police regulatory policies in line with the legislative reforms.

As the exchanges had the direct contact with the traders and investors, their role as self-regulators was implicit. Although this burst of regulatory activity suggested that the government was intending to take more control of the securities industry, the reverse was actually the case. The fact that the government limited its role to the establishment of a regulatory regime and initial legislative reform, reflected the market and government's overriding attitude at the time to intervention and regulation: ". . . the Government should not get deeply involved in attempts to regulate and supervise stock exchanges and dealings thereon."[13]

Inadequacy of the Initial Regulatory Framework

The early legislative reforms were ineffective to establish a workable regulatory regime for three reasons: the inadequacy of the supervisory framework, the lack of enforcement of the regulatory framework and a lack of understanding or indeed acceptance of regulation in the market. The supervisory framework was inadequate at all its three tiers.

The Commission in its composition was inadequate. It was perceived as lacking independence as its members included representatives from the Stock and Futures Exchanges. In its functioning, it was inadequate as it operated as a part-time body meeting infrequently and haphazardly. It delegated many of its functions to the Commissioner of Securities, whose office was severely understaffed and overworked.

The market considered the Commission of little relevance. It was not even consulted in the aftermath of the market collapse in 1987 in respect of the strategies undertaken to arrest the imminent demise of the capital markets.[14] No formal role in policy planning or development evolved from this Commission.

The Commissioner of Securities was the real regulator in the market. The market, however, treated the activities of the Commissioner with contempt and considered that his office's intervention hampered or impeded the market. To a significant degree this was true. The Commissioner, as a public servant and running an office directly under government control, was considered with suspicion by the market. His attempts to establish a workable regulatory regime were thwarted at every turn. Representative of and restricted by the interests of government, loaded with the responsibilities of the Commission and contemptuously received by the market, the Commissioner was perceived in the market as a "toothless tiger".[15] No policy direction for the promotion and development of regulation and therefore no effective strategy of policy planning or implementation was possible.[16]

The role of the Stock Exchange and Futures Exchange as self-regulators in the market was virtually non-existent. The original Hong Kong Stock Exchange had run utilizing a "London-style" format and set of practice codes.[17] Those practice codes, having their origins in the thirteenth century, enshrined self-regulation as the regulating face in the market. Although formalized regulation proliferated over time in the operation of the London Exchange, self-regulation remained a fundamental feature of the regulatory system. Tomasic considers this was made possible because of the "proximity, tradition, self-interest and culture of the English class system", which he notes in itself was a form of regulation imposing standards of conduct on the market participants.[18]

Ironically, the operation of the Stock Exchange in Hong Kong, especially after the uniting of the exchanges into the Hong Kong Stock Exchange in 1980,[19] was seen as nothing more than the running of a private club for the benefit of participating members with little or no regard to the interests of the general public investor and the concept of openness and fairness in the market.[20] The traditions of self regulation adopted in the English model had not made their way into the practices of the exchanges. The rot was present to the highest level. Indeed, the founding chairman of the united Stock Exchange, Ronald Li, was investigated, charged and found guilty of offences linked to prior allotment of shares in new company listing.[21]

The Establishment of the Securities Review Committee

In the wake of the world wide stock market crisis in October 1987, the government established the Securities Review Committee (the Committee). The Committee was charged with the responsibility of reviewing the constitution, management and operation of the Stock and Futures Exchanges and the regulatory bodies behind those exchanges.[22]

Recognizing the inadequacies of the system in terms of its structure and operation, the Committee set about structuring a new system that it believed would facilitate the re-establishment of confidence in the securities markets of Hong Kong. That the Committee was successful in having the majority of its recommendations implemented was a new phenomenon in the Hong Kong market. Reform of the securities market was demanded by all areas of the community, including investors, market participants, legislative council members and the media alike. This unique opportunity to implement real change in the securities market was not lost on the Committee. As a consequence of their deliberations, they prepared a detailed report[23] (the Hay-Davison Report) which avoided over emphasis on the allocation of blame for the markets' demise. It set about planning for the market's resurrection.

Fundamental to this process was the identification of the goals of regulation in the market. Here at last was a definitive statement on the objectives of regulation, framed in such a way as to allow for the initial development of policy planning for the implementation of the recommendations of the Committee. As the majority of the Committee's recommendations on the restructuring of the regulatory regime were implemented, the Hay-Davison Report became a fundamental starting point from which the identification and application of regulation could take hold.

What Makes A Securities Regulatory Regime Successful?

Any successful securities regulatory regime is dependent on a combination of factors. These factors include effective policy planning, workable legislative and regulatory regimes, adequate government funding and resource support, market perceptions and market acceptance. These factors are hinged on the ability of the market regulator to create an environment in which security regulation is seen as enhancing the securities market and not blanketing it in inefficient and ineffective regulation. Knowledge and participation by the market appears to be the key to the successful implementation of a workable regulatory regime. Without knowledge, acceptance and participation by the market, regulation will be ineffective in establishing the objectives of the market. Every securities market, therefore, needs to plan for, in a lucid and informative way, the role regulation is to play in achieving of the objectives of the market. Regulation itself is not the market's objective. Experience shows that through effective regulation the market's objectives have a better chance to manifest in achievements for the market. The Committee, after considerable deliberation, set out at the very beginning of the Hay-Davison Report what it perceived to be the objectives of the securities market in Hong Kong.

With those objectives in mind it set itself the task of creating a workable regulatory regime that would facilitate the establishment of the objectives. The objectives were formulated having special regard to the nature of the market in Hong Kong. The objectives may be summarized as:

(a) the establishment of Hong Kong as the primary capital market of the South East Asian Region;
(b) the encouragement of new market;
(c) the promotion of Hong Kong as an international financial centre; and
(d) the implementation of a regulatory framework instilling confidence and efficiency in the market.[24]

From this base, the Committee determined how regulation was to be utilized in achieving these objectives. It established lucid and cogent aims by which the regulation of the market could be gauged. It determined that stability, the orderly and smooth running of the market, fairness and protection of investors were the fundamental, requirements of the market to be achieved through regulation. These could be achieved through adequate risk management, implementation of appropriate levels of regulation (in which self-regulation would remain a part), the establishment of checks and balances within the system, all at a realistic cost both in terms of restrictions placed on the market and the price paid for the creation of this optimum regime.

Origins of Security Regulation in the Modern Financial Market

Securities Regulation and Policy

Whilst the early attempts at regulation of the Hong Kong securities market were ineffective, regulation in other securities markets has had a much longer and more illustrious presence. In the U.S., for example, from as early as 1929 regulation has played an important-indeed fundamental-role in the efficient operations of the securities market. It is the U.S. standard in regulatory controls that is accepted as the benchmark for adequate market regulation.

Mann notes that the U.S. Congress "determined that regulations designed to ensure the honesty and integrity of the securities markets were necessary and in the public interest".[25] All levels of the U.S. securities market play a role in the effective operation of securities regulation. Their knowledge and acceptance of regulation, and their compliance with its aims and objectives are fundamental to the facilitation of adequate and effective regulation of the market.

The concepts of "fair playing field" and investor protection are pivotal to the effectiveness of the market and are the "overriding goals" of the U.S. regulatory regime.[26] Regulation is not enacted for regulation's sake. It is recognized in the U.S. that markets need to be flexible enough to meet the emerging demands of the capital market. That the U.S. securities market is so dynamic illustrates how, with effective regulation, the aims of the market can be achieved without a burdensome cost placed on the market.

Mann recognizes the unique role regulator's must play in this context when he states:

"Regulators must constantly remind themselves that it is the markets, and not regulation that reflect the perceived value of securities. It is the market that has expanded globally to respond to the demands of business. And finally, it is the market, and not the regulators, that have developed new instruments to satisfy the desire of investors to hedge the risk."[27]

Through the primary securities regulator in the U.S. the Securities Exchange Commission (SEC), the regulatory environment creates a number of levels of supervision, all interdependent but which dovetail into a framework of regulation aimed at achieving market goals, as well as market responsibility. This environment sets a simple and effective philosophy by which the SEC regulates the market. These rules encompass the major premise that the market is established in an honest and fair environment aspiring to three qualities — openness, honesty and integrity — at all levels. Regulation becomes, not a by-product of market intervention, but a fundamental base through which codes of conduct (either regulatory or self imposed) elicit from the participants the appropriate standards of conduct.

In the facilitation of these aims, the market players are trusted to maintain a level of scrutiny in their conduct that can be simply stated as: do not lie, disclose fully and deal fairly.[28] Knowledge of the rules by which this conduct is achieved, understanding of the purpose of the rules and an application of the spirit rules is vital in such a system. Without these factors operating in unison within the market, regulation would not be effective and the orchestrated efforts to achieve the objectives of the market would be thwarted.

If adequate knowledge, understanding and acceptance are to be achieved, the regime itself must deal swiftly and effectively with those who do not conduct themselves in a manner sympathetic to the required standard. This encompasses the requirements of policing and effective sanctions imposed on those whose conduct deviates. Such policing and the imposition of sanctions must be seen to be administered fairly and evenly. The ability of the regulator to use its powers to protect the market participants is vital if those participants are to have confidence in the market.

The U.S. securities market is not free from incident or immune to scandal. In his book *Casino Capitalism?*, Tomasic notes that the SEC brought no fewer than 137 civil actions for insider dealing between 1977 and 1987. This represented a threefold increase in prosecutions for insider dealing over the previous 28 years.[29] Even with its long history of market regulation, public awareness, public and participants' acceptance, and a diligent regulatory authority, the U.S. securities market is still susceptible to financial scandals. Scandals including the demise of BCCI, the Savings and Loans scandal, market rigging and insider dealing exploits involving Michael Milken and Ivan Boesky were by no means small and their effects on the market were considerable. This is not to forget the potential developments in the wake of the Orange County bankruptcy, linked to its chief financial officer's disastrous derivative forays and the losses of Daiwa Bank of Japan (estimated at US$1.1 billion), from unauthorized trades made by Daiwa employee Toshide Iguchi over a period of 11 years, from Daiwa's New York office.

Securities regulation is, therefore, not effective in creating the perfect market. What must exist in the wake of this inadequacy is the recognition that the regulator is empowered, armed with the full weight of effective sanctions, to investigate and bring to justice those who breach the fundamental tenets of the system. The existence of the tenets and the understanding by the market of those tenets is, therefore, vital. This was recognized by the Committee when it recognized as ludicrous the establishment of a regulatory regime free from failure.

"Markets will continue to gyrate, sometimes widely, players will continue to fail and clients will continue to default. No free market system can or indeed should attempt to, prevent such events occurring. The important thing is to ensure that problems are localized and do not strike at the heart of the market."[30]

How Does Regulation Operate Effectively in the Market?

In the U.S. it is not possible for the SEC to monitor and investigate every transaction and foray that occurs in the market, nor is it able to monitor every action of the participants in the market. The market is enormous. The New York Stock Exchange alone has the highest turnover of all international markets on a daily basis.[31] There are over 8,000 securities firms across the country and thousands of employees operating in those firms. Then there are the companies in the market and the investors.

The imposition of regulation would be impossible if not for the acceptance by the market players of the principles of regulation and an understanding of the policy directing those principles. Coupled with this acceptance and knowledge is a regulatory structure that permeates all levels of market involvement. The hallmark of this regulatory structure is disclosure and enforcement.

Market perceptions of disclosure and enforcement are fundamental in establishing adherence to codes of conduct. If it is believed that the regulator is ineffective and little or no consequence will flow from the abrogation of a market participant's responsibilities, the system would be fundamentally flawed. The U.S. regime, on the other hand, is successful because the market perceives that failure to disclose will result in the full weight of the law, through enforcement and the imposition of sanctions, being dealt to the perpetrator.

Market Reform and the Securities and Futures Commission (SFC)

The Establishment of the SFC and the Role of Self-Regulation

The Committee, having severely criticized the existing regulatory structure, did more than give lip service to criticisms of the previous regulatory system. The Hay-Davison Report focused on and made recommendations for change to be implemented in the securities industry. Through these changes it was envisaged that Hong Kong would have the necessary structures in place to enable the objectives of the securities market to be achieved.[32]

The Hay-Davison Report identified the Hong Kong securities environment as based on a system of self-regulation. The market had, however, failed to ensure that self-regulation actively existed. This situation was compounded by the lack of policy direction from government or the regulators.[33] In reality, self-regulation was merely a victim of the overriding philosophy of laissez-faire.

Self-regulation was not rejected by the Committee. It was seen as an effective way in which regulation could be introduced allowing for flexibility, spontaneity and discipline to be part of the regulatory process. It was recognized that the laissez-faire approach had been abused, not that it had failed Hong Kong. Indeed it was emphasized that Hong Kong's success was based on the freedom of the market. What was needed was a regulatory system which redefined the role of regulation by the participants and which came with the necessary independent checks and balances to ensure that the system of self-regulation was working effectively. It is in the establishment of these checks and balances that we find the fundamental role envisaged for regulation in the Territory's securities industry. The report considered that a two tiered system should be established. The exchanges should be at the forefront of the first tier, instigating self-regulation of their members and their dealings. Above the exchanges, the Hay-Davison Report envisaged the establishment of a securities body whose role would be to oversee the market and its participants.[34]

This body, it recommended, should be independent of the government but adequately funded both by the industry and government to ensure its financial security. It recommended it be staffed by full-time professionals and support staff appointed outside the civil service. It recommended accountability — by the submission of a report prepared on an annual basis — to the Governor; and its accounts should be submitted to the Finance Committee for scrutiny. It should have a definite role in the development of policy and the implementation of market regulation. It should be empowered to investigate and where necessary prosecute infringements of the legislative regime. It should take an active role in the review of the operations of the self-regulators and in establishing codes of conduct for those self-regulators. Its power should be extensive and wide reaching, linked with its role as a watchdog of market regulation.[35]

The majority of these recommendations were enacted on May 1, 1989 in the Securities and Futures Commission Ordinance (Cap 24). Apart from its powers under the Ordinance, the SFC is empowered to carry out and exercise the duties and powers conferred on it by the Securities Ordinance and the overseeing of other protective and regulatory ordinances.[36]

Initial Reactions to the SFC

The market, still reeling from the stock exchange collapse, hailed the proposals the Hay-Davison Report as progressive and balanced. Criticism was present but generally, it was levelled at specific recommendations. Mr Henry Wu, the chairman of the Hong Kong Stockbrokers Association appeared as a lone voice when he expressed criticism of the Committee's report as "too academic", citing the failure to appreciate the potential financial burden on the market of funding the new commission and the lack of evidence showing that self-regulation was unworkable.[37]

The Stock Exchange and Futures Exchange had spent the time after the collapse of the market instituting what has become the major recommendation in the Hay-Davison Report, that they set about "placing their houses in order". Their reactions to the establishment the SFC was one of bipartisan support.

Over time, however, the market began to realize that the SFC was not a reincarnation of the previous regulators. It was establishing goals for the development of regulation, both overt regulation and procedures for the implementation and monitoring of self-regulation. It was taking active steps to implement such policies.

A Memorandum of Understanding was signed by the Stock Exchange and the new SFC in relation to the establishment of codes of conduct and the implementation of reviews to the structure of the Stock Exchange. This harmonious relationship was, however, short lived.

The market participants, unused to this type of intervention — even though they had welcomed, indeed demanded it some months before — reacted. Businessmen regarded the implication of the new securities rule as "*gweilo* nonsense".[38] They viewed the expansion plans of the SFC with suspicion and did not readily accept that western regulatory concepts had a place in the Hong Kong market. This market revolt was more a product of the realization that the SFC was, as a regulator, much more effective than had been its predecessor. The concept of change was much easier to deal with — upon the expectation that no net change would in fact occur — than what actually resulted. Interestingly this argument appears in direct conflict with the whole thrust of the reforms envisaged by the Committee. The Hay-Davison Report emphasized the need to develop regulation and control in the light of the unique local market forces at play, with a view to establishing acceptable market standards of practice and conduct, geared to protect the needs of the domestic investor but sufficient to attract the international investor. Why was it that the industry took exception to the dominating role the SFC planned to take in the regulation of the securities environment?

The role of the industry watch-dog is usually to act as an intermediary between the industry lobby and the investor lobby. The SFC, however, saw it's role as the representative of the interests of investors. It perceived the market was aligned towards the interests of the industry and not the interest of investors. In this regard, the first Chairman of the SFC, Robert Owen, said:

119

"In Hong Kong the investor lobby is there and one does hear it privately, but it is not very vocal or well organized, or articulate, whereas the industry lobby is extremely well organized, extremely, articulate, and extremely well represented in the places that matter. That tends to push you as a regulator, to the other side of the argument."[39]

This created suspicions of the SFC in the industry.

As a new regulator, the SFC encountered other problems, including defining limits to its role and the dividing up of responsibilities with other regulators so as to ensure that there was complete understanding of roles and responsibilities with as little duplication as possible. Although the SFC was established as an independent body funded by the government and industry, it was primarily under the control of the government for financial support and financial accountability. This gave antagonists in the market place a platform from which to launch attacks against the SFC.

The SFC came under direct criticism from the Legislative Council's ad hoc Finance Committee over its budgetary expenditure in 1989. This attack was accepted in part by the then Governor, Sir David Wilson, who authorized cut-backs in the SFC's budget. At such a critical point in the development of the SFC, this blow to its financial viability could have had serious consequences. The chairman of the SFC, however, maintained that the SFC would continue to streamline securities regulation and develop its monitoring and investigating roles. In an address to the press, the chairman gave a firm commitment that the SFC would continue to seek the maintenance of market integrity. He made no apology for the SFC's thrust towards establishing investor protections in the market aimed at enhancing the market for the greater protection of local participants as well as setting an acceptable international standard to attract overseas investors.[40]

The SFC established a mission statement, which it made publicly available, setting out the aims and objectives to be infused in its day to day activities. In these measures, the SFC was developing a public persona as an active, visible and influential regulator focused on the special needs of the Hong Kong market. The SFC made effective use of the media and took every opportunity to have its views expressed in print, on television and on radio. The Chairman took an active role in being identified as the face of the SFC.

For most of 1990 the SFC was in a constant battle with its detractors who took every opportunity to criticize its role, its functions and its activities. Errors in drafting,[41] the speed of reform and the open disputation between the SFC and the Stock Exchange[42] all took their toll. The SFC was, however, able to emerge relatively intact and during this time was able to continue to develop its role as a regulatory reformer and policy director of the securities industry.

Under the second chairman, Robert Nottle, the SFC made progress in streamlining its procedures as well as enhancing its monitoring role in the market. Its investigatory powers came under attack in a challenge mounted by a disgruntled company officer in the High Court, alleging such powers breached the Bill of Rights. This challenge was rejected and the court affirmed the SFC's investigatory powers as in accordance with the requirements of the Bill of Rights.[43]

It also moved beyond regulatory reform and stepped up its monitoring and enforcement activities. The role of policy growth and development has not been ignored. The SFC has focused on policy planning for the future development of the financial markets in Hong Kong. An example was the first successful listing of a PRC company on the Hong Kong Stock Exchange in 1993. This success was the culmination of two years of negotiations behind the scenes between the regulatory authorities in the PRC and the SFC.[44] Further, the signing of the Memorandum of Regulatory Understanding with the regulators in the PRC has set the scene for a continuation of policy focus and development geared towards the needs of the Hong Kong/ China market.

Current Role of the SFC and Recent Developments

The SFC has successfully developed from its early days into the paramount securities regulator in the Hong Kong market. It has maintained its independence and has been able to carve out for itself a role that, whilst not welcomed by everyone in the securities industry, is known and respected by the market participants. The SFC has, through its policy planning strategies and implementation, been able to instill in the market a level of acceptance which is quite phenomenal given its short history and the overt reluctance of the market to accept regulation. How has this occurred?

Market Expansion

The SFC has not been complacent. Robert Nottle trumpeted the cause of policy development as a key issue during his time at the SFC. He is on record as stating that policy direction and development should not be left to the SFC but should be driven by the market.[45] Whilst encouraging participation in policy planning, the SFC has taken the initiative in the role it plays in the market and the community at large. In this way the SFC has promoted both the interests of the market and its own presence in the market. In the establishment of new markets and the extension of its involvement in existing markets, the SFC has used all available means to promote itself.

The recognition of the growing importance of the PRC in the trading of securities prompted the SFC to develop a close working relationship with the China Securities Regulatory Commission. The promotion of this relationship was seen as vital to the establishment of a listings program for PRC companies on the Hong Kong Stock Exchange. The first "H" share listing occurred in 1993 and since that time 17 PRC companies have listed on the Stock Exchange. For such listings to occur, it was vital for the SFC to develop (with the Stock Exchange) procedures by which PRC companies would be able to comply with the regulatory requirements of the Hong Kong securities market without being seen to be compelling the PRC to institute a regulatory regime mirrored on Hong Kong's own.[46]

The derivatives market has caused worldwide concern in financial circles. The market in derivatives has grown rapidly. In light of the well publicized débâcles of Barclays Bank, Orange County and Daiwa Bank, and the growing potential for disputes between traders and clients — as exemplified by the derivative disputes (which were subsequently settled out of court) between Lehmann Bros and two PRC companies — the SFC is undertaking a review of the growing market and the question of regulation and monitoring of players, participants and transactions. The results of that report are due out in 1995.

After extended secret negotiation between the SFC and the Futures Exchange (to the exclusion of the Stock Exchange), the trading of stock futures contracts was established in November 1994. This market development was not applauded by all. The Stock Exchange, its members and a number of members of the Legislative Council reacted with stinging criticism of the action by the SFC in failing to consult with them. Concerns over the viability of futures trading and the inherent risk in the market fuelled the debate, which dragged on over October and November 1994. A slanging match between the SFC and the Stock Exchange did not help the situation.[47] The SFC's explanation of price sensitivity in the market and competition from overseas markets, notably Australia and Singapore, were the reasons the talks were commenced in secret. In retaliation, the SFC raised its concern over the Stock Exchange's apparent delay in developing an options trading floor, even though negotiations had commenced two years previously.[48]

In an address to the Hong Kong Business Summit 1994 organized by the Hong Kong General Chamber of Commerce, Ms Laura Cha, SFC executive director, emphasized that the "objective of securities regulators is to make it easier for companies to raise capital globally, and for markets to be able to operate freely, to price investments accurately whilst securing adequate levels of investor protection".[49] Again the SFC used the opportunity to inform as wide a market as possible that regulation does not exist in Hong Kong for regulation's sake but that it exists "to meet basic investor expectations of market transparency and fair dealing" and that unnecessary impediments to the regulatory framework are removed.[50]

Plans are a foot to extend the SFC's jurisdiction to place financial institutions, investment banking and securities trading businesses under its control. The first steps towards this goal have been taken by the signing of a Memorandum of Understanding between the Monetary Authority and the SFC. This Memorandum allows both authorities to co-ordinate supervision of financial institutions where they both have an interest. Previously, purely banking operations were under the control of the Monetary Authority, which, in some instances, lead to a lacuna in the monitoring and control of financial institutions' operations.

Growth in Regulation

Recently, a leading free market economist, Professor Pascal Salin, said that the Territory faced "an accelerating process of regulation, a loss of liberty, and less prosperity." He noted that "bureaucrats always have a possibility, of justifying more and more regulations [sic]."[51] The SFC is aware of these criticisms. It maintains, however, that — if regulation is dynamic and regulators are flexible — regulation will change to meet the demands by the market. This approach has been adopted by the SFC. With a sanction-backed legislatory regime together with non-statutory elements encompassing self-regulation, the market is able to adapt and develop without compromising its standards or goals.

Market Perceptions and Market Acceptance

Coupled with the development of policy is the need both to inform and raise debate within the market on policy issues. It has been the aim of the SFC to include, where appropriate, the market participants in the development of policy. More fundamental, however, is the use of education, media exposure and presence in the market to establish, firstly, the perceptions which the SFC hopes will be cultivated in the market and, secondly, acceptance of its growing role in the market.

In its enforcement strategies, the SFC has sought to establish itself as an effective market enforcer. It has used the media to promote its enforcement successes and to educate the market participants of their responsibilities in the market.

The use by the SFC of its investigation and enforcement powers to maximum effect by targeting highly visible companies such as MKI Corp Ltd, Peregrine Brokers Ltd and Standard Chartered Asia and

Standard Chartered Securities[52] illustrates its commitment to regulation and enforcement. It also illustrates the presence the SFC has in the market and how it will use the media to maximum effect in promoting both its role as a successful market manager and enforcer, treating all participants, be they big or small, the same.

Similarly, swift and decisive action against transgressors has defined the operations of the SFC as direct and effective. Two cases — including the first successful action resulting in the suspension of a forex trader in October 1995,[53] and a highly public investigation into another forex dealer, Canwell Forex International, resulting in the suspension of its licence and the placing of the company under administration in mid-October 1995—illustrate the wide and varied situations raising the interest of the SFC.

Criticism

Not all initiatives or actions by the SFC have been welcomed.

Efforts by the SFC to place financial advisors under its control caused a storm, with financial advisors claiming information required to be supplied may result in a breach of client confidentiality. These concerns were given wide press and raised alarm in the minds of the investing public, further raising the suspicion that the SFC was taking a big brother approach to the acquisition and dissemination of information. The SFC's claim that Securities and Futures Ordinance, section 59 prohibits the SFC from making the information public did little to placate the market.[54]

Criticism of the handling of the Canwell saga by investors and legislators has lead the SFC to agree to look into safeguards being established to protect forex investors. The measures undertaken immediately by the SFC to allay investor concerns were to ascertain the financial situation of all 34 forex traders in the market.[55]

The SFC is learning how to be an effective regulator in the market. Situations demanding swift action, balancing of interests, confidence or indeed secrecy to the exclusion of some participants will, predictably, occur again. The SFC must have in place lines of communication that are build on trust and understanding rather than alienation and suspicion. If such an environment should develop, the effectiveness of the SFC as the primary market regulator may be sorely tested.

Conclusions

The SFC has been successful in establishing itself as the primary securities regulator in the Hong Kong market. Through its implementation of policy planning it has been able to grow and develop regulation not for regulation's sake but in rising to the needs and objectives of the market. Hong Kong has come a significant way since the implementation of the recommendations of the Hay-Davison Report in establishing a securities market with the characteristics envisaged by the Report.

New markets have been developed, including the futures contracts and options trading, as well as the listing of PRC companies. The regulatory framework is constantly being reviewed and developed to ensure confidence and efficiency in the market. Commitment to risk management through establishing checks and balances exists, but this is not to say the SFC should assume total responsibility for regulation of the market. Whilst regulation is in an expansive mode, the SFC has firmly committed itself to ensuring that the market participants assume the major responsibility in the implementation of regulation in the market. Sometimes this results in confusion, for example, many brokers believe that the SFC pressures them to monitor and regulate the trading activities of clients. The brokers maintain, however, that they are entitled to act on instructions without questioning the motives behind such instructions. The role of the Stock and Futures Exchanges as active and independent monitors of participants is one way in which the SFC can maintain and develop control through its watch-dog activities without actively intervening and thereby undermining the role played by the internal market regulators.

The Hong Kong securities industry has successfully emerged from the market collapse of 1987. The role of the SFC and its implementation of regulation has, by all accounts, contributed to that success. The SFC is looking all the time at ways to promote Hong Kong as the primary capital market in the region. The current proposals to reduce the threshold limit for directors' disclosure — from 10 per cent to 5 per cent (reflecting the threshold levels of other international markets such as Britain, Australia and Singapore) — reflect this. In this and other examples the SFC is seeking to promote Hong Kong as a fair, open and honest market, ready and able to take its place on the world capital market's stage.

The current Chairman of the SFC, Sir Anthony Neoh Q.C., summed up both the intense market demands and the challenges for regulation in the future when he stated:

> "If I were to sum up Hong Kong's philosophy in the harnessing of economic opportunities in one sentence, I would say: 'it is the provision of a sound and level playing field so that those who play in it may without fear or favour reap their lawful rewards according to the risks that they have knowingly and willingly taken.' I subscribe fully to this philosophy but I will be the first to admit we are far from any state of perfection in this regard . . .

Mr Robert Gilmore, Deputy Chairman of the Hong Kong Securities and Futures Commission, puts it simply thus: 'In markets, you must have doors and exits. The more doors you have the more exits you have, the better is your market'. . . As regulators, our challenge for the future will be to ensure that as many doors and exits as possible are safely put in place and prudently used."[56]

Notes

[1] The Colony of Hong Kong was established by the signing of the Treaty of Nanking on August 29, 1842, becoming a Crown Colony on June 26, 1843. On March 26 and October 24, 1860, under the two conventions of Peking, Kowloon Point, the immediate surrounds and Stonecutters Island were leased "in perpetuity" to Britain. Finally, on July 1, 1898, the New Territories were leased to Britain for 99 years.

[2] Timothy E. Stocks,*Securities Legislation in Hong Kong*, p.1.

[3] Originally known as the Association of Stockbrokers it changed its name to the Hong Kong Stock Exchange in 1914. *Report of the Securities Review Committee* May 1988, (the Hay-Davison Report), Appendix 10, p.371.

[4] *ibid.*

[5] As remarked on by P. Lawton, in "Expanding Shareholder Control in Hong Kong" p.1, a paper presented at the Conference on Market Economy and Law, Hong Kong October 13–14, 1995, see p. 70 of this book, (in reference to a paper by E.L.G. Tyler, entitled "Does the Complexity of Companies Legislation Impede Entrepreneurship?").

[6] *ibid.*

[7] Hay-Davison Report, *op. cit.*, p.372.

[8] *ibid.* It is noted in the report that during 1973 there were 53 public offers and 48 placements of shares, bringing the total number of listed companies to 296.

[9] Hay-Davison Report, *op. cit.*, p.372.

[10] Report, *Asia Pacific — An Investment Guide*, p.76.

[11] Prior to this the Stock Exchange Control Ordinance was the primary tool by which the Government controlled the stock exchanges. It was repealed upon the enactment of the Securities Ordinance.

[12] Hay-Davison Report, *op. cit.*, Appendix 10, p.373.

[13] *ibid.* p.32 (from *Report of the Companies Law Reform Committee into the Protection of the Investor* (1971)).

[14] Hay-Davison Report, *op. cit.*, pp.229–230.

[15] The ineffectiveness of the Commissioner was demonstrated by his early attempts to unite the stock exchanges. It was plain that the operation of four exchanges was inefficient and made effective regulation difficult, if not impossible. His suggestions to unite the exchanges in 1975 and 1976 fell on deaf ears until such time as the markets' continued lackluster performances made the merger of the exchanges a sound economic proposition, based on the self-interest of exchange members. It took a further four years for the unification to occur, culminating in the Stock Exchanges Unification Ordinance (Cap 361) enacted in August, 1980.

16 Hay-Davison Report, *op. cit.*, p.230.
17 *ibid.*
18 Tomasic, *Casino Capitalism*? (1991), p.81 It is interesting to note that in 1986 the (U.K.) Financial Services Act was enacted to create a more rigid structure for the implementation and supervision of regulation in the market. The role of self-regulation was formalized by the establishment of licensing requirements for organizations within the established self-regulatory structure. These bodies (SRO's) were to be represented on a Securities and Investment Board (SIB) which itself was under the supervision of the Bank of England.
19 Stock Exchanges Unification Ordinance (Cap 361).
20 Hay-Davison Report, *op. cit.*, p.3.
21 *South China Morning Post* October 23, 1995. Mr Li was released from jail in 1994.
22 Hay-Davison, *op. cit.*, p.2.
23 *Report of the Securities Review Committee* May 1988, (the Hay-Davison Report).
24 *ibid.* pp.5–6.
25 Mann, "What Constitutes Successful Securities Regulatory Regime?" (1993) Vol. 3 No. 2 AJCL 178.
26 *ibid.*
27 *ibid.* p.179.
28 *ibid.* p.180.
29 *op. cit.*, at n.18, p.33.
30 Hay-Davison Report, *op. cit.*, p.31.
31 See appendix to Hay-Davison Report, *op. cit.*
32 Hay-Davison Report, *op. cit.*, pp.5–6.
33 *ibid.* p.3.
34 *ibid.* pp.31–35.
35 *ibid.* p.257.
36 Including the Securities (Disclosure of Interest) Ordinance (Cap 396), the Securities (Insider Dealing) Ordinance (Cap 395), the Protection of Investors Ordinance (Cap 335), the Companies Ordinance (Cap 32), and the Securities (Stock Exchange Listing) Rules as well as the non-statutory codes such as the Takeover and Mergers Code, and the Code on Unit Trusts and Mutual Trusts.
37 *Hong Kong Standard*, June 3, 1988.
38 As expressed in a confidential memo by Jardine Insurance Broker chairman, Mr Rodney Leach, leaked to the press. *South China Morning Post*, April 22, 1988.
39 *ibid.*
40 *South China Morning Post*, May 1, 1990.
41 Such as the admitted error in the drafting of the Code of Conduct for Unit Trusts and Mutual Funds.
42 In respect of an application for declarations as to the meaning of Stock Exchange Unification Ordinance s. 11.
43 Pursuant to an application for judicial review made by Lee Kwok-hung, High Court case unreported January 8, 1993.
44 The listing of Tsingtao Brewery Co. Ltd occurred on July 15, 1993. As at December 2, 1994 14 PRC companies had listed on the Hong Kong Stock Exchange. See Doreen Le Pichon, "The Listing of PRC Companies on the Stock Exchange of Hong Kong" (1995) Vol. 5 No. 3 AJCL 390.
45 *South China Morning Post*, January 1, 1995.
46 In an address to the Hong Kong Business Summit, Laura Cha, executive director SFC, stated that harmonization of regulation between the PRC and

Hong Kong meant the recognition of the diversities of the two legal systems, *South China Morning Post*, November 28, 1994.

47 *South China Morning Post*, October 26, 1994.
48 The first stock options on Hongkong Shanghai Banking Corporation Holdings were traded on September 8, 1995 *South China Morning Post*, September 9, 1995.
49 *South China Morning Post*, November 28, 1994.
50 *ibid.*
51 Speaking at a conference in the Territory, in reference to competition policies being promoted by the government, reported in the *South China Morning Post*, November 25, 1995.
52 The use of its winding up powers pursuant to Securities and Futures Commission Ordinance, s. 45 in an application to wind up MKI Corp on December 13, 1994 (after an investigation under the newly enacted Securities Ordinance s. 29A); disciplinary action taken against Peregrine Brokers following an investigation into alleged breeches of the Securities Ordinance linked to four new listing on the Stock Exchange; concerning four new listing; disciplinary action taken against SCA and SCS for alleged breaches of exchange listing regulations involving the creation of false markets in share dealings.
53 Against Cheng Tai-cheng, for breaching the Foreign Exchange Ordinance.
54 *South China Morning Post*, July 25, 1993.
55 *South China Morning Post*, November 25, 1995.
56 Sir Anthony Neoh Q.C., "The Capital Markets of Hong Kong: Opportunities and Challenges of the Future" (1995) Vol. 5 No. 3 AJCL 334 at 340.

PIERCING THE COMPANY VEIL AND REGULATION OF COMPANIES IN CHINA

Zhang Xianchu

Faculty of Law
City University of Hong Kong

Zhang Xian Chu, *M.C.L. and J.D. (Indiana University School of Law at Bloomington), is a lecturer at the City University of Hong Kong.*

Piercing the company veil is a judicial doctrine widely used in common law as well as civil law jurisdictions.[1] Under the doctrine courts will disregard the corporate entity in certain circumstances to hold the equity owners and others responsible for corporate debts.[2] The doctrine, however, has not been recognized in China in the Company Law of the PRC, which came into force on July 1, 1994. By the end of 1993, approximately 250,000 companies had been established in China.[3] Considering the various types of abuse of the company entity and the confusion in the judicial practice, a great number of concerns have been raised in recent years[4]. This paper addresses the question of whether the doctrine of piercing the company veil could or should be introduced into China during the conversion of the state owned and controlled enterprises to market orientated companies. The first section presents the major types of abuse of the company practice in China today. The second section examines the current legislative scheme against the company entity abuse. The third section illustrates, through case law analysis, the inconsistency of the court rulings in dealing with such abuses. The final section discusses the feasibility and urgency of introducing this doctrine into the company law regime in China.

The Background and the Major Types of Abuses

Company, as the form of modern business organization in the market economy, did not exist under the central planning economy system in China until the 1980s when the economic reform placed modernization of business organizations on the agenda. Since then thousands of state owned enterprises throughout the country under the direction of the government have been converted into the form of companies,[5] together with a large number of newly established ones promoted by the Communist Party or government branches. Unfortunately, due to the lack of experience and the ideological struggle over the pace and the extent of the reform, the company entity was extensively used before any effective regulatory regime was established. As a result, corruption and abuse of governmental power to make a fortune in an underdeveloped market system become a phenomenon particularly connected with the company practice. The tension between the people's anger and the government's tolerance as well as its ineffective regulation triggered the protests in Tiananman Square in 1989. With a short pause, during which more than 35,000 companies were closed down under the national campaign of reorganization and consolidation,[6] the company phenomenon came back with more intensity. In 1992 alone, 480,000 new companies made their business registrations. The number of companies in Beijing, Shanghai and Tianjin, the three biggest cities in China, all doubled in that single year.[7] Against this fast rate of development, effective legislation and enforcement fell behind. Even today companies that strictly meet the legal conditions under the Company Law are not many.[8]

The following are some major types of abuse:

(a) A large number of companies are established by the local Communist Party or government branches without any capital, or with insufficient borrowed money.[9] These branches have been using the company entity as an instrument to make a fortune in all kinds of businesses with their monopoly powers. In many instances, companies are operated as the treasure houses of these branches with the interlocked personnel to supply them directly with the money made on the market. Alternatively, the branches, as the owners, will receive various benefits from the companies under their control by the way of management fees.[10]

(b) Many private business firms without the independent status of legal person link up with state owned enterprises or companies. By this arrangement, the private business firms are shielded by the limited liability enjoyed by the state entities and at the same time bypass many state restrictions imposed on the private business. To appreciate such protection, they submit some profit to these enterprises or companies as part of the deal.[11]

(c) Switching-name companies are a hybrid of business entities and government branches. Without changing personnel, internal structure and function, the old government branches simply change their names into holding companies, then use their administrative powers to force the companies or enterprises under their control to join and squeeze profit from them. By switching name, the branches can get rich at the cost of the lower companies or enterprises; as legal persons they can directly engage in market activities, which they cannot do as the government branches.[12]

(d) It has become common that one or more companies are established to receive assets from a troubled company with the purpose rendering it an empty shell for future liquidation proceedings.[13] Also the registrations of some companies that have ceased operation are not cancelled in order to be used to escape from debts incurred by "new companies" with the same personnel and business.[14]

These abuses have troubled both the business community[15] and the judicial branch[16] for a long time. Although the phenomenon may be hard to imagine by those from other jurisdictions, it is quite understandable as an inevitable by-product of the struggle to turn a model of central planning economy under administrative control for forty years to one based on market discipline.

The Current Legal Framework against Abuses of Incorporation

The legal conditions for establishment of a legal person are provided in article 37 of the General Principles of Civil Law 1986 (GPCL): (a) to be established in accordance with the law; (b) to have necessary assets or capital; (c) to have its own name, organizational structure and place of business; and (d) to be able to assume civil obligations independently. Based on these conditions, the minimum registered capital is stipulated for different kinds of business by the law.[17]

Although article 61 of the GPCL provides that where a juristic act is held void because of fraud, deception, violation or unlawful purpose the party at fault shall return all properties it has obtained by the void act to, and compensate, the victim. Such civil liability, however, is limited by article 48, which stipulates that unless the law provides otherwise a state owned enterprise legal person shall be liable only to the extent of the property the state has granted it for operation and managment,[18] or in the case of collective and foreign investment enterprises to the extent of the property they own. Thus, despite the concepts "independent" and "limited" liability being held different in their meaning and substance,[19] the distinction seems less material in a piercing context where the issue is whether the liability should be limited to the independently owned or managed assets of the company or legal person in question.

The Company Law of 1993 also provides the minimum registered capital for companies engaged in different kinds of business.[20] In addition, it holds directors and managers liable for the serious losses caused to the company by any resolution adopted by them in violation of the law, regulations or the Articles of Association.[21] Moreover, it imposes legal liabilities against false reporting of the registered capital,[22] registration with deceptive means,[23] false capital contribution,[24] false asset or capital verification,[25] establishment or approval of registration of a company that does not meet the legal conditions,[26] and coercion of illegal registration[27] by fine, suspension of business, administrative discipline and criminal penalties. All the criminal liabilities are further specified later in the Decision on Cracking Down on Company Crimes adopted by the Standing Committee of the National People's Congress to battle the company crime wave.[28] The Company Law fails, however, to address the issue of piercing the company veil.

Indeed, in the past the Central Committee of the Communist Party and the State Council, by several notices, allowed imposition of civil liability against the owners or the upper level Party and government authority of the failed or illegally operated companies. In a joint decision issued in 1988, the Party and the government, after recognizing as a serious problem that many Party and government branches were directly involved in business operations to seek exorbitant profits by using their powers, ordered all companies established or promoted by any institutions of the Party, the Government, or the legislative or the judicial branches to be separated financially from such institutions and prohibited any profit taking by them from the companies.[29] In 1989, the Central Committee of the Party and the State Council jointly ordered the closure of a large number of companies and required the upper level authorities to liquidate the assets of the terminated companies.[30]

Nevertheless, after the Supreme Court expressed its opinion that terminated companies established by the Party or government branches should be liquidated by the direct "promoting or approval" authorities and that they should be liable for the unsettled debts,[31] the State Council issued its 68th Notice by the end of 1990 to give practical guidance for handling the debts of the terminated companies,[32] which apparently tried to qualify the holding of the Supreme Court. According to the notice, the upper level authorities shall be responsible for liquidation and disposition of the assets of the terminated companies;[33] they shall be liable for the debts of the terminated companies, if they have received any pecuniary or other benefits from the companies, to the extent of such benefits received;[34] the authorities that approved the establishment of the companies shall be liable, together with other investors, for the shortage in the registered capital;[35] and all the invested assets shall not be taken back until the debts have been paid off.[36] Without providing any definition and explanation, the notice, however, stipulates that the Party and government branches may bear their liabilities for the terminated companies only with their extra-budgetary assets.[37] Finally, it was declared that the rules stipulated by the notice would be automatically invalid when the national campaign of reorganization and consolidation was over.[38] All these quasi-piercing rules were just employed as temporary administrative measures, rather than the legal doctrine to be built into the regulative scheme for long term application.

In order to implement the Company Law and curb the abuses of incorporation, the Administration of Industry and Commerce issued an circular on company registration,[39] which provides that after the Company Law comes into force business entities that do not meet the legal conditions provided by the Company Law shall not be registered and named as companies.[40] From then on, any application for establishment of a company shall be filed directly by the investors and the approval of the the upper level authority may not be considered as a precondition for the registration.[41] Nevertheless, the legal effect of the circular seems crippled by its failure to provide clear rules governing re-registration of a large number of companies that were established before the Company Law came into force by the government or social organizations (the Communist Party belongs to this category), or registrations of new companies converted from state owned enterprises,[42] the main sources responsible for the abuse of incorporation.

A brief examination of the current legal scheme to prevent abuse of the company entity shows that most of the sanctions employed are of either administrative or criminal nature and that equitable remedy for company creditors in fraud or other abuse situations beyond the capital contribution is not available under the present legislation.

This scheme also proves ineffective to deter the abuses. Since 1988, the Central Committee of the Communist Party and the Government have tried to curb unlawful company practice by issuing notices and adopting laws and regulations. The abuses have not shown any sign of decreasing: the influences from, and the control by the Party and government branches are still strong;[43] more piercing cases are litigated;[44] and more concerns have been expressed by courts, economists, and legal scholars.[45] In practice, many cases show that once the Party or government authority decides to establish a company, other lower administrations such as registration offices may not be able to function independently.[46] As a result, the legal rules simply cannot be enforced strictly.

The rigid rules on company registration and criminal liability may not effectively stop all the abuses since a business entity may still enjoy the protection of limited liability without being named company as long as it is a legal person.[47] Moreover, the current law indicates that civil liability of a legal person shall be satisfied only from the assets granted to or owned by it and cannot be shifted to others.[48] As such, the imposition of administrative and criminal liabilities against abuses of incorporation may achieve very limited goals as they may be tangled with complicated high profile personal relations or require a higher standard of proof. In any event neither may prevent or correct unlawful or unjust enrichment.

The Judicial Practice on Piercing Company Veil Actions

It may be interesting to note first that all piercing cases confronted by the people's courts in recent years seem of contract setting, which is deemed in other jurisdictions a tougher situation for successful piercing than tort context.[49] The reason seems that contract disputes constitute the main part of the cases handled by the courts today and other disputes, such as labour, product liability, torts, bankruptcy, and environment, are quite often are handled through administrative channels.[50]

By following the State Council's guideline provided in the 68th Notice and having retreated from its previous holding, the Supreme Court held that the guideline of the State Council shall be applied to all the pending cases.[51] The Party or the government branches shall be in charge of liquidating the failed or terminated companies and are liable only to the extent of the benefits received and of making up the shortage of the registered capital of the companies with their own extra-budgetary assets.

By applying these rules, the Supreme Court denied the claim to pierce the veil of the defendant company on the ground that the Social Science Academy of Shanghai as the upper level authority was neither responsible for the defective establishment of, nor received any pecuniary or other kind benefit from, the dissolved company although it was operated within the Academy's body for almost two years without business registration. As a result, five creditors of one million yuan debt were left to the hopeless liquidation proceedings. *Re the Social Science Academy of Shanghai* (1991).[52]

Claimants did prevail in some piercing actions. In *Yue Hai Import-export Co. v. The People's Government of Yang Chuen County* (1992),[53] the Supreme Court agreed with the ruling of the High Court of Guangdong to direct the county government to repay the debts of 1.5

million yuan through its liquidating committee for the dissolved company where the company was found to be the instrument of the government without any invested capital. Although the general manager of the company was eventually removed from the government position and the new business licence was obtained pursuant to the State Council's decision as a steps to separate the company from the government, the fact that all employees of the company went back to the government after its dissolution without going through any liquidation procedure and that the government collected 20,000 yuan from the debtor of the company warranted the piercing finding.

In *Ping Ding Branch of Shanxi Oil Co. v. The Oil Development Group of Bai City of Jilin* (1991),[54] the Supreme Court held that the defendant's company veil should be pierced and the government office was liable to the extent of the registered capital based on the findings that the company, without any of its own capital, was established by the local government that provided the company with the asset certificate to enable the company to obtain its business licence, and that all the company's assets were transferred to another company later established by the same government office just before the execution of the first instance judgment in favour of the creditor plaintiff.

The Supreme Court in *The Union of Victory Oil Refinery v. The Trading Group of Mei County of Guangdong* (1992),[55] by reversing the decision of the High Court of Guangdong, directed it to conduct a new trial to find the upper level state-owned company liable for the debts of its failed subordinate company where the upper level company, as a minority shareholder, was found to make no capital contribution to the failed company, and to be liable for the company's wrong doing. Particularly, it pointed out as the important basis of piercing the company's veil the fact that the contract signed by the subordinate company with the creditor was void because it was *ultra vires* and the company had knowledge of its inability to carry out the contractual obligation.

From these rulings, it seems clear that the Supreme Court in piercing actions has paid close attention not only to the issues of undercapitalization and benefit taking, but also the issues of control and fraud.

The legal rules articulated by this line of cases seem to be blurred, if not contradicted, by the very unusual case *Ling Chuan Alloy Plant of Guangxi v. The Industry Holding Co. of Shangxi* (1993),[56] in which the Supreme Court had to make the second ruling to direct the High Court of Guangxi to reverse its piercing decision that had become final and effective and to deny the piercing claim after its first re-examination instruction was resisted by the High Court.

According to the plaintiff and the local courts, the defendant holding company composed of twelve local companies took the pre-

135

payment of one million yuan from the plaintiff and neither performed any contractual obligation, nor returned any money upon the plaintiff's repeated demands for almost two years after the conclusion of the contract and without the legal person registration and business license, but with full knowledge of its inability to perform the contract from the very beginning. The evidence also showed that certain members did not make any capital contribution and only 120 million of the 190 million yuan registered capital was actually paid in. An attachment to the Articles of Association of the company as well as the document issued by the approval authority further supported the finding that the company was jointly operated as a partnership.

The Supreme Court, nevertheless, held that the company obtained a legal person status with independent liability because its Articles of Association, as the evidence with the most weight, provided so and it was to be operated on a basis of independent accountability as indicated by another document of the government authority. With regard to other contradictory evidence, it found that as far as the observation of company formalities was concerned, the lack of legal person registration and business licence was not the fatal factor; that the document of the approval authority only meant to provide the company's structure rather than its nature; and that the undercapitalization might be cured by taking into account some know-how investment.[57] Most interestingly, the Supreme Court did not spill a single drop of ink on the issue of the fraudulent conduct raised by both the intermediate and the High Courts of Guangxi.

This decision may cause serious confusion not only because the literal reading of the case may lead to the prevailing of the Articles of Association and the operation methods over all other elements, rather than an overall examination; but also because the Supreme Court seems to deviate from the line of its previous rulings on the other piercing actions, particularly on the issues of fraud and undercapitalization. Although it may be argued that the court did not make any specific rules on these issues in this case, the attention of the court and the weight assigned to the issues apparently are sending a confusing, if not wrong, signal since some courts and judges are taking the incorrect position in their practice that a court shall not negate the legal personality of a business firm granted by the administrative authority[58] and that the doctrine of piercing the company veil shall not apply unless a crime has been found.[59]

With regard to the terminated enterprises established by promoting enterprises or companies, the Supreme Court held that the promoting company shall be jointed where the terminated company is undercapitalized or engaged in unlawful operation.[60] Later the rule was further articulated to mean that the terminated enterprises shall assume their civil liability by their own assets if they met all legal conditions at the time of establishment; where their paid-in capital satisfies the minimum capital requirement provided in the law, but falls short of the registered capital, the promoting enterprises or companies shall be liable to the extent of the shortage; the promoting entities shall be liable for all the debts of the terminated enterprises if they did not invest any their own capital or their own capital invested did not meet the minimum requirement.[61]

In this setting the Supreme Court seems to answer negatively again the question whether a company entity should be disregarded where the unlawful activities go beyond mere undercapitalization. In *The International Trust and Investment Co. of Liaoning v. Jingguang Co. of Shenzhen* (1991),[62] it denied the piercing claim where the defendant company with the capital registration of 600,000 yuan was dissolved with more than 12 million yuan debts. The evidence showed that the company was established and controlled by its upper level company with 40 per cent ownership; the defendant company never had its own independent organization as required by the law as a necessary condition for a legal person, but had interlocked personnel from the chairman of the board of directors and the general manager to accountants and secretaries. After the conclusion of the contract worth 15 million yuan with the creditor plaintiff, the defendant misappropriates the plaintiff's funds to pay its debts and make loans. Its products were found adulterated. When it finally broke down with deep debts, all its employees, except one manager, simply went back to the upper level company to resume their work. The majority of the High Court of Ningxia held the defendant was a sham. The Supreme Court, however, rejected the opinion of the High Court on the ground that the registered capital was actually paid up and as a result the defendant could enjoy legal person status with independent liability; it did further direct the High Court to impose criminal liability if any crime was found and to recover the funds unlawfully possessed by any other entities or individuals.

In addition to the confusion generated by these published decisions, the local courts are also vexed at many other problems. For instance, many Party or government branches, once involved in a piercing action, take advantage of their powers to hold the courts in contempt and make the proceedings difficult to continue.[63] Moreover, investigation and evidence collection become more and more difficult where the same group of persons who committed wrongdoing can hide behind several shields of companies by different names.[64]

To make the situation worse, local protectionism is also a factor hindering fair hearing of piercing actions. For example, an enterprise of Liao Yang in a contract action conducted locally was found to enjoy its legal person status with limited liability while its entity was disregarded in another contract dispute heard in another city.[65]

137

The Urgency of Introducing the Doctrine into China

Today China is in a period of transition from the traditional central planning economy to the market economy, which demands the establishment of a modern business organization system with independent accountability and the environment of fair dealing and competition based on equal market discipline, rather than excessive government control. The abuses aforementioned, on one hand, are new problems in the development of such a market economy; on the other, the phenomenon is really the resistance of traditional forces trying to keep control over the market activities. Against this background, the doctrine of piercing the company veil is the legal weapon urgently needed for the healthy development of the market economy, to deter and punish the unlawful intrusion by the administrative branches, as well as other practices using the form of company entity to evade the law.

The urgency of introducing the doctrine into China can be demonstrated by the facts of extensive abuse of incorporation and the ineffectiveness of the administrative and criminal liabilities imposed against these abuses. The confusion and inconsistency in the judicial practice further demand certain clear and stable legal principles and doctrines instead of administrative short term policy. These problems are the vivid reflection of the reality that the market development has forced the courts to deal with the abuses of incorporation regardless of the unavailability of any established principle or doctrine on the issue.

More importantly, neither of the administrative and criminal penalties provided by the law can address the very issue concerned by the market economy: equitable remedies for the victims of fraud, deception, abuse of powers and evasion of law. In the conditions of an underdeveloped market like China, creditors are very vulnerable to fraud and abuse because, even in a contract setting, very little information can be obtained through the official channels[66] and the monopoly created by the administrative powers may force some people to deal with a particular company. As such, the parties to a contract may not be able to detect all the risks and the free bargain theory of other jurisdictions may not be entirely applicable in China today. Further, under the current scheme, creditors are exposed to the risks of total loss in a failed transaction while the owners of companies to only limited civil liability without exception. Moreover, those Party or government branches are not only protected by the limited liability, but also by the extra-budgetary asset restriction even if the company veil is pierced.

On the other hand, the unavailability of piercing the company veil doctrine in the current legal scheme creates a loophole for the abuses since the absolute limited liability would raise a moral hazard problem and encourage and protect excessive risk taking, including abuse and fraud. As a result of ineffectiveness of administrative and criminal liabilities, the people or entities behind company entities may have a good chance just to walk away with the profit illegally or unfairly made if the doctrine is not employed. It has been reported that in some cases, court judgments in favour of creditor plaintiffs in piercing actions were rendereds mere scraps of paper where the Party and the government branches liable for the debts had no extra-budgetary assets for execution.[67]

Indeed, some policy arguments against the piercing doctrine have been advanced in other jurisdictions. For example, it is said that the unlimited liability under the doctrine would frighten some investors away and diversification of investment would be inhibited by unlimited liability.[68] Besides the theoretical analyses, there has not been any convincing evidence to show the negative impact of the judicial practice for decades of the doctrine on the business investment. Instead, it can be argued that a better market order can be created by using the doctrine to regulate market activities. The insurance system, the attractive method of providing protection to victims of tort or commercial risks and the device used to counter the adverse effects of limited liability in other jurisdictions,[69] is still at an early stage of development in China. As such, the principles of equity and fairness shall require the losses that cannot be effectively distributed to be borne by the party in fault, in breach, in violation, and in bad faith.

It is also true that the doctrine of piercing the company veil is the one that has been developed by courts in common law jurisdictions. Considering the strong civil law tradition in China where case law is not recognized as a legal source and *stare decisis* is not applicable in the judicial practice, the doctrine must be first recognized by the national legislation either by way of exception from the rule which confines the liability of shareholders for debts of a company to the capital invested by them,[70] or by direct codification of certain legal principles.[71] Without this legislative basis, the people's courts may not be able to create and further develop the doctrine. The inconsistency of the court decisions and the confusion in the judicial practice are apparently the reflection of lack of such legislative guidance and basis. More realistically, according to the State Council, the guideline could only be valid within limited period. Since the national campaign of reorganization and consolidation ended in 1992, the Supreme Court has not given answers to the questions of how long the guideline shall continue to be applied and what kind of legal rules shall be used after that.

In addition to the urgency, the conditions for the introduction of the doctrine into China seem ripe too. Both positive and negative lessons can be drawn from the Party and government documents for the introduction. Academic studies and research also supply the intro-

139

duction with a solid ground. The judicial decisions have prepared the courts for the further development of a more sophisticated doctrine in the area.

Based on the discussion above, it can be concluded that the doctrine of piercing the company veil should be introduced in China as soon as possible to deter the abuse of incorporation, to compensate effectively the victims of fraud and abuse, and to supply courts with clear legislative guidance. The introduction will also play an important role in safeguarding the healthy development of the market economy.

Notes

1. For the practice in common law jurisdictions, see Robert B. Thompson, "Piercing the Corporate Veil: An Empirical Study" (1991) 76 Cornell L.Rev. 1036; and P. Farrar's *Company Law* (1988) pp.73–81; For civil law jurisdiction see E.J. Cohn & C. Simitis, "Lifting the Veil in the Company Laws of the European Continent" (1963) 12 *International and Comparative Law Quarterly*, pp.189–225 and Liu, Xinshan, *Thesis on Commercial Law*.
2. Harvey Gelb, *Personal Corporate Liability* (1991), pp.2–4.
3. The figure only includes limited companies and joint stock companies. See Jiang, Ping, *New Company Law Textbook* (1994), 48. Many more business organizations that are not governed by the Company Law are also called companies in China, however.
4. Just to name some recent publications: Zhang, Gouming, "A study of Principle of Disregarding Company Personality" in *Hot Topics in Recent Studies of Civil Law and Economic Law* (1995), pp.274–315; Wang, Liming, "Certain Problems Concerning the Limited Liability of Company", *Tribune of Politics and Law (in instalments)* (1994), Vol. 3–4, pp.84–90, 87–93; The High Court of Zhejiang, "New Situations, New Problems and Their Handling" in *The Economic Division of the Supreme Court: Materials of Economic Trials and Comments on New Types of Cases* (1994), pp.255–69; also, Fu, Tingmei, "Legal Persons in China: Essence and Limits, Part III" (1993) 41 American Journal of Comparative Law, at 281–95.
5. The name and entity of company have been widely used since the economic reform began in the early 1980s. In 1992 the State Council adopted The Regulations on Conversion of Operation System for State-owned Enterprises with the goal of making them independent legal persons in the market. See article 2.
6. According the official report, among 294,946 companies registered at that time 23,367 were found undercapitalized and 35,575 were under illegal operation. See Ren, Zhonglin, *Report of the Administration of Industry and Commerce to the 9th Plenary Session of the Standing Committee of the 7th National People's Congress*; See *People's Daily*, August 30, 1989.
7. Zhang, Delin, *Property Rights: the Reform of State-owned Enterprises and Management of State Assets* (1993), at 41.
8. Zhang, Gonming, *op. cit.*, p.309.
9. Zhang, Delin, *op. cit.*, p.43.
10. Zhang, Gonming, *op. cit.*, pp.309–10.

¹¹ *ibid.* at 312.

¹² Zhang, Delin, *op. cit.*, pp.44–52; Zheng, Yang, "The Countermove against Switching Name Companies", Economic Daily, April 16, 1993 (7).

¹³ Ni, Jie, "The Phenomena of Evasion of the Law and Escape from Execution by Enterprises and Its Countermeasures", *Legal Daily*, May 28, 1995; and the High Court of Zhejiang, see above n.4, pp.261–62.

¹⁴ Zhang, Gonming, *op. cit.*, p.313.

¹⁵ Zhang, Delin, *op. cit.*

¹⁶ For examples: the High Court of Zhejiang, see above 4; and the High Court of Inner Mongolia, "Some Thoughts on Current Economic Trial practice" in *The Economic Division of the Supreme Court: Materials on Trials of Economic Cases and Comments on New types of Cases* (1994), pp.340–42.

¹⁷ See article 7 of the Interim Provisions on Company Registration 1985 and article 15 of the Detailed Implementation Rules of Enterprise Legal Person Registration Regulation 1988.

¹⁸ See also article 2 of Law on State-owned Enterprises and article 28 of Bankruptcy Law.

¹⁹ Fu, *op. cit.*, p.290.

²⁰ Article 23 and article 78.

²¹ Article 118.

²² Article 206.

²³ Article 206 and article 207.

²⁴ Article 208 and article 209.

²⁵ Article 219.

²⁶ Aricle 220 and article 222.

²⁷ Article 223.

²⁸ Adopted on February 28, 1995.

²⁹ Point 3 of the Joint Decision of the Central Committee of the Communist Party and the State Council of China on Reorganization of Companies of October 3, 1988.

³⁰ Point 6 of the Joint Decision by the Central Committee of the Communist Party and the State Council of China on Further Reorganization of Companies of August 17, 1989.

³¹ The Supreme Court reply to the High Court of Shanxi of August 29, 1987. See *The Bulletin of the Supreme Court* (1987), Vol. 4, p.21.

³² "The State Council Notice Concerning Liquidation of Terminated Companies in the Reorganization Campaign" of December 12, 1990.

³³ *ibid.* Point 2.

³⁴ *ibid.* Point 3.

³⁵ *ibid.* Point 4.

³⁶ *ibid.* Point 5.

³⁷ *ibid.* Point 7.

³⁸ *Ibid.* Point 11.

³⁹ "Certain Opinions Concerning Implementation of Company Registration Regulation of China" July 12, 1994.

⁴⁰ *ibid.* Point 1.

⁴¹ *ibid.* Point 4.

⁴² For the registration of these two kinds of companies, the circular only states that the State Council will adopt some regulations later, *ibid.* Point 20.

⁴³ For example, according to an official survey, of 14 rights provided by the law for enterprises, five can be enjoyed by most of them, another five can only be partially exercised and four are still dead words on the paper. See Gao, Fan, *Administrative Powers and Market Economy* (1995), pp.47–8. Also in the "Joint Decision by the Central Committee of the Communist Party and the State Council Concerning Acceleration of Service Business Develop-

ment" of June 16, 1992, government officers were encouraged to be engaged in business through separation from their offices and review and approval procedures were required to be "simplified". Point 14 of the Decision.

[44] Piercing action was never heard of in China until after late 1980s, but recent publications show that even the Supreme Court has had to hear quite a few cases of this nature every year since 1990. See the Research Office of the Supreme Court, *Collection of Judicial Interpretation of the Supreme Court (1949–1993)* (1994); the Economic Division of the Supreme Court, *Selected Economic Cases Heard by the Supreme Courts* (1994).

[45] See above n.4 and n.7.

[46] It was reported that some local government assign the number of newly established companies to the lower departments. See Zhang, Delin, *op. cit.*, pp.43–4.

[47] Currently, companies are just a small portion of legal persons in China.

[48] Zhao, Zhongfu, "Enterprise Legal Persons: Their Important Status in Chinese Civil Law" (1989) 52 *Law and Contemporary Problems* 1, at 4.

[49] It is sometimes argued that it should be harder for contract creditors than for tort creditors to prevail in piercing cases because of voluntary dealing and negotiation. Harvey Gelb, *op. cit.*, at 11–13.

[50] According to the *Supreme Court Working Report*, last year sales contract disputes alone made up more than 34 per cent of economic cases heard by the courts at all levels. See *People's Daily*, March 24, 1995.

[51] "The Notice Concerning the Application of 68th Notice of the State Council on Economic Trials by the Supreme Court" of March 16, 1991. See the Research Office of the Supreme Court, above n.44, at 1504.

[52] The Research Office of the Supreme Court, above n.40, at 1508–09.

[53] The Economic Law Division of the Supreme Court, above n.42, at 291–301.

[54] The Research Office of the Supreme Court, above n.44, at 1570–72.

[55] The Economic Law Division of the Supreme Court, above n.44, at 337–47.

[56] *ibid.* at 373–92.

[57] *ibid.* at 388–89. Article 24 and article 80 of the Company Law provide that intellectual property investment in a limited liability or joint stock company cannot exceed 20 per cent of its registered capital. The circular issued by the State Commission of Economic System Reform on May 15, 1992 on regulation of limited liability and joint stock companies had the same rule.

[58] Ren, Lichuen, "The Courts Shall Not Disregard The Entity of Enterprise Legal Person" in *Market Economy and Economic Judicature: Selected Articles Presented to 4th Economic Law Symposium* (1993), at 184–87.

[59] Wang, above n.4, Vol. 3, at 90.

[60] Reply to the High Court of Xinjiang by the Supreme Court of October 15, 1987 on the issue of who shall be named defendant where the company in question has been terminated. See *Bulletin of the Supreme Court* (1987), Vol. 4, at 22–23.

[61] Reply to the High Court of Guangdong by the Supreme Court on liability of promoting enterprises for their terminated enterprises on March 30, 1994.

[62] The Research Office of the Supreme Court, above n.42, at 1513–15.

[63] The Economic Law Division of the Supreme Court, above n.44, at 260–61.

[64] The High Court of Zhejiang, above n.4, at 261–62.

[65] Ren, Lichuen, above n.58, at 182–3.

[66] Even in the case listed companies in the exchanges, the problems have caused people recently to appeal that it is time information disclosure to be regulated. See HAN, Xiangquen, "Regulation of Information Disclosure of Listed Companies and Its Internationalization" (1995) 39 Securities Weekly 27.

[67] The High Court of Inner Mongolia, above n.16, at 341–42.

[68] Harvey Gelb, above n.2, at 67–69.

[69] Robert B. Thompson, "Unpacking Limited Liability: Direct and Vicarious Liability of Corporate Participants for Torts of the Enterprise" (1994) 47 Vanderbilt Law Review 1 at 21.

[70] See Cohn and Simitis, above n.1, at 190.

[71] For instance, article 101 of the Statute on Joint Stock Corporations of former West Germany provided that a person who, by exercising his influence on a company for the purpose of control, obtained for himself or a third party special advantages other than those which might naturally result from his participation in the company and thereby caused damage to the company, was liable to compensate the company and was responsible for all the company's debts that remain unpaided in consequence of the damage and to the extent of it. See Cohn and Simitis, *ibid.* at 192.

CONTEMPORARY MARKET ECONOMY AND MATHEMATICAL JURISPRUDENCE

Professor Liu Ruifu

Department of Law
Peking University

Professor Liu Ruifu, *LL. B. (Jilin University), in 1980 became an editor for the Education Publishing House. In 1988, he became a Professor of Law at Peking University. He has published numerous books and articles including* Introduction to Economic Law *(1981),* Economic Law *(1982),* New Economic Law *(1991), and* Economic Law: Law Governing Operation of National Economy *(1994).*

The development of a contemporary market economy has helped to enhance the existing human interest in natural science, particularly mathematics. As the market economy of China develops further and the legal system associated with it improves, there is a growing need for a legal foundation which is based on natural science.

The existence of an objective relationship among the economy, the mathematics and the law provides a firm foundation for establishing a "mathematical jurisprudence". This paper tries to develop the theory of "mathematical jurisprudence", with the objective of revealing the relationship between the three elements.

Mathematical Economy and the Law

The contemporary market economy involves the socialization of production, capital and labour. It has fundamentally changed economics, integrating the scattered and individual procedure into one uniform socialized production. During the socialization of production, individual capital is also combined together to realize the socialization of capital. At the same time, product has changed from the individual product to socialized product. Nowadays, especially since the 1970s, the socialization of production, capital and labour has been greatly developed in every respect of social life.

The relationship of socialized economy, which is a kind of socialized relationship, is established on the basis of mathematics. We cannot understand and analyze it out of its socialized nature. So it is a kind of mathematical relationship as well.

(a) The relationship between mathematics and economics is obvious. In general, there is a mathematical interdependence between economic phenomena. When one economic phenomenon varies mathematically, another will vary correspondingly. For example, when the amount of money supply tightens up, the speed and scale of infrastructure building will decrease. As the price of a commodity goes down, the volume of sales will increase. Given the promotion of salary, the profit of enterprise will drop. This relationship of mathematical economy can be divided into two kinds: one is that the value of reality relationship is fixed, which refers to functional relationship, another is that the value is variable, which refers to relative relationship. Thus, the mathematical interdependence is the foundation of the relationship of mathematical economy.

(b) Economic relationships are always changing, leading us to question the extent of the influence of independent variables upon dependent variables. To optimize the economic benefit is the object of economic activities. This optimization, which includes the optimum of revenue, cost and profit, is the procedure of analyzing the marginal influence of independent variables on dependent variables. It is the main principle of every economic subject.

(c) The subject of economic activities always effectively makes use of various input factors (production factor) to find the optimum relationship between input and output during the socialized production. Input refers to the consumed materials and labour in the production, and output correspondingly means the products and services from the production. Through the analysis of input and output, enterprises attempt to find an optimal way of combining input factors in order to reach the lowest level of cost. In addition, value relationship (the ratio of function and cost) and trade-off relationship all belongs to the relationship of mathematical economy.

(d) Because resources are limited, the allocation of resources must be rational. Economic activities always have production cost, so there are mathematical relationships between cost and profit. Governments must calculate the marginal profit of various resources, with the calculation based on mathematics, to get the rationalized way of allocation. The procedure of assessment is influenced not only by the coefficiency of objective functions, restricting conditions and constants but also by the number of restricting conditions and decision variables.

Mathematics can also be used to perform a quantitative study of economic processes which reveal the relationship between economic phenomena and the quantity to represent it.

Just as economics can be defined quantitatively, so can the law. A socialized economy requires unified legal regulation. This law must be based on mathematics. It could not be addressed by traditional legal studies without the help of mathematical jurisprudence.

Every enterprise develops economic activities and makes profits under the control of their concepts about legal regulation. If the field of their business is legal, we regard it as the judicial economic order. This is not always true. The following is the description of it in a quantitative way:

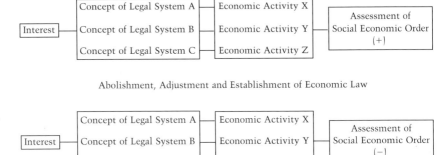

Abolishment, Adjustment and Establishment of Economic Law

We use A, B, C to represent the quantity of enterprises which carry on economic activities X, Y, Z with different concept of legal system respectively. If activity X and Y are legal according to the requirements of certain economic law, activity Z will be restricted. If activity X and Y are restricted on account of the abolishment, adjustment and establishment of this law, activity Z will be encouraged. It will cause the imbalanced interest between different enterprises. It is, therefore, important to catalogue enterprises and to determine the suitable model of economic activity. Then we can get the proper assessment of social economic order.

How to settle the boundary of legal and illegal? Let us use the environmental law as the example to reveal the relationship between the scientific reality, critical value and legal standardization. China has enacted the Environmental Protection Law in chapters two and three of which there are several stipulations, such as "To keep the quality of water" and "To limit the waste gas". So how to set these critical values?

From the point of view of natural science, there is no obvious difference between scientific reality and critical value. For example,

146

the average density per day of CO_2 is set at $150\mu g/M^3$. If real density is higher than this critical value which is often called value DO, it is considered as serious pollution. In some countries the value DO of water of first grade is set at 7 mg/l. According to this rule, water with value DO 7.1 mg/l is considered as first grade, but the value DO is not consistent with the certain differences between real data sets. We use subordinate function to explain it.

$$A_1(X) = \begin{cases} 1 & X \geq 7 \\ \frac{1}{2}(X-5) & 5 < X < 7 \\ 0 & X \leq 5 \end{cases}$$

The above formula is the subordinate of first grade water value DO, in which X is the observed value of DO. Obviously, the smaller the observed value of DO is, the greater the subordinate degree of first grade water is. Similarly, we can set the subordinate function of second grade water, too.

$$A_2(X) = \begin{cases} -\frac{1}{2}(X-7) & 5 \leq X < 7 \\ \frac{1}{2}(X-3) & 3 < X < 5 \\ 0 & X \leq 3, X \geq 7 \end{cases}$$

If X is 5.5 mg/l, A_1 (5.5) is 0.25 and A_2 (5.5) is 0.75, according to the principle of subordinate degree, this kind of water belongs to the second grade instead of the first grade. In reality, there are more than ten parameters of water quality.

There are several confused questions. Is it fresh air or not if the average density per day of CO_2 is 149.9 mg/M³? And is it first grade water or not if the value DO is 6.9 mg/l? In fact, there is hardly any difference between water quality of 7.1 mg/l and 6.9 mg/l.

In order to avoid the dispute between scientists and executive officials, law must clearly and definitely set the critical value. In 1906, the Congress of the United States enacted the Decree of Clean Foods and Medicines. From the view of Parliament Council, there is no need to determine in the proposal whether certain material is poisonous and harmful to the health or not, and it should be confirmed by the minister after most serious investigation, analysis, test, experiment and research under the direction of special and unprejudiced scientific authority. No matter whether scientists or ministers are given this right of decision making, it will cause severe abuses. On the basis of scientific demonstration, it is necessary to set the critical value by law.

From the above analysis, we can conclude that law strictly distinguishes between scientific reality and critical value which is determined on the foundation of the former, and marks the critical value as the definite boundary between legal and illegal economic activities.

During this dynamic procedure, mathematics not only urges the formation of legal system but also reveals the interdependence between the economic legal system and natural science.

The practical application of mathematics in the field of jurisprudence is the inevitable result of the unity between qualitative and quantitative nature. Through the research of quantity in the economy, we can reveal important relationships and proportions in the economic phenomena, then recognize its natural quality.

Characteristics of Mathematical Jurisprudence

In contemporary society, the enhanced tendency of science from the individual to the whole has brought up many frontier sciences on the cross of every field. Mathematical jurisprudence, which is the integration and infiltration of economics, mathematics and jurisprudence, is one kind of such frontier sciences.

It is considered that the rapid integration between natural science and social science is a typical characteristic of the development of contemporary science such as mathematical jurisprudence. Nowadays, science changes into productive forces directly and infiltrates into every field of social life. The unity of science, production and society not only combines nature and human society together but also joins the procedure of remaking them together. So we can conclude that the mission of modern natural science, on the one hand, remakes nature, on the other hand, remolds society, and the final aim of remaking nature is to remold human society. All of these are characteristics of the relationship between modern scientific technology and human society.

In the unity of science, production and society, natural science, which explores the development of nature and the law of this development, and social science, which probes the development of human society and the law of this development, have merged with one another. During the merging, the boundary between them gradually becomes unclear. The recognition of the truth that natural science will include social science in itself according to the extent of social science including natural science in the future, impels people to establish and to study mathematical jurisprudence.

Mathematical jurisprudence has its own research objective. It uses mathematical methods to adjust the legal system. The field of mathematical jurisprudence is relatively independent and different from general jurisprudence. The quantitative research of mathematical jurisprudence is based on the qualitative research of the whole legal system. Its simplicity and quantitative nature, uniting with economics and mathematics, can solve the problems which go beyond the general form of law.

The research object of mathematical jurisprudence should be given clear and definite description. The explanation is as follows:

(a) Mathematical jurisprudence studies not only the form of law and its structure but also its creation, development, transformation and abolishment.
(b) Mathematical jurisprudence investigates not only the adjustment of the law of social relationship but also the law of the relationship of mathematical economy and the inherent law of using legal systems to adjust this kind of relationship.
(c) Mathematical jurisprudence not only studies one certain field but also extends across the field of jurisprudence, economics and mathematics.

All the objectives stated above restrict, transform and infiltrate each other, being in the unity of mathematical jurisprudence. Any kind of science unity has its own logical starting point. The mechanism of relationship among economics, mathematics and law should be the logical starting point of mathematical jurisprudence, which is called the relationship of mathematical economic law. Its meaning is as follows:

(a) It is not the economic relationship or mathematical relationship but the legal relationship and is also the social relationship restricted by the legal system, so it is the logical starting point of mathematical jurisprudence.
(b) It is the legal relationship formed by the legal system from economic relationship which is the adjustment objective of law, namely economic legal relationship.
(c) It is the legal relationship formed by legal system from economic mathematical relationship which is not the general economic relationship.

The logical starting point of mathematical jurisprudence is, therefore, the relationship of mathematical economic law which is formed by legal system from mathematical economic relationship.

149

Whether an independent science has its own research objects and proper research methods or not is the important sign of its maturity.

The origination of frontier sciences has caused a great breakthrough in the area of research methods. On the one hand, research methods of parallel sciences are transforming each other, which means one specific method of a certain science can be applied in other fields of sciences. On the other hand, research methods of cross sciences, such as operation research, cybernetics, system theory and information technology, are infiltrating into every field of other sciences, which means the research methods of cross sciences can be used to analyze specific and common aspects of every science.

The great breakthrough in methodology caused by the rapid development of science has brought about the new principle of methodology and its scope. The interrelationship among sciences and the characteristics of cross science methodology determine the inevitable trend of this new methodology transforming and infiltrating to other sciences. It is also inexorable that mathematical jurisprudence, as a frontier science, applies mathematics, cybernetics, system theory and information technology to establish its whole structure.

The objective of mathematics is determination space formation and the quantitative relationship of the universe. The cognition law of science development has demonstrated that we need not only qualitative but also quantitative analysis to understand the nature of the world. Only when applying mathematics successfully is a science fully mature.

There are two closely related applications of mathematics in the field of mathematical jurisprudence. One is to apply the analytical methods of mathematics to process information and design the legal system; the other is to set up mathematical models to solve the problems of legal system in a quantitative way. Economic mathematical analysis makes use of abstract characters, such as mathematical equations, figures, tables and mathematical logic, to describe certain factors, variables and their interrelationship in the economic procedure, and to clear up all the uncertainties in the legal system.

Quantitative analysis of jurisprudence is on the basis of economic mathematical analysis. There are three steps in the principle of its methodology. First, to find out the main theme that penetrates into mathematics, economics and law. Second, to find out the media for communication that is the bridge between jurisprudence and mathematics. Third, to find out the formation of the unity which comes from the integration of every original part. This theoretical system is called quantitative analysis of jurisprudence. Its programme is as following:

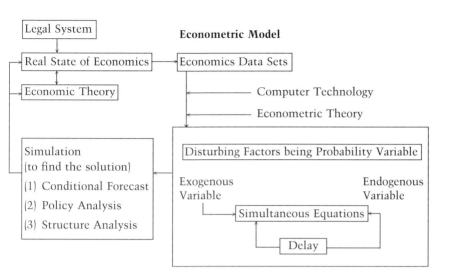

The practical applications for mathematical jurisprudence are numerous. There is the regulation of national economic development plan, including equilibrium technique, economic mathematical method and model; the regulation of infrastructure building, including linear programming, non-linear programming, dynamic programming, group cybernetics and matrix model; the regulation of financial credit, including balance sheet, mathematical model and automatic calculation; the regulation of scientific technology, including network model, network chart, indicator calculation and standardization; the regulation of agriculture, including balance sheet, matrix model, linear programming, solid geometry and plane geometry; the regulation of materials and means, including economic mathematical methods and modern computer technology; the regulation of resources, including balance sheet, automatic calculation, statistics and chart theory; the regulation of business, including balance sheet, statistics, demand elasticity and economic mathematical model; the regulation of labour, including indicator calculation, economic engineering, synthetic indicator, factor analysis, quota method and balance sheet; the regulation of price, including balance sheet, economic mathematical model, probability theory and demand elasticity; the regulation of enterprise, including mathematical model, linear programming and balance sheet.

It is lopsided to reject or accept completely the methods of mathematics in the research of mathematical jurisprudence. Mathematics is not the thought but the tool or the way of explaining the quantitative relationship between phenomena. It will not be able to reveal the nature of this relative relationship, the nature of economic and legal activities, but this limitation cannot prevent us from understanding and applying mathematics. The proper attitude for us to hold is to

151

analyze the relationship between application of mathematics and juris-prudence and then to find out the optimum ways and conditions of understanding and applying mathematics.

System theory, cybernetics and information theory, as typical cross sciences, have the function of methodology. The application of them in law is the reform in the field of jurisprudence theory.

The principal thought of system theory is to regard research objects as the unity of function, structure and behavior, and to emphasize the interaction among them. Its elementary characteristic is to examine objects as a whole according to the concept, configuration and nature of system.

Mathematical jurisprudence regards legal system and legal relation-ship in economy as the whole set in which their function, structure and behavior are integrated in accordance with certain objectives. The category system of mathematical jurisprudence includes general cat-egory, common category and self category. Since the introduction of general category and common category, the function, structure and behavior have changed so much. It is impossible to found mathemati-cal jurisprudence through the simple modification of concepts in the system theory.

In the face of application of system theory, the available and artifi-cial boundaries in the field of related jurisprudential will gradually disappear.

Cybernetics studies the direction, control, co-ordination, self-adjustment and feedback in the complicated dynamic system and reveals the synthetic attribute of the system. The methods of cybernet-ics use the control idea to investigate the law of system movement and evolution.

In the research of mathematical jurisprudence, the notion of en-tropy is utilized to fix problems about the direction and limitation of economic activities. The entropy function defined in the Second Law of thermodynamics is the effective determinants to describe the con-duction of heat. We do the experiment as follows: In the glass bucket, namely "Closed System", red balls and black balls are put level by level. Because of rolling and rocking, entropy has changed from the initial value. The movement of these balls is unceasingly becoming confusing. The maximum degree of confusion is the limitation of procedure, so the nature of entropy is the macro-measurement of micro-confusion.

In the legal system, one determined macro-state can be represented by numerous varied micro-states correspondingly. On account of changeable movements of economic activities, it is very difficult to determine which kind of micro-states will appear to represent the corresponding macro-state at a given time. In a certain macro-state, the greater the confusing state, the bigger the entropy of social economy. We apply entropy theory to judge different states of economic activities, such as spontaneous procedure, reversible procedure, unreversible procedure and impossible procedure, and determine the direction and limitation of economic activities within the creation period in order to make the legal system be in the optimum state. In addition, the notion of feedback is also utilized to examine the result of social economy after the law of economy is put into effect.

In brief, using cybernetics to adjust the regulation of national economy as a whole, mathematical jurisprudence probes into co-ordination and feedback relationship between a system and its sub-systems, explores the law of national economic control and direction, prospect for interaction between regulations and laws in the legal system, and finds the optimum adjustment of law within the normal movement of national economy.

Information theory is from cybernetics and independent of it. Infor-mation is the principal nature of objective world connecting all the procedures together. It studies information flow, information value, information system, information collection, information processing and information output. In order to understand and appraise the devel-opment of legislation and enforcement of law, we must apply method-ology of information theory to collect, analyze, arrange and decide these factors.

It is very necessary to study legislation, particularly the social consequence of law enforcement, to realize the phase and structure of the information system.

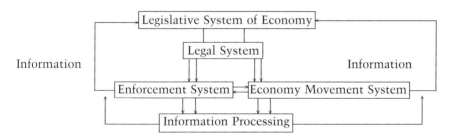

As in the above figure, information originates in the enforcement system and economy movement system. All the information, includ-ing internal and external, must be collected, classified and processed by the certain organization or functional departments. There is the problem of transmission during the whole procedure.

Information flow is realized through every organization of a information system. When we apply methodology of information theory to study mathematical jurisprudence, we must first set up the "hardware" of an information system, such as collection department, process department, transmission department and appraisal department.

153

Field and Mission of Mathematical Jurisprudence

It is of great immediate significance that mathematical jurisprudence, as an independent and special jurisprudence, forms a research field. The research field of mathematical jurisprudence can be classified into two aspects: macro-field and micro-field.

Macro-field

In the macro-field, mathematical jurisprudence studies the interaction between regulation and economy, and reveals the principal law of utilizing regulation to adjust mathematical economic relationship in the development of social economy. The relationship of mathematical macroeconomics, which is also called aggregation economic relationship, refers to integrated social economic relationship represented by corresponding economic variables, including economic growth, economic cycle, unemployment, inflation, national fiscal, international trade, gross national product, development speed, gross national income, social consumption, interest rate, employment, budget, deficit, import and export trade, international balance, etc. How jurisprudence adjusts aggregation economic relationship is the main field of mathematical jurisprudence.

Example One

Price is the important component in economic activities. In the price legislation, the adjustment of price is on the basis of the theory that supply varies directly with price and demand varies inversely with price. This is not always true. In fact, demand is not inversely proportional to price but reverse interdependent. Is there any law in this reverse interdependence? Why must the price legislation consider the reaction of demand to the adjustment of price?

Under certain conditions, price is the key factor in realizing value and adjusting the relationship between demand and supply. Thus, in the price legislation, especially in the legislation setting price and adjusting price, not only are commodity value and national economic policy considered, but also the elasticity of supply and demand, in order to determine the proper level of price and the suitable range of adjustment.

Generally, elasticity of price is in the range from -0.001 to -10. For the sake of making policy, elasticity of price, in accordance with its absolute value, is catalogued into elastic demand for $|e_p| > 1$, unit demand for $|e_p| = 1$ and non-elastic demand for $|e_p| < 1$. The marginal income is positive at the elastic part of the demand curve, negative at

154

the non-elastic part, and maximum at the point of unit elastic. Price reduction will, therefore, cause income declination in the range of non-elastic demand part.

We must examine the demand elasticity of price at the different price levels carefully in the legislation setting price and adjusting price. For example, it is impossible to get more profit through price reduction at the non-elastic part of demand curve. Even at the elastic part it is still uncertain. Whether the price reduction is advantageous or not depends on whether marginal income of increased amount is more than its marginal cost or not.

In the present price legislation, we will inevitably meet problems like elasticity of price. For instance, if price is set too high while elasticity is big, the manufacturing industry will be affected; if price is set too low while elasticity is small, it will be useless to the severe problem of fiscal allowance.

Besides the elasticity of price, the cross elasticity between price of minerals, raw materials and price of agricultural goods should be also considered for the purpose of well adjustment.

Cross elasticity is used to measure the extent of influence of one product's price variation on another product's demand variation. For example, the growth of coal price will increase the demand for electricity, but the expansion of oil price will decrease the demand for liquid gas. The extent of increase or decrease can be determined by the cross elasticity. The formula of cross point elasticity is as follows: when $i = c$;

$$e_c = \frac{\partial Q_y}{\partial X_c} \cdot \frac{X_c}{Q_y}$$

By means of the formula of cross arc elasticity, when $i = c$, we have:

$$\bar{e}_c = \frac{\Delta Q_y}{\Delta X_c} \cdot \frac{X_c'' + X_c'}{Q_y'' + Q_y'}$$

Besides measuring the extent of demand variation, cross elasticity can also determine whether the relationship between two kinds of products is substitutive or supplementary. If the price variation of one kind of product and the demand variation of another kind of product have the same trend, these two kinds are substitutive products and cross elasticity is positive $(e_c > 0)$. If the price variation of one and the demand variation of another have the reverse trend, these two kinds are supplementary products and cross elasticity is negative $(e_c < 0)$. If cross elasticity is approximately equal to zero $(e_c = 0)$, they are not coherent with each other.

The supply elasticity of price should be also noticed in setting and adjusting price legislation. It is used to measure the extent of influence of price variation on supply variation. The definition is as following:

$$\text{Supply Elasticity} = \frac{\text{Percentage Supply Variation}}{\text{Percentage Price Variation}}$$

$$= \frac{\Delta G_y}{\Delta X_p} \cdot \frac{X_p}{G_y}$$

The supply point elasticity of price is used to measure the elasticity of one point on the supply curve. The formula is as follows when $i = p$,

$$E_p = \frac{\partial G_y / G_y}{\partial X_p / X_p} = \frac{\partial G_y}{\partial X_p} \cdot \frac{X_p}{G_y}$$

The supply arc elasticity of price is used to measure the elasticity of arc between two points on the supply curve. By means of the formula of arc elasticity, when $i = p$, we have:

$$\bar{E}_p = \frac{\left(G_Y'' - G_Y'\right) \Big/ \dfrac{\left(G_Y'' + G_Y'\right)}{2}}{\left(X_p'' - X_p'\right) \Big/ \dfrac{\left(X_p'' + X_p'\right)}{2}} = \frac{\Delta G_Y}{\Delta X_p} \cdot \frac{X_p'' + X_p'}{G_Y'' + G_Y'}$$

Since resources are limited, it is necessary to keep a balance between varied production. By means of the regulation of price to increase the supply of certain product, it will be possible to decrease the supply of other products.

In short, the legislation of price should be on the basis of the theory of price elasticity. Whether the regulation is proper or not has an important bearing not only on supply or demand of products but also on the order of production and the development of national economy.

Example Two

Now let's probe into the application of elasticity theory in the legislation of social production.

Fundamentally speaking, an enterprise should organize production in accordance with the market demand during a certain period. Social production is restricted by the legislation of social production, achieving the purposes of legislation, such as expending production scale, adjusting industrial structure, increasing production force, meeting market demand. The market demand for products is affected by several demand factors, including price of product, income of consumer, price of relevant product, etc. We must exactly understand the factors that affect market demand for product and the elasticity of product.

If the price of the product changes and other factors affecting market demand keep constant, demand for the product will also change. The plan of production should be implemented therefore on the basis of market demand. Suppose elasticity of price e_p or $(\bar{e}_p)$ is given, we use formula $e_p \approx (\Delta Q_y/\Delta X_p) \cdot (X_p/Q_y)$ to get the approximate value of ΔQ_y:

$$\Delta Q_y \approx \frac{e_p \cdot \Delta X_p \cdot Q_y}{X_p}$$

If the price of the relevant product changes and other factors affecting market demand keep constant, demand for this product will change too. Modification of the production plan will be needed. Suppose cross elasticity e_c is given, we use formula e_c (or $\bar{e}_c$) to get the approximate value of ΔQ_y:

$$\Delta Q_y \approx \frac{e_c \cdot \Delta X_c \cdot Q_y}{X_c}$$

There are two cases for the application of income elasticity of demand in the legislation of social production. First, where average income has increased, for example the national promotion in accordance with the regulation of administration. In this case, the corresponding regulation should be utilized to adjust the capability of production on the basis of forecasting the market demand. Given the income elasticity e_i, ΔQ_y can be got through the formula e_i (or $\bar{e}_i$) as follows:

$$\Delta Q_y \approx \frac{e_i \cdot \Delta X_c \cdot Q_y}{X_i}$$

Second, average income is forecast to grow. In this case, according to the forecast, an enterprise must prepare for the extended production to meet potential demand in advance. Given the growth amount and income elasticity of income, the demand can be estimated. The formula is the same as above except ΔX_i here is the estimated value.

The formulas above are deduced from the extent of variation of certain independent variables on the variation of demand. Another way is to infer from the definition of point elasticity to get the relationship between the demand Q_y and the certain independent variable X_i affecting the demand. On the condition that variables except for X_i keep constant, the elasticity of demand Q_y to the certain independent variable X_i reflects the extent of variation of X_i on variation of Q_y. Thus, the formula of point elasticity can be written as follows:

$$e_i = \frac{dQ_y/Q_y}{dX_i/X_i}$$

the formula can be transformed into:

$$\frac{dQ_y}{Q_y} = e_i \frac{dX_i}{X_i}$$

to take indefinite integral on both sides:

$$\int \frac{dQ_y}{Q_y} = e_i \int \frac{dX_i}{X_i}$$

we have:

$$\ln Q_y = e_i \ln K \, (\text{K is constant})$$

that is,

$$Q_y = KX_i$$

It is the mathematical expression of the relationship between the demand Q_y and the certain independent variable X_i affecting the demand which is deduced from the definition of point elasticity. In the model, constant K can be calculated from the original value of Q_y and X_i. Because the above formula is a kind of approximate calculation, precise results can be got only when the variation of X_i is not great.

Example Three

The legislation of investment is the important topic in the field of mathematical jurisprudence.

For the purpose of increasing the supply of a product, capacity of production is expended through the continuous investment that is mainly determined by the amount of demand in the planning period. From the long term view, the amount of demand depends on the price of the product itself, the income level of consumers and the price of relevant products. If price and purchase power keep at the current level in the planning period, the amount of demand for products and the scale of investment can be easily estimated. If the variation of price and purchase power can be approximated, the corresponding scale of investment can also be predicted by the elasticity of demand. For example, if the price of a substitutive product increases, keeping other factors affecting demand constant, the amount of demand for the product planned for production will enlarge for sure. If it is a supplementary relationship, the amount of demand for the product planned to produce will decrease. The exact amount of variation can be calculated by means of cross elasticity.

If the price of product itself changes, keeping other factors constant, the extent of demand variation depends on the price elasticity of the product. During the energy crisis in the United States in 1973, power companies had to raise the price of electricity because of the increasing cost of fuel. But the problem came out intermediately. How would the increase in the price of electricity affect the demand for electricity, the capacity to produce electricity and the investment in power supply? The key to solving this problem was to estimate the price elasticity of demand for electricity.

If purchase power, which usually refers to the average income has greatly changed, it will certainly alter the amount of demand in the future. The extent of variation can be estimated by the income elasticity of demand.

In the investment legislation, the formula for calculating the amount of variation of demand is nearly the same as in the legislation on social production. The difference is only that in the legislation on social production it is used to estimate the amount of production; in the investment legislation it is used to predict the demand for capacity of production in the future.

Example Four

The equilibrium between supply and demand and the way of realizing it belongs to the marco-field of mathematical jurisprudence, too.

Usually, it is impossible to extend supply greatly to alleviate the situation when demand for products is in excess of supply. Under normal circumstances, there are only two regulations capable of reaching the equilibrium between supply and demand. One is to promulgate decrees to raise price; the other is to issue rational coupons. To choose which one depends on the price elasticity of the product at the current price level. In 1973, there was heated argument on how to solve the disequilibrium of oil products within the U.S. government during the energy crisis. One view was to increase price to depress demand, reaching the equilibrium. Another view was to use rational system to substitute the adjustment function of market. In fact, the nature of the dispute was the price elasticity of oil products.

159

Generally speaking, this kind of problem can be analyzed thus: Given that X_p is the current price of the product, Q_y is the demand corresponding to X_p for the product, X_y is the maximum amount of current supply, X_p is the price corresponding to Q_y, and e_p is the price elasticity of current price level, according to the formula of point elasticity:

$$e_p \approx \frac{\Delta Q_y}{\Delta X_p} \cdot \frac{X_p}{Q_y} = \frac{Q'_y - Q_y}{X'_p - X_p} \cdot \frac{X_p}{Q_y}$$

to get:

$$\Delta X_p = X'_p - X_p \approx \frac{\left(Q'_y - Q_Y\right) \cdot X_p}{e_p \cdot Q_y}$$

From the above calculation, if the price increment delta X_p is in the acceptable range, regulations for increasing price should be put into effect to reach the equilibrium state.

Micro-field

In the micro-field, mathematical jurisprudence studies how to utilize regulations to adjust the mathematical economic relationship among economy organizations, reveals that the relationship of mathematical microeconomics is the internal economic relationship of individual economic subject, such as enterprises, companies, etc. How jurisprudence adjusts the relationship of mathematical microeconomics is one of the important components of mathematical jurisprudence.

Example One

The establishment of an enterprise is the origination of its legal relationship. This establishment, which is related to the benefit of itself and the national economy, should be restricted by legislation. All the decisions depend on the analysis of risk.

Risk refers to the possibility or chance of meeting danger, suffering loss, injury, etc. Risk varies directly with the probability of unfavourable results occurring. In general, the legislation should depend on certain facts, but sometimes legislators have to make a choice among several drafts without knowing the results of putting this regulation into effect. It is very common that there are many uncertainties existing in the national economy, so we must apply risk theory to analyze quantitatively the problems in mathematical jurisprudence.

Two indicators, expected profit and expected utility are used as criteria in the decision-making of an enterprise.

For any kind of risky decision-making there are several natural states, drafts for choice, probabilities of natural state occurring and profits of drafts under the different natural states. Expected value of every draft is the weighted average, using the value of probability as weight. The formula is as follows:

$$V_i = \sum_{j=1}^{n} P_j V_{ij} \quad (i = 1, 2, \ldots m)$$

where: V_i is the expected profit of ith draft;
V_{ij} is the profit of ith draft under the natural state S_j;
P is the probability of natural state S_j.

The method of using expected profit as a criterion for decision-making involves two steps: first, to calculate expected profit of every draft; second, to choose the draft of which expected profit is the biggest.

The "decision tree" method is often utilized in the area of risky decision-making. It means that profits of every draft under every natural state and probability of every natural state are simply expressed in the one chart, and expected values are compared to find out the optimum draft. Because this chart looks like a tree, it is called a "decision tree".

The general structure of decision tree is as following:

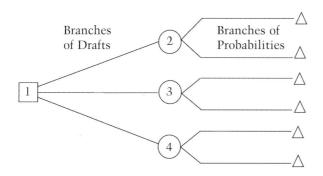

□ is the Decision Point. The branch from this point is the draft branch. If there is only one decision point in the decision tree, named single-phase decision-making, we merely make one decision. If there are several decision points, named multiple-phase decision-making, we need to make several decisions.

O is the Natural State. The branch from this point is the probability branch, representing different natural states. The value of probability must be marked near the point.

Δ is the End Point. It represents the profit of every draft under every natural state.

The standard deviation is used as criterion to measure the extent of risk of every draft. The procedure of calculating is as follows:

First, to calculate the expected value:

$$\text{Expected Value} \quad V = \sum_{j=1}^{n}\left(P_i V_i\right)$$

Second, to calculate the deviation:

$$\text{Deviation} \quad \Delta_j = V_j - V$$

Then, to calculate the variance:

$$\text{Variance} \quad \delta^2 = \sum_{j=1}^{n} P_j \left(V_j - V\right)^2$$

Finally, to calculate the standard deviation:

$$\text{Standard Deviation} \quad \delta = \sqrt{\sum_{j=1}^{n} P_j \left(V_j - V\right)^2}$$

For example, there are two drafts: one is to build a factory to produce hot products; another is to build a restaurant. We can use risk theory to make a choice between the two drafts. Although the net present value of the draft to build a restaurant is bigger than that of building a factory, the former is more risky. In addition, after considering other important factors like social environment, technology level and economic state, we can get the conclusion that the draft of building the factory is the feasible, so it is reasonable to set up regulations encouraging investment in the production.

Example Two

The input-output of an enterprise is the significant area of enterprise legislation which is on the basis of input-output analysis. It is important for legislators to study the relationship between the input amount of production factors and output, and the substitutive relationship among factors of input; but it is much more important to study the relevant relationship between factors of input and departments of production during the whole procedure of production. The effective tool for such problems is input-output analysis. Using this method, there are several steps: first, to create input-output tables reflecting the status of connection between factors and departments; second, to establish the mathematics model in accordance with the interdependence given by the tables. For input-output analysis of an enterprise, the static and opened value model is usually employed.

The basic structure of the input-output table of enterprise and the meaning of every symbol in the table is as follows:

Y_i is the production value of ith self-made product used for inventory and sales by the enterprise (the production amount is Z_i).

X_i is the total production value of ith self-made product (the total production amount is Q_i).

W_i is the purchase expense of ith outside product used for inventory and sales by the enterprise (the production amount is T_i).

U_i is the purchase expense of ith outside product used for producing ith outside product by the enterprise (the production amount is S_i).

X_{ij} is the production value of ith self-made product used for producing jth product by the enterprise (the production amount is Q_{ij}).

U_{ij} is the purchase expense of ith outside product used for producing Jth outside product by the enterprise (the production amount is S_{ij}).

R_j is the depreciation expense of jth self-made product.

H_j is the administration expense of jth self-made product.

V_j is the salary expense of jth self-made product.

M_j is the profit of jth self-made product.

The above table can be divided into five parts: The first part (consisting of X_{ij}) reflects the situation of self-made products used for production; the second part (consisting of Y_i and X_i) reflects the situation of products used for inventory and sales; the third part (consisting of U_{ij}) reflects the situation of sales products used for production; the fourth part (consisting of M_j and U_i) reflects the situation of outside products used for inventory and sales; the fifth part (consisting of R_j, H_j, M_j, X_j) reflects the situation of depreciation, administration expense, salary and profit.

Looking horizontally, the first and second parts reflect the usage of self-made products and labour; the third and fourth parts reflect the usage of outside products. Looking vertically, the first part reflects the amount of self-made products and labour input during the production;

Output \ Input	Input	Products in processing 1	2	...	n	Inventory	Sales	Sum	Total products
Products made by itself	1	X_{11}	X_{12}	...	X_{1n}			Y_1	X_1
	2	X_{21}	X_{22}	...	X_{2n}			Y_2	X_2
	$\vdots$	$\vdots$	$\vdots$	...	$\vdots$			$\vdots$	$\vdots$
	n	X_{n1}	X_{n2}	...	X_{nn}			Y_n	X_n
Products purchased from outside	1	U_{11}	U_{12}	...	U_{1n}			W_1	U_1
	2	U_{21}	U_{22}	...	U_{2n}			W_2	U_2
	$\vdots$	$\vdots$	$\vdots$	$\vdots$	$\vdots$			$\vdots$	$\vdots$
	m	U_{m1}	U_{m2}	...	U_{mn}			W_m	U_m
Depreciation fixed assets	of	R_1	R_2	...	R_n				
Business administration fee		H_1	H_2	...	H_n				
Salary		V_1	V_2	...	V_n				
Profit		M_1	M_2	...	M_n				
Total products		X_1	X_2	...	X_n				

the third part reflects the amount of outside products input; the fifth part reflects depreciation expense, administration expense, salary and profit. In brief, the input-output table shows clearly the structure of production value and cost of products in the enterprise.

The horizontal relationship can be expressed as the following equation set:

$$\left.\begin{aligned}
\sum_{j=1}^{n} X_{1j} + Y_1 &= X_1 \\
\sum_{j=1}^{n} X_{2j} + Y_2 &= X_2 \\
&\cdots \\
\sum_{j=1}^{n} X_{nj} + Y_n &= X_n
\end{aligned}\right\} \text{ and } \left.\begin{aligned}
\sum_{j=1}^{n} U_{1j} + W_1 &= U_1 \\
\sum_{j=1}^{n} U_{2j} + W_2 &= U_2 \\
&\cdots \\
\sum_{j=1}^{n} U_{nj} + W_n &= U_n
\end{aligned}\right\}$$

The vertical relationship can also be expressed as the following equation set:

$$\left.\begin{aligned}
\sum_{i=1}^{n} X_{i1} + \sum_{i=1}^{m} U_{i1} + R_1 + H_1 + V_1 + M_1 &= X_1 \\
\sum_{i=1}^{n} X_{i2} + \sum_{i=1}^{m} U_{i2} + R_2 + H_2 + V_2 + M_2 &= X_2 \\
&\cdots \\
\sum_{i=1}^{n} X_{in} + \sum_{i=1}^{m} U_{in} + R_n + H_n + V_n + M_n &= X_n
\end{aligned}\right\}$$

Defining coefficient of directly consuming a_{ij}, d_{ij},

$$a_{ij} = \frac{Q_{ij}}{Q_j} \quad (i,j = 1,2,\ldots,n)$$

$$d_{ij} = \frac{S_{ij}}{Qj} \quad (i,j = 1,2,\ldots,n)$$

a_{ij} is the amount of i*th* self-made product used for producing j*th* product.

d_{ij} is the amount of i*th* outside product used for producing j*th* product.

Using a_{ij} and d_{ij}, the equation set representing the horizontal relation can be modified as follows:

$$
\left.
\begin{aligned}
\sum_{j=1}^{n} a_{1j}Q_j + Z_1 &= Q_1 \\
\sum_{j=1}^{n} a_{2j}Q_j + Z_2 &= Q_2 \\
\ldots\ldots\ldots\ldots\ldots \\
\sum_{j=1}^{n} a_{nj}Q_j + Z_n &= Q_n
\end{aligned}
\right\}
\quad \text{and} \quad
\left.
\begin{aligned}
\sum_{j=1}^{n} d_{1j}Q_j + T_1 &= S_1 \\
\sum_{j=1}^{n} d_{2j}Q_j + T_2 &= S_2 \\
\ldots\ldots\ldots\ldots\ldots \\
\sum_{j=1}^{n} a_{nj}Q_j + T_n &= S_n
\end{aligned}
\right\}
$$

Suppose that:

P'_i is the internal price of i*th* self-made product $(i = 1, 2, \ldots, n)$;
p_i is the price of outside factory;
v_i is the salary rate;
h_i is the administration expense of the unit;
r_i is the depreciation expense of the unit;
π_i is the profit of the unit;
P_i is the price of i*th* outside product.

The equation set representing the vertical relationship can be modified as following:

$$
\left.
\begin{aligned}
\sum_{i=1}^{n} P'_i a_{i2}Q_2 + \sum_{i=1}^{\overline{m}} q_i d_{i2}Q_2 + r_2 Q_2 + h_2 Q_2 + u_2 Q_2 + \pi_2 Q_2 &= p_2 Q_2 \\
\ldots\ldots\ldots\ldots\ldots\ldots\ldots\ldots\ldots\ldots\ldots\ldots\ldots\ldots\ldots\ldots\ldots\ldots\ldots \\
\sum_{i=1}^{n} P'_i a_{in}Q_n + \sum_{i=1}^{\overline{m}} q_i d_{in}Q_n + r_n Q_n + h_n Q_n + u_n Q_n + \pi_n Q_n &= p_n Q_n
\end{aligned}
\right\}
\quad \text{or}
$$

$$
\left.
\begin{aligned}
\sum_{i=1}^{n} p'_i a_{i1} + \sum_{i=1}^{\overline{m}} p_i d_{i1} + r_1 + h_1 + v_1 + \pi_1 &= p_1 \\
\sum_{i=1}^{n} p'_i a_{i2} + \sum_{i=1}^{\overline{m}} p_i d_{i2} + r_2 + h_2 + v_2 + \pi_2 &= p_2 \\
\ldots\ldots\ldots\ldots\ldots\ldots\ldots\ldots\ldots\ldots \\
\sum_{i=1}^{n} p'_i a_{in} + \sum_{i=1}^{\overline{m}} p_i d_{in} + r_n + h_n + v_n + \pi_n &= p_n
\end{aligned}
\right\}
$$

165

The application of input-output analysis, which can calculate the cost, profit and price of various kinds of products in the planning period, is the foundation of enterprise legislation. For example, the formation of cost required by the cost regulation, the way of depreciation in the enterprise required by the depreciation regulation, the principle of setting price required by the price regulation, etc., all depend on the input-output analysis. It provides the legal premise for determining the items and data in the model of input-output analysis.

The relationship between mathematical macroeconomics and mathematical microeconomics is an unseparate unity, depending on each other and restricting each other. The united relationship of mathematical economics requires the united adjustment of law. The division between macro-field and micro-field in mathematical jurisprudence is only the division of abstract thought.

The origination of mathematical jurisprudence reflects the requirement of legislation and justice under conditions of contemporary market economy, and reflects the requirement of new development of jurisprudence. To meet such a need, mathematical jurisprudence should treat the following as its research mission: the relationship between jurisprudence and mathematical economy, co-ordinative development of jurisprudence and economy, the impact of the relationship of mathematical economy on legislation, the scientific foundation of legislation, the law of mathematical economics in other countries in regulating the economy, the optimum way of legal development, the comprehensive regulation of adjusting the contemporary social relationship, the search for the best framework for the rule of law by using mathematics, cybernetics, system theory and information theory, etc.

Branch, Structure and Future of Mathematical Jurisprudence

Like other sciences, mathematical jurisprudence consists of several branches. Nowadays, the application of natural science, jurisprudence and other relative subjects has infiltrated every field of mathematical jurisprudence.

In accordance with the area regulated by law, mathematical jurisprudence is classified into the following branches: mathematical national jurisprudence, mathematical economic jurisprudence, mathematical civil jurisprudence, mathematical executive jurisprudence, mathematical criminal jurisprudence and mathematical procedure jurisprudence. The principle of mathematical jurisprudence which studies the application of mathematics in jurisprudence such as legislative rule and legal procedure as a whole plays the leading and dominant role in all branches.

Mathematical national jurisprudence, regarding the national constitution and institution as an object, studies the origination, development, composition and structure, regulation and control of social system, political system and economic system, and also studies all the relationships among them and their impact on social development.

Mathematical economic jurisprudence, regarding laws regulating mathematical economy as an object, studies the mechanism and the law of interaction between jurisprudence and mathematical economy. Its branch includes juristical economics and economic jurisprudence which are the basis of mathematics.

Mathematical civil jurisprudence, regarding mathematical civil relations as an object, studies the mathematical relationship among the civil activities in everyday life, its formation and law on its transformation.

Mathematical executive jurisprudence, regarding mathematical executive relations as an object, studies the interaction among executive departments, executive behaviour and mathematics, to provide legal execution with the best legal environment.

Mathematical criminal jurisprudence, regarding mathematical criminal relations as an object, studies the mathematical basis of crime formation and punishment, the appraisal of harmfulness of crime to society, scientific prevention measurements for crime, also studies trends, factors, conditions of crime, prediction of short-term or long-term effect of crime on society.

Mathematical procedure jurisprudence, regarding lawsuit procedure as an object, studies mathematical relationships among economic, civil, criminal and executive procedures; it also studies the application of mathematics, system theory in the search for the best procedure draft, the appraisal of justice.

Law is an organic whole body including all complicated relationships among legislation, justice and enforcement. Although all branches stated above have their own characteristics and developed on their own, they integrate into only one unity, mathematical jurisprudence.

Given that the natural sciences, particularly mathematics, are now being increasingly applied to the area of legal studies, there is no doubt that mathematical jurisprudence will soon be established as a new and useful discipline, and that its theoretical base and methods will be further developed and enhanced.

Mathematical Jurisprudence stated above is different from "economic analysis of jurisprudence", "jurisprudence of economic analysis" or "juristical economics" established by the Columbia School of thought and the Chicago School of thought mainly in the object and field of studying. Both Columbia thought and Chicago thought emphasize "benefit", by means of mathematics and, on the basis of benefit, rationalizing the allocation of rights.

167

At the end of this paper, I want to review the history of my ideas about mathematical jurisprudence.

In September 1980, I raised the question on combining jurisprudence with the natural sciences in the Teaching Materials of Economic Law. As the continuation of this thought, the *Introduction of Economic Law* (May 1981) defined "economic analysis of technology" as the research method of jurisprudence. Since 1985, I have co-operated with a mathematics scholar to study the quantitative analysis of economic law. Because all the trials at that time were limited in the analysis of relations of mathematical economy, it was very difficult to establish the systematic theory of mathematical jurisprudence. Later, I realized from the experience that jurisprudence must use its own methods of quantitative analysis to study its own objects in order to achieve the transformation from "methodology category" to "theory itself". As a result, the *Theory of New Economic Theory* (1991) establishing "quantitative theory of economic law" was published. The further study should be on how to improve the whole system of concepts and logic of mathematical jurisprudence. This paper is only used as the introduction to futher study.

PART 3

BANKING AND CONTRACT

THE MARKET ECONOMY AND FREEDOM OF CONTRACT — ISSUES RELATING TO THE UNIFICATION OF CHINA'S CONTRACT LEGISLATION

Professor Wei Zhenying

Department of Law
Peking University

Professor Wei Zhenying, *LL.B. (Peking University), has been teaching at Peking University since 1960, holding the positions of assistant lecturer, lecturer, associate professor and Professor of Law. Since 1992, he has been the Dean of Peking University's law department; a member of the board of directors of the China Law Association; deputy director of the Civil Law and Economic Law Association; an arbitrator with the China International Economic and Trade Arbitration; and participated in drafting Civil Law, Contract Law, etc. He has published a number of books and articles, including* Civil Law, Principles of Civil Law, *and* Research on Hard Contract Cases.

Introduction

In today's China, there three laws related to contract: the Law of Economic Contract, the Law of Technology Contract and the Foreign Economic Contract Law.

Prompted by the development of the socialist market economy, and by proposals from a number of Chinese academics, work on the unification of the laws on contract was begun in 1993. This work is being carried out under the auspices of the Commission of Legislative Affairs of the Standing Committee, the National People's Congress, and resulted in the release of a Draft Contract Law with 34 chapters and 538 articles in January 1995.

The Draft Contract Law establishes five guidelines for the new unified contract law. The first guideline states that:

171

"In drafting the new law, it is essential to:
(a) take into consideration the reality of reform in China and the open-door policy, the development of the socialist market economy and the establishment of a nationally unified market and links with the world market;
(b) take into consideration all of China's current contract legislation, experience in judicial practice and achievements in theoretical studies;
(c) make broad reference to the experience of developed market economy countries in legislation, case law and legal theory;
(d) accept as far as possible the requirements of a modern market economy; and,
(e) keep the new contract law in conformity with relevant international conventions and practices."

This guideline offers a concise statement of the guiding principle behind the development of China's civil and commercial legislation. Given this statement, it is natural and logical that another principle the principle — of freedom of contract — should come into play.

The Development of the Principle of Freedom of Contract

Historical Development

A contract is a legal form for the exchange of commodities. Rules and institutions governing contracts have been in place since the days of ancient Rome. In ancient Rome the form of a contract was considered very important, with strict and complex requirements applied.

As the commodity economy developed, there was also rapid growth in the different categories of contracts. According to the *Digest Justinianus*, there were four types of contract, namely *contractus re*, *contractus verbis*, *contractus literis* and *contractus consensu*. The *contractus consensu* was the simplest, with the common consent of the parties involved sufficient for an effective contract; there were no requirements as to its form.

It was also in Roman law that legislation regarding the principle of freedom of contract first appeared.

The social transformation "from status to contract" advocated by Henry Maine was realized after feudal society was replaced by a capitalist society. Then laissez-faire was the dominant principle and structure for the capitalist market, in which contracts were widely adopted.

The development of the principle of freedom of contract was one of the inevitable products of laissez-faire capitalism. In the nineteenth

172

century when the Code Civil des Français was promulgated, individualism and liberalism were prevailing and the Code reflected the concepts of party autonomy and freedom of contract. Article 1134 of the Code provides: "Contracts made under the law are binding as the law on all parties to the contract." There were almost no legal or practical restrictions placed on contracts.

Defining the Principle

The principle of freedom of contract has been well-recognized in academic circles for some time, and in the civil and commercial laws of many countries. It is reflected in many different aspects of contract. A general summary of the principle follows

"Freedom of contract consists of the following five freedoms:
(a) the freedom of contracting, ie. one party is free to decide whether or not to make a contract with another party;
(b) the freedom of choosing a counterpart, ie. one party is free to decide with whom to make a contract;
(c) the freedom of deciding the contents of the contract, ie. the parties are free to decide the contents of the contract;
(d) the freedom to modify or discharge contract, ie. once a contract has been concluded, the parties are free to modify its contents as well as to discharge it by a new agreement;
(e) the freedom of form, ie. the formation of a contract does not necessarily depend on the performance of a particular form of the contract."[1]

The Principle in Practice

The above-mentioned five freedoms are concerned with the contractual actions of the parties. The fundamental point of freedom of contract, however, is the effect of contract, or the relationship between contract and contract law.

Under the principle of freedom of contract, contract legislation usually gives autonomy to the parties involved. Given that it is unnecessary and impossible to regulate all types of contracts currently in existence or which will come into existence in the future, legislation can only regulate general contractual relationships.

The law of contract does not prevent the parties, according to their own will and need, from entering into types of contracts which have not yet been regulated by the law (academically, contracts regulated by the law are referred to as *contractus re nominati*, while contracts not regulated by the law are called *contractus re innominati*). The parties may stipulate their contractual relationship either entirely under *contractus re nominati* or partly under *contractus re nominati* and *contractus re innominati*.

Under the principle of freedom of contract, when a judge hears a case any agreements between parties are applied first; the provisions of law are applied only where no agreements exist. The provisions in contract law and the presumption of will of the parties are supplementary to the expression of the parties' will.

Once concluded by the parties involved, the contract shall be binding and enforceable by law or, in other words, with legal effect, and judges should settle contractual disputes in accordance with the contract. They are not authorized to vary the parties' contract and have no power to alter or nullify it, even where the interests of the different parties are clearly imbalanced.

Academically, it is considered unnecessary for judges to consider whether terms of a contract accepted by the parties of their own accord are just or fair. According to the traditional theory of consideration in the common law, even one peppercorn given by one party to another is regarded as consideration. The court does not decide whether the consideration is sufficient. Even the phrase "I exchange my inheritance with you for a bowl of soup" is enforceable in law.[2]

> "For the 19th century judge, if freedom of contract means anything, it means that the parties are free to decide the self-estimated proper value for the promise made by themselves."[3]

Restricting Freedom of Contract

True freedom of contract can only be completely realized when the economic status of enterprises is equal and there is free competition. As enterprises have developed and, with them monopoly situations, the gap between the rich and poor has grown wider and the negative aspects of freedom of contract have begun to show themselves. Large enterprises in a monopoly position now have the power to reduce the freedom of smaller enterprises to select their counterpart in a contract and to stipulate the contents of that contract. For example, in the modern business of providing public facilities such as transport, water supply and electricity, and in insurance, standard contracts or adhesion contracts have become very popular. Effectively, consumers have little freedom of choice when entering into this type of contract.

Since monopoly situations can cause chaos in a social economy, the governments of capitalist countries have introduced legislation which allows intervention in the economy to protect fair competition and freedom of contract. In reality, they are restricting formal freedom of contract with non-freedom of contract.

In modern civil law and contract law adjustments to and restrictions on freedom of contract have become common. New concepts such as "socialization of contract", "justice of contract" and "social constraint on contracts" have appeared one by one.

Some academics have pointed out:

"Freedom of contract and justice of contract are both fundamental principles of contract law. To realize the function of contract, the two principles must support each other as well as complement each other.[4]

In today's German contract law, the principle of social constraint on contract and the principle of freedom of contract have become dependent on one another and neither should be omitted."[5]

It cannot be denied, however, in theory, that freedom of contract is still a fundamental principle of contract law.

"Freedom of contract is restricted to some extent, and the binding of contract is varied in some respects. But these restrictions and variety are mere exceptions to the general principle.[6]

The core of the law on obligation should be preservation of freedom of contract. Only under freedom of contract can civilians have the opportunity to satisfy their varying demands by a wide range of methods in a free community."[7]

China's Market Economy and the Implementation of Freedom of Contract

The Role of Contract in China

In China, studies and research on civil and commercial law have always attached great importance to general principles. Different stipulations on general principles have emerged over the years, reflecting the differing economic backgrounds, laws and politics of the time.

Under the planned economic system, academics have often regarded contract as an important tool in the implementation of the national economic plan. For a long time, the national economic plan was embodied as a general principle in civil and contract law, although its expression has varied with reform of the economic system.

The 1964 Draft Civil Law contained provisions "to strictly implement the uniform national plan". The 4th Draft Civil Law of May 1982 required that it should "follow the directive of the national economic plan". Finally, the General Rules of Civil Law promulgated in 1986 stipulate that "civil activities should respect social morality and not be allowed to damage public interest, do harm to the national economic plan, or make confusion in the social economic order."

China's path from a planned economy to a market economy can be traced through these stipulations. Some academics have connected the 1986 stipulation to the spirit of allowing greater autonomy in administration of enterprises, and have summarized it as "combining the direction of the national plan with the autonomy of the enterprises' administrators."[8]

In July 1982, the State Council published the Regulation on Changing the System of Administration of the Industrial Enterprises Owned by the Whole People. This regulation provides that:

> "The goal of changing the system of administration of the enterprises is: making the enterprises meet the requirements of the market, to become commodity-productive and administrative unities which are, under the law, with autonomy in administration, self-bearing in profit and loss, self-developing and self-restrained, as well as independent legal persons with civil rights and duties."

In addition, the Decision on Certain Issues in Establishing the Socialist Market Economic System, which was approved at the 3rd Central Committee Conference of the 14th National Congress of the CPC in November 1993, explicitly points out that enterprises "should become entities of legal person bearing civil rights and duties."

This was the first time the status of state-owned enterprises as civil subjects had been affirmed in the form of a decision by the Central Committee of the CPC. This policy and legal documents concerning further reform of the economic system are the guiding principle in the shaping of China's contractual legislation. The drafting of a uniform law on contract will play a key part in implementing this principle.

In this context, the principle of freedom of contract was, for the first time in China's civil and commercial legislation history, clearly specified by the draft law on contract.

Implementing Freedom of Contract in the Chinese System

A number of important questions on the implementation of freedom of contract remain to be answered and deserve serious consideration. For instance, under the conditions of the socialist market economy, what are the grounds for freedom of contract? How should the principle of freedom of contract be laid out in contract law?

The historical development of freedom of contract can make it difficult to reconcile with the reality of today's China. The theories and concepts of philosophy, economics, politics and law from which the principle derives often contradict the Marxist-based theories and concepts prevailing in China. Just as there are common rules of commodity economy in different communities, however, there are common rules in the contract laws of these communities. The principle of freedom of contract is one of these common rules.

The market economy focuses on market transactions, and contract is, in reality, the legal form of exchange of commodities. As Marx stated:

> "Transactions came first, then a legal system developed from the transactions ... This kind of practical relationship produced by and in the process of the exchange of commodities was subsequently given the legal form known as contract."[9]

The equality of the parties is a premise of contract and the accord of the parties, *i.e.* the parties' identical expression of their wills is a condition of contract. Contracts flourished under the free competition of capitalism, and the establishment of the principle of freedom of contract served to protect and promote the development of this capitalist economy.

The contract is also an important legal form in the socialist market economy. Under this system, the allocation of social resources is mainly carried out in the market, so the development of society is promoted by equal competition and by the recognition that the strong dominate. Equal economic competition requires appropriate legal institutions, and the contract, with its major characteristics being equality, autonomy and freedom, offers a highly suitable form.

The principle of freedom of contract is a legal principle which protects equal competition. If enterprises are expected to be autonomous in administration, self-bearing in profit and loss, self-developing and self-restrained, then they should also be allowed to decide independently their market activities. This is reflected in legal form as freedom of contract. As China evolves from a planned economy to a market economy, it is therefore necessary to establish clearly the principle of freedom of contract.

Restricting Freedom of Contract in China

While it is essential to establish the principle of freedom of contract, its implications should also be carefully limited so that it is in accordance with China's economic laws and legal regulations. The focus should be on promoting its positive factors and restricting or prohibiting the negative.

The implementation of equal competition in China will have the effect of widening the gap between the rich and the poor and may also lead to the development of monopolies. In this situation, it is possible that those in a position of power could take advantage of formal freedom of contract to damage the interests of others.

As a result, it is necessary to restrict freedom of contract to a certain extent with anti-trust (anti-monopoly) legislation, and legislation which protects against unfair competition and preserves the rights of consumers. In this way, true freedom of contract will need to be restricted somewhat to ensure that the benefits of freedom of contract are available to a wider cross-section of society.

The socialist market economy is based on the public ownership system. As a result, although the autonomy of enterprises should be promoted, macroscopic control over the economy should also be strengthened. To restrict freedom of contract to the proper extent, legislation on energy, materials, prices, finance, foreign exchange and foreign trade is required, as is legislation in the areas of public services such as transportation, water supply, electricity and medical care. In these fields, the needs of customers and consumers must be protected.

Given that state owned enterprises currently dominate the national economy, the state should administer these types of enterprises, and their freedom of contract should be restricted.

The fundamental principles of contract law are not the only principles to be considered. Under western civil and commercial law where a modern market economy is operating, faith and credit as well as public order and good customs have traditionally occupied an important position. In China's socialist market economy, the principles of civil and commercial law include equality, fairness and justice, and faith and credit, among others. While these principles will work well with the principle of freedom of contract, they will also serve to restrict it to a certain degree.

Issues Relating to Freedom and Restriction of Contract in China's Uniform Contract Law

The establishment of the principle of freedom of contract and restrictions to it should be embodied not only in contract law but also in administrative and economic law. This paper will focus only on contract law.

General Stipulations on the Principle of Freedom of Contract and its Appropriate Restrictions

The law of contract should contain definite general stipulations on the principle of freedom of contract and its restrictions. In traditional civil and contract law, although the principle of freedom of contract is generally recognized as a fundamental principle, there are no such definite general stipulations. Instead, the spirit of the principle underlies the clauses throughout. Accordingly, there is no definite general stipulations on restrictions in the relevant statutes.

Taking into account the experiences of other countries and combining them with China's specific needs, the principle of freedom of contract and its restrictions should be explicitly stipulated in the general provisions of the law of contract. This will assist the contracting parties and judicial personnel in understanding the reality and characteristics of the law on contract and in implementing it properly.

In China, the General Rules of Civil Law form the basis for civil and commercial law, and their general principles are equally applicable to the law on contract. As it is impossible to promulgate a civil code in the near future and there are no current plans to amend the General Rules of Civil Law, these general principles should be considered together with those in the law on contract to provide a comprehensive picture.

Stipulations on *Contractus re Innominati*

The law on contract should contain appropriate stipulations on the effect of *contractus re innominati*. Contemporary contract law can only stipulate those contractual relationships that often appear and have some general significance. As a general rule, contracts with titles and content differing from the provisions of contract law are still effective and enforceable provided they are not contrary to the law.

In practice, this is also the case in China, but there is no such provision in the law currently in force, although it is necessary for the correct implementation of contract law. In the theory of traditional civil and commercial law:

> "Law of obligation, in accordance with the principle of freedom of contract, allows the parties to create any contractual obligation with any content provided it is not contrary to public order and good customs."[10]

There is no clear legal stipulation to this effect, however, and it is usually reflected indirectly by the theory that property rights must be specified by law. For instance, article 175 of the Civil Code of Japan provides:

> "Property right (on the basis of the theory that property right must be specified by law) cannot be created except in accordance with this law or other statutes."

This statement indirectly implies that contractual obligation may be created by the parties on the basis of freedom of contract.

Given the experience of other countries in this area and the reality of current Chinese legislation, the uniform contract law should explicitly stipulate that contracts with title and content differing from the provisions of the present law are still effective and enforceable provided they are not contrary to mandatory legal provisions.

Stipulations on Form and Effect of Contract

The law of contract should contain explicit stipulations regarding the form and effect of contract. These stipulations will also relate to freedom of contract and its restrictions. In China, the Law of Economic Contract provides that "The economic contract shall be in written form, except when it is executed immediately."

There is, however, no stipulation on the effect of contract which is not in accordance with this provision. This leads to a wide range of different interpretations.

Given that a modern market economy depends on speed of transactions and efficiency, the uniform contract law should change the strict requirements for form of contract and confirm the freedom of form of contract. In order to ensure safe transactions and economic stability, however, it is necessary to provide certain forms of contract in some fields. The types of contracts which should be in legal forms should be laid out in detail in the law of contract so they can be easily applied. At the same time, with reference to both domestic and foreign experience, those contracts which are not in accordance with the legal forms but are otherwise sound and effective should be confirmed enforceable provided that one party has performed all (or the major) contractual obligations on his/her part, and demands such a confirmation.

Stipulations on the Time of Formation and Coming into Effect of Contract

The law on contract should also contain explicit stipulations on the time of formation and the time of coming into effect of contract. These are two different concepts with different legal significance and consequences.

Traditional contract law has no stipulation on conditions necessary for formation of contract or coming into effect of contract, but it does distinguish between the two. To date, there has been little comprehensive discussion on this topic, but recently some Chinese civil law academics have started to pay greater attention to the subject.[11]

Problems have resulted from the fact that there is no practical distinction made between the two times in China. Embodying stipulations regarding the time of formation and of coming into effect of contract in contract law will demonstrate the importance of properly ascertaining the formation, effect and legal consequence of a contractual relationship, as well as the regional jurisdictions for contractual cases.

> "Whether a juristic act has been formed is a question of ascertaining fact; it focuses on whether the juristic act has been in existence."[12]

According to general theory on contract law, a contract is formed when the parties agree on the major terms and conditions of the contract. The time of formation of contract is thus when the acceptance goes into effect. For *contractus re*, however, the time of formation is when the subject matter of the contract is delivered from one party to the other.

Formation of contract is a consequence of identical expression of the parties' will on the method of effecting of contract. If the parties agree to enter into a contract in a specified form (the agreed form), then an identical expression can only be proved by the specified form. The law of contract should, therefore, stipulate that, although a form of contract has been specified by the parties, the time of formation of contract is only when the specified form has actually been realized.

Article 161 of the Civil Code of Russia specifies:

> "While certain form is agreed on by the parties, the contract shall be deemed concluded at the time when the agreed form is realized, even though this kind of contract is not necessary in this form under the law."

In general, the time of formation is also the time of coming into effect of the contract if it is not contrary to any mandatory provision and no special requirement exists under the law. If special requirements do exist under the law, the contract comes into effect when these requirements have been satisfied. For example, if a contract is subject to approval of the authority, the time of coming into effect of the contract is when such approval is obtained.

Stipulations on Modification and Discharge of Contract by Agreement

The law of contract should contain explicit stipulations on modification and discharge of contract by agreement. No such stipulation is contained in traditional contract law.

Theoretically, discharge of contract is regarded as "making another contract for the purpose of discharging the previous contract, *i.e.* discharging the previous contract by a later one", and "according to the principle of freedom of contract, the formation of this kind of contract should not be prohibited under the law".[13]

Article 29, Chapter 1, Part III of the United Nations Convention on Contracts for the International Sale of Goods provides that "A contract may be modified or terminated by the mere agreement of the parties."

Contract law in China allows the parties to modify or discharge their contract through negotiation. This is consistent with the principle of freedom of contract and with the original provisions in the Law of Economic Contract and is helpful for understanding and implementing the law of contract.

The method of modifying or discharging contract through the agreement of the parties is through a later contract. The procedures for and the effect of such modification and discharge should be explicitly stipulated, and the relevant stipulations on formation of contract should be applied unless otherwise regulated under the law.

In addition, the law should stipulate that in a case where the interests of one party are damaged by the modification or discharge, the other party shall have an obligation to make compensation unless the law or the parties' agreement negates such obligation. This stipulation combines both the spirit of freedom of contract and the spirit of restriction on contract.

If one or both parties reserves in the contract the right to discharge the contract, they may do so once the conditions under which the reserved right comes into play are met. This is, in fact, a conditional juristic act and does not need to be stipulated in the law on contract.

Stipulations on the Effect of Contract of Adhesion

A contract of adhesion or adhesion contract is one in which all terms and conditions are determined by one party, with the other having only the choice to agree or not. The contract can only be entered into by the other party's agreement on all the terms and conditions as the result of the party's urgent needs.

The terms and conditions of adhesion contracts are usually determined by enterprises with great economic strength or public enterprises which deal with many counterparts. It is not convenient for these enterprises to negotiate individual terms and conditions for each contract, having standard terms and conditions makes transactions easier.

In reality, a contract of adhesion is a contractual relationship, not an administrative relationship, despite the ways in which it differs from other types of contract. As a result, the general provisions of contract law also apply to adhesion contracts.

Since the party determining the contract has the power to implement unfair terms and conditions, it is necessary to put restrictions on the terms and conditions allowable as well as on the effect of the contract. This is done largely through special statutes.

In addition, in order to protect the parties adhering to the contract, it is also necessary to provide certain general stipulations on this kind of contract in the uniform contract law. In principle, these stipulations would include: that the terms and conditions of the contract should be clearly presented in a manner which can be understood by the adhering party; and that where different interpretations of articles of contracts of adhesion occur, the interpretation against the drafter of the contract should be adopted.

Stipulations on Effect of Contracts Concluded by Fraud or Coercion

The Law of Economic Contract of China provides that contracts concluded by fraud or coercion are null and void. This stipulation is consistent with the corresponding provisions in The General Rules of Civil Law and is similar to the corresponding rule of the Civil Code of Russia. Traditional civil law and contract law, on the other hand, regard contracts concluded with fraud or coercion as avoidable instead of null and void. Comparatively speaking, the traditional rule is more reasonable.

While fraud and coercion violate the principle of freedom of contract, it is unnecessary for contracts concluded by fraud or coercion to be declared null and void under the law. In these cases, it is sufficient to protect the parties who have been defrauded or coerced by declaring the contract avoidable. Parties can then modify their contract through negotiation or, once the contract has been executed, enter into another contract which includes appropriate compensation for the injured party. Alternatively, the injured party may accept the effect of the fraud or coercion of their own accord.

The parties should have the legal right to deal with one another freely and flexibly, and as a result, it is inappropriate for the law to declare automatically the contract null and void.

Stipulations on Liquidated Damages and Deposits

There has been intense discussion regarding the nature of liquidated damages and deposit money and how they should be stipulated in Chinese law. Stipulations on liquidated damages, earnest money and damages and the relationships between them should also be in accordance with the spirit of freedom of contract with appropriate restrictions. The parties should have a right to decide, by agreement, the forms and amount of liquidated damages and deposits. In terms of the law, it is sufficient to provide directive and supplementary stipulations on these subjects. If the agreement of the parties on liquidated damages and deposits is obviously unfair, it should be handled in the same way an obvious civil act is handled.

It is often difficult to calculate damages, particularly those involving one party's prospective interest. The law of contract should stipulate that liquidated damages are regarded as compensatory damages unless otherwise agreed by the parties. At the same time, the law should stipulate that if the liquidated damages are much more or much less than the actual damage resulting from a breach of contract, either party can ask the court or arbitration tribunal to adjust the amount, or the court may do so of its own accord.

The provisions concerning the amount and proportion of liquidated damages in the By-Law of Economic Contract should not be incorporated into the new law. Allowing the parties to decide liquidated damages for themselves is both flexible and practical and is consistent with the principle of freedom of contract.

It is also unnecessary to stipulate the nature of deposits. The traditional stipulation on the result of a breach of contract should be incorporated. This provides for the non-refund of the deposit in an ordinary case or double refund of the deposit where the contract is breached by the party who received the deposit.

As there have been cases where deposits are confused with payment in advance and others where very large sums are involved, the law of contract should stipulate that, when calculating compensatory damages in a case where the deposit has been agreed on by the parties, the amount of the deposit should be deducted from the compensatory damages unless otherwise agreed by the parties.

In addition, the parties' agreement regarding the deposit should be supported even if the amount exceeds that of the compensatory damages. If the amount of the deposit exceeds the damages by too much, then either party can ask the court or arbitration tribunal to reduce the amount to a proper level.

Notes

[1] Wang Zhe Jian, *A Series of Books on Practice on Civil Law*, Vol.3, pp.69–70.
[2] Robert Kork and Thomas Yoran, *Law and Economics*, pp.296–298.
[3] P.S. Adia, *An Introduction to Contract Law*, p.85.
[4] Wang Zhe Jian, *op. cit.* p.71.
[5] Shao Jian Dong, "The Principle of Freedom of Contract and the Principle of Social Constraint on Contract in German Contract Law" (1994) *Nanjing University Law Review* 1 at 171.
[6] Yi Tian, "Conflict and Balance Between Freedom of Contract and Social Justice — the Decline of Party Autonomy in French Contract Law" in *A Selection of Articles on Civil and Commercial Law* (1994), Vol. 2, p.286.
[7] Lang Hui Xing, "On the Amendments to the Law on Obligation of the German Civil Code" in *A Study of Theories, Cases and Legislation in Civil Law* (1993), p.306.
[8] Wang Zuo Tang, *A Textbook of Civil Law*, p.206.
[9] *Collected Works of Marx and Engels*, Vol. 19, p.423.
[10] Shi Shang Kuan, *On Real Right*, p.11.
[11] Wang Jia Fu (Chief Editor), *Obligatory Rights of Civil Law* (1993), Chapters 9–10; Don An Sheng, *On Civil Juristic Acts* (1994), Chapter 4.
[12] *ibid.* pp.184–185.
[13] Zheng Yu Buo, *General Theories on Obligatory Rights in Civil Law*, p.349.

THE RELATIONSHIP BETWEEN COMMERCIAL BANKING LAW AND THE REGULATIONS OF THE PRC ON MANAGEMENT OF FOREIGN FUNDED FINANCIAL INSTITUTIONS

Professor Wu Zhipan

Law Department
Peking University

Professor Wu Zhipan, *LL.B., Ph.D., Master of Law (Peking University), is a visiting scholar at Harvard Law School. He is a Professor of Law, director of the Financial Law Institute and vice-dean of the law department of Peking University. He has published* Commercial Bank Law, Hong Kong Commercial Banks and Law, *and many articles.*

There are 123 branches of foreign banks and financial institutions that have obtained business licences in China, as have 393 foreign representative offices of foreign financial institutions in China. The number of the foreign banks that have branches in China with business licences exceeds that of our domestic banks.

Foreign banks, having entered China's financial market, have excelled in the foreign exchange markets by taking up a subsidiary part of the business, thus bringing much pressure on the domestic banks. They also competed with domestic banks for well educated personnel in the field. Why have foreign bank branches developed so quickly in China while domestic banks have to grow painfully? Let us look at the law regarding control and administratation of financial bodies: we can see that domestic banks and foreign banks have been facing two different legal environments. In fact, the difference in legal environment accounts for the divergence in the development of the two kinds of banks.

Origin and Development of the Legal Environment for Foreign Banks

Foreign bank branches did not begin business in China until 1982. Before that time, the setting for the domestic banks was a "whole people ownership" system, they were operated under a "state planned economy", This system and mode of management could hardly accommodate the business development of foreign banks, therefore, when foreign bank branches began to enter China's market, the Chinese Government established a new system specially for the control and administratation of foreign banks. From then on, two distinct administrative systems for financial institutes have existed. The foreign branch management system, which gradually evolved from 1949, can be divided into five periods:

Stage 1 (1949–1982)

After the establishment of the new Chinese Government in 1949, foreign banks and their branches left China one after another; but one branch of the Hong Kong and Shanghai Bank left its gate keepers to care for old building along the Yangzi river in Shanghai. For 30 years no other foreign banks or their branches opened in China. It was not until 1979 that a Japanese long term credit bank set up its first representative office in Beijing. Then Nanyang Commercial Bank opened a Shenzhen branch in 1982 as the first overseas branch bank of the PRC.

During this period, the Chinese Government did not issue any rules or regulations to administrate foreign branches or representative offices. Foreign financial institutions were to observe policies and rules laid down by the People's Bank of China.

Stage 2 (1982–1990)

During this period, foreign branches entered the Chinese financial market in increasing numbers. In order to meet the new situation, the People's Bank of China issued the Administration Procedure of Establishing Representative Offices by Overseas Chinese and Foreign-Invested Financial Institutes. On April 2, 1985, the State Council promulgated the Regulation on Foreign-Invested Bank and Joint Venture Bank in Special Economic Zone in the People's Republic of China (the Regulation on Foreign-Invested Bank and Joint Venture Bank in Special Economic Zone).

The requirements under the Regulation were rather lenient. The registered capital required of a foreign invested bank or a joint venture

187

bank in a Special Economic Zone is only an amount in foreign currency no less than the equivalent of RMB80 million or approximately US$9.4 million, which is almost the same required by U.S. laws. Furthermore, according to this Regulation, a foreign bank investor could establish a capital is not less than 50 per cent of its registered capital, equivalent to RMB40 million, or US$4.7 million.

The current mandatory amounts in this respect is 3.75 times higher than what is prescribed in the 1985 Regulation. It is still low, however, when compared to that for Chinese domestic banks. The minimum registered capital required of domestic banks now is 12.5 times higher than what is required of foreign banks in 1985.

Stage 3 (1990–1992)

Shanghai Pudong special economic zone was opened to outside institutions in 1990. On September 8 that year, after the examination and approval by the State Council, the People's Bank of China issued The Regulations of Foreign Financial Institutions and Sino-Foreign Joint Venture Financial Institute in Shanghai (the "Shanghai regulation").

The Shanghai Regulation was much stricter than the 1985 Regulation. The minimum registered capital required for foreign-invested banks must be no less than an amount in foreign currency equivalent to RMB200 million.

The opening up of Shanghai meant that the Hong Kong and Shanghai Bank, East Asia Bank, Standard Chartered Bank and Overseas Chinese Bank were permitted to re-open for business in Shanghai.

Stage 4 (1992–1994)

In the spring of 1992, Deng Xiaoping visited various parts of the Guangdong Province in south China, most significantly the Shenzhen special economic zone. He then made his now famous speech in Shenzhen commending the achievements that resulted from carrying out the policies that both reformed the local economic system and opened South China to the world. Deng's speech greatly encouraged the national economic reforms and intentionally accelerated the opening of the domestic market. In the same year, under the approval of the State Council, China opened another seven big coastal cities, *i.e.* Dalian, Tianjin, Qingdiao, Nanjing, Ningpo, Fuzhou and Guangzhou, adding to the first six Special Economic Zones (Shenzhen, Xiamen, Shantou, Zhuhai, Hainan and Shanghai). In 1992, the first foreign insurance company, an American Company, began its operation in Shanghai.

Stage 5 (1994–current)

On the January 7, 1994, the State Council promulgated the Administrative Regulations of foreign financial institutions of PRC. This Regulations came into effect on April 1 of the same year, abolished both the Regulations of 1985 and the Shanghai Regulations of 1990, and provided for new and uniform standards for the approved establishment of foreign-invested banks. Before the new Regulation came into effect, the mandatory registered capital for foreign banks in Shanghai was higher than those in other cities. The existence of a dual-standard in the same country could only be transitional. The birth of the new Regulation had ratified the proposal.

The Regulations of Foreign Financial Institutions of PRC cover five different kinds of foreign financial institutions:

(a) foreign banks registered in China. At present, there are four banks of such kind;
(b) Branches of foreign banks, of which there are 123,
(c) Sino-Foreign joint venture banks organized by a foreign bank and Chinese bank; there are six;
(d) Foreign financial companies in China, also called foreign-invested financial companies;
(e) Sino-foreign joint venture financial company organized by a foreign financial company and Chinese financial company.

In 1995, the Chinese government allowed foreign banks to establish their branches or institutions in another 10 big cities, including Beijing. In August of the same year, five foreign branches of foreign banks were permitted to operate in Beijing. On October 10, 1995, the Commercial Banking Law of PRC (the Banking Law) was adopted in the 13th Session Standing Committee of the Eighth Session of the National Congress, and came into effect on July 1, 1995.

Now foreign financial institutes are allowed to set up their representative offices in more than 20 cities in China but most of them gathered in the cities of Beijing, Shanghai, Guangzhou, Shenzheng and Dalian. More than half of them are in Beijing.

Special Characteristics of the Legal Environment for Foreign Banks

China still maintains two different systems in the control and administration of the two kinds of banks in China, that is the applicable law for domestic banks is the Banking Law, whereas the applicable law for foreign banks is the Regulation of Foreign-Invested Financial Institute, supplemented by the Banking Law.

The Banking Law was promulgated by the Standing Committee of the National Congress, but the Regulation of Foreign-Invested Financial Institute was passed by the State Council as just a kind of administrative policy for foreign banks. The Banking Law is supplemental in that, for matters not stipulated in the Regulations, foreign banks must apply the relevant sections in the Banking Law.

Special Requirements for Foreign Financial Institutes

Different requirements are set down for different kinds of application. The requirements for establishing a foreign-invested bank, a Sino-Joint Venture bank or a branch of a foreign bank are quite different from the requirements for establishing domestic banks in China. For the application of a domestic bank to be successful, the registered capital must be no less than RMB1 billion (Banking Law, article 13). Whereas, to establish a foreign bank or sino-foreign joint venture bank, the registered capital must be no less than convertible foreign currency equivalent to RMB300 million (Regulation of Foreign-Invested Financial Institute, article 5). The head office of the foreign bank shall allocate to the branch in China no less than convertible foreign currency equivalent to RMB100 million as working capital.

Now, there are four foreign solely invested banks, six Sino-foreign joint venture banks and 113 foreign bank branches in the mainland. To compare the two minimum capitals: the registered capital of domestic banks is three times higher than that of foreign banks. The distinction is based on the several grounds.

First, domestic applicants to establish a bank in China need not be a financial institute or a bank, need not have experience in bank operations and are not subjected to any mandatory capital limit. To establish a foreign solely invested bank or a head office of a Sino-foreign joint venture bank, the foreign or overseas applicant as well as its Chinese counterpart must be a financial institute. The foreign applicant must come from a country or area with a well-established supervision system; its total assets in the year before it submits its application must be no less than US$10 billion and it must already have a representative office in China. To set up a branch of a foreign bank, the total assets of the applicant's head office overseas in the year before the submission of the application should be no less than US$20 billion and the applicant should have maintained a representative office in China for at least two years. In the light of these stipulations, foreign applicants have to meet more stringent requirements than domestic applicants, although the mandatory minimum registered capital for foreign invested banks is lower than that imposed on domestic banks.

Secondly, China, pursuant to her open door policy, endeavours to attract more foreign or overseas investors, including foreign bankers, to do business in China. She is particularly keen on encouraging large foreign or overseas banks to set up branches in China. The Chinese government does not directly set any limit on the number of branches a foreign investor is allowed to establish. Under these circumstances, China, compared to Hong Kong, has created a more favourable environment for banking investments, although the latter is known to be the financial centre of Asia. Under Hong Kong law, foreign applicants are required to have total assets amounting to not less than US$20 billion and they are not allow to set up more than one branch in the territory because of the high density of banks there.

Thirdly, compared to other countries and regions, the amount of registered capital required of domestic banks under Chinese commercial banking law may be the highest in the world: ¥1 billion, equivalent to about RMB100 million, as registered capital is required according to Japanese commercial banking law, HK$150 million, RMB150 million approximately, as registered capital according to the Hong Kong Banking Ordinance, US$5 million (RMB42,500,000) according to American banking law, S$6 million under Singapore banking law, £5 million in the United Kingdom and DM5 in Germany, all lower than that stipulated by Chinese law. The minimum registered capital for joint-venture banks is the convertible foreign exchange equivalent RMB3 billion as stipulated by in China law is the highest in the world. The working capital for foreign branches is the convertible foreign exchange equivalent of RMB1 billion, which is also comparatively high.

In addition, for a domestic applicant to pass the capital inspection procedure, it is required that the registered capital be paid up at one go, but this does not apply to foreign banks. If the paid-up capital of a foreign bank is lower than its registered capital, it is required to allocate 25 per cent of the profit after tax of that bank every year to make up for the deficiency until the paid-up capital plus the reserve fund is equal to the statutory minimum registered capital.

Special Licence Procedures

The procedures for establishing a foreign-invested bank or a Sino-foreign joint venture bank are open to the public in China, whereas there are no publicly available details of the procedures for establishing a domestic commercial bank. For instance, the duration, of the licence a domestic commercial bank is not precisely specified in any regulations. This is one clear instance in which the procedures of establishing a foreign-invested bank in China are more transparent than that of domestic commercial bank.

The procedures for establishing a foreign-invested bank and Sino-foreign joint venture bank are as follows: the People's Bank of China will issue an formal application form to the foreign applicant after the preliminary examination of the relevant application materials. If a foreign applicant does not receive the formal application form within 90 days from the date of submission of his application materials, it means the central bank does not accept the application (Regulation on Foreign Financial Institute, article 13). The foreign applicant should fill in the formal form within 60 days from the date he receives it and send it back to the central bank, together with the other supporting documents (Regulation on Foreign Financial Institute, article 14). Within 30 days from the date the foreign applicant receives a licence from the central bank, he should raise funds or working capital and transfer them into China to go through verification procedure and taxation registration, and then get the Licence for Operating Foreign Exchange Business from the State Administration of Foreign Exchange Control.

Special Scope of Business

The business scope of foreign-invested banks, branches of foreign banks and Sino-foreign joint venture banks is:

(a) foreign exchange deposits;
(b) foreign exchange loans;
(c) foreign exchange bill discounts;
(d) foreign exchange investment upon approval;
(e) foreign exchange remittances;
(f) foreign exchange guarantees;
(g) import and export settlement;
(h) foreign exchange transactions for themselves or for other;
(i) conversion of foreign currencies and foreign exchange inducements;
(j) payment for foreign exchange credit cards;
(k) safe-keeping;
(l) credit rating and consultation; and
(m) standard currency business and other approved foreign exchange activities.

Domestic commercial banks may engage in the following business:

(a) receiving money deposits from the public;
(b) extending short, medium and long-term loans;

(c) providing domestic and international settlement services;
(d) discounting bills;
(e) issuing financial bonds;
(f) acting as an agent for issuing, cashing and underwriting government bonds;
(g) dealing in government bonds;
(h) inter-bank call-money business;
(i) dealing or acting as an agent in the foreign exchange transactions;
(j) providing L/C service and guarantee;
(k) acting as agent in collection and payment and insurance business;
(l) providing safe deposit box services; and
(m) other businesses approved by the central bank.

Why are foreign-invested banks not permitted to undertake RMB operations in China? An important official of the People's Bank of China gave three reasons at a press conference in 1994:

(a) since the financial system reforms are ongoing in China, the administrative system for financial markets in the mainland and the pertinent regulations and laws are not well-developed. Many elements have yet to be improved. At present, it is not appropriate for foreign-invested banks and Sino-foreign joint venture banks to join in the RMB market.
(b) State-owned commercial banks bear responsibility for favourable loans carrying high risk with low or no profit, while foreign-invested banks and Sino-foreign joint venture banks have no such responsibilities.
(c) The taxation rate differs among domestic banks and foreign-invested banks or sino-foreign joint venture banks. The rate for domestic banks is 55 per cent while the rate for foreign-invested banks and sino-foreign joint venture banks is 33 per cent. The cost of their respective business varies accordingly.

Today, the financial situation in China has been greatly changed. The income tax rate for both domestic enterprises and sino-foreign joint venture banks is now 33 per cent, that is the taxation margin between the domestic bank and foreign bank has been eliminated. Three state owned long term loan banks, namely the Import and Export Loan Bank of China, the State Development Bank and the Agriculture Development Bank of China, were established to operate the business of favourable loans, known as the state-policy loan business, so that purely commercial banks can specialize in commercial business. Now only solely state-owned commercial banks bear the responsibility to loan to state projects designated by the State Council. Other commercial banks that are fully state-owned, however, may develop their business independently in accordance with the need of the market, without the responsibility to loan to the above mentioned projects. Against this backdrop, therefore, whether China should open its RMB business market has become the point on which foreign banks and sino-invested joint venture banks focus. The central bank has not given any further indication on the question.

Special Rules for Business Control

Capital Adequate Ratio

The domestic banking law stipulates that domestic banks shall reserve their capital adequate ratio at no less than 8 per cent (Commercial Banking Law, article 39), however, foreign banks, Sino-foreign joint venture banks shall reserve 5 per cent adequate ratio. In other words, the Chinese require that foreign banks' total assets shall not exceed 20 times the aggregate amount of their paid-up capital and their reserve funds. The mandatory capital adequate ratio imposed on foreign banks is, therefore, 3 per cent lower than that imposed on domestic banks.

In my opinion, the two key reasons for the above mentioned 3 per cent disparity are: firstly, domestic banks that came into existence before July 1, 1995 are not obliged to observe the stipulation on capital adequate ratio of 8 per cent as in the now banking law. They are still waiting for the State Council to legislate on the date on which the 8 per cent rule shall be applicable to them; secondly, the domestic banks, especially the five biggest state owned banks are now keeping their capital adequate ratio at about 6 per cent. China would not, therefore, ask the foreign banks or their branches to maintain their capital at a level which is too high.

Deposit Reserve Requirement

All the foreign-invested banks and Sino-foreign joint venture banks on the mainland must maintain deposit reserves for all their deposits and savings accounts, except deposits in either domestic and overseas inter-bank market. The deposits reserve ratio for foreign banks is 5 per cent of all deposits and savings shorter than three months and 3 per cent of all the deposits and savings longer than three months.

The domestic banks implemented the deposit reserve system in 1983 when the People's Bank of China transferred its functions to the non-commercial central bank, and in 1994, the deposit reserve system was established in all banks in the mainland. Also in 1994, the central bank required different reserve ratios for different deposits: a reserve ratio for enterprise deposit of 20 per cent, individual savings of 40 per cent, and agriculture deposits of 20 per cent. The central bank controls 50 per cent of loan resources from all type of banks nationwide and the reserve ratio was very high taking into consideration the economic and financial situation in China at that time.

In 1985, China adjusted its deposit reserve policy. The varying deposit ratios were unified at 10 per cent. The "provisional" Regulations on Bank Management of PRC adopted in 1986 set the deposit reserve ratio at 13 per cent. The deposit reserve ratio for all types of deposits for city credit organizations was 10 per cent to 20 per cent. After 1989, the deposit reserve ratio was adjusted to 5 per cent to 7 per cent, which is the same as the ratio for foreign-invested bank and Sino-foreign joint venture banks.

The function of the deposit reserve ratio is mainly to enable the central bank to control the total supply of currency and credit and to strengthen the central bank's capacity to adjust cash circulation as well. Since China has not experienced any runs-on-the-back from 1949 to 1995, the Chinese people are not familiar with the consequences of banking bankruptcy or insolvency. In China, the benefit of deposit reserves in protecting payments by commercial banks has yet to be demonstrated, consequently, the deposits reserve ratio set by the authority is not as high as that of overseas banks.

Investment Limitation

According to Chinese law, the total capital of foreign-invested banks or Sino-foreign joint venture banks shall not exceed 30 per cent of the sum of paid-up capital plus its reserve funds. The term "investment" includes: bonds issued by both China and foreign countries; stocks and bonds issued by Chinese financial institutes; and bonds issued by non-financial institutes in China (Detailed Rules on of Foreign Financial Institutes, article 14). Except for in the circumstances mentioned above, foreign banks are not allowed to invest in other areas.

China's regulations prohibit foreign banks and Sino-foreign joint venture banks from investing real property not used by themselves and also prohibit investment in the field of stock and trust. Domestic commercial banks may invest in securities issued by governments. The interpretation of "government", however, is not restricted to the government of China, so "government" includes foreign governments as well. Obviously, when foreign-invested banks buy the bonds overseas they should get the permission from Chinese government.

Domestic banks are not allowed to invest in non-banking financial institutes or other enterprises. Is the same restriction also applicable to foreign-invested banks and Sino-foreign joint venture banks? Since the Regulations on Foreign-Invested Financial Institutes does not stipulate precisely, according to the Commercial Banking Law domestic banks should not invest in non-banking financial institutions. The term "non-banking financial institute" includes municipal credit organizations, agriculture credit organizations, trust investment companies, financial leasing companies and enterprises, financial companies, etc. Chinese law does not prohibit domestic bank investment in overseas business. Domestic banks are allowed to invest in other banks in China but owning more than a 10 per cent share requires approval from the People's Bank of China.

Restriction of Fixed Assets Ratio

The law of China stipulates that fix assets of foreign banks and Sino-foreign joint venture banks shall not exceed 40 per cent of the sum of paid-up capital plus deposits plus reserve. Here, "fixed assets" include both real property used by the investor and the real property not used by investor.

Although domestic banks may not invest in the real property not used by the investor, there is no restriction on the ratio of the value of the property to the total capital and deposit reserves. The ratio of fixed assets is indirectly controlled via the ratio of floating assets.

Limitations on Working Capital of Foreign Branches

According to Article 24 of the Regulation of the PRC on the Management of Foreign-Funded Financial Institutions, 30 per cent of the working capital of a foreign branch shall be in the form of interest-bearing assets designated by the central bank. The concept of a bank designated by the central bank includes any provincial branch in the same place where the foreign branch is located.

Domestic branches investments are not limited to interest-bearing assets designated by the central bank. The total working capital of branches must not, however, exceed 60 per cent of the registered capital of their head office.

Limitation of Liquid Assets

Legal requirements applicable to the liquid assets of foreign banks and Sino-foreign joint venture banks are similar to domestic banks' ratio of liquid assets to liquid liabilities which shall not be less than 25 per cent (Banking Law, article 39). The same ratio applies to foreign bank branches.

Although the ratio is similar for both domestic and foreign banks, the items constituting liquid assets are different for domestic and foreign banks. Domestic banks' liquid assets include all assets that can be cashed within one month, such as cash in accounts, deposits in the People's Bank of China, deposits in inter-bank account, Treasury Bonds, inter-bank loans due within one month, loans due within one month, bills accepted by banks becoming due within one month, and other securities approved by the central bank.

The liquid assets of foreign-invested banks, foreign branches, and Sino-foreign joint venture banks include cash, gold, deposits in the central bank, deposits of inter-bank accounts, and borrowed money and state bonds due within three months. Comparing the concept of "liquid assets" applicable to domestic banks and foreign banks, it is obvious that foreign banks' liquid assets are more flexible than those of domestic banks.

Limitations on Loans to Related Companies

The Regulations provide that foreign bank loans to one company and its related companies shall not exceed 30 per cent of the sum of the banks' paid-up capital plus its reserve. The term "related company" means: firstly, a company that holds more than 10 per cent shares in another company's registered capital; and secondly, each of two companies of which more than 20 per cent shares were held by the same shareholder.

Unlike foreign banks, domestic banks do not face precise limitations on loans to related companies. Article 39 of the Commercial Banking Law stipulates that sole loans to any one borrower shall not exceed 10 per cent of the registered capital of the bank. Although the regulations in China have given a precise definition of the term "related company", the same is not true of the term "the same borrower". In Schedule A of the Notice to the Supervision of Assets Debts Ratio on Commercial Bank (the Supervision Norm), "the same client" is clearly defined as any individual or any legal person. "Outstanding loans" to the same client shall not exceed 15 per cent of the banks' outstanding capital. Clearly, "the same client", "the same borrower" and "the related company" are three different legal concepts.

Article 39 of The Commercial Banking Law stipulates that "the ratio of loans to one borrower to the capital of the bank shall not exceed ten per cent" and Article 40 stipulates that banks shall not extend unsecured loans to related persons. "Related persons" means, first, the members of the board of directors, members of the board of supervisors, managerial personnel and staff of the credit business department of a commercial bank, and their close relatives; second, companies, enterprises or other economic organizations in which the aforesaid persons have made investments or assumed senior managerial positions.

In the rules of inspection of assets and liabilities ratio, "a client" is defined as an individual or a company.

It is clear that "related persons" is different from "a borrower" or "a client", and "a borrower" is different from "a client".

Limits to the Proportion of Deposits in Domestic Markets

Article 30 of the Regulations stipulates that the total amount of deposits from within the territory of China by a foreign financial institution shall not exceed 40 per cent of the total assets of the institution concerned. Domestic banks are not subject to the same limitation. In my view, this kind of limitation to some extent embodies market protectionism. Because a bank that takes deposits from the public must maintain the proper ratio of deposit reserves to protect the legitimate rights and interests of depositors, the limitation as the proportion of deposits to total assets of foreign banks is a double limitation based on the deposit reserve and working capital system. Weighing against this argument, however, is the fact that China's purpose in opening its domestic market to foreigners is to attract foreign capital to boost Chinese economic development. The limitations on foreign banks' capacity to take deposits from China's territory serves the same purpose.

The Commercial Banking Law Applied to Foreign Banks

Background of the Commercial Banking Law

The Commercial Banking Law was adopted by a 94.5 per cent vote at the 13th Session of the Standing Committee of the Eighth National People's Congress on May 10, 1995 and the law came into effect on July 1, 1995.

The Commercial Banking Law controls all banking business in China. Nonetheless, foreign banks and foreign branches are not covered primarily by the Commercial Banking Law, generally speaking, because the Regulations on the Management of Foreign-Fund Financial Institutions take precedence over the Commercial Banking Law. Only in matters on which the Regulations are silent and where the Commercial Banking Law is explicit does the latter apply.

Before 1949, several old Chinese governments issued a total of five banking laws. Some of these laws were not widely carried out in the country, and some were implemented but quite futile. The financial hardship at that time caused difficulty in their implementation, especially when old golden paper currency was issued, inflation escalated to as high as six-digits, leading to a general rejection of the currency. The Banking Law was soon nullified.

When the Commercial Banking Law was enacted, the Chinese economy was expanding and the inflation rate reached 15 per cent. After the Commercial Banking Law came into effect, the inflation rate dropped. One of the reasons was that the Commercial Banking Law imposes very strict requirements for commercial banks, more strict than many laws overseas in many aspects.

The main characteristics of the Commercial Banking Law are strictness and transition: China has adopted many international standards governing domestic banks; and five articles in the Commercial Banking Law do not come into effect until a future time to be decided by the State Council. These transition articles include article 17 on boards of directors; article 18 on boards of supervisors; article 39 on principles for loans and liabilities; article 41 on compensation by the State Council to a commercial bank for losses that result from loans to the special projects approved by the State Council; and article 44 on separate financial activities and controls on commercial banking business with other businesses such as trust investments, stock business, and investment in real property not for own use. These articles are not applicable to foreign banks in China.

The Conditions of Senior Managers in Banks

There are no required conditions for senior managers in foreign banks under the Regulations on Foreign-Fund Financial Institutes, however, the Commercial Banking Law does impose such standards on senior managers of foreign banks in the territory of China. The conditions are as follows:

(a) Positive condition: Senior managers must have the expertise and professional experience required by their positions.
(b) Negative conditions: A senior manager must not:
    (i) have been sentenced to imprisonment or deprived of political rights on account of graft, bribery, illegal possession of property, embezzlement of public property or disruption of social or economic order;
    (ii) have served as a director or manager of a company which

went bankrupt because of mismanagement, and have personally been responsible for the bankruptcy;

(iii) have been the legal representative of a company whose business licence was revoked on account of violation of the law, and have been personally responsible therefor; or

(iv) have failed to repay a fairly large debt already due.

Those conditions, especially the negative conditions, are tailored to foreign bankers in the territory of China.

No staff or manager in banks shall engage in any of the following:

(1) taking advantage of their positions to demand or accept bribes, or accept commissions or service fees under any pretext;

(2) taking advantage of their positions to commit graft, embezzlement, or illegal possession of the funds of the bank or of banks;

(3) providing loans or guarantee to relatives or friends in violation of regulations;

(4) holding positions concurrently at other economic institutions; and

(5) other acts in violation of the law, administrative decrees and regulations and rules for business management.

Protection of Depositors

The Regulations on Foreign-Fund Financial Institutions have no provisions on protection for depositors. In this regard, the Commercial Banking Law applies to foreign bank operation. In the Commercial Banking Law, there are two areas on protection of depositors: first, banks shall guarantee the payment of the principal and interest of every deposit and shall not delay or refuse the payment thereof; second, banks shall maintain depositors' confidentiality; and with regard to savings deposits of individuals, banks have the right to reject the demand of any department or individual for investigating, freezing, withholding or transferring a savings deposit, and with regard to deposits of any organization, banks have the right to reject the demand of any other organization or individual for investigation, unless it is otherwise mandated by the law or administrative decrees and regulations. Banks have the right as well to reject the demand of any other organization or individual for freezing, withholding or transferring such a deposit, unless it is otherwise permitted by the law.

In accordance with the law enacted by the national congress, there are six state organizations with the right to investigate, freeze, withhold or transfer both saving deposits owned by individuals and a current account's deposits. These are the Public Security Bureau, Procuratorial Bureau, People's Court, Security Bureau, Custom House and Taxation Bureau. In accordance with the administrative regulations issued by the State Council, there are six other state organizations with the right to investigate any deposits of organizations. These include the Industry and Commercial Administration Bureau, Audit Bureau, Supervisory Bureau, People's Bank of China, Foreign Exchange Control Bureau and State Price Management Bureau. Provincial laws and regulations also apply to foreign-fund banks in China.

Limitation on Current Account

In the Regulations on Foreign-Fund Financial Institutions, there is no requirement of checking accounts opened by organizations. The Commercial Banking Law limits the number of checking accounts in accordance with article 48 of the Law. The Law limits an enterprise or an undertaking unit to opening only one current account with a commercial bank of its own choice for daily transfer and settlement of accounts and cash receipt and payment. It shall not open more than one checking account in the territory of China.

It is difficult to find this kind of limitation in laws or regulations overseas. To apply the limitation on current accounts to foreign banks may not be appropriate. In China, the People's Court and the State Taxation Bureau hoped that such limitation would expedite the enforcement of the courts' judgments and that it would assist the State Taxation Bureau in its collection of tax.

Because of gaps in the Chinese taxation system, some enterprises and undertaking units attempt to avoid paying income tax in full by keeping deposits in secret accounts while maintaining no balance in their public accounts. The court is unable to enforce its judgment on some empty public accounts. Companies often have substantial deposits in their secret accounts, therefore, the Law limits the number of current accounts.

Regulation of Commercial Banks' Internal Management System

In China, in order to improve the quality of loans made by Chinese banks, especially state-owned commercial banks' loans, the Commercial Banking Law stipulates some rules to guide internal operating methods of banks. The regulations on foreign financial institutions are silent in this area, so foreign banks' internal management system shall follow the same explicit rules which include:

(a) Any commercial bank in China shall conduct its loan business in accordance with the need for development of the national economy and social progress and under the guidance of state industrial policy.

(b) Any commercial bank in China shall implement a system in which the examination and the actual extending of a loan are conducted by separate departments and the examination and approval of a loan are conducted at different levels.

(c) Any commercial bank shall extend loans against security, and conduct strict examination of the repaying capability, the ownership, and value of the mortgage or pledge, and the feasibility of the realization of the mortgage or pledge.

(d) Any commercial bank shall sign a written loan agreement with the borrower before extending a loan to the borrower.

(e) Any commercial bank shall dispose of the real property or stocks on mortgage or pledge within a year from the date of obtaining such security.

(f) The staff of a commercial bank shall not disclose commercial secrets acquired during their service in the bank.

(g) A commercial bank shall fix its business hours for the convenience of its clients and make public announcement thereof, shall conduct its business during its announced business hours, and shall not suspend business or shorten its business hours at will.

(h) A commercial bank shall not receive money deposits or extend loans by raising or lowering interest rates or by other unjustifiable means in violation of regulations.

(i) A commercial bank in handling settlements such as acceptance, remittance and collection shall make timely cashing and entries pursuant to relevant provisions without detaining bills or instruments nor dishonoring them in violation of regulations. The relevant provisions for the time limit for bill acceptance and entries in accounting books should be made public.

(j) A commercial bank shall abide by the principle of equality, fairness, honesty, and good faith in doing business with its clients.

(k) A commercial bank shall abide by the relevant provisions of the law and administrative decrees and regulations in doing business and shall not impair the interests of the state to the public, shall abide by the principle of fair competition in doing its business, and shall refrain from unfair competition.

Effects of Different Legal Environments

The legal environment for foreign bank investors is special and distinct from that for Chinese investors. The difference has a positive effect on economic development in China on the one hand, yet one may find some drawbacks on the other hand.

The Positive Aspect of Foreign Bank

It is beneficial for China to attract more foreign capital to support Chinese economic construction. There are more than US$14 billion in foreign banking assets in China and about US$5.6 billion taken by foreign banks as deposits from China at the end of 1994, therefore over US$9 billion in net banking assets come from the overseas financial market.

It is important that China raise the standard of financial management. Foreign banks which enter the Chinese market are larger banks in overseas markets and they have rich experience, advanced technology, efficient management methods and comprehensive management rules, which Chinese bankers lack. The Regulations of Foreign-Fund Financial Institutions stipulate that a foreign bank shall recruit at least one Chinese citizen into its upper management level in accordance with article 33. This enables Chinese banking personnel to learn from foreign bankers.

In general Chinese banks will benefit from exposure to the international financial market. Foreign banks come to China with international financial experience and management methods which Chinese banks lack. The more foreign banks come into China, the more the Chinese financial market becomes internationalized. In many international financial centres, such as New York, Tokyo, London and Hong Kong, local markets have merged into international markets. One of the characteristics of an international financial centre is that the number of foreign banks exceeds that of local banks. In this kind of environment, it is easier for Chinese bankers to learn from foreign banks their methods of management and their experience. In the future, Shanghai, the largest city in China with an increasing number of foreign banks, may become a financial centre in Asia.

Negative Aspects

Foreign banks in China would inevitably take up some business opportunities in the domestic market.

Well-educated Chinese professionals in domestic banks, attracted by better salary, flow into foreign banks. Chinese banks, especially the state-owned banks offer low salaries, which is consistent with China's status as a developing country; foreign banks from more developed overseas economies often offer higher salary. Foreign banks are able to take advantage of salary incentive to absorb well well-educated Chinese who are experienced and knowledgeable in domestic markets and administrative systems and can help them develop quickly in China.

Not only educated personnel, but also the market shares of Chinese banks may be drained in the competition with foreign counterparts, hindering the development of Chinese banks. Currently bankruptcy and business loss in some large and medium-sized state-owned industrial enterprises presents an even worse picture. It may be asked whether Chinese banks, especially the state-owned commercial banks, will in the future face the same bad situation as these industrial enterprises? In my personal opinion, if the state banking system reform is carried out too slowly and if the other reforms in interest management, banks' asset securitization, methods of bank management and personnel policy are not smoothly implemented, then the banking sector may experience greater difficulties.

Conclusion

Currently, China has established its own financial management system and built up its own independent foreign bank management regulation system. There are some respects in which bank management remains unsatisfactory. First, there aren't sufficient financial managers and controllers in the central bank, particularly compared with foreign countries and regions. Secondly, foreign banks do not have the right to bring administrative suits against improper punishment imposed by the central bank. Thirdly, there is a disparity between the ratio of adequate capital reserves for domestic banks and foreign banks. Finally, the Regulations of Foreign Banks and the Commercial Banking Law each give different interpretations and definitions as to the meaning of a number of legal turns of phrase.

The disparity between the regulations applicable to the two kinds of banks is an obstacle to the development of the Chinese financial and industrial sectors. For future development, the obstacle should be removed and uniform management systems should gradually evolve in order to protect the legitimate rights and interests of depositors and other clients, to standardize the behavior of commercial banks, to improve the quality of loans, to strengthen supervision and administration, to ensure the safety and soundness of commercial banking, to maintain a stable financial order, and hence, to promote the development of the Chinese market economy.

A STEP AWAY FROM THE MARKET? THE AUTONOMY OF NEGOTIABLE INSTRUMENTS AND THE NEW NEGOTIABLE INSTRUMENTS LAW OF THE PRC

Professor Derek Roebuck
and
Wong Wai-Ip

Centre for Chinese and Comparative Law
and
Faculty of Law
City University of Hong Kong
(respectively)

Professor Derek Roebuck, *M.A. (Oxon), M. Com. (Wellington), is Professor of Comparative Law at the Centre for Chinese and Comparative Law at the City University of Hong Kong. He is a solicitor in England and Hong Kong and a barrister and solicitor in Tasmania and Papua New Guinea. He was formerly a Professor of Law at the Universities of Tasmania and Papua New Guinea; and the Dean of the Faculty of Law at the City University of Hong Kong. He is the author, co-author or editor of 30 books on law, most recently* The Background of the Common Law *(2nd ed., 1990),* Cheques *(2nd ed., 1991),* Hong Kong Contracts *(with Pedley Chui) (2nd ed., 1994),* Law Relating to Banking *(editor and co-author) (2nd ed., 1994),* Digest of Hong Kong Contract Law *(1995),* Hong Kong Criminal Law *(1995),* Banking Law in Hong Kong: Cases and Materials *(with Srivastava and Zafrullah) (1995).*

Wong Wai-Ip, *B.Sc. (Eng) (Hong Kong University), M.Sc. (Dunelm), M.Sc. Dp (Ulster), PGDBIT, PCKHKL, M.A. Arb. D.R. (City University), Ph. D. candidate (City University), is an employee of the Hongkong Bank.*

Background

The seminars on Market Economy and Law, held jointly by the law schools of Peking University and the City University of Hong Kong, show the commitment of legal scholars in both jurisdictions to the improvement of mutual understanding of their legal systems. It may well be that the most effective way to achieve results in that difficult and never-ending task is to concentrate on identifying misunderstandings which are common in both senses of the word and explaining their causes and significance. It may be more fruitful to deal first with practical problems, whose size is comprehensible and where success can be realistically worked towards, rather than to attack the great ideological differences, where it is harder to find scholarly approaches to reconciliation or even willingness to concede points in argument.[1]

At last year's seminar I presented a paper written with my Ph.D. student and colleague, Wong Kwok-yuen.[2] Its purpose was to increase mutual understanding between legal scholars and practising lawyers in China and Hong Kong by showing how different ethical foundations could affect the enforcement of awards and judgments. This paper, too, written with the help of another Ph.D. student, Wong Wai-Ip, who has a wealth of experience of practical banking, hopes to dispel mutual misunderstandings, this time in relation to a common commercial controversy, the autonomy of a negotiable instrument.[3] Here too, different approaches to a legal problem provide another example of the effect of different ethical assumptions. These are no arid academic exercises. Differences of ideology produce different legal rules; when they are applied they cause serious misunderstandings between lawyers and between business enterprises. They can easily be assumed by each side to be evidence of the other's obtuseness or even lack of morality.

Chinese and Common Law Ideologies

It is a matter of surprise, of shock even, for scholars trained in systems other than the common law, when their comparative studies reveal to them that the common law has generally rejected the principle of good faith in contracts, both in creation and performance. In sales in particular, the English maxim *caveat emptor* is unknown to other systems. Despite its Latin dress, it is not to be found in Roman law or any of the systems which draw their legal principles from that source: "Whatever may have been the limits of the implied warranty of quality in classical law, the whole atmosphere of the contract of sale (which is alone in question in these cases) is one of good faith."[4]

The Catholic church's canon law reinforced the requirement of good faith; good faith was demanded by the customs of merchants, though they restricted its scope to fit their trades. German local customs, too, tended to make good faith in contracting a requirement for enforcement of an executory contract.[5] It is not surprising, then, that Chinese law, greatly influenced directly by German law at the time of its first modernization and later to a less extent at second hand through Soviet law, should demand *bona fides in contrahendo*.

But the main reason why Chinese law requires good faith is Chinese traditional thinking. Chinese law, like Chinese ethics, has always placed great stress upon fairness in contracting. This is part of the emphasis which Chinese legal thinkers and Chinese judges place upon traditional attitudes which emphasize substantial justice. The law is legitimated by the support it receives from generally accepted standards of fairness. If it produces a result which offends those standards, there is something wrong with the law. There has been less concentration on procedural regularity than has been usual in the common law tradition.[6] Marxism-Leninism Mao Tse Tung thought reinforces the emphasis on fairness above procedural regularity, to which the writings of Mao Tse Tung ascribe little weight.[7]

The present law reflects its historical sources. China's current Foreign Economic Contract Law provides:

"Article 3: Contracts shall be concluded in accordance with the principles of mutual benefit and equality, and reached by unanimity through consultation . . .

Article 10: Contracts that are concluded by means of deception or coercion are invalid."

The Supreme People's Court interprets deception and coercion broadly; for example, if one party withholds a material fact from the other, the contract is invalid.[8]

Planned Economies and Market Economies

In a planned economy, the government answers the questions of how to organize production, what should be produced by whom, for whom, where, when, in what amounts and at what prices. These answers are part of long-term plans, which the government requires to be fulfilled. In a planned economy, if performance of an economic agreement turns out to be more onerous than the parties thought it would be when they made the agreement, the efficient response may well be to ensure that the change of circumstances has the least possible destructive effect, not only on the party receiving the performance but the party whose performance then falls short of what was agreed. More important, the overarching criterion may well be the effect on the larger or smaller community affected by the reduction of performance.

207

A market economy, on the other hand, is interpreted by its theore-
ticians as encouraging, if not ensuring, all economic transactions
which make the participants better off. The result should be that all
potential opportunities for the participants to do business are ex-
hausted. The driving force of the market economy is self-interest.

One of the essential elements of a market economy is that the
system should encourage the participants to take carefully assessed
business risks. Those risks need to be fixed so that they may be
quantified. It follows that, in a market economy, the most important
value is not that contracts be fair but that the parties may rely on
their strict performance. It becomes the paramount duty of the state
to enforce them: "The foundation of contract is the reasonable expectation which the person who promises raises in the person to whom
he binds himself; of which the performance may be extorted by
force."[9]

That person may not, of course, use personal force. The state has a
monopoly of enforcement. The basis of contractual liability at common law may be economic self-interest, but that is the highest good in
the eyes of at least one judicial theorist, still not atypical or old-
fashioned:

> "If there is one thing more than another which public policy
> requires, it is that men of full age and competent understanding
> shall have the utmost liberty of contracting, and that their con-
> tracts when entered into freely and voluntarily shall be held sacred
> and shall be enforced by courts of justice."[10]

There are those in China now who espouse and promote the view
that the law should in future aspire to that principle, though it is
doubtful whether they would elevate it to the level of religious dogma
— "contracts . . . shall be held *sacred*"— nor are they likely to insist
that good faith shall play no part in the requirements of the formation
of a valid contract.

Of course, if the economy is not planned, then businesses must be
able to rely on the state enforcing contracts. In a capitalist society,
business would be impossible if a company could not rely on the
contractual obligations of its suppliers to provide it with raw material,
its bank to supply it with finance, its workers to provide labour of all
kinds and its customers to buy its products. The state cannot interfere,
however, too drastically with the ways in which businesses ensure
that reliance. They must be left to take advantage of their economic
power in working out their contract liabilities. Yet *caveat emptor* is
not a necessary part of capitalist law; it is not found in those jurisdictions that have never adopted the common law but have preferred civil
law principles to govern their contracts. There is no noticeable difference in the effect which the capitalist economic systems of Germany

and the United States, or of France and England have on their legal superstructures.

The Need for Autonomy

One way a seller can be sure of a continued healthy cash-flow and avoid becoming a full-time collector of bad debts is to demand payment before delivery. That leaves the buyer with the job of getting the price back, or a part of it as damages if the goods are faulty. Otherwise, the seller may have to wait for any payment, and then get only part, until the courts have finished with a dispute about timely performance or compliance of the goods with the contract description.

It is a heavy and unnecessary burden for a buyer to have to find cash in advance. For centuries, market economies have found ways of accommodating the needs of both seller and buyer. The business of banks is to make money by providing just the lubricant that sales require. For a commission, they pay the seller before the buyer pays them. In other words, they lend the price. The essential characteristic of this money-lending service, though, is that the seller should get paid before the buyer gets the goods. The seller does not care whether payment is in cash or by some other means so long as it is as good as cash, but sellers will not settle for less. It is the buyer who requires the bank's help. If a buyer cannot arrange the bank's assistance, then the buyer will have to pay in cash and raise a loan. Of course, *because* buyers can raise the money to buy in this way, sellers make sales they would not otherwise have done. Everybody wins. There are snags, however. If the goods or the performance do not comply with the contract, the buyer cannot withhold the price. That was the point of the bank's intervention.

The problems that the seller has of judging whether to extend credit to the buyer — and which the buyer has of ensuring that the goods are delivered in accordance with the terms of the contract — are exacerbated when the parties are in different jurisdictions, particularly in international trade. This paper is concerned specifically with the seller's determination not to extend credit to the buyer but to ensure that it receives payment before the buyer has any chance to refuse to pay on the ground that the delivery does not conform to expectations.

There are four main ways in which sellers accept payment in international trade: advance payment, open account trading, documentary credits and documentary collections.

Advance payment causes no problems for the seller. The buyer merely pays the price at the time of the contract, or at least before the seller ships the goods. The buyer takes the risk of the goods not conforming and relies on the right of action in damages which that breach would provide.

In open account trading, the seller takes the risk of the buyer failing to pay on the due date. Open account trading, therefore, relies on the trust generated from a longstanding or regular course of dealing between the parties and from close knowledge not only of the buyer's business but the stability of the country from which payment is to come. About 60 per cent of trade between buyers and sellers in the United Kingdom and one of the other European Union countries is on open account.

In its urge to encourage exports, the exporters' government may reduce the exporters' risk by offering export credits insurance, as is done through the Export Credit Guarantee Department in the United Kingdom and the Export Credit Insurance Corporations (ECIC) of Hong Kong and Singapore. There is an economic cost for their services: not only is a premium charged, but the Hong Kong ECIC indemnifies its policy holders only up to 90 per cent of their losses arising from the buyer's refusal or inability to pay.

But the buyer usually needs to borrow the money to pay the price, and the usual lender is a bank. Banks can finance buyers by granting the buyer a specific loan for a particular shipment or by allowing the buyer an overdraft; or they can finance the seller by making premature payment to the seller, discounting or purchasing bills of exchange drawn by the seller on the buyer in the seller's favour.

Bills of Exchange

One of the oldest methods of securing payment before performance is the bill of exchange.[11] The seller draws a bill on the buyer for the amount of the price, the buyer accepts it — that is undertakes to pay its full amount — but only after a period, perhaps long enough to resell the goods or otherwise get the value out of them. The seller discounts the bill with a bank, that is accepts the amount of the bill reduced by the bank's charges for standing out of payment until the bill matures. This scheme depends on the effectiveness of the bill being quite separate from the contract of sale. The whole point of it is to give the seller payment before the buyer has a chance to argue about performance.

The seller runs the risk that the buyer may countermand payment before the bill is accepted or may fail to honour it later. The seller who has sold or discounted it will then be liable to recompense the bank, being left with only a right to sue the buyer on the bill.[12] In such a case, English and Hong Kong courts have refused to allow the buyer any defence on the bill arising from the buyer's allegations of the seller's faulty performance. Indeed they allow fast and simplified procedures for recovery under the Rules of the Supreme Court, Order XIV.[13]

The *York Airconditioning* Case

In *York Airconditioning and Refrigeration v. Lam Kwai Hung* [1995] 1 HKC 287, Kaplan J. had to decide a dispute arising from a buyer countermanding payment of a bill of exchange (in this case a cheque). The seller sought summary judgment under Order 14 of the Rules of the Supreme Court, which required it to show that the defendant had no arguable defence. Kaplan J. held that the seller was entitled to summary judgment, even though the sales contract was subject to Chinese law and contained an arbitration clause. In doing so he also found that Chinese law respected the autonomy of the bill of exchange: that it provided a cause of action to the payee separate from the sales contract. He accepted expert evidence that the relevant law in the PRC was the Procedures for Bank Settlements promulgated by the People's Bank of China in 1988, article 22 of which states:

"Where a payment instrument which in accordance with these Procedures is transferable by indorsement suffers dishonour by reason of non-payment, the holder of the instrument is entitled to exercise a right of recourse against the drawer, indorsers and other persons liable [on the payment instrument]; all persons liable on a payment instrument are jointly and severally liable to the holder."

These Procedures, said Kaplan J., created "a new category of obligations distinct from and independent of the obligation of the parties under civil law or economic law arising from the underlying transaction."

The expert evidence which the judge preferred was given by Professor Anthony Dicks Q.C., Head of the Department of Laws of the School of Oriental and African Studies, University of London. It was strongly opposed by that of Professor Chen An, Dean of the School of Politics and Laws, Xiamen University. They, like Kaplan J., are both members of the panel of arbitrators of the China International Economic and Trade Arbitration Commission (CIETAC), as are the other experts who supported Professor Chen, Professor Yao Zhuang of the International Research Institute of the Foreign Affairs School and Mr Guo Xiaowen, Vice-President of CIETAC's Shenzhen Division.

Professor Chen's evidence stressed that nowhere in the Chinese law was there any mention of the "autonomy of the bill of exchange". Moreover, the Procedures for Bank Settlements had been misunderstood. Section 3 provides:

"The issue of a commercial bill of exchange must be based on a lawful commodity transaction; the issue of a commercial bill of exchange in the absence of a commodity transaction is prohibited."

Professor Chen argued that it was clear that unless the bill was linked to a sale, indeed based on it, it was illegal and void *ab initio*. The bill in this case, linked as it was to the sales contract for its very legal existence, could not possibly be autonomous. The policy of the law was to ensure that any dispute arising out of the deal *as a whole* should be dealt with either by the agreement of the parties; or, if that was not possible, by mediation or arbitration according to the arbitration clause in the sales contract; or, in default of such a clause, by an application to the People's Court. In reality, the dispute about the bill, which was only a method of payment, had no existence in the eyes of the Chinese experts unless it was a dispute arising out of the sales contract, of which payment was an integral and inseparable part.

The New Chinese Law

Whatever the law might have been, the position has been clarified by new legislation. The Law of the People's Republic of China on Negotiable Instruments came into effect on January 1, 1996. It draws a distinction between an action on the bill brought by an immediate party and one brought by an indorsee. Article 13 provides:[14]

> "The debtor on an instrument shall not set up against the holder of it any defence founded on his relation with the drawer or a party prior to the holder, unless the holder acquired the instrument with knowledge of the existence of the defence.
>
> The debtor on an instrument may set up a defence against a holder who has a direct credit-debt relationship with the debtor but who has not performed the stipulated obligation.
>
> The defence referred to in this Law is the act of the debtor on an instrument who refuses performance of the obligation to the creditor in accordance with the provisions of this law."

This provision applies only to the original parties to the instrument, who must be also the parties to the transaction which gave rise to the payment instrument. The debtor on the instrument has no such defence to an action brought upon it by an indorsee or other third party who holds it.

It is clear that the model for this new legislation has not been found in the English common law.[15] Those who advise foreign sellers will now need to consider carefully how they are to ensure payment. What the new law may do is to drive all those engaged in international trade with China as sellers to more expensive forms of transferring the price, such as documentary letters of credit (DLCs). If those too fail to provide the protection the seller requires, they may be driven to even more costly or inconvenient stratagems.

Documentary Letters of Credit

The purpose of a DLC is to take away any chance of the buyer countermanding payment. By issuing a letter of credit, the buyer for-goes the right to withhold the *price*, accepting instead a right of action in damages (with whatever other rights may be available) against the seller. The buyer's bank issues a document which in effect guarantees payment to the seller.[16] The seller is secure unless the bank fails. Of course, the bank charges; that amount adds to the cost of the goods but the overall cost is reduced by the removal of the uncertainty of payment.

DLCs are used in international trade. An international convention promoted by the International Chamber of Commerce provides a scheme of international law to govern their use. The latest version is UCP500, which applies in those countries that have adopted it. Many countries were slow to adopt previous UCPs, including the United Kingdom and the U.S.;[17] but now the major trading nations accept the benefit of the uniform practices and law which UCP500 provides and imposes.

Hong Kong has adopted UCP500; China has not.[18] When a Chinese business wants to make use of DLCs, it often asks the Bank of China to provide them; that is possible through the Bank of China's Hong Kong branch. The Bank of China is a member of the Hong Kong Association of Banks (HKAB). According to article III(i) of the General Rules, August 1995, made by the Committee of HKAB, under powers given to it by the HKAB Ordinance (Cap 364), s. 12(1): "All members shall establish their DLCs in conformity with the UCP in force from time to time. DLCs shall bear indications to this effect." The Basic Law provides that: "International agreements to which the People's Republic of China is not a party but which are implemented in Hong Kong may continue to be implemented in the Special Adminstrative Region."[19]

Conclusion

If the courts cannot keep bills of exchange separate from the sales transaction, sellers will insist on DLCs. They cost more. If Chinese courts do not accept the separateness of DLCs, overseas suppliers are likely to invent some other equivalent of advance payment. Whatever it is, its newness will make it even more expensive. If PRC law and Hong Kong law diverge, sellers will take care that Hong Kong law applies. Artificial elements may creep into enforcement law and practice.

It would not be too difficult, perhaps, to get the required result by cheap and easy means. All that the seller needs to do is to delay releasing the goods to the buyer until the bill has been safely indorsed to a third party. It should not be assumed, however, that a Chinese court or arbitrators will allow the kind of subterfuge which immediately springs to the mind of a common lawyer. It would be easy to make sure that a cheque or bill or, if necessary, a negotiable DLC was immediately on receipt indorsed to the creditor-seller's bank. To do so, however, may not always be easy, and it could easily be overlooked by those who are used to English common law and assume it applies to their transaction.

It is not likely that the Common Lawyers of Hong Kong and the Civil Law experts of the People's Republic of China will easily or quickly accept one and the same view of good faith in contracting. It may take a while, for those who have been brought up to take for granted the advantages of planned or market economies, to resolve their differences or agree to differ. Neither of these long-term goals, assuming they are desirable, are necessary for the solution of immediate problems. What is needed is a system of ensuring payment of the price of goods in international transactions, without which trade would be artificially inhibited or made more costly. That is a task well within the skills of those who now advise clients, both buyers and sellers, in international trade between the People's Republic of China and Hong Kong and other countries. It should be done quickly, in consultation with the banks who provide the credit, and preferably before the common law jurisdiction of Hong Kong becomes once again an integral part of China.

What may be most encouraging is the fact that the law in the U.S. is the same on this point as that in China. There, too, the bill of exchange is not autonomous from the transaction that gives rise to it, at least as between the original parties. It would not seem, therefore, that there are profound ideological barriers to a rapprochement between the Common Lawyers of Hong Kong and the Civil Lawyers of China.

Notes

1 There is much current activity, in both macro- and micro-legal research, for example that represented by the publications in (1995) 141 *China Quarterly*.

A recent example of a paper which comprehends both approaches is Guiguo
Wang and Stephen Foo, "The Banking Law Reforms in China — Difficulties
and Prospects" (1995) 18 *World Competition* 13–53.

2 K.Y. Wong and D. Roebuck, "The Enforcement of Foreign Arbitral Awards
in the People's Republic of China: the Influence of Traditional Morality",
now published in Chinese in *Market Economy and Law* (1995), pp.272–92.
See also D. Roebuck and K.Y. Wong, "Rapid Change and Traditional Morality: Enforcement of Foreign Arbitral Awards in the People's Republic of
China" (1995) 5 *Australian J of Corporate Law* 342–355 and D. Roebuck,
"Courts, Judges and Arbitral Awards in the History of the Common Law and
in China Today" published in Chinese in (1995) *Jurists' Review* 24–30.

3 The courts in Hong Kong have often had to deal with the problem and have
repeatedly endorsed the principle: "It is trite law that a promissory note or
bill of exchange is to be treated as cash and honoured unless tainted by fraud
or total failure of consideration", *per* Barnett J. in *Chevalier v. Rotegear
Development* [1994] 3 HKC 457, 461. See also *Suen Ho Sun v. Kamenar
International* [1989] 1 HKC 135; *Plaza v. Tso Kar Yin* [1959] HKLR 390, F.C.;
Bank of Canton v. Mak Lai Ting [1923] HKLR 27. *A fortiori* in relation to
documentary letters of credit: *Cic-Union Europeenne International v. Wing
Sun* [1985] 1 HKC 568.

4 W.W. Buckland and A.D. McNair, *Roman Law and Common Law: a Comparison in Outline* (2nd ed., 1952), 211. But the Common Law no longer
prevails in this form in North America, see E.C. Chiasson, "Is Gateway a
Floodgate: Canadian Law Embraces the United States Contractual Obligation of Good Faith and Fair Dealing", and the references there cited, *American Bar Association ADR Newsletter* (1996).

5 The literature is vast but a neat summary is in O.F. Robinson, T.D. Fergus
and W.M. Gordon, *European Legal History* (2nd ed., 1994), pp.88–91.

6 Wong and Roebuck, *Market Economy and Law*, pp.351–353.

7 Ding Xueliang, *Post-Communism and China* (1994), p.8.

8 Answers to Certain Questions on the Application of the Foreign Economic
Contract Law, Clause 3(7), issued October 19, 1987.

9 Adam Smith *The Wealth of Nations*.

10 Sir George Jessel M.R. in *Printing and Numerical Registering v. Sampson*
(1875) L.R. 19 Eq. 462.

11 There is evidence of bills of exchange in reported decisions of the Mayor's
Court of the City of London from about A.D. 1300 but they did not come
into regular use in England until the middle of the fifteenth century, J.
Milnes Holden, *The History of Negotiable Instruments in English Law*
(1955), p.21. For the Chinese history, Lien-sheng Yang, *Money and Credit in
China: a Short History* (1952).

12 The legal position where the bill has been negotiated to others is ignored
here. In such a case there are other arguments in favour of this thesis, most
a fortiori. But see below on the new PRC Negotiable Instruments Law.

13 *Nova (Jersey) Knit v. Kammgarn Spinnerei* [1977] 2 All ER 463; [1977] 1
WLR 713.

14 The translation we have is unsatisfactory. We have, therefore, made some
necessary changes to improve comprehensibility and avoid unidiomatic
expressions, at the risk of mistranslation.

15 Perhaps it is to be found in German law; or in the U.S. Uniform Commercial
Code; more comparative work needs to be done.

16 Once a bill drawn under a DLC has been accepted by, or negotiated to the
bank which issued the DLC, the bill is governed exclusively by the law
relating to bills of exchange. The purpose of the DLC is then spent and the
special rules that apply to DLCs no longer apply to the bill. If an issuing

bank has been put in funds to honour bills of exchange that it accepts under a DLC before they fall due, the bank must pay the beneficiary, and when it has done so may claim reimbursement from the applicant for the DLC.

[17] The law on the autonomy of payment instruments varies among western trading nations. Even the larger common law jurisdictions, notably the U.S. and the U.K., do not agree. Among the commercially developed western jurisdictions, only the USA has codified its law on DLCs, see Uniform Commercial Code, art. 5.

[18] The UCPs are adopted by Bankers' Associations or by individual banks. It is through membership of an association or individual accession that the UCP becomes binding, Filip De Ly, *International Business Law and Lex Mercatoria* (1992), p.177.

[19] The Basic Law of the Hong Kong Special Administrative Region, article 153.

THE ROLE OF THE CENTRAL BANK OF CHINA

Dr D.K. Srivastava
and
Wang Chenguang

Faculty of Law
City University of Hong Kong

D.K. Srivastava, *M.A., LL.M. (Banaras), Ph.D. (Monash), is an associate professor with the Faculty of Law at the City University of Hong Kong.*

Wang Chenguang, *M.A., LL.M. (Peking), LL.M. (Harvard), is an associate professor with the Faculty of Law at the City University of Hong Kong.*

Introduction

The adoption of the Law of the PRC on People's Bank of China (hereafter referred to as the Central Bank Law) at the third Session of the 8th National People's Congress on March 18, 1995 marks a watershed in the banking reform of China. The new Law seeks to ensure the position and functions of the People's Bank of China (PBC) as the country's central bank, to guarantee the correct formulation and implementation of monetary policies, to establish and improve a system of macro adjustments by the PBC and to strengthen the supervision and management of the financial sector. Although the PBC began to perform some of the functions of a central bank over a decade ago, it did not have any real powers. It functioned as a ministry of the State Council. Its role and powers as the country's central bank were not defined under the law. To facilitate China's goal of maintaining a socialist market economy, the PBC has now been given wide ranging powers and functions, in many respects similar to those exercised by central banks in other countries. The PBC is no longer an accountant carrying out the instructions of the various government bodies.

Like other central banks the PBC is authorized to supervise all financial activities in China. It formulates and implements the monetary policy; issues legal tender and manages its circulation; approves the establishment of financial institutions and supervises and administers the financial markets; drafts and promulgates the rules and regulations on the supervision of the financial sector; holds and controls the country's financial reserve; manages state treasury; conducts normal operation and maintenance of payment and clearing system function; is responsible for the formation and collection of statistics, surveys, analyses and forecasts of the financial sector; participates as the country's central bank in international financial activities; and performs other duties as assigned to it by the State Council. It exercises those powers and functions under the leadership of the State Council. The Bank's president is a member of the State Council and is appointed and removed in the same way as any other minister. It is also required to submit working reports to the Standing Committee of the National People's Congress (NPC) on monetary policies and the supervision and management of the financial sector.[1]

Given China's commitment to transform its planned economy system to a market economy, the passage of the new law is timely. If effectively implemented, China will be able to streamline its banking system and achieve a great measure of success in its market oriented reform and its bid for modernization of the banking sector. Since the implementation of the new regime of banking law, which is a major part in the overall reform project, inflation has been nearly halved and China's overheated economy has shown signs of improvement with an increase in the GDP.

This paper will examine the evolution of China's banking system, analyze the main provisions of the new law, in particular examining the role of the PBC with respect to the ongoing economic structure reform. It will also examine the achievements and deficiencies of the new law. It will conclude by making general observations pointing out, *inter alia*, that the new law is likely to set a pace for a new economic order based on market oriented forces.

The Role of the PBC in the Planned Economy

After the founding of the PRC, the leaders of the country adopted a Stalinist type highly centralized economic scheme based on state planning. The national economy was organized, managed and controlled by and through the state plans which were drafted by government bodies and officials at various levels and approved by the State Council with the assistance of the State Planning Commission. The state plans determined the financial and monetary policies and the PBC was subject to such plans and the government bodies and officials responsible for drafting and implementing those plans. If a plan demanded the expending of a certain amount, the PBC had to print and issue the required amount of money. Under that scheme of state planning, the PBC was then merely an accountant and a cashier for the government. Its role in the management of the country's financial and monetary policies was thus minimal.

Patriarch Deng Xiaoping saw that the planned economy system could in no way redress the poverty and economic problems which plagued the country in the 1960s and 1970s. After his return to power, he started the Economic Structure Reform with a view to streamlining the economic set up. In his new scheme (officially described as the Socialist Market Economy), he urged that "the bank should function as a lever for economic development".

To fulfil that goal, a new financial system with multiple banks and financial institutions under the leadership of the PBC was gradually set up. Although the PBC's role was strengthened, it still was not established as a central bank. From 1985 to 1992 further steps were taken to establish the PBC as a central bank. Finally in 1993, the State Council's Decision on Financial Reform set out the role of banks, especially of the PBC as the country's central bank, with a view to achieving a smooth transition to a socialist market economy. The Central Bank Law of 1995 contains most of the provisions of the Decision on Financial Reform.

It must be reiterated at the outset that the PBC functions under the leadership of the State Council. Acting as the central bank the PBC has three major functions to perform, namely to lay down monetary policy, exercise prudential supervision over other banks and to manage the State Treasury. The Central Bank Law stipulates several particular functions of the PBC which shall be discussed below.

The Organization and Structure of the PBC

The Law stipulates the structure of the PBC. The top senior management of the PBC consists of one president and seven vice-presidents. The president must be nominated by the Premier of the State Council. That nomination must be approved by the National People's Congress or, when it is in recess, by its Standing Committee. The appointment of the PBC's President is made by the President of the PRC. The appointments of vice-presidents are made by the Premier of the State Council.[2]

The PBC has four tiers of offices; its head office is in Beijing. At the provincial level, it establishes branch offices; below these branch offices are the secondary branch offices which are set up at the prefecture level; the PBC's sub-branches, which are the lowest level of the PBC, are established at the country and the city level.

The PBC seeks to practice centralized and unified control over its branches throughout the country.[3] Article 12 of the Central Bank Law will certainly change the past practice, which gave much more power to the local government and governmental organs.

The Central Bank Law stipulates the establishment of a Monetary Policy Committee by the PBC whose functions, constitution and working procedures are to be regulated by the State Council and submitted to the Standing Committee of the National People's Congress for record or information.[4]

Previously, the government organs made decisions following the state plans.[5] The PBC had no say in the making of the plans concerning the monetary policies of the country. It is noteworthy that it is widely believed now the Monetary Policy Committee, which is part of the PBC, will determine the appropriate monetary policies by taking into account the prevailing market forces rather than the state plans.[6]

Formulation and Implementation of the Monetary Policy

The objectives of the monetary policy are to maintain the stability of the Renminbi (RMB) and promote the economic development of China.[7] To achieve those objectives the PBC is empowered to make decisions in respect of annual money supply, interest rates, exchange rates and other matters stipulated by the State Council but its decisions are required to be approved by the State Council prior to their implementation.[8] So far as the PBC's decisions in respect of other matters of the monetary policy are concerned, they can be put into operation immediately after their adoption and the only condition stipulated in the law is that such decisions must be reported to the State Council.[9] It is of great significance that the PBC has been granted the power to make decisions concerning certain matters of monetary policy without the approval of the State Council. The Central Bank Law, article 7 states that under the leadership of the State Council the PBC shall independently formulate and implement the monetary policies free from any interference from any local governments, government departments (at various levels), social entities and individuals. This provision has a history. Previously, local administrative organizations used to interfere with the operations of the PBC with a view to obtaining more capital for their region. Moreover, the ministries, commissions and other administrative organs of the central government also interfered with the operations of the PBC. Now, although the PBC is required to formulate and implement its monetary policies under the leadership of the State Council, no other government bodies, central or local can interfere in the work of the PBC. The Central Bank Law, article 6 requires, however, the PBC to submit working reports to the Standing Committee of National People's Congress (NPC) of China on the situation concerning monetary policies and the supervision and management of the financial sector. It would appear that article 6 is designed to empower the NPC to use its legislative powers in an exceptional situation where it feels that the PBC is not discharging its duties and functions in the best interests of the country.[10]

Issuance of Renminbi (RMB) and Management of its Circulation

The issuing of the legal tender in a country is usually vested in the country's central bank. The sole authority to issue, reissue or cancel RMB including coins has also been vested in the PBC together with the power to print the currency. It must be noted that this power has been vested in the PBC to prevent the widespread practice of some government organs of issuing RMB substitutes.[11] The role of the PBC as the country's central bank has been further strengthened by giving it power to control all the newly printed and excess notes not intended to be in circulation. The amount of RMB to be put in circulation is decided by the PBC upon prior approval by the State Council.

The Establishment of the Financial Institutions and the Supervision and Management of Their Operation

Financial institutions include banks, such as commercial banks, and non-bank institutions, such as investment companies, insurance and trust companies. The Central Bank Law, article 31 states that the PBC shall approve the establishment, alteration and closure of financial institutions and its business.[12] The PBC sets minimum requirements for capital investments for different financial institutions. The detailed procedures for establishing a financial institution will be drafted by the PBC. The previous regulations and rules issued by the PBC shall continue to have effect until the new rules come into operation. According to the existing regulations, an application to establish a national financial institution with the word "China" or "Chinese" in its name must be forwarded to the headquarters of the PBC for examination and approval. An application to establish a non-national bank, a financial company, urban credit co-operatives, a branch of a bank, an insurance company, a subsidiary of a financial institution, an experimental financial institution shall be examined by a branch of the PBC at the provincial level. An application to establish a sub-branch or a business office of a bank, a sub-subsidiary or an office of a financial institution shall be examined and approved by a local branch of the PBC at the provincial level, but before its establishment the approved application shall be sent to the headquarters of the PBC. If the headquarters of the PBC do not raise any objections within 30 days, the approval shall be deemed to be final. Applications to establish an urban credit co-operative shall be examined and approved by a local branch at the provincial level and sent to the headquarters of the PBC for filing. Financial institutions other than those mentioned above shall be examined and approved by a local branch of the PBC at the provincial or lower level (with the authorization of the PBC's provincial level branch).

The establishment procedure consists of two stages. The first involves preparation and establishment. At this stage, the promoters must send the application and the necessary documents to the PBC which shall respond within three months. If the application is approved, the promoter takes steps to establish the institution that must be completed within six months. If after six months the institution cannot start its operation, the original approval becomes automatically invalid, but with approval from the PBC, the period can be extended up to one year. After establishment, the institution on initial approval is requested to submit an application for the commencement of operation and the PBC shall decide within 30 days whether to approve the application.

The PBC adopts a licence system for financial institutions. It provides a "Permit of Legal Person for Financial Institution" to applicants who are legal persons and a "Permit of Business Operation for Financial Institution" to applicants who are not legal persons. A branch of a financial institution is not qualified to apply for licence as a legal person. The Notification Concerning Several Issues of Examination and Approval of Financial Institutions empowers the PBC to set minimum requirements of capital investment for different financial institutions. It provides that the minimum registered capital for a national bank without branches shall be 1 billion RMB; a national bank with branches must have a minimum of 2 billion RMB. The requirements may be changed according to the situation of the financial market. Recently the PBC has raised the capital requirement for a national investment and trust company from 50 million RMB to 100 million RMB, and for a provincial company from 10 million RMB to 50 million RMB.

Besides the authority to approve the establishment of financial institutions, the PBC also has the power to supervise the operation of the financial institutions. The Central Bank Law states that the PBC shall have the right at any time to inspect and audit the financial institutions in respect of the deposits, loans, settlement of accounts and bad debts. And, increases or decreases in interest rates on deposits and loans must be authorized by the PBC.[13] The PBC also has the right to require a financial institution to submit its balance sheet, profit and loss statement and other financial accounting statements and data,[14] the right to guide and supervise the financial business of the State policy banks and the right to impose administrative sanctions on banks and individuals.[15]

The PBC may on finding a financial institution guilty of violating any law or regulation concerning its operations order that institution to rectify the breach. The PBC can cancel a financial institution's permit or licence to operate as a financial institution.[16]

It should be noted that most financial institutions have been established by decrees of the State Council.[17]

The Supervision of Financial Markets

China's securities and bonds markets reflect an attempt to substitute the planned economy system by a "State managed capitalism" in which the PBC is to play a significant role. The device of raising capital by issuing stocks and bonds first started in the nineteenth century. According to Karmel, foreigners traded the first foreign securities in China in the 1860s; and in 1894 and 1898. The Quing dynasty floated national government backed public bonds to pay war debts and modernize the naval force.[18] During the first quarter of this century stock markets opened in various provinces and in Beijing. The stock markets in China survived the First and the Second World Wars, but after the communist takeover in 1949 stock exchanges were closed and no securities were issued during the Cultural Revolution. Although national domestic bonds were issued six times in the first decade after the commencement of communist rule, they did not provide much revenue to the government. When the government stopped the issuance of national bonds, it authorized local governments to issue local bonds, but local bonds did not play any consequential role in the national economy.

The demise of Mao and the succession of Deng Xioaping not only brought philosophical changes in the economic structure of the country but marked the beginning of a new era for securities and bonds markets. The first national treasury bonds (Guokuzhai) were issued by the State Council in 1981. The Ministry of Finance also issued key construction projects bonds and finance bonds. National bonds were also issued by other national bureaux and organizations. Since the PBC has emerged as the country's central bank it is vested with considerable authority to supervise the stocks and bonds markets and see to it that such markets function in a way that supports the country's monetary and economic policies.

The financial market is one item in the market oriented reform. It includes the interbank market, the foreign exchange market, and the securities and bonds market.[19] The PBC has the power to regulate the business operations of the monetary market or interbank and foreign exchange markets. However, the role of the PBC in the securities and bonds markets is not very clear. Previously, it had the power to regulate and control the securities and bonds markets,[20] but since October 1992 that power has been vested in the CSRC and the Securities Supervision and Administration Commission under the State Council. Recently the Securities Commission ordered the closure of the State treasury bonds futures trading.[21]

Although the supervision and control of the business operations of the securities and bonds markets has also passed under the jurisdiction of the Securities Commission and the Securities Supervision and Administration Commission, the establishment of the securities institutions are still within the exclusive jurisdiction of the PBC. Securities companies, securities exchange bourses, financial companies and financial futures companies cannot commence their business unless their applications for that purpose are approved by the PBC and it issues them a licence to do business. The Securities Commission and the Securities Supervision and Administration Commission are, however, in a better position than the PBC to monitor the day to day business activities of the securities institutions and thereby protect the interests of the investors and safeguard the nascent capital and securities market. Moreover, banking prudence is not required to monitor such activities. China is moving in the same direction as other developing countries.[22] Indeed, China has to be complimented for adopting such a rational and pragmatic approach.

It will, however, be noted that the PBC in order to carry out its monetary policies may use the tool of trading in treasury bonds, *e.g.* buying and selling treasury bonds, other government securities including bonds and foreign exchange in the open market, but it cannot directly subscribe or purchase or underwrite treasury bonds or other government securities.[23]

Bonds, including treasury bonds, are issued with a view to raising capital. Bondholders are like creditors who lend money at a fixed rate of interest. Some treasury bonds carry an interest of 14.5 per cent which is 2.26 per cent higher than bank deposit yields for the same term.[24] The treasury bonds are sold to further China's economic reform and are the safest investments available as the repayments are fully guaranteed by the Ministry of Finance. Although no one can be compelled to buy such bonds, the government makes all possible efforts to sell whatever bonds have been issued.[25] Treasury bonds in particular are increasingly being used by the government to raise funds for its expenditure. In 1994 the Ministry of Finance issued treasury bonds worth 100 billion RMB. In 1995 it planned to issue treasury bonds worth 150 billion RMB to finance its budget deficit.[26] The more the bonds are sold the more money is available to the government for investment. Bonds which are registered in the buyer's name are a particular kind of property; they are not directly transferable but can only be inherited. Bonds of small denominations do not bear the buyer's name and are transferable like negotiable instruments. Those who sell bonds issue certificates evidencing the bondholders' rights in that they state the face value of their bonds, the repayment period and the right to receive interest. The treasury bonds in China are similar to the U.S. Series E Bonds.

In China there are two kinds of treasury bonds, namely certificate treasury bonds and standard treasury bonds. The standard treasury bonds are mainly sold to the institutional buyers. The rates of interest on treasury bonds vary; for example, enterprises or institutions receive less interest than individual buyers.

Apart from treasury bonds, the central or a provincial government may issue some bonds. In certain cases, bonds may be issued by enterprises with the prior approval of the PBC. There are several kinds of government bonds besides the treasury bonds, *e.g.* investment bonds, financial bonds, key construction bonds and enterprises bonds. Investment bonds are issued by the Industrial and Commercial Bank to support basic industrial and infrastuctural projects and important technical renovations.[27] Financial bonds are issued by banks and financial institutions to individuals to realize money for giving loans to newly established enterprises with sound economic operations and for infrastuctural projects requiring cash. Key construction bonds are issued to institutions and individuals, including the state owned enterprises, central and local government organs, for the purpose of collecting money for key construction projects. Further, there are non-government bonds that are issued by enterprises that are legal persons.[28] The issuance of other government bonds, such as financial and construction bonds, is decided by the PBC with the approval of the State Council by taking into consideration the overall financial and credit plans, but such bonds are issued by the commercial or specialized banks. The construction bonds are issued by the Construction Bank of China (CBC) and financial bonds are issued by the Industrial and Commercial Bank of China (ICBC). The China Investment Bank (CIB) also issues several other kinds of bonds. After consultation with the State Council, the PBC may authorize a local government to issue bonds. Guangzhou announced in 1995 that it planned to issue bonds worth 300 million RMB.[29] Important state enterprises which comply with certain capital requirements may also be authorized by the PBC to issue bonds.

The PBC plays an important role in controlling the bonds market. In the case of financial bonds the amount of such bonds and the quota for each bank responsible for issuing such bonds, including the branches of the PBC, are determined by the PBC. In the case of key construction bonds — although their issuance and repayment are implemented by the CBC, Agricultural Bank of China (ABC) and the Industrial and Commercial Bank of China (ICBC) — the PBC exercises an effective supervision on these banks as regards issuance of such bonds. In the case of enterprises bonds, every year the PBC along with the Ministry of Finance, the State Planning Commission and the Securities Commission determines the amount of such bonds to be issued. The PBC together with the State Planning Commission also determines whether or not an enterprise can issue bonds. Further, the PBC along with the State Planning Commission[30] determines the issuance of bonds by enterprises.

The PBC plays an important role in organizing the bonds market as bonds are an effective means of attracting large amounts of funds when inflation is running high and there are only a limited number of institutional investors who are prepared to invest. Since China has embarked upon a policy of market reform the PBC must see to it that a balance is maintained between what public money or institutional investment goes to the government through bonds and what public money businesses — including private sector — receive for various purposes. Any unhealthy competition between the government and the business sector can have an adverse affect on the economy. Put simply, the more available public funds government has, the less of it businesses will have. Moreover, the more that is realized from the sale of bonds the greater will be the financial burden of interest payments on the government; this could affect other developments. The present trend of issuing excessive treasury bonds could prove counter productive, therefore. There is a risk that China could fall into "a vicious cycle in which it will be forced to issue new bonds to service previous governmental will while at the same time incurring more interest payments and debts."[31]

Reserve Funds

Ever since the PBC became the central bank, the mechanism of reserve funds has been instituted as a major and effective device to control liquidity. The Central Banking Law, article 22(1) gives the PBC the authority to require financial institutions to contribute to the deposit reserves fund.

The reserve funds contain deposits made by banks and non-bank financial institutions to the PBC according to the ratio specified by the PBC. The PBC, by changing the ratio of the reserve funds, is able to control the lending capacity of banks and non-bank financial institutions and, therefore, to loosen or tighten money supply according to the financial situation.

In 1984, the reserve ratio was 20 per cent on enterprise deposits, 25 per cent on agricultural deposits, and 40 per cent on savings deposits. These relatively high ratios were subsequently unified and reduced to 10 per cent in 1985 and 1986; and 13 per cent in 1988–1990.[32] At present it still is 13 per cent but for foreign banks the ratio is only 5 per cent. The banks and financial institutions in urban areas are required to adjust and deposit their reserve funds every 10 days, whereas the banks and financial institutions in rural areas are required to make adjustments every month.[33] The required reserves are calculated on the basis of deposits at the end of each of these periods. Any shortfall or delay in handing over reserves in this process is subject to a penalty interest rate of 0.02 per cent per day.[34]

The mechanism of reserve funds is necessary for the macroeconomics control of the economy. This is also a common method and is widely used by many developed countries, for the position of reserve fund is a good economic indicator.[35]

Re-discount

The Central Bank Law, article 22(3) authorizes the PBC to re-discount commercial and financial papers (they being equivalent to what is known as bills of exchange in the common law jurisdictions) for those financial institutions which have accounts with the PBC. Usually commercial and financial papers are given to settle debts for the price of goods. The seller draws them on the buyer in favour of a bank. The seller by this method obtains immediate funds. The bank buys the commercial and financial papers at a discount. The bank, however, has to wait for the commercial and financial papers to mature. Until then the bank cannot receive any payment on it. The discount is calculated like a rate of interest at so much for each day the bank is out of money.[36] When banks and financial institutions need funds urgently the PBC may re-discount the commercial and financial papers by providing a loan. This is done to support ailing banks and financial institutions and the re-discount interest rates are lower than the ordinary lending rates by 5–10 per cent.[37]

Shanghai was the first city to start re-discount business in China. It is an important lever for the PBC to control bank credits and adjust monetary policies by taking into account the financial needs of the country. The PBC may use the re-discount rate for loosening or tightening the money supply.[38]

Interest Rates

Interest rate is the rate at which banks and other financial institutions and individuals borrow or lend money. The basic idea is that the lender must not lose the benefits he would have had otherwise. The result of raising the interest rates is to increase the cost of borrowing which in turn restrains the demand for loans. By the same token the rise in interest rate would naturally encourage more deposits. The interest rate as an economic lever plays an important role in resource mobilization, resource allocation and reallocation, developing the economy and activating the market.[39] Today interest rates are connected with a complex of other financial activities and scenarios. It must take into account the rate of inflation, the value of currency and the position of foreign exchange reserves. Low inflation, sluggish money supply and a slow down in the economy often leads to easing of the interest rate with a view to boosting the economy. In Germany there was a move to cut interest rates to deal with the downturn in the economy.[40] Canada's central bank slashed its interest rates six times in the summer of 1995 as Canada's economy remained very weak.[41]

The determination of interest rates in China is perhaps more complicated than anywhere else. Factors to be taken into account are not only those stated above but also the government's preference for key projects in different agricultural and industrial sectors and economic returns from such investments. The PBC, upon approval by the State Council, determines the basic interest rates on loans by banks to business organizations and individuals[42] and deposits.

Since such matters are under the control and supervision of a country's central bank, it is but necessary to vest the power of determining interest rates on loans and deposits with it.[43] Thus, the PBC determines the amount, duration (which cannot exceed one year), interest rate and the mode of its loans to the commercial banks. It also has the authority to prescribe the interest rates payable for borrowing from foreign sources. This is done with a view to offering protection to local entities, which for the sake of obtaining foreign money could agree to pay a much higher rate of interest without having the ability to pay.

It is important to establish a floating, sophisticated and market oriented interest rate system without which the economic progress cannot be realistically sustained.[44] In China, however, it has not been possible to achieve it, at least for the present. Over the last eight months the consumer price inflation rate has fluctuated between 27 per cent and 15 per cent. Obviously depositors cannot expect to get such interest as would offset the effect of inflation. The PBC, therefore, provides for the payment of interest rate subsidies to reassure the depositors that their savings will not be eroded by inflation.[45] This policy of giving subsidies encourages depositors to put their money in long term deposits, which would result in savings and thus accelerate economic growth.

Loans

The Central Bank Law, article 22(4) states that in order to carry out the monetary policy, the PBC may provide loans to the commercial banks. Further, according to article 27 the PBC may, when it deems necessary for carrying out such policy, decide on the amount, duration, interest rate, and mode of its loans to the commercial banks. Nevertheless, the term of such loans shall not exceed one year.[46] The giving of loans to commercial banks will enable them to make loans to individuals and entities for commercial purposes. Article 32, as stated before, provides that the PBC shall have the right at any time to inspect and audit the financial institutions in respect of their deposits, loans, settlement of accounts and bad debts and it shall have the right to inspect and supervise the financial institutions in respect of any unauthorized increase or decrease of interest rates for deposits or loans. In July 1993, the PBC issued a three point directive to state owned banks, restricting interbank loans, ordering a curb on reckless interest rate increases and on investments in enterprises run by the financial houses themselves. Recently the PBC sacked and disciplined eleven senior bank officials who acted in violation of this directive.[47] The PBC also has the power to launch investigations into loans granted by other banks. The transactions relating to 280,000 clients of the Construction Bank of China (CBC) who have received fixed asset and working capital loans from the bank are under investigation.[48] Article 47 makes it an offence to provide loans in violation of article 29(1) as mentioned above. In China a distinction is maintained between budgetary loans and loans for commercial purposes. The budgetary loans are mainly long and medium term loans to finance key construction projects, *e.g.* the Three Gorges Dam, railway systems and power stations. Since the establishment of policy banks the budgetary loans are provided by these banks and loans for commercial purposes by the commercial banks.[49] In fact the policy banks were formed for the purpose of providing budgetary loans.

On August 22, 1995 the PBC proclaimed a detailed set of rules on loans called the General Rules on Loans. They are to ensure the security and profitability of loans. Under the new rules only those with the ability to repay the loan and who have not previously defaulted in paying back existing loans will be qualified to apply for loans.

The object of allowing the PBC to give loans and regulate lending by financial institutions to the commercial banks and to local governments, departments at various levels, non-bank financial institutions, entities or individuals (with the approval of the State Council) is to create a new investment environment and to rationalize the credit system in China. Further the PBC must try to improve risk management by setting limits on high risk loans, improving loan efficiency and rationalizing and streamlining the quality of services to the customers. There are, however, some inbuilt constraints on the power of the PBC. It cannot grant loans to commercial banks for more than one year and cannot provide loans to the local governments, departments, non-bank financial institutions, entities or individuals except with the approval of the State Council.[50] Thus the PBC is still subject to the administrative discretion of the State Council in the matter of granting loans to local governments and other non-bank financial institutions.

Accounts for Financial Institutions and Clearing Services

Article 25 provides that the PBC may, as it deems necessary, open accounts for financial institutions, but may not provide overdraft facilities to the financial institutions. The PBC is thus a banker to such institutions. These institutions may use their accounts to settle transactions between them and the PBC arising from the purchase of securities such as treasury bonds and certificate bonds, foreign exchange, notes and coins. These rules are designed not only to enable the PBC to monitor the commercial activities of the financial institutions having an account with them but also serves the purpose of providing the PBC with some reserve funds from the outstanding credit balances of these institutions.

The PBC is empowered under the Central Bank Law, article 26 to organize and co-ordinate the clearing system among the financial institutions and provide the necessary services for that purpose. It is further responsible for laying down the procedure for the operation of the clearing system. The clearing system as used in many countries is a device by which accounts between different banks are settled. Cheques or drafts received by banks for collection are brought to a common place where they are balanced against each other, giving a total picture of outstanding deposits and withdrawals on a particular day.

Conclusion

Apparently the position of the PBC is quite similar to that of other central banks. It has most of the powers of a central bank. These powers, however, are to be exercised under the leadership of the State Council and some matters are to be reported to the NPC for information. Such checks are not unique to China, for other central banks even under a free market economy system also function under a similar framework.

In China, it may be noted that the superimposition of the authority of the State Council and the NPC has occurred because China is in the phase of transition from a planned economy to a socialist market economy. The leaders of the country, to use the well-known words of Deng Xiaoping, "want to cross the river by touching the stones".

Another reason for not removing the control of the State Council and the NPC is because of the uncertainties which multifarious ongoing reforms have brought in their train. The power division between the central, provincial and local governments are undergoing adjustments. The structure of new economic zones may require changes and financial institutions are still not free from local interferences.

It is, however, hoped that the new law will foster further economic and industrial growth in China and will be a forerunner of a more organic and technologically advanced central bank law, which the country would need in the near future as China's socialist market economy is firmly established.

Notes

[1] In comparison, the position in other countries such as the U.S. and Australia is that their central banks report directly to their respective parliaments; the central banks of Japan and Britain are directly under their respective finance ministries.
[2] Central Bank Law, art. 9.
[3] *ibid.* art. 12.
[4] *ibid.* art. 11.
[5] Since 1984, the PBC has had a Policy Formulation Committee. That committee was established when the PBC was made the country's central bank and its commercial functions were transferred to other banks. The Policy Formulation Committee consisted of the governor and deputy governors of the PBC, a deputy finance minister, deputy minister of the State Planning Commission and the heads of the four largest specialized banks.
[6] Regarding the functions of the Monetary Policy Committee, see Wang Shengming, "The Bank Law, A Milestone Marking the Transition of the PBC into a Central Bank" (1995), 2 *China Law, Chinese and English Quarterly*, pp.71–72.

7 Central Bank law, art. 3. The objectives of the Reserve Bank of Australia as set out in the Reserve Bank Act, s.10(2) are similar. It is required to contribute to the stability of the Australian currency, maintain full employment and the economic prosperity and welfare of the people.

8 Central Bank Law, art. 5.

9 *ibid.*

10 The law in the U.S. gives the Congress the power of inspection of activities of the Federal Bank relating to monetary and financial policies.

11 Similar power of issuing the currency is given to the Federal Bank of the U.S., where it was basically a question of removing the difficulty of dealing in too many bank notes issued by the various States in the U.S. before the incorporation of the Federal Bank, see Edward L. Symons, Jr and James J White, *Banking Law, Teaching materials* (3rd ed. 1991), pp.11–12.

12 The People's Bank of China Administration of Financial Institutions Provisions 1994, article 2 states that the PBC and its branches shall be the authorities in charge of financial institutions. They shall independently exercise their duties of examination and approval of the establishment, termination and changes in respect of all kinds of financial institutions according to law and be responsible for the supervision and control of the financial institutions. No local government or work unit or department may engage in its own examination and approval or interfere with such examination and approval. Article 2 further prohibits any financial institutions from providing any services such as account opening, credit settlement and cash for any financial institutions that have been established or any entity that engages in financial business without the approval of the PBC.

Article 8 requires a financial institution applying for establishment upon the PBC's approval to satisfy several conditions:

"To apply for approval to establish a financial institution, the following conditions shall be met:

(1) the applying institutions shall possess at least the minimum amount of renminbi monetary capital or operating funds must conform to the regulations of the People's Bank of China: where the institution is to engage in foreign exchange business, it shall additionally possess foreign currency capital or operating funds that conform to the regulation: the specific limits shall be determined by the People's Bank of China;

(2) its legal representative chairman and vice-chairman of the board, ('bank president, deputy bank president, general manager, deputy general manager, director and deputy director thereafter, primary responsible person') shall possess the qualifications for their positions as determined by the People's Bank of China, and at least 60 per cent of its employees must have previous work experience in the financial business or are graduates of universities, colleges or specialized schools in finance;

(3) it shall have a business site that meets the conditions determined by the People's Bank of China and be equipped with complete antitheft, alarm, communication and fire fighting facilities, etc; and

(4) other conditions that are required by the People's Bank of China are met."

13 Central Bank Law, art. 32.

14 *ibid.* art. 33.

15 *ibid.* arts. 44, 45 and 47.

16 Recently the PBC's Shenzen branch ordered the closure of Shen Zen Jinwei Urban Credit Cooperative for operating its business before receiving a permit, *Ming Bao*, May 31, 1995. There is some overlapping between the

powers of the PBC and those of the Securities Commission and Securities Supervision and Administration Commission.

[17] For example, the Agricultural Bank of China, People's Construction Bank of China, Industrial and Commercial Bank of China, Bank of Communications, China International Trust and Investment Corporation Industrial Bank and China Merchant Bank have all been established by the State Council decrees.

[18] For an interesting account of the development of the stocks and bonds markets, see Solomon M. Karmel, "Emerging Securities markets in China: Capitalism with Chinese Characteristics", *The China Quarterly*, December 1994.

[19] For a detailed discussion of the operation of these markets, see Dipchand, Zhang and Ma, *The Chinese Financial System*, Greenwood Press (1994), p.31.

[20] PRC *Interim Regulations on Administration of Banks* 1986; PRC *Interim Regulations on Administration of Bonds* 1987.

[21] *Ming Bao*, May 29, 1995.

[22] In India a similar development has occurred. Earlier many of the powers under legislation were vested with the central government. They have now been transferred to the Securities and Exchange Board of India for regulation of all activities connected with dealings of securities. The main objects of the Indian legislation are to protect the investors and safeguard the emerging securities market.

[23] See Central Bank Law, arts. 22(5), 28.

[24] *China Daily* August 10, 1995.

[25] D. Owen and Nee Jr in *Doing Business in China* (Williams (ed.), Sept 1993), pp.12–37.

[26] *South China Morning Post*, June 28, 1995.

[27] State Council Notification Concerning issue of Government Investment Bonds 1991, art. 1(b).

[28] Regulations Concerning Administration of Enterprises Bonds 1993, art. 2.

[29] *China Daily* August 12, 1995.

[30] Regulations Concerning Administration of Enterprises Bonds (Revised) 1993, art. 10.

[31] *South China Morning Post* June 28, 1995.

[32] Dipchand, Zhang and Ma, *The Chinese Financial System*, Greenwood Press (1994), p.39.

[33] Wu Zhipan, *On Financial Law* (Chinese), p.24, Peking University Press (1993). In India, adjustments are done on the basis of an average daily balance of time and demand liabilities.

[34] *China Finance*, China Finance Press (1990), p.45.

[35] World Bank, *A World Bank Country Study: China* (1990), p.41. *China Finance*, p.45. Cecil Dipchand, Zhang Yichun and Ma Mingjia, *The Chinese Financial System* (1994), p.39. Greenwood Press. The authors of the last book also expressed their suspicion to the function of reserve fund in controlling the economy in China.

[36] Wu, p.206.

[37] Wu, p.25.

[38] In September 1995, the PBC Shanghai branch lowered its discount rates on loans to commercial banks. The commercial banks will correspondingly lend at lower rates. In fact they cannot charge more than 0.15 per cent above the PBC's discount rates.

[39] Beijing Institute of International Finance, *The Banking System of China* (1993), p.24.

[40] *South China Morning Post* August 9, 1995.

233

[41] *ibid.*
[42] Central Bank Law, art. 22(2).
[43] As the Hong Kong dollar is linked to the U.S. dollar, Hong Kong does not have much flexibility to adjust its interest rates.
[44] Gao Xiang, *Reform of the Chinese Financial Management* (Chinese), p.290, China Fiance Press (1991), p.290.
[45] The rates offered were: January 9.84%, February 10.38%, March 11.87%, April 11.475%, May 12.27%, June 12.92%, July 12.995%, August 12.64%. The holders of three, five and eight year deposits would now receive an extra 12.64% interest above the set rates of 12.24% for three year deposits, 14.94% for five year deposits, and 17.64% for eight year deposits.
[46] See art. 29(1) which restricts the power of the PBC to give loans to local government departments and non-financial institutions.
[47] *Far Eastern Express* March 22, 1995.
[48] *South China Morning Post* September 4, 1995.
[49] Decision of the State Council on Reform of the Financial Structure 1993.
[50] See Central Bank Law, art. 29(1).

RECONCEPTUALIZING CHINA'S CONTRACT LAW — THE PROBLEM OF INTERPRETATION OF CONTRACT

Ling Bing

Faculty of Law
City University of Hong Kong

Ling Bing, *S.J.D. candidate (Michigan), LL.B. (Peking University), LL.M. (Michigan), Diploma (The Hague Academy of International Law), is an assistant professor at the Faculty of Law, City University of Hong Kong, and formerly assistant lecturer of law at Peking University.*

The development of China's contract law has been inspired, to a large extent, by China's economic reform. China's contract law at present is bothered by a perplexingly complicated order of norms with varying authoritativeness. Apart from the General Principles of Civil Law,[1] there are three laws enacted by the supreme legislature that govern economic contracts,[2] foreign-related economic contracts[3] and technology contracts[4] respectively. There are dozens of administrative regulations made by the State Council and its subsidiary commissions and ministries.[5] There are also numerous regulations, decrees and rules made by local authorities. On top of all these, the Supreme Court and various administrative commissions and ministries frequently issue opinions, orders and instructions that are of norm-creating character. The complexity of this normative structure is worsened by the fact that unpublished rules are often invoked by the authorities as the controlling norm. This makes the determination of applicable law in a particular case a daunting task. It obscures the predictability of commercial transactions and shortchanges rule of law in this area. China needs to develop a clear and definitive set of conflict of law rules to put the system in order. The enactment of a uniform Contract Law does not necessarily solve the problem.[6]

The work on the uniform Contract Law,[7] however, does provide an opportunity for China to streamline its contract law and, more significantly, to develop the substance of law in order to address the requirements posed by the newly- and rapidly-emerging market economy. Unlike the amendment of the Economic Contract Law in 1993 (which only made minor changes to the old law), the uniform Contract Law should be able to reform substantially the normative landscape of China's contract law. This paper discusses the problem of interpretation of contract. It is an area that current Chinese contract law has so far failed to address,[8] but the problem is of great importance to the integrity of contract law and to the stability of business transactions.

The Relevance of the Problem

Legal texts operate only through interpretation. Interpretation of contract involves much more than explanation or clarification of what is included in a contract.[9] It is a process shaped by the value judgment of the interpreting party toward a desired end. Especially where the intent of a party differs from the expression thereof, interpretation recreates the factual and normative context in which the party's expectations under the contract are to be effected. A proper interpretation under defined rules contributes to the stability of transactions and the realization of the parties' expectations.

Contract law doctrines and rules cannot operate without interpretation of contract or of extrinsic statements and conduct. The conclusion of contract requires, under China's Economic Contract Law, the agreement between the parties on the principal clauses of the contract.[10] A contract is voidable if it violates the law or the public interest or is obviously unfair.[11] The damages for breach of contract may not exceed the loss which the breaching party should have foreseen at the time of the conclusion of the contract as a possible consequence of the breach.[12] Interpretation of contract is indispensable to the operation of those rules in Chinese law. It comes as a surprise, therefore, when one finds that no Chinese law or regulation contains any even general guidelines as to how a contract is to be interpreted, nor do the Supreme Court opinions or most textbooks touch upon the problem.

One should not exaggerate the negative consequences of this legal vacuum, since interpretation of contract is invariably a problem the solution of which calls for judicial resilience and creativity, with or without authoritative guiding principles.[13] Good contract drafting also helps avoid problems of interpretation, but it is also true that the total lack of normative standards in contract interpretation leaves too much discretion to the courts and increases the incidence of disputes that may vitiate the stability of transactions. A cynical view on the necessity of interpretational standards in Chinese contract law would only do disservice to the improvement of the legal system.

It may be interesting to note that major industrialized countries in common law systems and civil law systems follow quite different approaches to contract interpretation. The United Nations Convention on Contracts for the International Sale of Goods (CISG Convention) adopts a mixed approach that applies to international sales contracts. I will briefly survey those different approaches before I comment on the recent draft articles in the uniform Contract Law on interpretation of contracts and the approach that I think China should consider taking to fulfil the professed aims of its contract law.

The Civil Law Approach

Contract results from the free exercise of will by the parties and it is a party's intent or consent that defines his contractual obligations. Under that theory, civil law countries stress the importance of finding the true intent of the parties in the interpretation of contract. A broad interpretative approach is adopted without confining the court to the literal terms of contract. The German Civil Code, on declaration of intention, provides that "[i]n interpreting a declaration of intention the intention shall be sought without regard to the declaration's literal meaning".[14] On interpretation of contract in particular, the German Code emphasizes the requirement of good faith.[15] The Swiss Code of Obligation provides that interpretation should be based on the common intent of the parties without regard to vague expressions and terms.[16] The French Civil Code also provides that "[i]n agreements we must endeavour to ascertain what was the common intention of the parties, rather than to adhere to the literal sense of the terms".[17] In accordance with the idea of consensualism in French civil law, the general principle of interpretation is to determine the will of the parties to the contract, and the common intention of the parties prevails over its outward formulation.[18] Professor Barry Nicholas noted that "French law, influenced no doubt by the doctrine of the autonomy of the will and more concerned for justice in the individual case than for commercial expediency, often takes account of the true state of mind of one of its parties."[19] Greater emphasis on vitiating elements of contract (mistake in particular) and on the requirement of good faith and the lack of parol evidence rule all attest to this tendency.[20]

A purely subjective approach may easily run into difficulties where it is impossible to ascertain the disputing parties' intent but through their own testimonies.[21] The essence of the approach, however, does not lie in the adherence to the mythical intent of parties, but in its emphasis on good faith requirement and its allowance for the consideration of a wide range of relevant circumstances in order to determine the intent of the parties.

The Common Law Approach

The common law approach to interpretation of contract was staunchly stated by Oliver Wendel Holmes as follows: "The law has nothing to do with the actual state of the parties' minds. In contract, as elsewhere, it must go by externals, and judge parties by their conduct."[22] Although different judges have differing degrees of faith in the reliability of language, in a dispute over contract interpretation in common law countries each party tries to establish that the language should be given the meaning that that party attaches to it at the time of dispute.[23] It is the language as a form of objective expression of intent that is the focus of interpretation. To ensure the integrity of interpretation, common law courts developed the parol evidence rule to exclude extrinsic materials that should not even be interpreted. Professor Farnsworth argued that the parol evidence rule, if aptly used, has much to commend it, as:

> "[t]here are many instances in which the parties, after concluding their negotiation, want to simplify the administration of the resulting contract and to facilitate the resolution of possible disputes by excluding from the scope of their agreement those matters that were raised and dropped or even agreed upon and superseded during the negotiation. It is often useful to be able to replace the negotiations of yesterday with an authoritative agreement of today."[24]

The interpretation centres on the literal terms of a contract, but in determining the meaning of the language in a contract, common law courts look to all the relevant circumstances surrounding the transaction, including all the written and oral statements and other conduct by which the parties manifested their assent, together with any prior negotiations between them and any applicable course of dealing, course of performance, or usage.[25] The purpose of the parties, where ascertainable, is given particular weight.[26]

The CISG Approach

The CISG Convention was based on the work by the United Nations Commission on International Trade Law (UNCITRAL) and was adopted in Vienna on April 11, 1980. China ratified the Convention on December 11, 1986 and the Convention thus became part of the Chinese law of contracts. The Convention embodies uniform rules for international sales contracts and, on many aspects, compromises differing theories of civil law and common law. The rule on interpretation of contract is no exception.

Article 8 of the Convention provides:[27]

(a) For the purposes of this Convention statements made by and
other conduct of a party are to be interpreted according to his
intent where the other party knew or could not have been
unaware what that intent was.

(b) If the preceding paragraph is not applicable, statements made
by and other conduct of a party are to be interpreted according
to the understanding that a reasonable person of the same kind
as the other party would have had in the same circumstances.

(c) In determining the intent of a party or the understanding a
reasonable person would have had, due consideration is to be
given to all relevant circumstances of the case including the
negotiations, any practices which the parties have established
between themselves, usages and any subsequent conduct of
the parties.

The provisions in article 8 are based on a graduated concept of
intent, *i.e.* firstly, the common intent of the parties; secondly, if this is
not applicable, the intent of one of the parties provided that the other
party knows about this intent; and thirdly, if neither is applicable, the
understanding of a reasonable man.[28] Since common intent of the
parties will be lacking wherever there is a need to interpret, the Convention adopts the second and third concepts.[29]

The apparent civil-law focus on the subjectivity of intent in Paragraph 1 is obviated by the requirement that the other party "knew or
could not have been unaware of that intent. The hypothetical reasonable man referred to in Paragraph 2 reinforces the objectivity of interpretation and places the burden on one who makes a statement or
drafts a contract to communicate clearly to a reasonable person in the
same position as the other party.[30] Paragraph 3, however, defies the
traditional common law approach by allowing a court to give due
consideration to "all relevant circumstances of a case".[31] By doing so,
the Convention removes all bars against relevant but extrinsic evidence and implicitly excludes the application of parol evidence rule in
international sales transactions.[32]

The Draft Articles on Interpretation of Contract in the Uniform Contract Law

In the July 1995 draft of the uniform Contract Law, there is a
separate chapter including six articles that formulate, for the first time
in China's legal history, rules on interpretation of contract. It is worth
translating the whole chapter as follows:

Chapter 9 Interpretation of Contract

"Article 159 The common true intent of the parties shall be sought in the interpretation of contract and the interpretation shall not be limited to the terms used.

Article 160 Each contract provision shall be interpreted by reference to other provisions in order to determine the correct meaning of each provision in the contract as a whole.

Article 161 Where two interpretations are possible of the terms used in a contract or of a particular provision, one that better suits the purpose of the contract shall be adopted.

Article 162 Where the meaning of the terms used in a contract is ambiguous, reference shall be made to the habitual usage of the parties.

Article 163 The interpretation of contract shall follow the principle of fairness.

In interpreting a gratuitous contract, the meaning shall be adopted that would impose lighter obligations on the obligor. In interpreting a non-gratuitous contract, the meaning shall be adopted that would be fair to both parties. Where disputes arise over a contract that was made on the basis of provisions decided by one party alone, the meaning shall be adopted that would be against the interests of the party who decided the contract provisions.

Article 164 The interpretation of contract shall follow the principle of good faith."

The emphasis on the intent of the parties in article 159 resembles the approach followed in major European civil codes (as mentioned above). The inner intent of the parties may well be elusive, and it is its outward manifestations (words and other conduct) that are within judicial cognizance as a practical matter. Business contracts often affect the interests of third parties, and the security and predictability of transactions, to a large extent, depends upon avoiding the confusion that may be caused if the interpretation of contract is to be controlled by the secret intent shown subsequently in defiance of the express language of a contract.[33] The "common true intent" as referred to in the article is probably difficult (if not impossible) to ascertain in most contract disputes, and one needs to adopt the objective reasonable man standard to reach a fair solution. The other draft articles, apart from the vague reference to the principles of fairness and good faith in articles 163(1) and 164, fail to specify where and how the inquiry should go beyond the language of the terms of a contract, and those articles are primarily concerned with rules on determining the meaning of the language of the terms in a contract. This, perhaps, belies the general focus on subjectivism.

The holistic approach stressed by article 160 is, in principle, beyond reproach.[34] Its actual operation may, however, present problems not expected by law-makers. Instead of gathering the intent of the parties from the language of the terms, a judge may conceivably attempt to justify a preconceived "intent" by straining and manipulating the language of various parts of an agreement.[35] The reference to the purpose of a contract in its interpretation, while essentially sound, may present the same problems.[36]

If the meaning of a term of a contract is ambiguous, article 162 points to the "habitual usage" *of the parties*. Thus, "habitual usage" refers to the special meaning, *i.e.* different from the ordinary meaning, that the parties habitually attribute to a certain term. This article probably does not apply to a contract between two strangers where one may not find any habitual usage between the parties. It is not clear whether this article will be applicable if the ordinary meaning of the term in question is *not* ambiguous. The "common true intent" standard of article 159 will probably direct to the application of "habitual usage".[37] The really difficult problem is where the parties do not agree on the "habitual usage" of a term and attach different meanings to that term. It is in those cases one has to adopt the reasonable man standard to achieve a sensible result — but the draft articles fail to specify such a standard.

Given the lack of more specific standards, the principles of fairness and good faith in articles 163(1) and 164 provide a court with some general guidelines to deal with difficult cases. Article 163(2) provides rules that apply the principle of fairness to certain types of contracts.[38] The recognition of the time-honoured rule of *contra preferentem* will probably serve to protect the interests of weaker parties (especially consumers) who have to enter into transactions on the basis of pre-determined terms prepared by the stronger parties. The rule, however, should be so qualified that it is only applicable where the meaning of the term in question is doubtful or ambiguous.[39]

The draft articles of the uniform Contract Law are still open to comments, and one may expect a fair number of changes before the draft is passed into law. I will set out briefly the approach China should take for contract interpretation in the final part of this paper.

Conclusion

In developing its approach to contract interpretation, China has the luxury of being able to review and compare the different approaches employed by different legal systems. As China endeavours to reform its contract law to promote the development of the market economy, several points may be noted here.

An objective approach to interpretation based on the language of a contract serves to ensure the security of business transactions and reduce the likelihood of disputes. It also induces the parties to attend closely to the details of the contract and the transaction and develop their business sophistication.

All relevant circumstances may be considered to determine the proper meaning of the language in a contract. While the parol evidence rule needs not to be imported into Chinese law, careful legal analysis is required in weighing extrinsic evidence for the purpose of interpretation. The parol evidence rule, as Professor Corbin noted, essentially affirms the principle that subsequent agreements should supersede antecedent contracts and preliminary negotiations.[40] The principle is nothing novel to Chinese law.

Established rules and maxims in aid of interpretation should be incorporated into Chinese law, most properly through judicial decisions. Such rules as that in favour of business efficacy, that of "against the profferer" and that "the expression of one thing is the exclusion of the other" are generally accepted in both civil law and common law jurisdictions and can serve as useful tools in aid of interpretation.

The intent of the parties should be a controlling element in contract interpretation in cases not involving arm's length transactions, particularly consumer cases. The abuse of written documents to entrap weaker parties and of standardized form contracts may be dealt with not only by virtue of article 59(2) of the GPCL but also by such methods of interpretation as stress mutual assent and understanding, as exemplified by the CISG approach.

The formulation of interpretation standards in legislation is of limited assistance. It is much more important that the courts, especially the Supreme People's Court, apply those standards to cases in an imaginative and yet principled manner. The Supreme People's Court can play an important role in this area of law-making by providing exemplary cases and opinion on the application of rules of contract interpretation.

Notes

1 General Principles of Civil Law of the People's Republic of China, adopted by the National People's Congress on April 12, 1986, has its English translation in *The Laws of the People's Republic of China (1983–1986)*, p.225. A better translation, by Whitmore Gray and Henry R. Zheng, appears at 52

Law and Contemporary Problems 27 (No. 2, 1989). The Supreme People's Court issued *Opinion (for Trial Use) on Questions Concerning the Implementation of the General Principles of Civil Law of the People's Republic of China* on January 26, 1988. It is regarded as the authoritative interpretation of the law. Its English translation, also by Gray and Zheng, appears at 52 *Law and Contemporary Problems* 59 (No. 2, 1989).

2 Economic Contract Law of the People's Republic of China was first adopted by the National People's Congress on December 13, 1981. The English translation appears at *The Laws of the People's Republic of China (1979–1982) op. cit.* at 219. The Law was amended by the Standing Committee of the National People's Congress on September 2, 1993. The English translation of the amendments appears at 7 *China Law and Practice* 40 (No. 4, November 1993).

3 Foreign Economic Contract Law of the People's Republic of China, adopted by the Standing Committee of the National People's Congress on March 21, 1985, has its English translation at *The Laws of the People's Republic of China (1983–1986) op. cit.* at 162. The Supreme People's Court issued its interpretation of the law in the *Answers to Certain Questions on the Application of the Foreign Economic Contract Law* on October 17, 1987. The Chinese text appears at *Zuigao Renmin Fayuan Gongbao [Gazette of the Supreme People's Court]* 3 (No. 4, 1987).

4 Technology Contract Law of the People's Republic of China, adopted by the Standing Committee of the National People's Congress on June 23, 1987, has its English translation at 1 *China Law and Practice* 32 (No. 7, August 1987). The State Council, on February 15, 1989, issued the Implementation Regulation of the Technology Contract Law.

5 Some of the major regulations include Regulation on Contracts for Sale of Industrial and Mineral Products, Regulation on Contracts for Sale of Agricultural Products, Regulation on Contracts for Processing Work, Regulation on Contracts for Property Insurance and Regulation on Loan Contracts. Provisions governing specific types of contracts can also be found in several laws, *e.g.* Maritime Law, Copyright Law, Railway Law, Sino-Foreign Equity Joint Venture Law and Sino-Foreign Contractual Joint Venture Law.

6 Article 538 of the draft Contract Law of the People's Republic of China provides that Economic Contract Law, Foreign Economic Contract Law and Technology Contract Law shall be repealed when the uniform law comes into effect. This provision does not mention pre-existing administrative regulations and other contract law rules made by various government organs, and it is likely that new contract regulations (if not laws) will be adopted by governmental authorities at various levels even after the adoption of the uniform Contract Law.

7 For an account by a noted scholar of the general background of the uniform Contract Law, see Liang Huixing, "From Trinity' toward a Uniform Contract Law" [in Chinese] *Zhongguo Faxue [Chinese Legal Science]* 9 (No. 3, 1995)

8 For discussions of the problem by Chinese scholars, see Liang Huixing, "On Methods of Legal Interpretation" [in Chinese] in *Minfa Xueshuo Panli yu Lifa Yanjiu [A Study of Civil Law Doctrines, Cases and Legislation]* at p.20 (1993); Dong Ansheng, *Minshi Falü Xingwei* (1994) [*Civil Legal Act*] 236–252.

9 Often what should be the subject matter of interpretation may give rise to legal controversies, as is addressed by the parol evidence rule in common law jurisdictions.

10 Chinese Economic Contract Law, art. 9.

11 Chinese General Principles of Civil Law, arts. 58(5), 59(2).

12 Chinese Foreign Economic Contract Law, art. 19.
13 The contexts in which the interpretation rules operate vary greatly, and the subject matter of interpretation may range from unwitnessed telephone conversations to elaborate written agreements formally executed. For that reason, rules of interpretation as formulated in a statute are necessarily general and open to flexible application.
14 German Civil Code, art. 133.
15 *ibid.* art. 157.
16 Swiss Code of Obligation, art. 18.
17 French Civil Code, art. 1156.
18 Michel Alter, *French Law of Business Contracts: Principles* (1986), p.51.
19 Nicholas, *The French Law of Contract* (1992), p.42.
20 *ibid.*
21 It may happen that the parties with different intent will agree on the same imprecise language used in the contract. A well-known example is *Raffles v. Wichelhaus* (the *Peerless case*) 159 Eng. Rep. 375 (1864). Sometimes the parties may have overlooked certain specific points in the contract and may have no "intent" at all on those points. Especially where a contract is based on pre-determined standard terms, it is often not realistic to assume that the parties intended the legal consequences of all the apparently agreed terms.
22 Holmes, *The Common Law* (1963), p.262. Objectivist statements abound in common law literature. For instance, Learned Hand remarked in *Hotchkiss v. National City Bank* 200 F. 287, 293 (S.D.N.Y., 1911),

"A contract has, strictly speaking, nothing to do with the personal or individual intent of the parties. A contract is an obligation attached by the mere force of law to certain acts of the parties, usually words, which ordinarily accompany and represent a known intent. If, however, it were proved by twenty bishops that either party, when he used the words, intended something else than the usual meaning which the law imposes upon them, he would still be held, unless there were some mutual mistake, or something else of the sort. Of course, if it appear by other words, or acts, of the parties, that they attribute a peculiar meaning to such words as they use in the contract, that meaning will prevail, but only by virtue of the other words, and not because of their unexpressed intent."

Lord Wilberforce stated in *Reardon-Smith Line Ltd. v. Hansen-Tangen* [1976] 1 W.L.R. 989

"When one speaks of the intention of the parties to the contract one speaks objectively — the parties cannot themselves give direct evidence of what their intention was — and what must be ascertained is what is to be taken as the intention which reasonable people would have had if placed in the situation of the parties."

23 *Farnsworth on Contracts* (1990), p.502.
24 *ibid.* at 469. Tindal C.J. justified the rule in *Shore v. Wilson* [1842] 9 Cl. & F. 355, as follows:

"If it were otherwise, no lawyer would be safe in advising upon the construction of a written instrument, nor any party in taking under it, for the ablest advice might be controlled, and the clearest title undermined, if, at some future period, parol evidence of the particular meaning which the party affixed to his words, or of his secret intention in making the instrument, or of the objects he meant to take benefit under it, might be set up to contradict or vary the plain language of the instrument itself."

25 *Farnswarth, op. cit.,* at 511.

[26] Restatement of Contracts (Second), § 202(1).

[27] Article 7 is no doubt applicable to a unilateral statement (or other act) by a party; a contract, as shown in a single document, may be regarded as the product of two unilateral acts (offer and acceptance) and is also within the scope of application of article 7. See the Secretariat Commentary on article 7 of the 1978 draft of the Convention, reproduced in J. Honnold, *Documentary History of the Uniform Law for International Sales* (1989), p.408.

[28] See G. Eörsi, "General Provisions" in *International Sales: The United Nations Convention on Contracts for the International Sale of Goods* (Galston & Smit ed., 1984), pp.2–17.

[29] As article 7 is specifically addressed to *unilateral* acts of a party, the issue of ascertaining common intent is, therefore, not dealt with. See the Secretariat Commentary, *supra* n.27.

[30] See J. Honnold, *Uniform Law for International Sales* (1991), p.165.

[31] It has, however, been stressed that "[i]n determining the intent of a party or the intent a reasonable person would have had in the same circumstances, it is necessary to look first to the words actually used or the conduct engaged in"; but the interpretation is not limited to such words or conduct, even if they appear clear and unequivocal. See the Secretariat Commentary, *supra* n.27.

[32] However, the so-called "integration clause" may probably still have its effect by virtue of article 6 of the Convention which allows the parties to vary the effect of most rules of the Convention.

[33] See Lord Devlin, "Morals and the Law of Contract", as quoted in Kim Lewison, *The Interpretation of Contracts* (1989), p.8.

[34] *cf.* French Civil Code, art. 1161, "all clauses of agreements are interpreted the one by the other, giving to each the sense which results from the entire act."

[35] See *Leader v. Duffey* [1888] 13 App. Cas. 294, *per* Lord Halsbury L.C.

[36] See Kim Lewison, *supra* n.33, at 6–7, 10–15.

[37] See Restatement of Contracts (Second), S. 201(1), "Where the parties have attached the same meaning to a promise or agreement or a term thereof, it is interpreted in accordance with that meaning." Article 8(1) of the CISG Convention compels the same conclusion.

[38] Compare the Chinese rule on gratuitous contracts with French Civil Code, art. 1162, "in a doubtful case, the agreement is interpreted in favour of him who has contracted the obligations."

[39] See *Birrell v. Dryer* [1884] 9 App. Cas. 345, *per* Earl of Selbourne L.C.

[40] *Corbin on Contracts* (1960), p.574.

PART 4

THE ROLE OF GOVERNMENT IN MARKET ECONOMY

A COMPARATIVE STUDY ON THE ACT OF STATE DOCTRINE — WITH SPECIAL REFERENCE TO THE HONG KONG COURT OF FINAL APPEAL

Professor Wang Guiguo

Faculty of Law
City University of Hong Kong

Professor Wang, *JSD (Yale), LL.M. (Columbia), is the Dean of the Faculty of Law, City University of Hong Kong and Visiting Professor of Law at the People's University of China. He is an arbitrator with the China International Economic and Trade Arbitration Commission, Beijing; and the China and British Columbia International Commercial Arbitration Centre, Canada. Professor Wang has published more than a dozen books and a number of academic articles on international commercial law, comparative law and Chinese Law. His most recent publications include* Business Law of China; International Monetary and Financial Law; *"Economic Integration in Quest of Law: Chinese Experience",* Journal of World Trade; *"The Banking Law Reforms in China — Difficulties and Prospects",* World Competition: Law and Economics Review *and "Taxation Law of China",* Taxman.

In June 1995, the Chinese and the British Governments reached an agreement on the establishment of the Court of Final Appeal of Hong Kong (CFA) before July 1, 1997.[1] To implement the agreement, the Hong Kong Government enacted the Court of Final Appeal Ordinance,[2] clause 4 of which provides:

"JURISDICTION OF THE COURT
(a) the court shall have the jurisdiction conferred on it under this Ordinance and by any other law.
(b) the court shall have no jurisdiction over acts of state such as defence and foreign affairs.

(c) the court shall obtain a certificate from the Governor on questions of fact concerning acts of state whenever such questions arise in the adjudication of cases, and that certificate shall be binding on the court.

(d) before issuing such a certificate the Governor shall obtain a certifying document from the Government of the United Kingdom of Great Britain and Northern Ireland."[3]

Before the adoption of the Court of Final Appeal Ordinance but soon after the publication of the Court of Final Appeal Bill (CFA Bill) based on the agreement between China and Britian, lots of comments were made on the Bill, particularly on the concept of "acts of state". Some of them claimed that Clause 4 of the CFA Bill would weaken the independence of the judiciary, for the Chinese Government might use this clause to take away the jurisdiction of the CFA. As a result, Chinese enterprises and institutions in Hong Kong such as the Bank of China might be able to avoid their obligations that would not be eluded otherwise.[4] Other comments mention that the Chinese definition of "acts of state" differed from that of common law countries;[5] and that the words "such as defence and foreign affairs" were too wide and indefinite to be interpreted.[6]

Clause 4 of the CFA Ordinance follows article 19 of the Basic Law of Hong Kong which provides: "The Court of the Hong Kong Special Administrative Region shall have no jurisdiction over acts of state such as defence and foreign affairs." Accordingly the interpretation of Clause 4 of the CFA Ordinance will depend on the interpretation of Article 19 of the Baisc Law of Hong Kong. The Basic Law of Hong Kong itself does not further elaborate on the concept of acts of state. Article 8 of the Basic Law, however, provides that:

"[T]he law previously in force in Hong Kong, that is, the common law, rules of equity, ordinances, subordinate legislation and the customary law shall be maintained, except for any that contravene this Law, and subject to any amendment by the legislature of the Hong Kong Special Administrative Region."

It is, therefore, obvious that the common law approach towards the acts of state will have a direct bearing on the interpretation of the acts of state under the Basic Law and the CFA Ordinance. This article examines the judicial practice of the courts of the common law and civil law jurisdictions, the laws of China in respect of the acts of state and the potential operation of the Hong Kong Court of Final Appeal regarding cases involving the acts of state.

Acts of State under the Common Law

Like the other aspects of the common law, the U.S. and the United Kingdom have played an important role in developing the doctrine of acts of state. The American statement of the acts of state doctrine appears to have taken root in England as early as 1674 in *Blad v. Bamfield*.[7] This case was considered as evidence to prove the origin of the acts of state doctrine by the U.S. Supreme Court.[8] There were differences of opinion on the basis and scope of the doctrine, but on the point of its origin the court was unanimous. The doctrine can be traced from Lord Nottingham's passage:

> "[T]he plaintiff hath proved letters patent from the King of Denmark for the sole trade of Iceland; a seizure by virtue of that patent; a sentence upon the seizure; a confirmation of that sentence by the Chancellor of Denmark; an execution of that sentence after confirmation; and a payment of two-thirds to the King of Denmark after that execution. Now, after all this, to send it to trial at law, where either the court must pretend to judge the validity of the King's letter patent in Denmark, or of the exposition and meaning of the articles of peace; or that a common jury should try whether the English have a right to trade in Iceland, is monstrous and absurd."

This general principle was:

> "started in English law, adopted and generalized in the law of the United States of America which is effective and compelling in English courts. This principle is not one of discretion, but is inherent in the very nature of the judicial process".[9]

According to Lord Denning M.R.,[10] the first acts of state case decided in England was the *Duke of Brunswick v. The King of Hanover*,[11] which involved an action of one sovereign against another under an authority. The essential issue was an instrument executed by King William IV in 1833 which was confirmed by the German Diet. According to that instrument the respondent was made guardian of the appellant. The respondent was the British subject and was present at the material time in England. Under the authority of guardianship the respondent sold immovable and movable properties of the appellant. Against that action of the respondent, the appellant prayed the court to declare the instrument of 1833 null and void and claimed money and other properties from the respondent. By holding in favour of the respondent, Lord Cottenham L.C. stated:

251

"A foreign sovereign coming into this country cannot be responsible for an act done in his Sovereign character in his own country; whether it be an act right or wrong, whether according to the constitution or not, the courts of this country cannot sit in judgement upon an act of a foreign Sovereign effected by virtue of his sovereign authority abroad, an act not done as a British subject, but supposed to be done in the exercise of his authority vested in him as a Sovereign."[12]

This passage thereafter became the guiding principle in respect of cases involving the acts of state in the nineteenth and the first half of the twentieth century. The United Kingdom position in *Hanover* was restated by Fletcher Moulton L.J. in *Salaman v. Secretary of State for India*:[13]

"An act of state is essentially an exercise of sovereign power, and hence cannot be challenged, controlled, or interfered with by municipal Courts. Its sanction is not that of law, but that of sovereign power . . . [I]t is a catastrophic change, constituting a new departure. Municipal law has nothing to do with the act of change by which this new departure is effected. Its duty is simply to accept the new departure . . ."[14]

In both cases the United Kingdom court took the view that the municipal court must give full recognition to the acts done by a foreign sovereign. They did not, however, decide the issue of liability, if any, arising from such acts. In both cases, the acts involved were acts of foreign governments. The same rule would apply to the acts done by the government of the country where the court is located.

In a leading case, *Secretary of State for India-in-Council v. Kamachee Boye Saheba*,[15] the Privy Council took an absolute view of the acts of state. The respondent brought an action against the appellant, in the Supreme Court of Madras, praying for the declaration that the estate of her husband should be inherited by her and the seizing of the property by the East India Company was illegal. The husband of the respondent was the King of Tanjore, a small state of India and was a sovereign having treaty relations with the East India Company which was an agent of the British Government. The King died without any issue. The East India Company merged the kingdom in the British Empire.[16] The Supreme Court of Madras gave its decision in favour of the respondent. Against the decision of the Court the Secretary of State of India appealed to the Privy Council contending that the seizure of the property was an act of state and the Supreme Court of Madras could not inquire into it. He also contended that the act done by an agent of a government, when it is ratified and adopted by the government afterwards, must be taken as if it had been done under its previous authority. Having accepted the contention of the appellant and declared that the transactions between independent states were governed by laws other than those which municipal courts administered and that such court had neither the means of deciding what was right nor the power of enforcing any decision they might make, the Privy Council stated:

"The result, in their Lordships' opinion, is that the property now claimed by the respondent has been seized by the British Government, acting as a sovereign power, through its delegate, the East India Company; and that the act done, with its consequences, is an act of State over which the Supreme Court of Madras has no jurisdiction. Of the propriety or justice of that act, neither the Court below nor the Judicial Committee have means of forming, or the right of expression, if they had formed any opinion. It may have just or unjust, politic or impolitic, beneficial or injurious effects taken as a whole to those whose interests are affected. These are considerations into which Their Lordships cannot enter. It is sufficient to say that even if a wrong has been done, it is a wrong for which no municipal court of justice can afford remedy."[17]

Whilst commenting on *Secretary of State v. Bai Rajbai*,[18] Lord Dunedin[19] stated that when change of sovereignty occurred the right of inhabitants might be affected and that such acts must be recognized. Specifically, he said:

"When a territory is acquired by a sovereign state for the first time that is an act of state. It matters not how the acquisition has been brought about. It may be by conquest, it may be by cession following on treaty, it may be by occupation of territory hitherto unoccupied by a recognized ruler. In all cases the result is the same. Any inhabitant of the territory can make good in the municipal courts established by the new sovereign only such rights as that sovereign has, through his officers, recognized. Such rights as he had under the rule of predecessors avail him nothing. Nay more, even if in a treaty of cession it is stipulated that certain inhabitants should enjoy certain rights, that does not give a title to those inhabitants to enforce these situations in the municipal courts. The right to enforce remains only with the high contracting parties. This is made quite clear by Lord Atkinson when, citing the Pongoland case of *Cook v. Sprigg*,[20] he says: 'it was held that the annexation of territory made an act of state and that any obligation assured under the treaty with the ceding state either to the sovereign or the individuals is not one which municipal courts are authorized to enforce.'"[21]

253

The above principle in respect of the acts of state was summarized by Lord Sumner in *Johnstone v. Pedlar*:[22]

"municipal courts not to take it upon themselves to review the dealings of State with State or Sovereign with Sovereign. They do not control the acts of a foreign State that done within its own territory, in the exercise of sovereign power, so as to criticize their legality or to require their justification."[23]

The principle of non-justiciability of acts of state by the English court was followed in Britain until the mid-twentieth century. *Bank Voor Handel en Scheetvaart v. Slatford*[24] represents a turning point. That case involved a decree issued by the Royal Netherlands Government, then exiled in London during the occupation of Holland by the Germans in 1940. The object of the decree was to entrust to the State the property belonging to the persons who were resident in the occupied Netherlands so as to prevent it from being used in a manner against the interest of the Netherlands. Under that decree even properties in the form of gold and bank balances should be transferred to the Netherlands State. It was held that the United Kingdom courts would not recognize foreign legislation as having effect in the United Kingdom; and that whether foreign legislation might be recognized or not on the ground of public policy was a matter not for the court to decide but for the legislature. Still later the United Kingdom courts gradually imposed restrictions on the act of state doctrine by holding that an act of state might be pleaded as a defence (not as a matter of non-justiciability) and whether the defendant was successful or not depended on the courts' willingness to restrain themselves from exercising jurisdiction.

A leading case representing the shifting of position of the United Kingdom courts from non-justiciability to judicial restraint was *Buttes Gas and Oil Company v. Hammer*.[25] In that case both the plaintiff and the defendant were oil exploration companies which were granted oil concessions in Persian Gulf from two different rulers. The plaintiff was given concession from the ruler of Sharjah and the defendant was given concession from the ruler of Umm al Quaiwain. A dispute arose over a rich oil area. The defendant made a slander on the disputed area in England against which the plaintiff brought a suit in the English court. The defendant pleaded the defence of fair comment and justification based on a decree issued by the ruler of Sharjah and other government instructions. The defendant also filed a counterclaim in which he claimed damages for the alleged conspiracy between the plaintiff and the ruler of Sharjah and others to cheat and defraud the defendant. In response to the counterclaim, the plaintiff argued that the justification and counterclaim raised by the defendant were based on the decree of the ruler of Sharjah and other government instructions into which the court had no jurisdiction to inquire and that hence the justification and counterclaim must be struck out.[26] In this case Lord Wilberforce held:

"[T]here exists in English law a more general principle that the courts will not adjudicate upon the transactions of foreign sovereign states. Though I would prefer to avoid argument on terminology, it seems desirable to consider this principle, if existing, not as a variety of act of state but one for judicial restraint or abstention."[27]

Nevertheless, judicial restraint or abstention will only be exercised in extraordinary cases as declared in *Nissan v. Attorney-General*:[28]

"Any ordinary governmental act is cognisable by an ordinary court of law (municipal not international): if a subject alleges that the governmental act was wrongful and claims damages or other relief in respect of it, his claim will be entertained and heard and determined by the court. An act of state is something not cognisable by the court: if a claim is made in respect of it, the court will have to ascertain the facts but if it then appears that the act complained of was an act of state the court must refuse to adjudicate upon the claim. In such a case the court does not come to any decision as to the legality or illegality, or the rightness or wrongness, of the act complained of: the decision is that because it was an act of state the court has no jurisdiction to entertain a claim in respect of it. This is a very unusual situation and strong evidence is required to prove that it exists in a particular case."[29]

Thus the United Kingdom courts decided to restrain from exercising jurisdiction except in cases where no commonly accepted judicial or manageable standards by which to judge are available. Following the precedent, the courts should also restrain from exercising jurisdiction where "the court would be in a judicial no-man's land", such as "making war and peace making treaties with foreign sovereigns and annexation and cessions of territory."[30]

In the U.S., the act of state doctrine can be traced back to *The Schooner Exchange v. M'Faddon*[31] decided in 1812. M'Faddon, an U.S. citizen, was the owner of an armed vessel that was captured by certain persons acting under the authority of Napoleon, the emperor of France, while it was sailing peacefully and lawfully to Spain from Baltimore. The vessel was then brought to the U.S. where the owner filed a case and requested the court restore the vessel to him. The main issue involved in the case was whether an U.S. citizen can assert in an U.S. court a title to an armed national vessel found within the waters of the U.S. The court turned down the request and held that a public armed ship of a friendly power came into the American territory under an implied promise that she should be exempt from the jurisdiction of the country. In the opinion of the Supreme Court, the Chief Justice John Marshall declared:

> "One sovereign being in no respect amenable to another, and being bound by obligations of the highest character not to degrade the dignity of his nation, by placing himself or its sovereign rights within the jurisdiction of another, can be supposed to enter a foreign territory only under an express license, or in the confidence that the immunities belonging to his independent sovereign station, though not expressly stipulated, are reserved by implication, and will be extended to him."[32]

It must be noted that *The Schooner Exchange* only stated that as a matter of policy the U.S. must respect the independence and sovereignty of other nations. No mention of acts of state was made in that case.

The first case involving the act of state doctrine dealt with by the U.S. Supreme Court was *Underhill v. Hernandez*.[33] Underhill was an U.S. citizen doing construction work in Bolivia under a contract between him and the government of Venenzuela. General Hernandez was the civil and military chief of the city of Bolivia. Underhill requested Hernandez to issue a passport to him so that he could leave the country but the request was refused. Ultimately, Underhill got the passport and reached America. Thereafter, he brought an action to recover damages for the detention caused by reason of the refusal to grant him the passport; for the alleged confinement in his house and for certain alleged assaults and affronts by the soldiers of Hernandez's army. In this case the Supreme Court, affirming the judgment of the Second Circuit Court for the defendant, held:

> "The immunity of individuals from suits brought in foreign tribunals for acts done within their own states, in the exercise of governmental authority, whether as civil officers or as military commanders, must necessarily extend to the agents of government ruling by paramount force as a matter of fact. . . . The acts complained of were the acts of a military commander representing the authority of the revolutionary party as a government which afterwards succeeded and was recognized by the United States. We think the circuit court of appeals was justified in concluding 'that the acts of the defendant were acts of the government of Venezuela and as such are not properly the subject of adjudication in the courts of another government.'"[34]

With regard to the issue of jurisdiction related to sovereign act, the Supreme Court stated:

"Every sovereign state is bound to respect the independence of every other sovereign state; and the courts of one country will not sit in judgement on the acts of the government of another done within its own territory; the acts of a foreign government done within its own territory cannot be brought into judgment in the courts of this country."[35]

The principle stated in *Underhill* had been followed by the U.S. courts till the 1950s, although the terminology used was different. This is not to say, however, that the U.S. courts subsequent to *Underhill* failed to follow the development of the principle of the act of state doctrine. On the contrary the courts tackled the act of state doctrine from different perspectives. For instance, in *American Banana Co. v. United Fruit Co.*,[36] the Supreme Court stated:

"The fundamental reason why persuading a sovereign power to do this or that cannot be a tort is not that the sovereign cannot be joined as a defendant or because it must be assumed to be acting lawfully . . . The fundamental reason is that it is a contradiction in terms to say that within its jurisdiction it is unlawful to persuade a sovereign power to bring about a result that it declares by its conduct to be desirable and proper. It does not, and a foreign court cannot, admit that the influences were improper or the results bad. It makes the persuasion lawful by its own act. The very meaning of sovereignty is that the decree of the sovereign makes law."[37]

Oetjen v. Central Leather Co.[38] involved a seizure of hides from a Mexican citizen as a military levy by a general acting on behalf of his government. Later those hides were sold to a Texas corporation. The plaintiff in the court instituted the case for claiming back those hides alleging that the seizure was illegal as it was contrary to the Hague Conventions. The U.S. Supreme Court rejected the plea and held:

"The principle that the conduct of one independent government cannot be successfully questioned in the courts of another is as applicable to a case involving the title to property brought within the custody of a court, such as we have here, as it was held to be the cases cited, in which claims for damages were based upon acts done in a foreign country, for it[s] rests at last upon the highest considerations of international comity and expediency. To permit the validity of the acts of one sovereign state to be reexamined and perhaps condemned by the courts of another would very certainly 'imperil the amicable relations between governments and vex the peace of nations'".[39]

It is, therefore, fair to say that before the U.S. changed its position on sovereign immunity, that is from the absolute immunity to restrictive immunity, the courts adopted more or less the same approach as that in *Underhill* towards the act of state doctrine.

A fundamental change of the U.S. Supreme Court towards the act of state doctrine took place in *Banco Nacional de Cuba v. Sabbatino*[40] decided in 1964. The defendant was an U.S. national who agreed to purchase a certain quantity of sugar from a Cuban corporation which was principally owned by U.S. residents. It was agreed that the payment for the sugar would be made in the U.S. upon delivery of certain relevant shipping documents. Subsequently the Cuban government expropriated the Cuban corporation under a Cuban nationalization law and insisted the purchaser enter into an identical contract according to which the payment must be made to a Cuban bank. The plaintfiff to which the bank (the Banco Para el comercio Exterior de Cuba) had assigned the bill of lading instituted an action in an U.S. court for the recovery of the proceeds of the bill of lading as it had been denied. The main issue in the case was the act of expropriation by the Cuban government, which was pleaded as an act of state. The Supreme Court declared, for the first time in history, that the act of state doctrine had constitutional underpinnings. Commenting on the act of state doctrine, the Court stated:

> "[I]t arises out of the basic relationships between branches of government in a system of separation of powers. It concerns the competency of the dissimilar institutions to make and implement particular kinds of decisions in the area of international relations. The doctrine as formulated in past decisions expresses the strong sense of the Judicial Branch that its engagement in the task of passing on the validity of foreign acts of state may hinder rather than further this country's pursuit of goals both for itself and for the community of nations as a whole in the international sphere."[41]

Apparently one of the reasons for the *Sabbatino* court's reluctance in exercising its jurisdiction over the case was lack of applicable rules of international law. This was implied by the Supreme Court when it stated:

> "It should be apparent that the greater the degree of codification or consensus concerning a particular area of international law, the more appropriate it is for the judiciary to render decisions regarding it, since the courts can then focus on the application of an agreed principle to circumstances of fact rather than on the sensitive task of establishing a principle not inconsistent with the national interest or with international justice."[42]

In fact one should not be surprised at the departure of the *Sabbatino* decision from the traditional views towards the act of state doctrine. Even in *Ricaud v. American Metal Co.*[43] and *Shapleigh v. Meir*[44] the Supreme Court already started changing the principle announced by the *Underhill* Court. In *Ricaud* the court stated that the act of state doctrine:

> "does not deprive the courts of jurisdiction once acquired over a case. It requires only that, when it is made to appear that the foreign government has acted in a given way on the subject matter of the litigation, the details of such action or the merit of the result cannot be questioned but must be accepted by our courts as a rule for their decision. To accept a ruling authority and to decide accordingly is not a surrender or abandonment of jurisdiction but is an exercise of it."[45]

In *Shapleigh* Justice Cardozo went even further by saying:

> "The question is not here whether the proceeding was so conducted as to be a wrong to our nationals under the doctrines of international law, though valid under the law of the situs of the land. For wrongs of that order the remedy to be followed is along the channels of diplomacy."[46]

The *Sabbatino* decision was therefore just a natural result of the development of *Shapleigh*.

The U.S. Supreme Court decision in *Sabbatino* was much criticized for not being firm in dealing with issues of expropriation, in particular the presumption adopted by the *Sabbtino* court that a foreign act of state should not be questioned but the court should obtain indication from the executive branch.[47] Apparently *Sabbatino's* hesitation in finding the applicable rules of international law was one reason for the adoption of the Hickenlooper Amendment to the Foreign Assistance Act 1961, which in substance reversed the *Sabbatino* decision. The Hickenlooper Amendment declared that no court shall decline to adjudicate a case on the merits in dealing with any claim of title acquired through a foreign expropriation measure that violated international law. At the same time, the Amendment was expressly made inapplicable in cases where the expropriation in question is lawful under international law or where the executive branch of the United States determines that the act of state doctrine should apply.[48]

After *Sabbatino*, U.S. courts basically followed the position of the executive branch in dealing with acts of state. For the purpose of keeping in line with the political decision of the executive branch, U.S. courts often found themselves under the pressure of justifying the political decisions with legal reasoning. A case on this point is *Alfred Dunhill v. Republic of Cuba*.[49] The plaintiffs (Americans) were importers of cigars from a Cuban company owned by Cuban nationals. In 1960 the Cuban government confiscated the business and assets of the Cuban cigar company and started to operate the business of the seized Cuban concern. The Cuban Government continued to export cigars to the U.S. importers. In the meantime the original owner of the Cuban concern fled to the U.S. and instituted several proceedings in the court claiming the properties and amount due from the importers. The amount due for the pre-intervention period was made to the interventors under the impression that they were entitled to that. Later the importers demanded from the interventors those monies. The issue before the court was whether the failure of the respondent to return to the petitioner funds mistakenly paid by the petitioner for the cigars that had been sold to them by the expropriated Cuban cigar businesses was an act of state by Cuba which preclude an affirmative judgment against respondents. The Supreme Court stated:

> "The major underpinning of the act of state doctrine is the policy of foreclosing court adjudications involving the legality of acts of foreign states on their own soil that might embarrass the Executive Branch of our Government in the conduct of our foreign relations. But based on the presently expressed views of those who conduct our relations with foreign countries, we are in no sense compelled to recognize as an act of state the purely commercial conduct of foreign governments in order to avoid embarrassing conflicts with the Executive Branch. On the contrary, for the reasons to which we now turn, we fear that embarrassment and conflict would more likely ensue if we were to require that the repudiation of a foreign government's debts arising from its operation of a purely commercial business be recognized as an act of state immunized from question in our courts."[50]

Thus commercial activities conducted by a foreign government would no longer be considered by the U.S. courts as an act of state. This policy adopted by the U.S. Supreme Court was in line with the then U.S. position on sovereign immunity to be discussed later.

The *Dunhill* court admitted that "there may be little codification or consensus as to the rules of international law concerning exercises of governmental powers, including military powers and expropriations, within a sovereign state's borders affecting the property or persons of aliens."[51] The Supreme Court for the first time linked acts of state to sovereign immunity and found itself compelled to follow the policy of the executive branch in respect of sovereign immunity. The Court declared:

"The United States abandoned the absolute theory of sovereign immunity and embraced the restrictive view under which immunity in our courts should be granted only with respect to causes of action arising out of a foreign state's public or governmental actions and not with respect to those arising out of its commercial or proprietary actions.[52] This has been the official policy of our Government since that time as the attached letter of November 26, 1975, confirms.

Moreover, since 1952, the Department of State has adhered to the position that the commercial and private activities of foreign states do not give rise to sovereign immunity. Implicit in this position is a determination that adjudications of commercial liability against foreign states do not impede the conduct of foreign relations, and that such adjudications are consistent with international law on sovereign immunity.

Repudiation of a commercial debt cannot, consistent with this restrictive approach to sovereign immunity, be treated as an act of state; for if it were, foreign governments, by merely repudiating the debt before or after its adjudication, would enjoy an immunity which our Government would not extend them under prevailing sovereign immunity principles in this country. This would undermine the policy supporting the restrictive view of immunity, which is to assure those engaging in commercial transactions with foreign sovereignties that their rights will be determined in the courts whenever possible."[53]

It should be noted that in *Dunhill* the legal advisor to the Department of State, Mr Monroe Leigh, wrote to the Attorney General suggesting the Court to overrule the holdings of *Sabbatino* so that the Court would adjudicate acts of state according to international law and the executive branch would not be embarrassed in relation to foreign affairs. The *Dunhill* Court, however, did not give importance to that suggestion. In the view of the Court, the circumstance of the case did not require the Court to undo the decision of *Sabbatino*. The Court then decided the case on the basis of commercial activity exceptions to the act of state doctrine. The Court's refusal to take notice of the suggestions forwarded by the executive branch indicated that the U.S. judiciary might not abstain from adjudicating a case upon receiving instructions from the executive branch, rather the U.S. courts would regard such instructions as facts and then proceed. If a case was found to involve acts of state, the court would restrain from adjudication. This practice is similar to that of the English courts as shown in *Buttes Gas* case.[54]

Having said the above, it does not mean that the U.S. courts were not under influence of the executive branch of the U.S. government. Actually, the U.S. courts were under instant pressure when adjudicating cases involving foreign governments. The end results of such practice are inconsistent court decisions in cases with similar material facts.[55] In fact even for the same case courts in the U.S. came to different conclusions.

The *Republic of Philippines v. Marcos(I)*[56] and *Republic of Philippines v. Marcos(II)*[57] exemplify this point. The facts and circumstances of both cases are similar. The Republic of Philippines filed a complaint against the former president of the country, Marcos, alleging that he used illegal means and his position for procuring fortunes while he was in power. It was also alleged that he had purchased lots of immovable properties in the U.S. in a friend's name that were in fact the property of the government. In addition, Marcos was allegedly involved in the conspiracy of misappropriation of public money. The plaintiff sought preliminary injunction restraining the defendant from liquidating or transferring the assets and property situated in the U.S. In the second case, *Marcos (II)*, the petitioner relied on the law promulgated by the former president under which it was alleged that he made fortunes by misusing the law. In both cases the prayer of the petitioner was exactly the same. The Philippine Government challenged a wide variety of Marcos' activities, including but not limited to accepting payments, bribes, kick-backs, expropriating outright private property for the benefit of persons beholden to or fronting for Marcos, the said expropriation at times effected by violence or the threat of violence or incarceration; arranging loans by the Philippine Government to private parties beholden to and fronting for Marcos; direct raiding of the public treasury.[58]

The defendant pleaded act of state defence. The Ninth Circuit Court and Second Circuit Court came to different conclusions. In the Ninth Circuit's opinion the act of state doctrine was applicable as a defence for Marcos for two reasons.[59] In the first place, Marcos' traditional governmental actions were sufficiently public to invoke the act of state doctrine.[60] Secondly, in order to avoid interference with the foreign relations of the U.S. the act of state defence by Marcos must be permitted.[61] In other words, by refraining from dealing with foreign policy matters the Court tried not to embarrass the executive branch. The only possible embarrassment or interference the Court's resolution might have had, however, was to find that the Philippine Government under Marcos, which was considered by the United States as a close ally for many years, "was actually a criminal enterprise under our law."[62] At the same time, the Second Circuit held that the act of state doctrine did not apply because Marcos had not met the burden of proving that what he did was within his official capacity.[63] The Second Circuit Court also gave two further reasons for not permitting the act of state defence. First, Marcos was no longer president of the Philippines, therefore, the rejection of the act of state defence raised by Marcos would not interfere with the foreign relations of the U.S.[64]

Secondly, the act of state doctrine reflects the respect for the sovereignty of foreign countries, it is therefore less justifiable for a court to allow the act of state defence when the foreign government in question asked the U.S. court to examine its action.[65] The court added that "the United States has made it clear that it does not fear embarrassment if the courts of this country were to take jurisdiction of this and other appeals between the Republic of Philippines and ex-President Marcos."[66]

The inconsistency of the U.S. courts in applying the act of state doctrine is also demonstrated in *United State v. Noriega*.[67] In this case the Grand Jury indicted Noriega, who was head of the Panamanian armed forces, on various criminal charges, *e.g.* international conspiracy, drug trafficking, etc. Noriega pleaded the defence of act of state and sovereign immunity as he was former *de facto* head of the state. The court held that: (a) the act of state doctrine was different from head of state immunity (the latter was a question which went with the jurisdiction of the court while the former was a function of separation of powers);[68] (b) the act of state doctrine did not apply to the private and unofficial acts of government officials even if the actor was a dictator;[69] and (c) the act of state doctrine was originally couched in terms of sovereign immunity, but did not rest on the principle of international law or respect for sovereign independence; instead it was a function of the system of separation of powers in that its purpose was to preclude judicial examination of the acts of state which might otherwise hinder the executive's conduct of foreign relations.[70] This conclusion has an obvious bearing of *Sabbatino* case, but it is not consistent with the U.S. court decisions subsequent to *Sabbatino*.

Despite the inconsistency of the U.S. courts as well as the United Kingdom courts regarding the act of state doctrine, the change of position occurred in the mid-twentieth century. One may wonder, having applied the act of state doctrine for more than a century, why did the U.S. and other developed countries decide to change their position? In the early 1950s, a number of things happened. In the first place, the U.S. emerged from the Second World War as the most powerful country, virtually dictating the establishment of the United Nations, the World Bank and the International Monetary Fund. It became clear then that without the participation of the United States no international organization could function properly. The failed attempt to establish the World Trade Organization at that time was a case in point. Secondly, the U.S. adopted a policy against the former Soviet Union and the former East European countries forming a bloc capable of challenging the authority of the U.S. and its allies. Thirdly, the governments of the former East European bloc countries engaged in commercial activities through bodies or corporations controlled by those governments. That caused fear among merchants as well as the governments in western countries in respect of their dealings with

263

these government controlled organizations. They were afraid that private enterprises would be at disadvantage if such government controlled institutions and corporations were granted sovereign immunity or would be able to plead the act of state doctrine as defence.[71] In order to deal with the situation, on May 19, 1952, Acting Legal Advisor Jack Tate for the State Department issued a letter announcing that the U.S. would follow the restrictive theory of sovereign immunity by excluding commercial activities from the cases where sovereign immunity would apply. The Hickenlooper Amendment was actually an extension of the Tate Letter from sovereign immunity to the act of state doctrine. By issuing the Tate Letter and adopting the Hickenlooper Amendment, the U.S. made it clear that it decided to take the lead in formulating the laws of nations. This was better expressed at the Senate hearings of the U.S. For instance, Judge Jennings stated that the domestic courts should extend their jurisdication to certain international issues:

> "The prime importance of the domestic jurisdiction in international law cases . . . is that it provides the only considerable area of compulsory judicial determination of public international law issues. The sovereign state of course enjoys immunity from jurisdiction, except insofar as it chooses to waive it, in the international sphere, and to an important extent also in domestic courts. But public international law issues increasingly arise in ordinary civil cases between individuals or corporations in which the state is not in any sense a defendant. In this kind of case the International Court has no jurisdiction at all. The domestic court does commonly have jurisdiction; and its exercise of it is backed by the sanction of the state machinery of enforcement. So quite clearly, we have here a facet of jurisdiction which is of prime importance to international law and international lawyers."[72]

Judge Jessup agreed with Judge Jennings and called upon the national courts to contribute to the development of international law.[73] No matter how such statements were phrased the purpose thereof was pure and simple, that was to serve the interests of the U.S. and other developed countries.[74] This was candidly put by Professor McDougal:

> "[I]n a world without centralized legislative, executive and judicial institutions most of the decisions about the development and application of international law must continue to be made, as during the past several hundred years, by the officials of particular nation-states. Any suggestion that our courts are not competent to continue to participate in the development and application of an international law, whether related to economic affairs or to other

affairs, is fundamentally inimical to our own long-term national interests and the comparable interests which we share with other states."[75]

Whether or not the advancements made by the U.S. are shared by other nations or to what extent are shared by other nations, the U.S. has played an important part in shaping the rules of international law regarding the act of state doctrine. As a world leader, the U.S. has influenced the policy-making of the industrialized countries both of common law and civil law jurisdictions.

Acts of State under Civil Law

Continental countries basically follow the principle adopted by the common law countries in respect of acts of state, although the terminology used may differ. Instead of "acts of state", "acts of government" and "non-justiciable acts" were, as to be discussed later, adopted by the courts and laws of the continental countries. French law does not allow any challenge in a court of acts involving the French government and foreign governments or the relationships between French government and international organizations. A typical example in this regard is the negotiation, conclusion and implementation of international treaties and agreements.[76] Some scholars have attempted to draw a distinction between "act of government" and "act of state": the doctrine of act of state is a legal concept of mainly common law origin which precludes assessment by the courts of the legality of "sovereign acts" of foreign states, whilst the concept of act of government refers to acts of the state in which the court is situated. The doctrine of act of state is mainly concerned with public international law and private international law, whereas act of government arises mainly in the sphere of domestic public law.[77]

Under French law, the acts of French authorities in the conduct of foreign relations are not subject to judicial review[78] and are therefore not justiciable.[79] This general theory of immunity is, however, tending to shrink as a result of development of the theory of detachable act and acceptance of the principle of no fault liability of the state arising from duly concluded international agreements. Under the detachable act theory, if the French authorities have discretion or independent choice with regard to the procedures by which they perform their international obligations and can themselves take the initiatives as regards the means by which they comply with the obligations, such acts may be adjudicated by the court.[80] Examples in this regard include deportation, extradition of aliens, etc.[81] The condition for the application of the principle of no fault liability is that the alleged damage is abnormal and special and that reparation is not precluded by their agreement itself.[82]

In giving effect to the acts of foreign governments, French courts took a view that such acts must not violate the public policy of France. The decision of the French cour de cassation dealing with the Spanish government's confiscation of goods situated in Spain was a case in point.[83] The Montpellier Court of Appeal took a view that the confiscation was an act by the government of Spain in its capacity as a sovereign state and that the Court had no authority to judge the validity of such acts. Since the Spanish government failed to pay compensation for the confiscation, the French court should not recognize or give effect to the expropriation of the property right.[84] Such view is similar to that taken by the courts in the United Kingdom and the U.S.

The German position in respect of acts of state is not as clear as one would have hoped. In the first place, there is no concept of acts of state in German law. Secondly, there is a notional difference of opinion between German court and legal theorists on acts of government (*Regierungsakte*) or non-justiciable acts (*justizfreie Hoheitsakte*), although the two views lead to almost the same result.[85] In practice, any action brought by an individual to a German court will be admissible if the act complained of harms his personal rights. Major policy making acts seldom have such an effect though.[86] Such acts may therefore either be labelled as acts of government or non-justiciable acts. No matter how they are labelled, the courts will not exercise jurisdiction in cases where such acts are in dispute. In general, however, the German Government enjoys much discretion in conducting external relations, "because Federal German government must in particular be in a position to take the reactions of its international partners into consideration when adopting decisions."[87] German practice shows that relations with friendly nations is a prime factor which controls the justiciability of foreign governments' acts in the German court. This practice is similar to United Kingdom practice and comparable to recent U.S. practice which give emphasis to the embarrassment of the executive branches in their foreign relations with other countries. The German Government has equal discretion in matters concerning defence as well. An example is the judgment of December 16, 1983 by the Bundesverfassungsgericht concerning the decision of the Federal German Government to authorize the installation of Pershing missiles.[88] The court held that "certain claims could not give rise to judicial review because of the margin of discretion enjoyed by the public authorities in the conduct of defence policy".[89] The court, after considering whether there existed any rule of international law forbidding such activities by the German Government, concluded that the German Government had the discretion to make decisions regarding defence matters.[90] This result is not surprising as under German law, unless a government measure harms private or individual interests, it will not give rise to judicial review.[91]

Under the Italian Constitution, individuals are entitled to bring cases against the government.[92] Nevertheless, no case is allowed to be brought against governmental measures which have been adopted in the exercise of political powers by the government.[93] Under Italian law, the exercise of political powers includes the conclusion of international treaties and measures relating to international relations which enjoy absolute immunity.[94]

With regard to the laws and acts of foreign governments, the Italian courts have adopted a similar view to that of the French and German courts. The *Anglo-Iranian Oil Company*[95] case illustrates the Italian view in this regard. The Anglo-Iranian Oil Company (A.I.O.C.), the plaintiff in the case, had concessionary rights in the Persian Gulf regarding extraction of oil from that area. In 1951 the Persian government, pursuant to its Oil Nationalization Law, nationalized the petroleum industry which affected the ownership of AIOC over the petroleum extracted from the concessionary area. After the nationalization, the defendant purchased oil in Persia that was shipped to Italy. The Plaintiff applied for judicial sequestration (an order for interim custody) in this case and contended that the Italian court could not enforce the Oil Nationalization Law in Italy and that, moreover, the law had no effect on the particular cargo of oil which was bought and brought by the defendant to Italy. The defendant argued that granting of such type of judicial order would annul the law of a foreign state over which the court has no jurisdiction.

The Court of Venice decided the case against the plaintiff. At the same time the Court also rejected the argument of the defendant that the court had no power to examine the law of a foreign state. The court found that the Persian Law was not contrary to Italian "public order" and so the plaintiff could not claim the ownership of oil. The Court stated:

> "[The respondent's objection] can easily be refuted by the fact that in view of the provisions of the Italian Civil Code relating to private international law (Articles 16–31 of the Preliminary Rules), the Persian Oil Nationalization Law would in any case be subject to examination to ascertain whether or not it could be regarded as coming within the limits contemplated by Article 31 of the above-mentioned Rules, the intention of which is — as is well-known — to prevent foreign laws or acts from taking effect on Italian territory if such laws are contrary to public order; it is clear that, although such an examination might prevent the Persian Law from being applied, it could never cause the 'annulment', 'revocation' or 'destruction' of that Law, which would in any case remain effective within Persian territory."

The Italian Court emphasized that it did not intend to consider whether a foreign law was in compliance with the public policy of Italy. It rather regarded foreign law and the consequences thereof as a matter of fact. Specifically the Court stated:

"According to the most authoritative writers and case-law, it would appear redundant to enquire whether the principles adopted by a foreign Legislature are contrary to those adopted by our Legislature. If the acts contrary to public order have taken place in a foreign country, seeing that the proceedings before the Italian Court deal only with the juridical consequences of these acts, the acts themselves having — from a legal point of view — been finally concluded abroad.

The oil which forms the subject of the present dispute was taken by the Persian Government in Persia by virtue of the Nationalization Law, and in Persia it was disposed of in favour of S.U.P.O.R. by a contract of sale: all this was in conformity with the judicial system of the Persian Government, on whose territory these acts (expropriation and sale and purchase) took place, with the legal and material consequences flowing therefrom. The recognition in Italy of the validity of the effects which these acts had already had in Persia cannot be termed co-operation to make them become effective; it constitutes no more than an acknowledgment that the effects have indeed taken place, i.e., accepting the effects produced, which in themselves — and considered separately from their cause — are in no way contrary to public order. The Nationalization Law should not, therefore, be examined from the point of view of public order."

In Belgium the question whether the theory of acts of government has been accepted by the domestic court is debatable. The cases clearly demonstrate that matters concerning foreign relations, including the conclusion of commercial agreements, may not be questioned. In several cases, the Belgian courts gave judgments for damages brought by individuals against the State. In the case concerning the Belgian State's and the United Nations' intervention in Katanga,[96] the court stated that "the Courts have no power to assess diplomatic action taken by the executive".[97] In another case where the alleged wrongful acts were in connection with the grant of independence of the Congo without previously arranging for transfer of the colonial's debt to the new state.[98] The court considered the matters concerning the independence of the Congo as an act of government which was not subject to judicial control.[99]

The Portuguese law stipulates that political acts such as negotiation and approval of international agreements as well as diplomatic actions taken by the government are not subject to judicial control.[100]

The position of Danish law on the act of state doctrine is not clear. Nevertheless, it would seem that in no circumstances may a private individual call for judicial review or bring an action for damages in respect of the conclusion of a treaty.[101]

Apparently the continental countries have adopted a position that political acts, including acts relating to foreign relations and defence of the governments, are not subject to judicial review. When private or individual interests are affected, the continental courts may adjudicate cases involving acts of government. In such circumstances, the courts are very cautious in exercising jurisdiction on such matters.[102] With regard to acts of foreign governments or states, courts in continental countries have a tendency not to exercise jurisdiction. A case decided by the court in Amsterdam is an example. In that case, the plaintiffs were the owners of tobacco stored in 1923 at Galata. A British peace force removed and sold the tobacco by public auction. Later on, when the goods were shipped by the buyer to Amsterdam the plaintiffs claimed possession of the goods. The court of first instance held that:

> "were the court to declare the acts whereby the property of the plaintiff had been seized as unlawful and in view thereof to order the restitution of such goods to the plaintiff, then the court would undo the act which had been done; as these acts were done by the said GOC in his capacity of representative of the occupying Powers and thereby had the character of authoritative acts of a sovereign Power, the Court would thereby violate such a sovereignty."[103]

The court refused, therefore, to exercise jurisdiction over the case. When the case was appealed to the Court of Appeal Amsterdam, it was held:

> "These questions would by international law be withdrawn from the Dutch Court if any one of the Powers in occupation of Constantinople had itself been a party to the suit in which the legality of its sovereign acts was questioned, but not in the case under consideration where their legality is questioned in a suit between two private individuals. The District Court was wrong in holding that by pronouncing such acts illegal it would have negatived acts which had been done by the occupying Power; on the contrary, all those acts would remain in force, notwithstanding the decision of the Dutch Court. So it is impossible to consider as a violation of foreign sovereignty the decision of a Dutch Court, that such acts of the occupying Power constituted acts of embezzlement under Turkish law. The Dutch tribunal being an independent organ of the State of the Netherlands, . . . cannot be deemed to engage the

international responsibility of that State by a judicial decision pronouncing illegal certain acts of a foreign Government."[104]

Since the Second World War, Japan's foreign policy has borne the obvious influence of the U.S. With regard to the act of state doctrine, the Japanese courts also seem to follow the approach adopted by the U.S. and other developed countries. In the *Anglo-Iranian Oil Co. v. Idemitsu Kosan*[105] case which involved the Oil Nationalization Law of Iran. The Tokyo District Court stated:

"It may be undeniable that there exists a principle in international law that any act of a state confiscating rights and interests within its territory of an alien without compensation constitutes a wrong in violation of international law. Hence it is easy to understand that the alien whose property has been confiscated, or the home country of such alien, which has the right to protect the rights and interests of the alien, may try to hold the state responsible for the latter's illegal act of confiscation and claim indemnity. Whether or not a court of a third country is allowed to decide that such an act of the state is invalid and deny its effect, is a different question on which this Court hesitates to assert that there exists a definite and universally applicable principle of international law. Unless the performance of such an act is to be within the territory in which the law of Japan pervades, or unless recognition of the validity of the act in question actually disturbs its domestic order, this Court, in conformity with the requirements of international comity due to the necessity for mutual respect for the sovereignty of independent and sovereign states and for the maintenance of friendly relations, considers itself to be in no position to deny either the validity of the laws and ordinances concerned of a state where they were enacted as conforming to the interest of that state, or the effect of the said laws and ordinances, which has already been produced within that state."

As discussed earlier, the developed civil law countries have essentially adopted the traditional position on acts of state in respect of foreign affairs, political matters and defence. The recent trend is to make commercial activities an exception to the act of state doctrine. In this regard, the practice of the developed civil law countires is similar to that of the U.S. and Britain. At the same time, the act of state doctrine has not been developed in these civil law countries to the same extent as that in common law jurisdictions. For instance, neither a comprehensive definition of the acts of state nor detailed exceptions to the doctrine have been formulated. Courts in these countries consider acts relating to foreign affairs and defence non-justiciable unless private interests are affected.

The Chinese Position

China is a civil law country, judgments of the courts are not regarded as precedents with binding force. China's legal system suffered a fundamental set-back during the Cultural Revolution.[106] Its current legal system has been built up from the late 1970s. Not much practice of the court in relation to acts of state can be spoken of therefore. The concept of the act of state was formally introduced into Chinese law through the adoption of the Administrative Procedure Law of the People's Republic of China (Administrative Procedure Law).[107] Article 12 of the Administrative Procedure Law provides that the People's Court shall not accept suit brought by citizens, legal persons, or any other organizations against any of the following matters: "(1) act of the state in areas like national defence and foreign affairs . . ."

It must be pointed out that the Administrative Procedure Law mainly deals with the relationship between the Chinese government and Chinese nationals. As regards acts of foreign governments, it appears that China follows the principle of absolute sovereign immunity. As a result, the courts in China will not exercise jurisdiction over acts of foreign states unless special arrangements are made between the parties concerned.

China's attitude towards the acts of state can be inferred from China's relations with other countries. For instance, on April 23, 1958, China concluded the Treaty of Trade and Navigation with the former Soviet Union. Article 4 of the Annexture stipulated:[108]

> "The trade delegation shall enjoy all the immunities to which a sovereign state is entitled and which relate also to foreign trade, with the following exceptions only, to which the Parties agree:
>
> (a) Disputes regarding foreign commercial contracts concluded or guaranteed under Article 3 by the trade delegation in the territory of the receiving state shall, in the absence of a reservation regarding arbitration or any other jurisdiction, be subject to the competence of the courts of the said state. No interim court orders for the provision of the security may be made;
>
> (b) Final judicial decisions against the trade delegation in the aforementioned disputes which have become legally valid may be enforced by execution, such execution may be levied only on the goods and claims outstanding to the credit of the trade delegation."[109]

This provision reveals that in the view of the Chinese Government commercial activities can be excluded from sovereign immunities, but such exclusion must be agreed upon by the parties concerned. The

Chinese view seems not having changed much over the last forty years. In *Jackson v. People's Republic of China* et al.[110] (the *Huguang Railway Bonds* case), after the U.S. District Court for the Northern District of Alabama delivered a default judgment, the Chinese Embassy in Washington issued a memorandum to the U.S. State Department on November 9, 1982 stated:

> "In accordance with the principle of equality of all countries as stipulated in international law, the People's Republic of China, as a sovereign state, is entitled to enjoy judicial immunity. It will accept no suit filed against it by any person at a foreign court, nor will it accept judgment against it by any foreign court."

Later the Chinese Government restated its position:[111]

> "Sovereign immunity is an important principle of international law. It is based on the principle of sovereign equality of all states as affirmed by the Charter of the United Nations. As a sovereign state, China incontestably enjoys judicial immunity. It is in utter violation of the principle of international law of sovereign equality of all states and the UN Charter that a district court of the United States should exercise jurisdiction over a suit against a sovereign state as a defendant, make a judgment by default and even threaten to execute the judgment. The Chinese Government firmly rejects this practice of imposing US domestic law on China to the detriment of China's sovereignty and national dignity. Should the US side, in defiance of international law, execute the above-mentioned judgment and attach China's property in the United States, the Chinese Government reserves the right to take measures accordingly."

The Chinese position towards acts of state and sovereign immunity is determined by its economic and political powers and its influence at international level. It also reflects its experience in the past. As the U.S. State Department stated in the *Huguang Railway Bonds* case,[112] "China's adherence to this principle [absolute sovereign immunity] results, in part, from its adverse experience in extra-territorial laws and jurisdiction of Western powers in the 19th and 20th centuries."[113] In the view of China, the restrictive theory of sovereign immunity has not yet become a rule of international law, because only a small number of nations which by and large do not include developing countries have adopted the principle of restrictive sovereign immunity.[114] China believes that the restrictive theory of sovereign immunity will do more harm than good to developing countries.

In fact, to a large extent, the Chinese position in relation to sovereign immunity and act of state reflects the view of developing countries.[115] The reason for the developing countries' preference for the absolute sovereign immunity and absolute act of state doctrines is protection of national interest. In theory, under the restrictive theories of sovereign immunity and act of state doctrine courts of every country may adjudicate cases involving commercial activities and cases involving human rights that in the view of the courts are in violation of international law even though a foreign government or state may be a party. In practice, however, the courts of developing countries may not be able to exercise jurisdiction over cases involving strong economic and political powers in the world. Even in very few cases, where courts of the developing countries exercise such jurisdiction, they may not have the means to enforce their judgments. The difficulty in ascertaining the rules of international law, which are obviously influenced by the developed countries, is another reason for the developing countries to adhere to the restrictive theory of the act of state doctrine.

The Chinese position on acts of state may change with the growth of its economy and the increase of mutual understanding among members of the international community. In this regard, signs of improvement of mutual understanding between China and Western countries have already been seen. The Chinese scholars' view on acts of state has become similar to that of Western scholars and courts. According to Professor Luo Haocai, Vice-President of the Supreme People's Court of China:

> "Chinese legal scholars hold two views on the definition of acts of state. One view considers that the acts of state only include national defence and foreign affairs, other acts cannot be regarded as acts of state. According to the other view which is broader, acts of state include acts of government or acts of the ruling body, related to all kinds of decisions made by the central government of a country through exercising its sovereign function to the outside world as well as inside the country".[116]

Professor Luo then continued that an act of state is "a political act accomplished in the name of the state by the administrative organ of the state or its executive department, according to the constitution and laws, or upon authorization or delegation of power by the competent organ of the state."[117] Other characteristics of acts of state according to Luo include "manifestation of sovereignty of state which is conducted in the interest of the whole state and for the basic interest of the people."[118] The above view is similar to that held by Devlin L.J.[119] who divided the Government's acts into two categories: (a) those which a government does for the public good in the interests of the country as a whole; and (b) those which it does to avoid its own liabilities under a particular contract or contracts. So far as the first category is concerned, a government cannot fetter its duty to act for the public good.

It cannot bind itself, by an implication in the contract, not to perform its public duties. The first category was illustrated by *Commrs of Crown Lands v. Page*.[120] So far as the second category[121] is concerned, it appears that a government can bind itself to perform a contract with an implication that it will not do anything with or in connection with that particular contract so as to hinder or prevent the performance of its obligations thereunder.[122]

In China's legislative practice, it seems a change is taking place toward the act of state doctrine. An example is the adoption of the Regulations on Diplomatic Privileges and Immunities of the People's Republic of China.[123] These regulations grant foreign diplomats general immunities and privileges. At the same time, it is stipulated that a foreign diplomatic agent shall not enjoy immunity from civil and administrative jurisdiction of the Chinese courts in cases where the diplomatic agent is acting as a private person or conducting professional or commercial activities or unofficial functions. Since foreign diplomats do not enjoy immunity in respect of commercial and professional activities and unofficial functions, it can hardly be argued that they may plead the act of state defence. It is, therefore, a significant step taken by the Chinese Government in adopting these Regulations.[124]

With regard to the nature and characteristics of an act of state, Professor Luo stated:

"The act of state is an exercise of sovereignty, representing the highest interest of the country in question, so the political nature is its main characteristic. To judge whether or not an act is an act of state depends mainly on the following three factors: whether the act is done with a political objective, whether it concerns the exercise of sovereign power and whether it represents the fundamental interests of the whole people. In any event, whether an act should be considered an act of state should not be determined merely according to the nature of the organs which have undertaken the act."[125]

This argument is generally in compliance with the practice of the common law jurisdictions.

According to Chinese scholars, an act of state may fall into three categories: foreign affairs, national defence and public interest. According to these scholars, acts relating to foreign relations may include: "recognition of foreign governments, establishing and breaking off the diplomatic relations with foreign countries, concluding international treaties and agreements, annexation and cession of the territories, important decisions concerning foreign trade, etc." What constitutes an "important decision" of foreign trade, however, is not clear.

With regard to acts in relation to national defence, it has been argued that they include the various administrative measures adopted for the safety of the state, the territorial integrity and the important military activities such as construction of military installations and military bases, test of strategic weapons, preparation of war, mobilization, guaranty of military manoeuvres, conscription and the transport of military supplies.[126]

Acts concerning public interest have not been stipulated as acts of state under Chinese law. Nevertheless, scholars in China are in general agreement that such acts by the administration may not be challenged or judicially reviewed by the court. Examples given in relation to such acts include enforcement of martial law limited to certain provinces, autonomous regions or municipalities directly under the central government, special measures adopted for dealing with emergency or disaster relief, important actions for guaranteeing the implementation of major construction projects of the country and important decisions for promoting national economic development.[127]

Under the Administrative Procedure Law other matters that are not subject to judicial review include administrative rules and regulations, regulations or decisions and orders with general binding force formulated and announced by administrative organs; decisions of administrative organ on awards or punishments for its personnel, or on the appointment or relief from duties of its personnel.[128]

On the whole, the Chinese position on acts of state is similar to that of the Continental countries. Taking into account the traditional link between the Chinese legal system and those of the Continental countries, it is natural for China to adopt a similar view. China's position also bears some influence of the common law countries, such as the U.S.[129] This is so because the concept of acts of state was directly borrowed from the common law. When the Basic Law of Hong Kong was drafted, "acts of state" was suggested by the Hong Kong members of the Basic Law Drafting Committee to be incorporated into the draft.[130] Actually when final approval was sought at the former Hong Kong Basic Law Drafting Committee, some of the members from the mainland side opposed the incorporation of act of state for lack of specific definition. Although the Administrative Procedure Law was adopted earlier than the Basic Law of Hong Kong, the concept and wording in respect of act of state of the Administrative Procedure Law came from the Basic Law of Hong Kong (draft). When the Administrative Procedure Law was debated, a question on the basis the incorporation of the concept of act of state was raised. Mr Wang Hanbing, now Vice-Chairman of the National People's Congress, who was then introducing the bill, simply answered, "The Basic Law of Hong Kong (draft) has such a provision, we think it should also be included in the Administrative Procedure Law." With that, the law was passed. Scholars who write on or interpret the provision of "act of state" have been almost exclusively trained in common law countries. Professor Luo himself also studied in the U.S. It is not surprising, therefore, that the Chinese interpretation of acts of state has the underpinning of common law.

Synthesis of the Act of State Doctrine

The act of state doctrine has always had an international law implication. The doctrine was first invented out of the principle of equality and mutual respect of nations. Subsequently, the application of the act of state doctrine was either defended or rejected, but it has always been done on the basis of international law. At the same time, the act of state has always been related to sovereign immunity. That is, when absolute sovereign immunity prevailed, application of the act of state doctrine was not restricted in any sense. Once the theory of restrictive sovereign immunity was introduced, exceptions to the act of state were created. As a result, commercial activities have ceased to be recognized as acts of state.

Another feature of acts of state is that the developed countries have been playing a dominating role. In the past, the court practice in relation to the act of state doctrine was almost exclusively confined to the developed countries, which have strong economic and political powers but are small in number in the international community. Although these countries are small in number, their practice is diversified. As discussed earlier, the practice of the courts even of the same country may vary from case to case.[131] At the same time, various principles have developed. In such circumstances courts may often find it difficult to determine which principle should apply to a given case. This is especially true for common law countries. For instance, a British court decided in *Buron v. Denman*[132] that as a matter of principle the Crown may plead act of state as a defence to an action in tort brought by an alien for torts of damage inflicted in the King's dominions. In *Walker v. Baird*,[133] however, it was held that the subject was under the protection of the King and was, therefore, entitled to bring an action against the Crown. In other words, the King cannot use act of state as defence to an action arising from loss or damage inflicted upon a British national within the territory of Britain. This rule was subsequently extended to friendly aliens lawfully within the jurisdiction of Britain.[134] The question of whether the alien in question is friendly or unfriendly is likely to be subject to the discretion of the court or the executive branch.

The complexity and diversity in relation to the principles adopted by and the practice of the courts of the members of the international community make it difficult to define the scope, content and applicability of the act of state doctrine. Nevertheless, the practice of various countries influenced each other in this highly interdependent world. As a result, there are certain common features of the court practice of the international community that can help define the act of state doctrine. Also writings by scholars and professionals are helpful in this regard.

According to Western literature, "An act of state includes not only an executive or administrative exercise of sovereign power by an independent state or by its authorized agents or officers, but also its legislative and judicial acts, such as statutes, orders, or judicial pronouncements."[135] In most cases, however, acts of state are conducted by the executive branch of the government. They include "the execution and denunciation of treaty, the annexation of foreign territory, the seizure of property upon conquest, declarations of war and of blockade, the detention perhaps of enemy aliens in wartime, and the torts of Crown employees in some circumstances."[136] It is perhaps futile to attempt to list exhaustively acts that may be considered as acts of state. Generally speaking, acts of state may be subdivided into two categories, one in relation to foreign nations and foreign nationals, and the other in relation to the citizens of the country that does the act. The major difference between the two categories of the acts lies in the jurisdiction of the court, that is remedy. Lord Atkin stated in the *Eshugbayi Eleko v. Government of Nigeria*,[137]

> "As applied to an act of the sovereign power directed against another sovereign power or the subjects of another sovereign power not owing temporary allegiance, in pursuance of sovereign rights of waging war or maintaining peace on the high seas or abroad, it may rise to no legal remedy. But as applied to acts of the executive directed to subjects within the territorial jurisdiction it has no special meaning, and can give no immunity from the jurisdiction of the Court to inquire into the legality of the act."[138]

In addition, whether a particular act should be regarded as an act of state, it "depends upon the nature of the act and (sometimes) at any rate upon the intention with which it was done, and the intention is to be inferred from the words and conduct and surrounding circumstances."[139]

Acts of government officials for private interests may not be regarded as acts of state. It is commonly agreed that an act of state may be conducted by government officials or officers. In such cases, the officials or officers must perform in accordance with their authorization and powers, otherwise their acts may not constitute acts of state. This was confirmed by the Fifth Circuit Court of the U.S. which in *Jimenez v. Aristeguieta*[140] held

277

"Even though characterized as a dictator, the appellant was not himself the sovereign-government-of Venezuela within the Act of State Doctrine. He was chief executive, a public officer, of the sovereign nation of Venezuela. It is only when officials having sovereign authority act in an official capacity that the Act of State Doctrine applies.

Appellant's acts constituting the financial crimes . . . were not acts of Venezuelan sovereignty . . . [E]ach of these acts was 'for the private financial benefit' of the appellant. They constituted common crimes committed by the Chief of State in violation of his position and not in pursuance of it. They are as far from being an act of state as rape . . .[141]

Likewise, the Second Circuit Court of the United States in *Republic of Philippines v. Marcos(I)*[142] stated that privately motivated acts of government officials were outside the reach of the act of state doctrine.

The act of state doctrine refers to the actions taken by the government of the state rather than the effect of such actions by the government. This was reiterated in *Czarnikow Ltd. v. Rolimpex*,[143] which involved a decree of the Polish Government prohibiting the export of sugar. The defendant relied on the Polish decree, arguing that it was an act of state of Poland, therefore, its non-performance of contract should not give rise to any action. The United Kingdom Court of Appeal relying on the findings of the arbitrators that sugar was available in the world market and that contract could have been performed by the defendant by purchasing sugar from the world market, without questioning the intent of the Polish decree dismissed the appeal. The House of Lords affirmed the decision of the Court of Appeal. Also in *Central Hanover Bank & Trust Co. v. Siemens & Halske Aktiengesellschaft*[144] the Second Circuit Court of the U.S. rejected the defence of unsuccessful attempt to obtain the governmental approval required to pay obligations to the foreign creditors.[145]

Acts of state have a territorial boundary. Traditionally the act of state doctrine as an extention of the principle of sovereign immunity developed out of respect for independence and territorial integrity of sovereign states. Accordingly, an act of state may not and should not have effects beyond the territory of the state which performs the act. The underlying reason is that sovereign immunity is mutual in nature among all the nations in the world. Accordingly, the act of state doctrine will not be applied where the "foreign government's act is directed at the property outside its territorial boundary. When the parties and the res are outside the foreign government's territorial boundaries, the foreign government does not possess the ability to alter the legal status of the parties related to the res."[146] This was precisely stated by Professor Beale: "Within his own territory the jurisdiction of the sovereign is exclusive . . . On the other hand, a sovereign has in general no power or jurisdiction outside his own territory; and he can confer upon his legislature no greater power than he himself possesses."[147]

Non-recognition of the extra-territorial effect of an act of state, as a rule of international law, can be traced back to early days. In the early twentieth century, this rule was announced in unequivocal terms in *Luthers v. Sagor*[148] that the "court of one state does not, as a rule, question the validity or legality of the official acts of another sovereign or official or officially avowed acts of its agents, at any rate in so far they purport to have taken effect within the sphere of the latter's state's own jurisdiction".[149] To put it in more positive terms, the courts of Britain announced in the mid-twentieth century that foreign legislation purporting to have effect over property within the territory of the United Kingdom will not be recognized by the British courts, it being immaterial: (a) whether or not the legislation was confiscatory; and (b) that it was the legislation of an allied government made for the purpose of keeping property out of the hands of a common enemy. Whether or not foreign legislation having extraterritorial effect should be recognized is, therefore, a political question to be decided by the legislature on the ground of public policy.[150] This view was shared by the international community at large.[151]

Taking property under the colour of legal title may not be regarded as an act of state. Under this principle, if a government has acquired legal title on the property, such acquisition should not be considered an act of state. This view was vividly stated by the Privy Council in *Forrester v. Secretary of State.*[152] The widow of a French soldier was conferred with an estate together with the public revenue thereof by the Scindia government (a princely state) on the condition that she had to maintain a military force which could be called up for the service of the Scindia government. Later the princely state was conquered by British nationals but the position of the widow remained unchanged till her death. Upon her death the property was resumed by the order of the government. On the basis of a will by the widow in favour of a lunatic person a suit was brought against the Government of India claiming the possession of the widow's estate. The government of India pleaded the defence of act of state and argued that the municipal court was barred for want of jurisdiction. Rejecting the plea of act of state, Lord Hatherly L.C. stated:

> "The act of Government in this case was not the seizure by arbitrary power of territories which up to that time had belonged to another sovereign State; it was the resumption of lands previously held from the Government under a particular tenure, upon

the alleged determination of that tenure. The possession was taken under colour of a legal title; that title being the undoubted right of the sovereign power to resume, and retain or assess to the public revenue all lands within its territories upon the termination of the tenure under which they may have been exceptionally held rent-free. If by means of the continuance of the tenure or for other cause, a right be claimed in derogation of this title of the Government, that claim, like any other arising between the Government and its subjects, would *prima facie* be cognizable by the municipal courts of India."[153]

The application of the above principle as an exception to the act of state doctrine was later extended by the courts of other countries into government measures in respect of their own subjects.[154]

Commercial activities may not fall within the sphere of acts of state. As discussed earlier, the act of state doctrine and sovereign immunity evolved hand in hand over the last century and more. Before the movement of decolonization and independence in the 1950s and 1960s, absolute sovereign immunity was asserted by the world powers. The act of state doctrine was likewise regarded as an absolute bar to jurisdiction of the court. Soon after the Second World War, in particular when the former colonies became independent, the restrictive theory of sovereign immunity was pushed forward by the developed countries. This gave rise to a further exception to the act of state doctrine, *i.e.* commercial activities. Under this theory, if the act in question is commercial in nature the act of state doctrine will not apply. Needless to say, whether or not the act should be considered commercial is often disputed. An additional issue is the relationship between the commercial act and public interest. In other words, if the state government in question takes a measure for the betterment of the society, even if the act itself is commercial in nature, should the doctrine of act of state apply? Although meeting some resistance, the trend in the international community is to adopt the restrictive approach. The reason for this development is the need for the flow of capital and technology among nations in the world, in particular from the developed countries to the developing countries, and business transactions between individuals and private enterprises and foreign governments.

For developing countries, for the purpose of protecting their sovereignty on the one hand and carrying out economic exchanges with other countries on the other hand, through national law they have established business enterprises with the state government as the sole owner. Such enterprises do not enjoy the status of government bodies, therefore, they can neither claim sovereign immunity nor plead for act of state defence.

The commercial activity exception to the act of state doctrine has also a contractual dimension. This was stated by Lord Denning M.R.:[155]

> "When the government of a country enters into an ordinary trading transaction, it cannot afterwards be permitted to repudiate it and get out of its liabilities by saying that it did it out of high government policy or foreign policy or any other policy. It cannot come down like a god on to the stage — *the deus ex machina* — as if it had nothing to do with it beforehand. It started as a trader and must end as a trader. It can be sued in the courts of law for its breaches of contract and for its wrongs just as any other trader can. It has no sovereign immunity."[156]

Some have argued that conduct by foreign governments in violation of fundamental human rights should not be recognized as act of state to bar jurisdiction of the court. This has been written into the *Restatement (third) of Foreign Relations Law of the United States*[157] which reads:

> "A claim arising out of an alleged violation of fundamental human rights — for instance, a claim on behalf of a victim of torture or genocide — would (if otherwise actionable) probably not be defeated by the act of state doctrine, since the accepted international law of human rights is well established and contemplates external scrutiny of such acts."[158]

Unlike the legal title and commercial activity exceptions, it may take a long time for the international community to reach a consensus on the human rights exception to the act of state doctrine. Obvious difficulties include the differences of culture, history, economic and political systems, social and moral values, etc. among various nations that will lead to different standards of human rights. The same act that is considered a violation of international law in relation to human rights in one country may be considered as being in compliance with such rules. Also, the developing countries fear that the developed countries may use human rights as a pretext to interfere with their sovereignty and their internal affairs. To say the least, the human rights exception is most controversial and will continue to be debated among members of the international community.

In any event, no consensus in respect of the application of the act of state doctrine has been reached among countries with different culture, history and political and legal system, and among countries at different stages of economic development. In fact, even courts and scholars within the same country may find it difficult to give a precise definition of the act of state. This issue may not be resolved in the foreseeable future.

Acts of State and the Basic Law of Hong Kong

Under Article 19 of the Basic Law, while adjudicating cases in which a defendant pleads act of state as a defence, the CFA must obtain a certificate from the Chief Executive on the questions of fact. The certificate issued by the Chief Executive has binding force on the court. In addition, before issuing the certificate, the Chief Executive must obtain from the Central People's Government a certifying document on the matter.[159] That is to say, unless the Central People's Government confirms the facts in relation to foreign affairs and national defence, the Chief Executive cannot issue any certificate. This arrangement is similar to the practice of the developed countries such as the U.S. where the executive branch, which is in charge of foreign relations for the country, may issue documents to the court in cases involving acts of state. The difference is that the Chief Executive of the Special Administrative Region must first obtain a certifying document from the Central People's Government. The ground for the arrangement seems to be the provisions of the Basic Law, which stipulate that the Central People's Government is responsible for the defence and foreign affairs of the Hong Kong Special Administrative Region. As such, it is the Central Government, not the Chief Executive, that is in the best position to confirm the relevant facts and circumstances in cases where actions are alleged to have been acts of state. This may happen, for instance, in relation to the recognition and enforcement of foreign judgments and arbitral awards to which one of the parties is a foreign government, the seizure or expropriation by a foreign government of the properties of the residents of Hong Kong. Likewise where someone claims to be acting on behalf of his/her government and, therefore, the court should not have jurisdiction over the act conducted by him or her, the Central Government would be in a position to confirm the official status of the person; the Chief Executive could then issue a certificate to the court.

The certificate issued by the Chief Executive and the certifying document issued by the Central Government should only concern facts and must not concern the interpretation of law. In other words, such certificates should not state what constitutes an act of state or give interpretation to Article 19 of the Basic Law. The certificate should only state the related facts or factual situation of the event such as whether or not the foreign country in question has diplomatic relations with China, whether China recognizes the foreign government, whether a state of war exists between China and the foreign country, etc. This appears also to be the understanding of the Chinese Government. The Chinese Convenor (from the mainland) of the Political Affairs Sub-group of the Preliminary Working Committee of the Preparatory Committee of the Hong Kong Special Administrative Region, Professor Xiao Weiyun, said after the sub-group's meeting in May

1995 that distinction between "acts of state" and the "facts concerning acts of state" should not be blurred. He gave an example: A person who was alleged to have committed an offence claimed to be a foreign diplomat. Whilst the CFA was not certain about the person's status, a certificate from the Chief Executive ought to be sought.[160] Professor Xiao also agrees that the acts of state doctrine is a concept of common law countries and that it is seldom used in China. In his view, acts of state include recognition of states, declarations of war, engagement of war, signing of treaties, etc. Any act conducted and any exercise of administrative powers by the state government would constitute an act of state, said Professor Xiao.[161] It should be noted that Professor Xiao's argument reflects the traditional view of act of state doctrine, which is likely to be the view of the Chinese Government on the issue. A potential question then arises that whilst in the view of the Chinese Government a given act should not be adjudicated by the court, under common law — according to the restrictive act of state doctrine — the act may be tried by the court in Hong Kong; should the court in Hong Kong exercise jurisdiction under that circumstance? With regard to defence matters, the certificate should stipulate if the organ or individual has the authority to carry out the act or to use a given facility, for example, a military vessel. In such cases, the CFA must accept the fact and factual situation provided through the certificate as conclusive and hence no further inquiry into the existence or non-existence of facts will be needed. The power of the CFA is then restricted to determining whether the act in question constitutes an act of state.[162] For example, the People's Liberation Army stationed in Hong Kong carry out an exercise in which the property of a local resident is damaged. When a lawsuit is brought by the local resident to the CFA and the act of state defence is raised, the CFA must request a certificate from the Chief Executive. The certificate should only deal with the facts, *i.e.* whether it was a military exercise. In order to avoid potential problems, the CFA may make its request very specific. The CFA may even draft a certificate for the Chief Executive to confirm and sign. The Basic Law does not prohibit the CFA from so doing. Whether in practice the CFA can play its role to that extent depends on the relationship between the Central People's Government and the Government of the Special Administrative Region. In any event, the more pro-active the role regarding the interpretation of the act of state doctrine the CFA plays, the less likely the chances of misinterpretation of the doctrine.

Under the Basic Law, while adjudicating cases involving an alleged act of state, the CFA should handle the case in the same manner as adjudicating other cases except to be bound by the certificate issued by the Chief Executive. Article 8 of the Basic Law stipulates that the laws previously in force in Hong Kong, *i.e.* the common law, rules of equity, ordinance, subordinate legislation and customary law, shall be maintained. Common law will play therefore a major role in determining what does and what does not constitute an act of state. In other words, in adjudicating cases involving an alleged act of state, the CFA may still apply common law in deciding whether the act in question constitutes an act of state. It is submitted that instead of applying the principle of judicial abstention, the CFA should apply the principle of judicial restraint.[163] For instance, an unit of the Central Military Committee of China enters into a contract with an enterprise in Hong Kong to supply leather jackets for the army. Later the Hong Kong trader is informed by the Chinese party that the contract cannot be performed for lack of foreign exchange. A certificate is issued by the Chief Executive confirming the affiliation of the Chinese party and the intended use for the goods. In such circumstances, instead of not exercising jurisidction, the CFA should examine the facts contained in the certificate in accordance with the common law principles and international law rules and decide if the breach of contract constitutes an act of state. If the answer is Yes, then the court should refrain from adjudicating the case. Of course, it may be argued that the CFA may be under much pressure in case the certificate issued states in unequivocal terms, *e.g.* that the act in question was done by a state organ and should be considered an act of state. As a court of a developed market economy and with common law tradition, the CFA should tackle the issue of act of state in the same way as courts of developed countries do.

The CFA should have independence in adjudicating cases under the Basic Law. It could be argued that since the Basic Law is a Chinese law and, according to the interpretation principles in China, the Basic Law is subject to the interpretation by the Standing Committee of the National People's Congress, the understanding of the Standing Committee of the act of state doctrine may differ from that of the courts of common law jurisdictions. For instance, when a certificate issued by the Chief Executive contains both facts and opinions of the Government, is the CFA empowered not to take into account the non-factual parts of the certificate? There is obviously no ready answer to this question. It is submitted that the CFA should only take into consideration the parts concerning facts.

Conclusion

After the end of the cold war era, the world has become politically more multi-polarized and economically more interdependent. This circumstance has been coupled with China's economic success of the last two decades through its policy of economic reforms and opening to the outside world. With a stronger economy, China is more willing to interact with its counterparts at the international and regional level and is more open to the influence of other cultures. Even in the establishment of its legal system, China has transplanted concepts, values and practices of foreign jurisdictions into its own laws. With the increasing integration of the international community, the laws and principles adopted by the Chinese legislature and the practice of the Chinese courts are bound to be more and more compatible with those prevailing over the international community. This process of integration will achieve a better mutual understanding between other countries and China. This will in turn make China, which suffered at the hands of the world powers in the past, more willing to accept the norms and practices of other countries. The current Chinese legal system has developed almost entirely since the late 1970s. Detailed principles and rules in respect of the act of state doctrine still need to be developed. Whether or not China is willing to accept the exceptions to the act of state doctrine such as commercial activities still needs to be seen. Any development of this nature will directly or indirectly affect the interpretation of the Basic Law and likewise the concept of the act of state. As regards the acts of state doctrine, although China is still in the early stage of development, its willingness and commitment — demonstrated in international treaties to compensate in cases of nationalization and its effort in separating state ownership from the legal entities with legal person status — have paved the way for China to develop detailed rules. This will help to ensure the correct interpretation of the Basic Law of Hong Kong in general and acts of states in particular. Taking into account the origin of the act of state doctrine under the Chinese law, the above conclusion is not over optimistic.

Notes

[1] This agreement is the execution of the earlier agreement reached in the Joint Liaison Group between China and Britain (JLG) in September 1991.
[2] The idea to set up the Hong Kong Court of Final Appeal before the change over of sovereignty in 1997 was first initiated by Britain in 1988. The JLG then held talks and in September 1991 reached an agreement on the establishment of the CFA at an appropriate time before 1997 with the purpose of enabling the Court to accumulate some experience before the change over of sovereignty.

The agreement reached in 1991 was not endorsed by the Legislative Council of Hong Kong. Although Britian was constitutionally in a position to take measures to make the agreement into law, it did not do anything because of its deteriorating relationship with China. Discussion on this matter was resumed among Expert Groups of the JLG in March 1995. At the same time, the Preliminary Working Committee of the Preparatory Committee of the Hong Kong Special Administrative Region (PWC) which was established by China was also discussing the matter. On May 17, 1995, the Political Affairs Sub-Group of the PWC announced its own eight point proposals for the setting up of the CFA. These proposals stuck to the principles of the 1991 agreement. Subsequently, China suggested the CFA be set up before 1997 by the Chief Executive of the Hong Kong Special Administrative Region (designate) and his/her administration with the participation and assistance of Britain.

On June 9, 1995, China and Britian reached an agreement to amend the CFA Bill which had been published subsequent to the 1991 agreement. The two sides agreed that the amendment should be based on the eight point proposals of the Political Affairs Sub-group of PWC and should incorporate Article 19 of the Hong Kong Basic Law on acts of state. It was also agreed that the CFA would start to function on July 1, 1997.

[3] It is anticipated that the word "Governor" will be replaced by "Chief Executive" and the "Government of the United Kingdom of Great Britain and Northern Ireland" will be replaced with the "Central People's Government" after 1997.

[4] *South China Morning Post*, June 10, 1995.

[5] *South China Morning Post*, June 10, 1995.

[6] *South China Morning Post*, June 10, 1995.

[7] 3 Swans 604, 36 E.R. 992.

[8] *per* Justice Harlan in *Banco Nacional de Cuba v. Sabbatino* 376 U.S. 416 at 816.

[9] *Buttes Gas and Oil Company v. Hammer* [1982] A.C. 888 at 932, H.L.

[10] Lord Denning M.R. made this comment while deciding *Occidental Petroleum Corp. v. Buttes Gas & Oil Co.* [1975] 1 Q.B.557 at 572D.

[11] [1844] 6 Beav 1, [1848] 2HL Cas.1.

[12] *ibid.* at 17.

[13] [1906] 1 K.B. 613.

[14] *ibid.* at 639–40.

[15] 7 MIA 476.

[16] In India, the general practice prevalent at that time was that only son of a king could succeed his throne. The British Government took advantage of that social practice and enacted a law that whenever a King died without issue the state would lapse into British government.

[17] *ibid.* at 540.

[18] (1915) 42 I.A. 229.

[19] The decisions of *Cook v. Sprigg* [1899] App. Cas. 572 and *Secretary of State v. Bai Rajbai* (1915) 42 I.A. 229 was discussed by Lord Dunedin in *Vajesinghji Joravorsingji v. Secretary of State* (1924) 51 IA 357. His passage has been repeatedly cited with approval.

[20] [1899] A.C. 572. This case was cited by Lord Atkinson in (1915) 42 I.A. at 237–38.

[21] (1924) 51 I.A. above at 360–1.

[22] [1921] 2 A.C. 262.

[23] *ibid.* at 290.

[24] [1951] 2 All E.R. 779.

[25] [1982] A.C. 888.

[26] This is an unique case in which the issue of act of state was raised by the plaintiff and not by the defendant as usually happens in such cases. The issue of act of state is in almost all cases raised as a matter of defence, *i.e.* by the defendant. Here the plaintiff was defending the counterclaim of the defendant at the same time he was fortifying his case against the plea of justification and fair comment made by the defendant.

[27] [1982] A.C. 888 at 931.

[28] [1970] A.C. 179.

[29] *ibid.* at 237, *per* Lord Pearson with whom Lord Wilberforce agreed.

[30] *per* Lord Wilberforce in [1982] A.C. 888 above at p.938.

[31] 7 Cranch, 116.2.

[32] *ibid.* at 137.

[33] 168 U.S. 250 (1897).

[34] *ibid.* at 252–254.

[35] *ibid.* at 252.

[36] 213 U.S. 347 (1908).

[37] *ibid.* at 358, *per* Justice Holmes. He based his reasoning on the *ratio* propounded by Justice Fuller in *Underhill.* In continuation of the dictum he added his reasoning and extended the dictum of Justice Fuller.

[38] 246 U.S. 297 (1918).

[39] *ibid.* at 303–304, 62 L. Ed. at 732.

[40] 376 U.S. 398.

[41] *ibid.* at 423.

[42] 376 U.S. at 428; see also *OPEC* 649 F.2d at 1361 (the lack of international consensus on the propriety of cartels).

[43] 246 U.S. 304.

[44] 299 U.S. 468.

[45] 246 U.S. 304 at 309.

[46] 299 U.S. 468 at 471.

[47] For detailed discussion, see F.A. Mann, "The legal consequences of Sabbatino" (1965) 51 Virginia. L. Rev. 604; Kline, "An Examination of the Competence of National Courts to Prescribe and Apply International Law: The Sabbatino Case Revisited" (1966) 1 U.S.F.L Rev. 49.

[48] The Hickenlooper Amendment was adopted in 1964 as an instrument to control the Foreign Assistance Act of 1961, Pub.L. No. 88–663, 301 (d)(4), 78 Stat.1013 (1964). The pertinent part of the Amendment reads as follows:

"[N]o court in the United States shall decline on the ground of the federal act of state doctrine to make a determination on the merits giving effect to the principles of international law in a case in which a claim of title or other right is asserted by any party including a foreign state . . . based upon . . . an act of that state in violation of the principles of international law, including the principles of compensation . . . provided that this subparagraph shall not be applicable (1) in any case in which an act of a foreign state is not contrary to international law . . . or (2) in any case with respect to which the President determines that application of the act of state doctrine is required in that particular case by the foreign policy interests of the United States and a suggestion to this effect is filed on his behalf in that case with the court . . ."

[49] 425 U.S. 686.

[50] *ibid.* at 697, 698, *per* Justice White.

[51] *ibid.* at 704, *per* Justice White.

[52] This practice of the U.S. was declared in a letter (the Tate Letter) written by Jack B. Tate, the acting legal adviser, on behalf of the Secretary of State to the Attorney General in 1952.

[53] 425 US 686 at 698, 699.

[54] [1982] A.C. 888.

[55] See The Court of Appeals of the State of New York in *Salimoff & Company v. Standard Oil Company of New York* 262 N.Y. 220 (1993) and the Supreme Court of Aden in *Anglo-Iranian Oil Co. Ltd. v. Jaffrate* [1953] 1 WLR 246, which decided the other. The cases were almost identical but the

two courts came to opposite conclusions. One may of course justify this by saying that one case was decided by a U.S. court while the other case was decided by a court which follows U.K. practice, despite the fact that both courts were of common law jurisdictions.

[56] 806 F 2d 344 (1986), 81 ILR 581.

[57] 862 F 2d 1355 (1988), 81 ILR 609.

[58] As stated by the court in the *Republic of Philippines v. Marcos(II)* 818 F 2d 1473.

[59] *ibid.* at 1489. Judge Kozinski wrote the majority judgement, while Judge Nelson dissented.

[60] *ibid.* at 1485–89.

[61] *ibid.* at 1487.

[62] According to Judge Kozinski, this was one of the points on which the resolution of *Marcos (II)* would have embarrassed the United States. The Republic of Philippines alleged the former President of the country as a main instrument in making the government of the country a racketeer-influenced enterprise under the Racketeer Influenced and Corrupt Organizations Act 18 USC Sections 1961–1968.

[63] *Marcos (I)* at 593–4. The Second Circuit Court distinguished this case from its earlier decisions barring suit against a foreign sovereign, see *Bernestein v. Van Hyghen Freres, S.A.* 163 F. 2d 246; *Banco de Espana v. Federal Reserve Bank* 114 F. 2d 438. Those cases relied on the principle of sovereign immunity rather than the act of state doctrine, see *Marcos (I) ibid.* at 359. Moreover, the Supreme Court in *Sabbatino*, based on the separation of power rationale, established that the balance of considerations may shift against a ruler of a former government because the political interest of the United States would be lessened.

[64] *Marcos (I)* 806 F. 2d at 359.

[65] *cf. Re Grand Jury Proceedings John Doe No.700* 817 F.2d 1108, 1111 (4th Cir.) noting failure to honour government's waiver of former dictator's head of state immunity would undermine international comity.

[66] *Marcos (I)* 806 F.2d at 356. This conclusion was reinforced by a declaration of Michael H. Armacost, Undersecretary of State for Political Affairs, made on March 15,1986, submitted to the United States Court of International Trade in connection with a pending suit before that court which was also recorded in *Marcos(I)* court. Armacost's declaration pointed out the political, economic and military relationship of the United States with the Philippines. It also indicated the strong future relationship with the Aquino government. In short, the U.S. government did not want to spoil its relationship with the Aquino government and committed itself to honour the Philippine government's requests at the earliest possible time.

[67] 808 F. Supp. 791 (1992); 99 ILR 143.

[68] *ibid.* at 163–64.

[69] *ibid.*

[70] *ibid.* at 165.

[71] At that time courts of the developed countries began to adopt the restrictive theory of sovereign immunity, which denied immunity to commercial activities carried out by state governments or government bodies. Because the respect for sovereignty underlies both the act of state doctrine and the doctrine of sovereign immunity, these courts applied the same reasoning in both contexts, *i.e.* that commercial acts were not sovereign acts and thus might warrant denying the act of state protection. See, *e.g. Hunt v. Mobil Oil Corporation 550 F. 2d 68, 73; Bokkelen v. Rumman Aerospace Corp. 432 f. supp. 329, 333–4.* See also J. Sweeny, C. Oliver & N. Leech, *International Legal System* (2d ed., 1981), pp.365–7.

72 Jennings, The Sabbatino Controversy, Senate Hearings (The Foreign Assistance Program: Hearings Before the Senate Comm. on Foreign Relations) 89th Cong. 1st Sess. (1965) at 739–40.

73 Jessup, "Has the Supreme Court Abdicated one of its Functions?" (1946) 40 AJIL 168.

74 The reason behind the adoption of the restrictive theory of sovereign immunity was apparently different in the USA and U.K. A number of U.S. corporations had invested large sums of money in other countries. It was, therefore, of the utmost importance to protect those investments by excluding commercial acts from sovereign acts otherwise the U.S. corporations might have lost their investment. The second reason was that the USA invested in the development of natural resources of other countries to such an extent that those countries started depending heavily on the USA and put themselves indirectly under the control of the USA. In order to release themselves from such foreign control, developing and newly developed countries started to nationalize foreign controlled concerns in the 1950s. As a result, a good number of cases related to expropriation started reaching the U.S. courts. This phenomenon gave impetus for the USA to formulate the laws relating to acts of state and sovereign immunity according to its own interest. The extraterritorial reach of antitrust law was also a contributory factor in this area.

In U.K. the court as well as the government shifted to the restrictive theory of sovereign immunity because of the fact that disputes related to contract might involve private and government concerns and in that situation the government might plead the defence of act of state. The case of torts in which government was involved also came up a number of times where the court got an opportunity to shape the interpretation of the act of state doctrine and sovereign immunity. See Michael Singer, "The Act of State doctrine of the United Kingdom: An Analysis, With Comparisons to United States Practice" 75 AJIL 283.

75 Senate Hearings at 751–52.

76 For consistent line of case-law, see *Conseil d'Etat* (CE) February 5, 1926 *Dame Caraco* p.125; CE March 16, 1962 *Prince Sliman Bey* p.179; CE July 13, 1979 *Cofarex* p.319.

77 See Ergec: "Le controle juridictionnel de l'administration dans des matieres qui se rattachent aux rapports internationaux" *Revue de droit international et de droit compare* 1986 p.73 in particular at 74. Similarly it has been said that act of state is a "secondary conflict of laws rule", Flack, quoted by Buzyova in "Reflections on immunity of States from the point of view of international law" *Questions of International Law*, Vol.3, Dordrecht, 1986, p.46. The act of government doctrine has at least occasionally been subject to criticism. One commentator even suggested that the "act of government" should be banished from the system of public law of all civilized countries'. See Duguit, *Traite de droit institutionnel* (3rd ed., III 1930). On the other hand this doctrine has also been defended, with the reason that without it there would otherwise be a lack of court jurisdiction to deal with governmental activities as distinct from administrative activities. See Chapus, "L'acte du gouvernement, monstre ou victime?" D. 1958, Chr. p.5. Other authors consider that the court's lack of jurisdiction is a consequence of the mixed character of the act. Virally, "L'introuvable acte de gouvernement", RDP 1952, p.338.

78 Some commentators maintain that "Whilst international treaties obviously concern the relation of the French state with foreign states, they are not acts of government. Apart from that they are not acts of municipal law, since they do not emanate from the French government alone, the rules

applying to them are 'completely different from those applying to acts of government'." Chapus, *Droit administratif general,* 1985, p.618 and 619.

[79] Examples of non-justiciable acts of government include: suspension of navigation in maritime safety zone in order to conduct nuclear tests (CE July 11, 1975; *Paris de la Bollardiere* p.423); intervention with a foreign state to protect the goods or interests of a French national (CE March 2, 1966 *Cramennel* p.157.; refusal to take proceedings before an international court (CE January 9, 1952 *Geny* p.17); refusal to communicate to a union proposals addressed to an international body (CE February 10, 1978 CFDT p.61).

[80] Opinion delivered by Odent in the *Tribunal des conflicts, February 2, 1950, Radiodiffusion françaize* RDP 1950, p.423, in particular at p.427.

[81] For examples relating to French practice of non-justiciability of act of government with full authority, see *Maclaine Watson v. EC Council and Commission of the European Communities* (Case C 241/87), May 10, 1990.

[82] *Conseil d'Etat, Compagnie generale d'energie radio electrique* March 30, 1966 Rec. Lebnon p.257; on that judgement see AJDA, June 20, 1966, "Chronique Puissochet et Lecat", p.349; the decision marks the extension to international agreements of no fault liability arising from laws.

[83] Cass. Civ., March 14, 1939, Clunet (1939), 615.

[84] The cour de cassation retorted that, outside the proprietor's consent and without a just and previous indemnity, the French courts of justice should not recognize any expropriation of the property right.

[85] M.P. Singh, *German Administrative Law in Common Law Perspective,* Springer-Verlag Berlin, Heidelberg 1985.

[86] See *Maclaine Watson v. EC Council and Commission* at p.215.

[87] *ibid.* p.216.

[88] *Archiv des Volkerrechts,* 1984, p.220.

[89] *ibid.*

[90] In this case the court examined whether there existed any rule of international law under the meaning of Article 25 of the Grundgesetz which prohibits the possession and use of nuclear arms.

[91] Jurisprudentially this is a fundamental ground for instituting legal proceedings but what is remarkable under German practice is the concept that major policy making acts generally do not infringe private or personal rights.

[92] Article 113 of the Constitution provides for the protection of individuals against acts of public authorities.

[93] Article 28 of the law concerning the corte constitutionale provides that the court's power of control does not include any political assessment of the discretionary power of the parliament.

[94] The corte di cassazione plainly indicated that the responsibility of the organs of government for international acts was political and could not be raised before the courts. See *Rivista di diritto internazionale,* 1969 Vol. II, p.583, especially at p.586.

[95] *Anglo-Iranian Oil Company Ltd. v. S.U.P.O.R. Company* (Unione Petrolifera Per'L'Oriente, S.P.A.) (The Miriella), Italy, Court of Venice, March 11, 1953. (Mastrubuono).

[96] September 15, 1969, *Pasicrisie belge,* p.247.

[97] *ibid.* p.249.

[98] December 4, 1963, JT December 15, 1963, p.782, see also Civ. Brussels, September 23, 1964, JT October 25, 1964, p.600.

[99] The cour d'appeal held that "the claim is directed, if not at the legislative power, then at the executive, whose sovereign decisions are not subject to

censure by the courts", December 4, 1963, JT December 15, 1963, p.782.

[100] See Article 4(1) of the Estatuto dos Tribunais Administrativos e Fiscais (ETAF) which precludes any proceedings directed against political acts. It should be noted, however, that Article 20 of the Constitution grants the rights of protection by the courts against any act affecting "lawfully protected rights and interests".

[101] See *Maclaine Watson v. EC Council and Commission* at p.215.

[102] The Dutch Hoge Raad decided that despite the very wide margin of discretion accorded to the state in giving effect to a treaty, any act which directly affected personal rights and liberty could not escape the jurisdiction of the court. March 2, 1951, NJ 51.217.

[103] District Court Amsterdam, April 17, 1925, *Annual Digest (1925–26)*, No. 19.

[104] Court of Appeal Amsterdam, March 13, 1928, *Annual Digest* (1927–8); No. 17.

[105] Decided by Tokyo District Court on May 27, 1953, 1 JAIL 56 (1957).

[106] The Cultural Revolution, which has been severely criticized, started in 1966 and ended in 1976 in China after the death of Chairman Mao Zedong.

[107] Adopted at the Second Session of the Seventh National People's Congress on April 4, 1989 and effective as of October 1, 1990.

[108] The annexure was reprinted in *Materials on Jurisdictional Immunities of States and Their Property*, U.N. Leg. Series 1982 (ST/LEG/SER.B/20), pp.135–136.

[109] *ibid.*

[110] 794 F 2d 1490 (1986).

[111] See *aide mémoire* by Chinese Minister of Foreign Affairs Wu Xuequian to U.S. Secretary of State George Shultz on February 2, 1983.

[112] 596 F. Supp. 386 (1984).

[113] *ibid.* at 152.

[114] *ibid.* at 152. China forwarded its view while defending the case by raising the plea of absolute sovereign immunity.

[115] For instance, in *Promod Chandra v. Orissa*, the Supreme Court of India held: "'Act of State' is the taking over of sovereign powers by a State in respect of territory which was not till then a part of its territory, either by conquest, treaty or cession, or otherwise, and may be said to have taken place on a particular date, if there is a proclamation or other public declaration of such taking over. As an act of State derives its authority not from a municipal law but from ultra-legal or supra-legal means, Municipal Courts have no power to examine the propriety or legality of an act which comes within the ambit of 'act of State'. Whether the act of State has reference to public rights or to private rights, the result is the same, namely, that it is beyond the jurisdiction of Municipal Courts to investigate the rights and wrongs of the transaction and to pronounce upon them, and, that, therefore, such a Court cannot enforce its decisions, if any." (1962) Supp. 1 S.C.R 405, ('62) A.SC. 1288.

[116] Prof. Luo Haccai (Ed.), *The Chinese Judicial Review System*, Peking University Press, Beijing (1993), at p.308.

[117] *ibid.*

[118] *ibid.*

[119] *Commrs. of Crown Lands v. Page* [1960] 2 All E.R. 726.

[120] *ibid.* at 735–736.

[121] The second category was illustrated in *Board of Trade v. Temperley Steam Shipping Co. Ltd.* [1926] 2 Lloyds' List L.R. 76, 78.

[122] These two views were succinctly set out by Lord Denning M.R. in the Court of Appeal hearing of *Czarnikov v. Rolimpex* [1978] 1 All E.R. 81.

123 Adopted at the 7th Session of the Standing Committee of the 6th National People's Congress of China on September 5, 1986.

124 One may argue that these Regulations were adopted in accordance with 1961 Vienna Convention on Diplomatic Relations to which China is a party. Nevertheless, it was the first time for the Chinese law to exclude commercial activities from diplomatic immunities.

125 See Luo Haucai, *op. cit.*, at p.309.

126 *ibid.*

127 *ibid.*

128 Article 12 of the Administrative Procedure Law.

129 For instance the courts in the U.S. have adopted a view that courts are barred from adjudicating political actions taken by the administration.

130 Interview by the author with Professor Xu Chungde, a member of the former Hong Kong Basic Law Drafting Committee on October 25, 1995.

131 It varies even in cases where the facts and parties are similar. See *Marcos (I)* and *Marcos (II)*, *op. cit.* Also see the above text dealing with acts of state under the common law.

132 (1848) 2 Ex 167.

133 [1892] A.C. 491.

134 See *Johnstone v. Pedlar* [1921] 2 A.C. 262.

135 See S.A. Williams and Alc de Mestral, *An Introduction to International Law chiefly as interpreted and applied in Canada* (2nd ed.), particularly the chapter on "State Responsibility", p.174 at p.181. Also see F.A. Mann, "The Sancrosanctity of Foreign Acts of State (1943) 59 L.Q.R. 42.

136 Hugh M. Kindred, "Acts of State and the Application of International Law in English Courts" in *The Canadian Yearbook of International Law* (1981) at p.272.

137 [1931] A.C. 662.

138 *ibid.* at 671.

139 *ibid.* at 212 F.213A. *per* Lord Pearson in *Nissan* [1970] A.C. at 238A. Only Lord Reid in the same case felt that political considerations precluded judicial inquiry into the motives of the crown.

140 (1962) ILR 33, 311 F.2d at 557–58.

141 *ibid.* at 557–58.

142 806 F.2d 344 (1988) at 358–59.

143 [1979] A.C. 351.

144 15 F. Supp. 927 (S.D.N.Y 1936), 299 US 585 (1936).

145 It is to be noted that the court in this case applied the private international law principle of choice of law in rejecting the act of state defence.

146 See Kenneth L. Miller, "Debt situs and the Act of State Doctrine: A Proposal for More Flexible Standard" (1985) 49 *Albany Law Review*, pp.653–54.

147 Joseph H. Beale, "Jurisdiction of a sovereign State" (1923) 36 Harv.L.Rev. 241, 245. Prof. Beale was also the Reporter for the *Restatement (First) of Conflict of Laws.*

148 [1921] 3 K.B. 532.

149 Oppenheim was of the view that this was the proposition for which the case stands for but later on the learned editor introduced an additional qualification — that the act must not be contrary to international law. See Oppenheim 1, *International Law* (8th ed., Lauterpacht 1995), p.267.

150 See *Bank Voor Handel en Scheepvaart v. Slatford* [1951] 2 All ER 779.

151 The U.S. courts uniformly denied the expropriatory effect of foreign decrees. Only in exceptional cases involving matters of significant national interests, public policy may be used "to gave extra territorial effect to

foreign decrees that would not otherwise be given." 62 *Columbia Law Review* (1962), p.1293.

[152] 12 Rang LR 120.

[153] *ibid.* at 150.

[154] It is to be noted that the U.K. courts are of the opinion that the defence of act of state cannot be raised by the state where the affected party is a British subject. In other words, between the Crown and its subjects, the plea of act of state does not exist. See *Nissan v. Attorney-General* [1970] A.C. 179. The limit and extent of this position, *i.e.* non-applicability of act of state as defence is not settled with regard to the question whether the act of the Crown should be confined to the territorial boundary of Britain. See J.G. Collier, "Act of State as a Defence against a British Subject" [1968] C.L.J. 102.

[155] *I Congresso del Partido* [1980] 1 Lloyd's List L.R. 23.

[156] *ibid.* at 32.

[157] 443,cmt.f (1987).

[158] *ibid.*

[159] *ibid.*

[160] See *Ming Po Daily*, May 17, 1995.

[161] *ibid.*

[162] The same approach has been taken by the EC courts and the U.K. courts as demonstrated in the *Maclaine Watson case*. There the court took the provisions of a treaty as a matter of fact and then decided the case accordingly. In other words, the treaty as such was taken as a piece of evidence for the determination of the case.

[163] This seems to be the prevailing approach of the courts in the common law countries. See *Buttes Gas and Oil Case, op. cit.*

THE FUNCTION OF LEGAL EVASION IN CHINA'S ECONOMIC REFORM — FROM A SOCIO-LEGAL PERSPECTIVE

Dr Zhu Suli

Department of Law
Peking University

Zhu Suli, *LL.B. (Peking University), LL.M. (McGeorge School of Law), Ph.D. (Arizona University), has been a lecturer and associate professor at Peking University. He has published and translated many books and articles in the sociology of law.*

Issues

Much research suggests that a unified and rationalized legal system is both beneficial to and prerequisite to the market economy and a unified national market, and that, as the market economy evolves, such a legal system will evolve and be firmly established.[1]

The current experience coming out of China's market-oriented economic reform appears to contradict this theory, however, as this goal is proving difficult to achieve in practice. Although many academics have pointed out the importance of a unified legal system and effective law enforcement in building the socialist market economy, and more and more people are solving their disputes in court, some studies show that a number of civil, commercial and sometimes criminal conflicts are still being settled privately.[2]

Private settlement refers to settlements reached not according to state law but negotiated between the conflicting parties. This is not necessarily restricted to private individuals, but also includes state-owned enterprises and sometimes local government officials. In addition, these settlements sometimes go against state law and government policy.

The explanation for this phenomenon most often offered by Chinese academics is that China is a country without a modern western-style legal tradition or formal rationalized law.[3] Historically, Chinese society had no formal and unified civil and commercial law and most civil and commercial affairs were regulated by informal, customary rules which evolved within Chinese society and its folk culture.

In addition, China's law and judiciary have historically been considered more often as a method of dispute resolution than a formal institution, in contrast to the Western tradition.

In the context of China's market-oriented economic reform, I would argue that this kind of socio-legal phenomenon — private settlement or legal evasion — is inevitable. This is due to the fact that China's economic reform began with a decentralization of power. Many reform measures were initiated by individuals, enterprises or local governments with the explicit or implicit permission of the central government, and many were actually in conflict with, at least in some aspects, current legal provisions and the established legal system. As a result, private settlement, legal evasion and locally adopted measures (tu zhengce) have become very common among individuals, enterprises and even some local government officials during the process of social economic reform.

As one economist points out,

> "[M]any substantive economic reform measures in China were conducted without reforming formal institutions or changing the terms. As a result, people initially went against the formal rules, changed a varity of behavioral constraints, and created various new economic relationships, from which many people had an opportunity to profit."[4]

This pragmatic approach to China's reform has proved effective, successful and even necessary given the country's social and cultural climate. It has also, however, damaged the authority and unity of the legal system, which is, according to historical experience, essential to the formation of a unified national market and integration of the national legal system.

In a practical sense, therefore, China's legal system is in a Catch 22 situation. On the one hand, economic reform demands a break from the old legal and institutional framework; while on the other, a national market needs a unified legal system in order to operate effectively.

The pressing issue to be addressed is how to avoid the damaging effects of economic reform on legal authority and unity, while maintaining a situation of balanced social and economic development.

There is also a theoretical question to be answered, in terms of why private settlements or legal evasion have managed to become more common in China, when the market economy demands a unified and rationalized legal system, and until current times at least, they haven't hindered, instead have promoted the development of market economy. If private settlements can be considered to be rational, then what are the reasons and conditions for their existence?

With this in mind, this paper will analyse a case of private settlement, which is a common Chinese practice, particularly in rural areas. Through this analysis, it attempts to demonstrate the reasonableness of private settlements and their potentially positive role in transforming and building a legal system conducive to China's socialist market economy.

The paper then explores the theoretical and practical implications of the case for legal researchers and attempts to show a possible way forward for China's legal transformation and development.

A Case of Private Settlement

A young boy, X, fell in love with a young girl, Y, of another village. One day, X asked Y for a date and Y accepted. During the date, X asked for sex, Y refused, and subsequently X raped Y. After returning home, Y told her parents of her experience, and her parents reported the crime to the local police.

Before the police could formally arrest X, X's parents came to Y's family and asked for a private settlement. Under the settlement, X would marry Y and an additional payment of RMB3,000 would be made. In return, Y would withdraw the charge against X.

Y and her family agreed to the offer in principle, but demanded payment of RMB10,000. Negotiations followed, with a final payment of RMB5,000 agreed to. Although neither X nor Y had reached the statutory age for marriage, they obtained a marriage licence with the help of a family friend. At the end of the day, however, the matter was pursued by the local police. The marriage was then nullified and X was charged and sentenced to prison.[5]

This type of apparently simple legal evasion has been quite common in Chinese society for many years. In some ways, however, it represents the dilemma faced in reforming China's legal system. From this perspective alone, it deserves closer examination. In addition, the fact that it represents a common practice in China means that analysis of it may assist in understanding the development of China's legal system.

Folk Law

Many Chinese legal academics would explain this case by saying that these rural people were ignorant of the law or did not have access

296

to legal information.[6] They would suggest that the priority in strengthening the legal system and eradicating such phenomena would be to popularize legal information (referred to as popular legal education in China), and to improve law enforcement and legal services.[7] The premise is to know the Law. Popular legal education in China has followed this logic since the mid-1980s.

This argument is, however, not convincing in this case. The very fact that Y had reported the case to the local police and X had asked that the charge be withdrawn clearly demonstrates that both the offender and the victim knew the behaviour was unlawful and punishable by state law.

This collaboration to evade the law is full of cultural meaning. Although an illicit act not conforming to the rule of state law, it was not a random act, but one guided by cultural norms. Without such norms or rules to follow, such a peaceful settlement would probably not have been achieved. Y's family might have sought revenge of one kind or another; and X might not have considered his own behaviour a criminal act and not voluntarily initiated a private settlement.

Without rules to guide them, it is unlikely these people would have reached an agreement at all, with so many alternatives open to them. Just as people must share a common language in order to communicate, so they must share some common cultural norms to come to an agreement. It is these norms or rules which define the agreement as socially just, reasonable or at least acceptable to the participants.

Even more important is that this kind of conflict resolution is not uncommon in rural China. Given that it is a commonly used method of resolving conflicts and plays an important role in restoring and maintaining order in Chinese society, it might even be termed a "folk law", evolved within and accepted by society. Its use and acceptance leads to a situation usually defined as legal pluralism.[8]

In a situation of legal pluralism, people must choose which set of norms and rules apply. In this case, folk law was chosen over state law. This is hardly surprising from the point of view of the offender. What is surprising is that this was also the choice of the victim and her family, despite their awareness of the formal legal protection offered by state law. They voluntarily accepted folk law or customary law as the *better* legal protection.[9]

Reasons for Private Settlement

In this case, the state law, which is supposed to be the best protection for the people, was voluntarily and willingly abandoned by these people. The question is, Why?

The elitist view that the people involved did not understand their best interest is unacceptable. This rationale implies that only trained lawyers or governmental officials are in a position to know what is in people's best interests. This argument has a strong authoritarian tone, which, if not contained, will deprive common people of their freedom of choice.[10] It may not serve but frustrate attempts to improve China's legal system either.

Given the context of the case and Chinese society, the victim's choice can be viewed as a reasonable one. Putting aside other considerations, such as the victim's feelings for the offender, and the relationship between the two families, the victim might still consider the settlement an acceptable alternative.

In Chinese culture, especially in rural areas, female virginity is highly prised, making life very difficult for victims of sexual crimes.[11] They may find it difficult to find a satisfied husband, and be discriminated against. In reality, therefore, it is not always in the victim's best interest to demand strict enforcement of the law.

By accepting the settlement, however, the victim would not only save her reputation, but also earn what would be considered a substantial amount of money for her family. If you consider that, in this case, she may also have had conflicting feelings for the offender, her actions must be seen to be rational and reasonable, although illegal.

It is reasonable to conclude, then, that this legal evasion is not proof of the victim's ignorance of the law or lack of access to legal services, but strong proof of their rationality. It may also illustrate the imperfections in some aspects of the state law given China's current social and economic conditions. At least in this case, the law that was intended to protect victims would have cost them more than they were willing to pay.

However, calling the victim's choice justified is not saying that the attempted result would have been just in a legal sense. We are not here to pass a moral judgment on the case, but to consider if the state law is expected to alter people's behaviour, how should the law itself be improved?

It is unlikely that either moral education or legal information alone would be sufficient to eradicate this kind of phenomenon. Instead, it is necessary to alter people's behaviour and attitudes toward the law within the legal structure.

The Role of State Law

Although some Chinese academics might recognize the rationale behind the actions of individuals in this case, most would consider that the state law was evaded and played no part in the settlement. In fact, this is not true. A closer examination of the case reveals that state law played an important if largely invisible role throughout this process of legal evasion.

It was only the victim's report to the police (the representative of state law in this case) that forced the offender to settle privately. Without the prospect of this state power and potential legal punishment, it is unlikely the offender would have voluntarily proposed a settlement. In addition, without the relatively certain and definite legal penalties for rape existing under state law, neither party would have had a basis for negotiation. In other words, the effectiveness of folk law was actually dependent upon the invisible presence of state law, and it could be said that state law played a role in resolving this social conflict through folk law.

Furthermore, given that state law provides a basis for negotiation, the party with more definite knowledge of state law would have more power to control or manipulate the negotiation and settlement. If the victim's demands is beyond the offender's financial capability, the offender might have been more willing to go to court. The victim must, therefore, bargain within the limits of what can be borne by the offender.

In defining these limits, both parties would benefit from learning something about the law. In this sense, the process of private settlement becomes one of legal education. Evading state law requires knowledge of state law, and the more people work to evade it, the more they will have learnt from and about it. In addition, even where state law is effectively evaded, its influence will remain. The knowledge acquired about state law through the evasion will have some limited but not negligible influence upon the future behaviour of both parties and others connected to them. This influence is not negligible because it means that state law is penetrating society, even though unconsciously, and reshaping the fabric of folk law. In the long term, this process will eventually have the effect of completely transforming folk law.

Final Analysis

The analysis of this legal evasion is useful in understanding the problem concerning the legal model in China's market-oriented reform.

Many of the economic reform measures currently being initiated by individuals, enterprises and local government officials could be considered to be a kind of legal evasion. By this definition or analogy, these reform measures are both helping to build the unity of the legal system and the unified national market economy, and at the same time helping to destroy it.

I have argued elsewhere that China's socialist market economy and the corresponding legal structure cannot "naturally" evolve as it did in western countries, but must be transformed from a planned economic structure.[12] This implies that the economic system must be reformed, and that the old legal-economic framework must be broken down, allowing for some private settlements which do not conform to state laws.

On the other hand, in order to build a market economy, particularly a national market, a unified, authoritative legal system is required. This represents a fundamental paradox, and it is necessary to maintain a certain amount of tension between these two interests. Even though the legal system was constructed within the planned economic structure that is to be reformed, some formal elements of the legal system, such as the unity of law, law enforcement and social order, have important value beyond the substance of the law itself and beyond the planned economic structure.

The phenomenon of legal evasion could, therefore, be considered instrumental to the reform of China's economy and the development of its legal system. As illustrated in the case above, a private settlement is a rational method used by individuals to solve their problems and evade laws which may damage their interests. This negates the old legal structure and offers something new in its place. It helps to break down the old system and, through rational choice, shape a new system and form new rules. In addition, because Chinese law is sketchy and law enforcement often ineffective, it would appear that the phenomenon of legal evasion is inevitable in China at the present time.

This pragmatic approach will also, however, have the effect of harming the development of the legal system. Permitting legal evasion or private settlement helps to erode the authority of the law. In addition, different local rules or norms are bound to result from legal evasion, which will make a unified national law impossible. Widespread use of legal evasion may also make the public accustomed to taking the law into their own hands, thus preventing the establishment of rule of law. In fact, recent media reports of local economic protectionism and ineffective law enforcement are symptomatic of a serious weakening of central government authority and unity of law. Ultimately, this will not be beneficial to China's economic reform.

The case analyzed here suggests that when legal evasion is unavoidable, its use may not be *so* serious, and it can actually affirm the existence of state law and its authority, and help state law to influence the public (it charges the state law as well). It becomes a serious problem, however, while those involved act *without any awareness* of legal authority. The authority of the central government and state law are prerequisite to legal evasion, the penetration of state law into society, and the eventual nation-wide transformation of folk law.[13]

The case analysis also helps us revisit some widely accepted thoughts on Chinese society and culture. One is that China has no legal tradition. If we acknowledge that law is not restricted to legal codes and western-style legal institutions, then we must recognize that a number of para-legal norms are present in Chinese society. Yet our opinions on law make them an invisible part of everyday life. These norms only become visible when a different law is imposed by the state or by other external powers, resulting in the choice of legal evasion.

This also leads us to re-evaluate the conclusion that the failure to introduce a western-style legal system to China is the result of the conservative nature of Chinese society, and the lack of awareness among common people of their rights.

Finally, we must reconsider the theory of Legal Transplanting which is popular in China currently and we should bear in mind the words of Justice Holmes, who once said that the law embodies the story of a nation's development through the centuries, and cannot be dealt with as if it contained only the axioms and corollaries of a book of mathematics.[14] Likewise, Savigny said the law is the embodiment of a nation's spirit.

Since the beginning of this century, China has been working to reform its social system along the lines of the western model. While it has not been a total failure, the newly introduced legal system is far-removed from the Chinese people, particularly those living in the rural areas. Many people do not follow the law — one reason being that they will gain nothing from it. As the case above suggests, more attention should be paid, therefore, to the rules and norms followed by the Chinese people, particularly during this period of economic reform. We should work to understand these norms, rather than just passing judgment on them. This does not suggest that all these rules and norms are necessarily good, but that we should not attempt to oversimplify the complexity of the issues faced by Chinese society. Close observation and analysis are bound to reveal new and relevant issues and interpretations.

Notes

[1] For example, Max Weber, *On Law In Society and Economy* (1956).

[2] *cf.* Yang Deqing and Shao Jingan, *Why Enterprises Do Not Litigate in Commercial Disputes Reference of Economy, Jinji Cankao Bao*, August 9, 1993, p.4.

Sometimes, even the formal legal system is compromised. For example, local economic protectionism is currently a serious problem in China acknowledged at both the central and local government levels.

³ Chinese academics often describe China as a country *without* a legal tradition. This is an inaccurate statement based on western views. Strictly speaking, China has a long tradition of law, but no tradition of western-style law, which represents only one form of law.

⁴ Fan Gang, "Chinese Culture and Economic Development" *Bulletin of Market Economy*, Vol. 2, 1995.

⁵ This case was fabricated by the author after collecting information on several similar cases. Its circumstances, however, are very common in many parts of contemporary rural China.

⁶ This interpretation of legal evasion of this kind is commonly accepted by most Chinese academics.

⁷ Many academics emphasize legal information while neglecting effective law enforcement and the provision of legal services. Some legal evasions are not the result of a lack of legal information, but ineffective law enforcement and a lack of legal services. This, however, is another issue not to be addressed here.

⁸ Sally Engle Merry, "Legal Pluralism", *Law and Society Review*, May 22, 1988, p.869.

⁹ The term "best" used here is from the victim's perspective, not that of a trained lawyer, government official or others. This definition is consistent and compatible with the economic analysis of law, which refuses a universally applied standard of utility or profits, but considers that the individual is the best judge of his/her best interests.

¹⁰ I am not suggesting that folk law or individual liberty is present in all such private settlement cases. I believe that government intervention in some such cases is necessary, due to the fact that all voluntary choices are to some extent culturally informed and framed, and are a reaction to the existing cultural and legal pattern which may change or need to be reformed. See further discussion later.

¹¹ On the other hand, this aspect of Chinese culture has also historically protected women from sexual crimes to a certain extent. This viewpoint is often neglected by legal sociologists analysing the effects of the importance of virginity. They emphasize its negative effects, but almost unanimously neglect the rationale behind such a custom. For further analysis, see Sir James George Frazer, *The Devil's Advocate, A Plea for Superstition* (1927).

¹² Suli, "Reform, Local Resources and Modern Legality", *Zhongwai Faixue* (1995), Vol. 5.

¹³ The Chinese government and CPC seem to have acknowledged this point. They have emphasized macro-regulation of the economy; granted the People's Bank of China a semi-independent status (independent from all local government but under the authority of the State Council); and re-emphasized the system of democratic centralization in a resolution of the fourth session of the 14th Central Committee Meeting of the CPC.

¹⁴ O.W. Holmes, *The Common Law*, Little Brown and Company (1948), p.1.

RECENT DEVELOPMENTS IN CONSUMER PRODUCTION — AN UPDATE

Henry W.L. Chen
and
Stephen Foo

Faculty of Law
City University of Hong Kong

Henry W.L. Chen *is an assistant professor of the Department of Professional Legal Education of the Faculty of Law, City University of Hong Kong. He is admitted to practise at the State Bar of California and as a solicitor of the Supreme Court of Hong Kong.*

Stephen Foo *is a lecturer in the Faculty of Law at the City University of Hong Kong. He is a barrister-at-law of the Supreme Court of Hong Kong.*

Consumer protection has been developing and evolving in several different directions in Hong Kong. This paper will discuss the developments and events in consumer movement in recent years, including legislative measures, Consumer Council actions, and events and developments in Hong Kong and China that affect Hong Kong consumers.

Development of Consumer Movement in Hong Kong

In February 1990, the Law Reform Commission of Hong Kong published its *Report on Sale of Goods and Supply of Services* in which the state of consumer protection law in Hong Kong was described as being "far behind other Commonwealth jurisdictions in the development of consumer protection law."[1] Not only did the Commission address the law on sale of goods and supply of services and the need to

303

control the use of exemption clauses and standard contracts,[2] they also raised their concern over the general issue of consumer protection.[3] It concluded that the government should review and examine the wider aspects of consumer protection law so that the position of consumers in Hong Kong could be improved. As a result of the recommendations of the Law Reform Commission, several consumer-oriented ordinances were passed by the legislature.

In the past, the Hong Kong Government has been criticized for not having a unified policy on consumer protection. There had been no legislation specifically aimed at consumer protection and there was no quick and effective system of redress for consumers such as a compulsory consumer arbitration tribunal, which would provide an efficient and effective way to resolve consumer disputes.[4] One suggestion is that the Consumer Council is one institution which fulfills that role.[5] Nevertheless, experience shows that the Consumer Council has not been very effective in that regard.

It took almost 10 years after the establishment of the Consumer Council in Hong Kong and the adoption of the Unfair Contract Terms Act in the United Kingdom for the Hong Kong Government to mandate the Law Reform Commission to review the laws of Hong Kong on unconscionable contract terms. During this time, the Sale of Goods Ordinance (Cap. 26) (the "SOGO") was the principal statute governing sale of goods,[6] in other words, consumers when pursuing their claims had only the general laws on contract and torts to rely on.

Consumer movement has a much longer history in other jurisdictions such as the U.S., the United Kingdom, Canada, Denmark, Switzerland, and other Asian countries, namely Japan and Singapore. Many of these countries have enacted separate legislation for consumers and commercial sales.[7] In 1993, China also adopted the Law of the People's Republic of China on Protection of the Rights and Interests of Consumers (the "PRC Consumer Protection Law").[8]

In Hong Kong, following the Law Reform Commission's *Report on Control of Exemption Clauses* 1986, the Control of Exemption Clauses Ordinance (Cap. 71) (the "CECO") was enacted in 1990. The CECO opened a new chapter in the history of the consumer movement in Hong Kong. The year 1994 could very well be remembered as the watershed of consumer protection laws in Hong Kong. Four pieces of legislation were enacted, namely the Consumer Goods Safety Ordinance (the "CGSO"),[9] the Sale of Goods (Amendments) Ordinance,[10] the Supply of Services (Implied Terms) Ordinance (the "SOSITO")[11] and the Unconscionable Contracts Ordinance (the "UCO").[12] They became law on October 20, 1994 and will undoubtedly be the cornerstone in the future development of consumer protection in Hong Kong.

Formulation of a Set of Consumer Legislation in Hong Kong

The term "dealing as consumer" was initially introduced into the laws of Hong Kong through an amendment to the SOGO in 1977,[13] but the change did not receive much attention, and it had, in practice, little impact on the overall development of consumer protection in Hong Kong. The enactment of the four pieces of legislation has, however, reinforced the concept of consumerism and has perhaps turned a new leaf in the annals of the Hong Kong consumer protection movement.

"Dealing as Consumer"

The term is now contained in various ordinances, namely the SOGO,[14] the CECO,[15] the UCO[16] and the SOSITO.[17] Accordingly, special protection is accorded to consumers through specific provisions in these ordinances. The most important point is perhaps these ordinances are now more in favour of consumers in that they require that the person who contends the other does not deal as consumer has the burden to prove to the contrary.

Under the statutory definition, a party to a contract "deals as consumer" if:

(a) he neither makes the contract in the course of a business nor holds himself out as doing so;
(b) the other party does make the contract in the course of a business; and
(c) the goods passing or services provided under or in pursuance of the contract are of a type ordinarily supplied or provided for private use, consumption or benefit.

The Court of Appeal in the United Kingdom had the opportunity to consider the definition of "consumer" in *R & B Customs Broker Co Ltd v. United Dominions Trust Ltd.*[18] In this case, the court decided that a business may be entitled to the protection given to individual consumers if the transaction in question is not a regular one.

In *R & B Customs Broker*, the plaintiffs bought a car for the use of a director from the defendant finance company. A term in the contract purported to exclude a statutory implied term that the goods be fit for the purpose. The issue was whether the plaintiffs dealt as "consumer" as the implied term could not be exempted if the contract was a consumer sale. If the plaintiffs did not deal as "consumer", the exemption clause would only be effective if it satisfied the test of reasonableness and in this case it did. Thus the finding on "consumer" was decisive.

Dillon L.J. drew a distinction between an one-off transaction and a regular one.[19] He found that as the purchase of the car was not a frequent transaction, and thus unless "a degree of regularity"[20] could be established, the plaintiffs had to be treated as a consumer and were, therefore, entitled to the same protection as if they were an individual consumer.

The interpretation of the term "dealing as consumer" is, therefore, crucial in that it determines the scope of protection offered by the foregoing ordinances, under which consumers are entitled to greater protection. These ordinances are examined below.

The Control of Exemption Clauses Ordinance (the "CECO")

The public policy has always been that one should have freedom to contract.[21] In the past, there has been little statutory intervention on freedom of contract, people are free to make whatever contracts they want. The idea of a free exchange of promises remains central to the theory of contract and the law would only step in if it arises out of "necessity" of trade in the context of a market economy. The existence of unequal bargaining power often defeats that classic principle. That inequality has been getting more recognition in recent years is evident in the laws on labour[22] and consumer protection.[23]

In the case of *Schroeder v. Macauley*, Lord Diplock opined:

> "The terms of this kind of standard form of contract have not been the subject of negotiation between the parties to it . . . They have been dictated by the party whose . . . position . . . provides . . . classic instance of superior bargaining power."[24]

Although *Schroeder v. Macauley* was a case on labour law, it illustrates that a consumer, being a contracting party with weak bargaining power, often becomes the victim of the contract if there is an absolute party autonomy.[25] In 1978, the *Hong Kong Law Journal* in its editorial remarked that "the idea that a contract necessarily represents an agreement reached by parties bargaining from equal positions was long ago abandoned" in Hong Kong.[26]

It is beyond question that we need more stringent statutory control over exemption clauses, especially where they are contained in standard-form contracts. The old principles in common law, *i.e.* the notion of "fundamental breach"[27] and the *Harbutt's Plasticine* rule,[28] are no longer acceptable.[29] An exemption clause would only be upheld if the clause is clear and unequivocal.[30]

It is worth noting that the old section 57 of the SOGO even provided a positive recognition for the use of exemption clauses. Section 57 stated:

> "Where any right, duty, or liability would arise under a contract of sale by implication of law, it may be negatived or varied by express agreement or by the course of dealing between the parties, or by usage, if the usage be such as to bind both parties to the contract."

Following the lead of the Unfair Contract Terms Act 1977 of the United Kingdom, section 57 of the SOGO was amended in 1977 so that in the case of a sale of goods other than a consumer sale, exemption clauses were only effective insofar as they satisfied the test of reasonableness. The guidelines for the test were set out in section 57(5):

> "(a) the strength of the bargaining positions of the seller and buyer relative to each other, taking into account, among other things, the availability of suitable alternative products and sources of supply;
> (b) whether the buyer received an inducement to agree to the term or in accepting it had an opportunity of buying the goods or suitable alternatives without it from any source of supply;
> (c) whether the buyer knew or ought reasonably to have known of the existence and extent of the term (having regard, among other things, to any custom of the trade and previous course of dealing between the parties);
> (d) where the term exempts from all or any of the provisions of sections 15, 16 or 17 if some condition is not complied with, whether it was reasonable at the time of the contract to expect that compliance with that condition would be practicable;
> (e) whether the goods were manufactured, processed, or adapted to the special order of the buyer."

In the case of a consumer contract, exemption clauses were void regardless of whether they were reasonable or not. This was the first time the term "dealing as consumer" was incorporated into the laws of Hong Kong.

In addition to the 1977 amendment to section 57 of the SOGO, statutory controls over specific types of contracts are also to be found in the following ordinances, namely the Landlord and Tenant (Consolidation) Ordinance (Cap. 7), the Bills of Sale Ordinance (Cap. 20), the

Law Amendment and Reform (Consolidation) Ordinance (Cap. 23), the Apprenticeship Ordinance (Cap. 47), the Employment Ordinance (Cap. 57), the Contracts for Overseas Employment Ordinance (Cap. 78), the Hotel Proprietors Ordinance (Cap. 158), the Pawnbrokers Ordinance (Cap. 166), etc. For example, the Misrepresentation Ordinance (Cap. 284) prohibits any contracting party from avoiding liability for misrepresentation unless it is reasonable for the purpose of section 3(1) of the CECO.[31]

The aforesaid statutory control exists only in relation to certain contracts. The position of consumers had not changed very much. In the *Report on the Control of Exemption Clauses*, the Law Reform Commission reached the following conclusion:

> "... the use of exemption clauses leads to abuse, especially where the parties are not in positions of equal bargaining strength, and we believe that the benefits of some measure of control outweigh any economic disadvantages which may be caused by this limited interference with the freedom of contract ... We recommend that the relevant provisions of the UK Unfair Contract Terms Act 1977 should be adopted in Hong Kong with appropriate amendments."[32]

Four years after the Commission's report, its recommendations were implemented in the CECO which is closely modelled on the Unfair Contract Terms Act 1977 of the United Kingdom. It reflects the judicial tendency to move away from protecting commercial interests to that of protecting consumer interests.[33] The objectives of the CECO are "to limit the extent to which civil liability for breach of contract, or for negligence or other breach of duty, can be avoided by means of contract terms and otherwise, and to restrict the enforceability of arbitration agreements."[34]

The key provisions of the CECO, *i.e.* sections 7–12, apply to "business liability" only.[35] The term "business liability" refers to liability for breach of obligations arising from things done in the course of business or in relation to one's business premises. With regard to tortious liability, section 7 provides that no liability for death or personal injury resulting from negligence may be excluded or restricted by any contractual term or notice. For other losses or damages, exemption clauses would only be operative if they pass the test of reasonableness. With regard to contractual liability, Part III of the CECO restricts the application of the CECO in the following manner:

(a) where the contract is an international supply contract;[36]

(b) where the proper law of the contract is the law of Hong Kong only by choice of the parties;[37]

(c) where the proper law of the contract is the law of some other jurisdiction by express term;[38]
(d) where such exemption clause is authorized or required by the express terms or necessary implication of an enactment;[39] and
(e) where such exemption clause is made with a view to compliance with an international agreement which applies to Hong Kong.[40]

Save for the above-mentioned contracts, section 11 of the CECO reiterates the principle in the old section 57 of the SOGO that liability for breach of contractual obligations arising from sections 15–17 of the SOGO cannot be restricted or excluded unless they satisfy the test of reasonableness. Section 11 also makes such obligations non-excludable in consumer contracts.[41]

The test of reasonableness under the CECO is more or less the same as the one under the old section 57 of the SOGO. For an exemption clause to be operative in non-consumer contracts, such terms must be "fair and reasonable . . . having regard to the circumstance which were, or ought reasonably to have been, known to or in the contemplation of the parties when the contract was made." The guidelines for application of the reasonableness test are referred to the Second Schedule,[42] which is a more liberal application of the old section 57 of the SOGO.

Section 6 of the CECO empowers the Legislative Council to amend the schedule by resolution. Judging from the composition of the 1995 Legislative Council which is dominated by more liberal and democratic elements, later amendments to the CECO if any are likely to be more consumer-oriented.

Special reference is also made to consumer contracts. For example, section 8 prohibits exclusion of liability arising in consumer contracts except in so far as the term meets the requirement of reasonableness.[43] Unreasonable indemnity clauses,[44] and clauses which purport to exempt or restrict liability for loss or damage arising from consumer goods,[45] or liability under section 14 of the SOGO,[46] are also prohibited. Section 15 further provides that no arbitration agreement as against a person dealing as consumer is enforceable unless:

(a) the party (who deals as consumer) signifies, in writing, his consent to arbitration after the differences in question have arisen; or
(b) he has himself had recourse to arbitration in pursuance of the agreement in respect of any differences.

Accordingly, a party dealing as consumer may not be forced to resort to arbitration as the only mode of dispute resolution, even though there is an arbitration clause in the contract, they are entitled to have their disputes resolved in a court of law.

The Supply of Services (Implied Terms) Ordinance (the "SOSITO")

Unlike the United Kingdom, prior to 1994, there was no statute setting out the essential obligations of a supplier of services in Hong Kong.[47] The Law Reform Commission recommended the introduction of law along the lines of the Supply of Goods and Services Act of the UK to Hong Kong.[48] The SOSITO is one such piece of consumer legislation passed in 1994.

The SOSITO applies to "contracts for the supply of a service". A "contract for the supply of a service" means a "contract under which a person agrees to carry out a service".[49] Section 3(2)(b) of the SOSITO stipulates that a contract is a "contract for the supply of a service" regardless of whether the goods are hired or transferred, hence, contracts for work and materials fall within its scope.[50]

Part II of the Ordinance, the integral part, sets out the terms implied into contracts for the supply of services where a supplier is acting in the course of business. First of all, a supplier must carry out the service with reasonable care and skill.[51] If a contract for the supply of services contains no express provision as to the time for performance and consideration, sections 6 and 7 will be implied into such contracts.[52] Section 6 provides that the supplier should carry out the service within a reasonable time[53] whilst section 7 states that the supplier should be paid a reasonable charge.[54]

What is reasonable is a question of fact[55] and the court will have to consider all the circumstances at the time when the contract was made. For instance, a delay of three weeks in the repair of a car which should only take five weeks was held unreasonable.[56]

It should be noted that the court has no power to re-open an agreement if a party has made a bad bargain, even in cases of "blatant exploitation".

Subject to the CECO, parties to a contract for the supply of services may by express agreement, or by the course of dealing between them, or by such usage as binds both parties, contract out the obligations under the SOSITO.[57] If one is dealing as a consumer, however, the liability under sections 5–7 could not be excluded.

Section 9 preserves any rule of law which imposes a stricter duty on suppliers in contracts for the supply of services.

The Unconscionable Contracts Ordinance (the "UCO")

Despite the recognition of the concept of unconscionability in *Fry v. Land*,[58] the judiciary is still of the opinion that the doctrine of freedom to contract is paramount and any restriction should be left to the decision of the legislature.[59] The legislature realizes that the disparity in economic strength and resources between the consumer and the seller (who may be a large corporation or a distributor for a manufacturer) often puts the consumer in a very disadvantageous position when he complains about the goods or services supplied. The UCO was therefore enacted to empower courts to give relief to consumers[60] who are affected by unconscionable contracts.

Where the court finds a contract or any part of a contract to be unconscionable, section 5 of the UCO confers on the court power to grant the following reliefs:

(a) refuse to enforce the contract;
(b) enforce the remainder of the contract without the unconscionable part; or
(c) limit the application of, or revise or alter, any unconscionable part so as to avoid any unconscionable result.

Accordingly, the court may strike down or even rewrite an unconscionable contract (or parts of it).

It should be noted that the test of unconscionability is a very stringent one. The onus of proof of unconscionability of a contract rests upon the person claiming that the contract is unconscionable.[61] It is envisaged that the UCO would only apply to extreme cases. In determining whether a contract is unconscionable, the court will, *inter alia*, consider:[62]

(a) the relative economic positions and bargaining powers of the parties;
(b) whether the consumer was required to comply with conditions that were not reasonably necessary for the protection of the legitimate interest of the other party;
(c) whether the consumer was able to understand the documents;
(d) whether the consumer was subjected to any undue influence or pressure, or unfair tactics; and
(e) the availability of any substitute from the open market.

The court may also consider other relevant circumstances relating to the contract at the time it was made. Although post-contract matters are of no relevance in the determination of unconscionability of a contract, in considering the exercise of powers to grant relief under section 5, the court may take into consideration the conduct of the parties after the formation of the contract.[63]

The UCO contains provisions similar to section 17 of the CECO to prevent evasion of the application of the UCO.[64]

311

The Consumer Goods Safety Ordinance (the "CGSO")

The lack of legislation governing product safety in Hong Kong has attracted much criticism. The Toys and Children's Product Safety Ordinance (Cap. 424) was passed in 1993 but its application is limited to toys and children's products only. Essentially it has incorporated the prevailing international safety standards for toys into Hong Kong law.[65]

In 1994, the government attempted to tackle the wider concern on consumer protection regarding product liability by enacting the CGSO "to impose a duty on manufacturers, importers and suppliers of certain consumer goods to ensure that the consumer goods . . . are safe and for incidental purposes."[66] "Consumer goods" are defined as "goods which are ordinarily supplied for private use or consumption",[67] excluding those listed in the Schedule and those exempted under section 3 of the CGSO.[68]

The general safety requirements for consumer goods are set out in section 4 of the CGSO under which consumer goods must be reasonably safe with regard to *inter alia*:

(a) the manner in which the goods are presented, promoted or marketed;
(b) the use of marks, instructions or warning given for the keeping, use or consumption of the consumers goods;
(c) the reasonable safety standards published by a standards institute; and
(d) the existence of any reasonable means to make the goods safer.

The Secretary of Trade and Industry may by regulation approve a safety standard or safety specification applicable to consumer goods or a class of consumer goods.[69] Section 6 of the CGSO provides that no person may supply, manufacture or import into Hong Kong any consumer goods which fail to comply with the general safety requirement (under section 4) or a standard approved by the Secretary of Trade and Industry (under section 5).

Part III of the CGSO confers power on the Commissioner of Customs and Excise to control the safety of consumer goods, the Commissioner may:

(a) require a person (a supplier, manufacturer or importer of consumer goods) to publish a warning at his own expense that the consumer goods may be unsafe;[70]
(b) issue a prohibition notice, prohibiting the supply of unsafe consumer goods for a specified period;[71]

    (c) serve a recall notice requiring the immediate withdrawal of unsafe consumer goods if there is a significant risk that the consumer goods will cause a serious injury;[72] and

    (d) require by written notice:

        (i) testing, in a specified manner, of those consumer goods suspected of non-compliance with the requirement or standards;

        (ii) necessary modifications to ensure compliance with the requirement or standards; and

        (iii) warning notices in advertisements or withdrawal of advertisements.[73]

Any person who is aggrieved by a decision or action of the Commissioner may, under Part III, within 14 days after the decision or action, appeal to the Appeal Board.[74] Nevertheless, an application for an appeal will not stay the execution of the Commissioner's decision.[75] After hearing the appeal, the Appeal Board may:[76]

    (a) confirm or revoke the decision or action of the Commissioner;

    (b) make any decision that the Commissioner could have made; or

    (c) order the Commissioner to take any action within his powers.

Part VI of the CGSO sets out the specific powers given to authorized officers for the purpose of enforcing the provisions of the CGSO, including the power to enter premises, inspect and seize consumer goods and documents, etc.

A number of offences are stipulated under section 22 of the CGSO, for example, the failure to comply with a notice issued by the Commissioner. Criminal sanctions are provided by the imposition of a fine of up to HK$500,000 and imprisonment of up to 2 years.[77] The defence of due diligence is available to the person who acted on the default of another, or relied on information given by another, and also who took reasonable steps to avoid committing the offence.[78] To invoke this statutory defence of due diligence, the person must serve a notice on the authority seven days before the hearing.[79]

The Sale of Goods (Amendments) Ordinance 1994

The SOGO is a collection of law relating to sale of goods. The amendments generally follow the recommendations of the Commission Report, Topic 21. The term "merchantable quality" is expanded to include certain elements of consumer protection. Under section 2(5), goods sold must be reasonably fit for a common purpose; with the appropriate standard of appearance and finish; free from defects; and safe and durable. Meanwhile, persons dealing as consumers are not, under the amendments, always afforded a reasonable opportunity to examine the goods they are buying.

The Consumer Council

The leading advocate of consumer protection in Hong Kong is the Consumer Council. The Council is a government-subvented body established in 1974 and was later incorporated under the Consumer Council Ordinance (Cap. 216) (the "CCO") in 1977. It aims at enhancing, protecting and promoting consumer rights.[80] Its functions are set out in section 4 of the CCO which include:

(a) to collect information on the prices of a selected range of commodities and on the workings of the wholesale and retail markets in them;[81]
(b) to receive and consider suggestions and complaints, including complaints of profiteering; and
(c) on the basis of its conclusions on (a) and (b),
   (i) to publish the facts;
   (ii) to act on public opinion to deter clear-cut cases of profiteering; and
   (iii) to advise the Government if scope for effective official action is discovered.

One of the major criticisms of the Council is that it is not empowered with any real authority. For a long time, the Council has been dubbed a "toothless" dog because of the lack of legal power to sanction.[82] Very often, when the Council finds there is a valid complaint, they are unable to do much for the consumers. They cannot mediate or arbitrate if there is a lack of consensus between the parties. At most, they could only expose the malfeasance (if there is any) in the media and the complainants have to pursue their remedies in court at their own expenses.

In the past, certain goods and services provided by the entities listed in the Schedule of the CCO are exempted from the Consumer Council. The 1994 amendments to the CCO repealed section 4(3)(a)(ii), (4) so that such bodies will not longer be outside the purview of the Consumer Council.

The Consumer Legal Action Fund

The Consumer Council has received numerous complaints in which the rights of consumers have been infringed as a result of malpractice or unconscionable conduct by a common defaulting business. In many cases, the Council can only advise the complainants to seek redress in court as the Council itself is not empowered to settle consumer disputes. Under the current system, legal aid is only available to those who could satisfy the means test. Besides, most consumer claims are of amounts under HK$15,000, the minimum figure specified in the Legal Aid Ordinance. Many consumers may not be able to benefit from the system.

We have seen that recent enactments have bolstered the law on consumer protection, but, no matter how good the legislation is, its objectives are often defeated because of the lack of access to legal advice. Legislation alone is no panacea if it cannot be effectively enforced. Since 1990, the Council has been investigating the feasibility of introducing into Hong Kong a procedure which would assist groups of consumers to assert their rights through legal proceedings, particularly in cases involving common defendants and common circumstances or where legal action is likely to benefit the public generally.

The government has injected HK$10 million into the fund. Initially, it is recommended that the fund be restricted to cases that relate to consumer transactions and fall within the purview of the Consumer Council's statutory functions; or that involve significant public interest and injustice; and for which court action is the most effective means of resolution.

Pre-sale of Land in Hong Kong and China

During 1993 and 1994, activities in China's property market heated up because of the shift of investment by Hong Kong property investors and the opening up of the Chinese property market. The move was prompted by the rise of property price in Hong Kong and the relatively low price of properties located in the special economic zones and other areas in the Pearl River Delta. Most of the purchases involve pre-sale of uncompleted buildings and almost all the investors made their purchases without proper investigation of title or ownership of the developments. They relied instead on the representations of agents or advertisements alone.

In Guangdong, after the central government's decision to cool down the overheated market and the economy in 1994; many of these developments failed, and many investors lost out on their investment, some could not obtain good title to their properties, some projects did not get completed, or even get started. Many buyers did not get what they contracted for in terms of quality and size of their properties.

There are a number of explanations of the seemingly irrational behaviour of these investors. One is that consumers or property buyers in Hong Kong have for a long time been quite well protected in their purchase of pre-sale or uncompleted flats. They believed, therefore, that they would be protected the same way.

Since the early 1960s, the Hong Kong Government has through their conditions of sale or government leases restricted the ability of landowner-developers to pre-sell flats. It does so by providing in the Crown Leases a condition that government's consent is required before a pre-sale can take place. Advertisements must be pre-approved, and each stage of construction monitored and completed[83] before money can be transferred to the developer.[84] Without the consent and evidence of full compliance, title of the property will be defective.[85] Besides, in Hong Kong, all property transactions must be completed with the services of solicitors.[86] They are under a legal duty to ensure that the title of the property in question is good and the title is being transferred to the purchaser.

Another factor which could have led consumers to a wrong belief is the practice of requiring the notarial service of a China-appointed notary public to attest the relevant instruments at certain stage of the purchase. As some of these notaries are also Hong Kong solicitors (or barristers) and the process takes place in solicitors' offices, consumers may believe that the solicitor is providing legal services as in the case of a sale of Hong Kong property.

One further explanation is that these consumers were caught in the frenzy of then very heated activities.

Advertisement and Sale of Properties Located in China

Presently, there is no law regulating advertisements of sales of properties located outside Hong Kong, nor are there regulations concerning pre-sale of properties outside Hong Kong. Although China has laws and regulations on advertisement, for example, the Law of the People's Republic of China on Advertisements,[87] the Law of the People's Republic of China on Anti-unfair Competition[88] and the PRC Consumer Protection Law,[89] the question of jurisdiction remains: Can a Hong Kong consumer go to a People's Court contending that he has been misled by advertisements put in Hong Kong media promoting sale of Chinese properties?

The recent case involving Ong's Property (China) Consultants presents a roundabout way of enforcement by the Hong Kong authorities. In this case the Securities and Futures Commission of Hong Kong fined the company for unauthorized advertising. The advertising that appeared in Hong Kong related to the sale of units in the Giant Building in Zhuhai. It included a guarantee to buyers that their properties would increase by 80 per cent in value or the developer would buy back at 180 per cent of the original price. The Protection of Investors Ordinance (Cap. 335) requires that offers involving a buy-back guarantee be authorized by the Commission.[90]

Conclusion

The recent developments in consumer protection in Hong Kong indicate that it is evolving steadily and the gap between Hong Kong and European and U.S. jurisdictions is narrowing; but it still depends very much on the development of other areas of consumer protection such as consumer awareness, access to various systems of consumer redress, consumer education and the willingness of the consumer to utilize the existing system of law to further the cause of consumer protection in Hong Kong.

Notes

[1] The Law Reform Commission, *Report on Sale of Goods and Supply of Services* [Topic 21] (the Commission Report, Topic 21), para. 8.8. See also Ho Suk-ching, *Consumer Protection (or Lack of It) in Hong Kong*, Working Paper Series of CUHK, 1984.
[2] See the Law Reform Commission's *Report on Control of Exemption Clauses* [Topic 13] (the Commission Report, Topic 13), (December 1986).
[3] The Commission Report, Topic 21, para. 8.8.
[4] For discussions on these mechanisms, see Aster Camille Elms, "Consumer Protection in Hong Kong: Is the Proposed Legislation Enough?" (1994) 1 HKSLR 1 at 19–23.
[5] The Consumer Council is a government-subvented body established in 1974. One of the functions of the Consumer Council is to receive and consider suggestions and complaints, including complaints of profiteering. See Consumer Council Ordinance s.4(1)(b).
[6] Although some other ordinances contain consumer protection elements, they seldom serve this purpose. Dr David Campbell pointed out that some legislation, despite clear legislative intent to offer consumer protection, has been used almost exclusively by businesses to their interest, see David Campbell, "The Merits of Legislation Against Restrictive Practices and Cartels: Should Hong Kong Legislate?". His view echoed the opinion of the

Law Reform Commission. See the Commission Report, Topic 21, para. 8.3.7.

7 For example, a series of consumer protection statutes were enacted by the U.K. in the 1970s and 1980s, namely the Supply of Goods (Implied Terms) Act 1973, the Consumer Credits Act 1974, the Unfair Contract Terms Act 1977, the Sale of Goods Act 1979, the Supply of Goods and Services Act 1982, and the Consumer Protection Act 1987.

8 Adopted at the 4th Session of the Standing Committee of the 8th National People's Congress and promulgated by the President of the Country (Order No.11) on October 31, 1993 with effect from January 1, 1994.

9 Ord. No.84 of 1994.
10 Ord. No.85 of 1994.
11 Ord. No.86 of 1994.
12 Ord. No.87 of 1994.
13 SOGO, s.57(7).
14 SOGO, s.2A.
15 CECO, s.4.
16 UCO, s.3.
17 SOSITO, s.4.
18 [1988] 1 All ER 847, C.A.
19 *ibid.* at p.853.
20 *ibid.* at p.854.

21 In *Printing and Numerical Registering Co v. Sampson* (1875) LR 19 Eq 462 at 465, Sir George Jessel M.R. said, "If there is one thing which more than another public policy requires it is that men of full age and competent understanding shall have the utmost liberty of contracting, and that their contracts when entered into freely and voluntarily shall be held sacred and shall be enforced by Courts of Justice". For an account of the interplay of economic and social doctrines and the law of contract, see Atiyah, *The Rise and Fall of Freedom of Contract* (1979).

22 David Campbell, "The Undeath of Contract: A Study in the Degeneration of a Research Programme" (1992) HKLJ 20; in the article Dr Campbell stated that the distinction between voluntary and imposed obligation is entirely bankrupt in labour law.

23 It was suggested that exemption clauses were not the subject of negotiation between the parties and that they were weapons of consumer oppression. See Yates, *Exclusion Clauses in Contracts* (2nd ed., 1982), at p.2.

24 [1974] 3 All ER 616 at 624.

25 Very often, the party seeking to impose exemption clauses has overwhelming economic bargaining strength that leaves no room for negotiation or the party with stronger bargaining power allows few opportunities for the party with weaker bargaining power to negotiate or read the contract. For further discussion on the justification of statutory control, see Aitken Lee, "The Control of Exemption Clauses Ordinance" (1990) HKLJ 381, pp.381–389.

26 (1978) HKLJ 284.

27 If a party does not comply with a fundamental term so that the performance becomes totally different from what the contract contemplated, the contracting party cannot rely on the exemption clause to exempt himself from his liability. See *Photo Production Ltd v. Securicor Transport Ltd* [1980] 1 All ER 556. When construing an exemption clause, the *contra proferentum* rule entitles the court to construe an exemption clause in a way unfavourable to the person who put it into the contract. See *Alexander v. Railway Executive* [1951] 2 All ER 442.

28 *Harbutt's Plasticine Ltd v. Wayne Tank & Pump Co Ltd* [1970] 1 All ER 225. In this case, Lord Denning M.R. accepted that the principle which said

that no exclusion clause could excuse a fundamental breach was not a rule of law but a rule of construction when the non-defaulting party affirmed the contract. It would only be a rule of law if the non-defaulting party elected to repudiate the contract on the ground of fundamental breach. *Harbutt's Plasticine* was, however, overruled by *Photo Production* and by the Unfair Contract Terms Act 1977.

[29] The courts are reluctant to strike down exemption clauses on the ground of unreasonableness alone. For instance, in *Ailsa Craig Fishing Co v. Mavern Fishing* [1983] 1 WLR 964, the House of Lords upheld exemption clauses under which the parties agreed to apportion the risk of occurrence of certain events even though on the "fundamental breach" approach, the non-performance by the party at fault went to the root of the contract. See Aitken Lee, "The Control of Exemption Clauses Ordinance", above, pp.381–382.

[30] *Houghton v. Trafalger Insurance* [1954] 1 QB 247. See also Yates and Hawkins, *Standard Business Contracts: Exclusions and Related Devices* (1986), p.89.

[31] Misrepresentation Ordinance, s.4.

[32] The Commission Report, Topic 13, paras. 4.10 and 5.20.

[33] Pun Ho-cheung and Leung Kwai-Ho, "A Study on the Control of Exemption Clauses Ordinance", (Research Paper), at p.1.

[34] The Preamble to the CECO.

[35] CECO, s.2(2). In other words, the common law principles governing exemption clauses prior to the commencement of the CECO continue to apply to "non-business" transactions.

[36] CECO, s.16.

[37] CECO, s.17(1).

[38] CECO, s.17(2); unless the court or the arbitrator is satisfied that the whole or main purpose of such terms is to evade the operation of the CECO, or one of the contracting parties was a consumer habitually resident in Hong Kong and the essential steps necessary for the making of the contract were taken in Hong Kong.

[39] CECO, s.18(1)(a).

[40] CECO, s.18(1)(b).

[41] SOGO, ss.15–17 orelate to implied terms to conformity with description or sample, and quality or fitness for purpose. For further discussions, see Atiyah, *The Sale of Goods* (8th ed., 1990).

[42] CECO, s.3(2).

[43] This section also applies to standard terms business contracts.

[44] S.9 of the CECO.

[45] S.10 of the CECO.

[46] S.11(1) of the CECO.

[47] The U.K. Supply of Goods and Services Act 1982 applies to contracts for sale of goods and supply of services.

[48] The Commission Report, Topic 21, paragraph 6.7.

[49] S.3(1) of the SOSITO.

[50] Note that under s.3(3), the Governor-in-Council may by order exempt specified services from one or more of the implied terms under the SOSITO.

[51] S.5 of the SOSITO; *cf.* s.13 of the Supply of Goods and Services Act. See also *Bolam v. Friern Hospital Management Committee* [1957] 2 All ER 118, where McNair J. decided that in deciding whether a supplier discharges his obligations the standard of care required should be an objective one. At p.121, he stated, "The test is the standard of the ordinary skilled man exercising and professing to have the special skill . . . it is well-established law that it is sufficient if he exercises the ordinary skill of an ordinary competent man exercising that particular art."

[52] SS.6 and 7 operate as the residual provisions in that they are only applicable if the contract contains nothing as to the time for performance and consideration. For further discussions, see Murdoch, "Contracts for the Supply of Services under the 1982 Act" [1983] LMCLQ 652, at 660. If there is an express provision in the contract, no party may rely on the SOSITO to attack its reasonableness.

[53] cf. s.14 of the Supply of Goods and Services Act.

[54] cf. s.15 of the Supply of Goods and Services Act.

[55] SS.6(2), 7(2) of the SOSITO.

[56] Charnock v. Liverpool Corporation [1968] 1 WLR 1498.

[57] S.8(2) of the SOSITO.

[58] (1888) 40 Ch D 312.

[59] National Westminster Bank v. Morgan [1985] 1 All ER 821. See Aster Camille Elms, "Consumer Protection in Hong Kong: Is the Proposed Legislation enough?" supra, at p.8.

[60] The UCO only applies to contracts in which one of the parties deals as consumer. See s.5(1) of the UCO.

[61] S.5(2) of the UCO.

[62] S.6(1) of the UCO.

[63] S.6(3) of the UCO.

[64] S.7 of the UCO. See also note 17.

[65] S.3 of the Toys and Children's Product Safety Ordinance.

[66] The Preamble to the CGSO. For discussions on the current law on product safety in the U.K., see Cartwright, "Product Safety and Consumer Protection", The Modern Law Review, Vol.58 (March 1995), pp.222–31.

[67] S.2 of the CGSO.

[68] The CGSO does not apply to goods in transit, consumer goods in the course of transhipment or consumer goods manufactured for export.

[69] S.5 of the CGSO.

[70] S.7 of the CGSO.

[71] S.8 of the CGSO. The period must, however, not exceed 6 months unless the Commissioner has taken proceedings against the person for the prosecution of an offence under the CGSO or for the destruction of seized or detained the consumer goods.

[72] S.9 of the CGSO.

[73] S.10 of the CGSO.

[74] S.13(1) of the CGSO.

[75] S.13(3) of the CGSO.

[76] S.17(2) of the CGSO.

[77] S.28 of the CGSO.

[78] S.24 of the CGSO.

[79] S.24(2) of the CGSO.

[80] Consumer rights were classified by the late U.S. President JF Kennedy in his address to the Congress, "Consumer's Protection and Interest Programs" (1962), into four main categories: the right to safety, the right to be informed, the right to choose and the right to be heard.

[81] Consumer information in relation to the selection of goods and services is provided in the Council's official monthly magazine Choice. The results of regular testing of comparative quality and performance of specific products are published in Choice.

[82] Ho Suk-ching, Consumer Protection (or Lack of It) in Hong Kong, supra, at p.7.

[83] The requirements are the completion of the foundations and piling work and the Building Authority's consent having been secured under s.14 of the

Building Ordinance (Cap. 123). See paragraphs 1–3 of Land Office Circular Memorandum No.57.

[84] Developer's solicitor acts as stakeholder in Consent Scheme transactions. Details of the release of fund are found in condition 15 to the Annexure to Land Office Circular Memorandum No.57.

[85] It is because the Crown will have the right to re-enter the land on the ground of breach of the Conditions of Sale.

[86] S.47 of the Legal Practitioners Ordinance (Cap. 159).

[87] Adopted by the 10th Session of the Standing Committee of the 8th National People's Congress on 27 October 1994, promulgated by the President of the Country (Order No.34) on 27 October 1994, and became effective as of 1 February 1995.

[88] Articles 9 and 24 of the Law of the People's Republic of China on Anti-unfair Competition. The Law was adopted by the 3rd Session of the Standing Committee of the 8th National People's Congress on 2 September 1993, promulgated by the President of the Country (Order No.10) on 2 September 1993 and became effective as of 1 December 1993.

[89] Articles 19, 22 and 23 of the PRC Consumer Protection Law.

[90] S.4(2)(g)(ii) of the Protection of Investors Ordinance.

PART 5

CORRUPTION, MARKET REFORM AND CRIMINAL JUSTICE

PERFECTING CHINA'S LEGAL SYSTEM TO FIGHT CRIMES OF BRIBERY

Professor Chu Huaizhi

Department of Law
Peking University

Professor Chu Huaizhi, *LL.B. (Peking Institute of Politics and Law), began teaching in 1955 at the Peking Institute of Politics and Law. In 1979 he moved to Peking University, becoming Professor of Law. Between 1981 and 1982 he was a visiting scholar at the Chicago Law School. He has published* American Criminal Law, On Crime Control *and numerous articles.*

Definition of Concepts

The definitions of the two terms "corruption" and "bribery" often appear simultaneously. In other parts of the world, corruption and bribery are simply different names for the same crime. In mainland China, however, they refer to different crimes under criminal law.

In China, corruption refers to the embezzlement of public property by state personnel. State personnel include the staff at all levels of state bodies, administrative bodies, judicial bodies, the armed forces, state enterprises and state institutional organizations, as well as all other personnel engaged in public service according to the law. Bribery, on the other hand, refers only to the act of giving or accepting bribes.

In other countries, the crime of embezzlement, including both official and business embezzlement, is stipulated under criminal laws. Official embezzlement is equivalent to corruption in China. It is considered to be an independent crime.

In the meantime, the crime of embezzlement referred to in the Decision Regarding the Punishment of Crimes of Violating Company Law (February 1995) is equivalent to that of business embezzlement in other countries. As a result, corruption is considered to be different from embezzlement under China's Criminal Law.

Under the Criminal Law of the PRC accepting bribes only refers to official bribery. Prior to February 1995, accepting bribes was only a criminal act when committed by state personnel and those engaged in public service. Business bribery was added in the above-mentioned February 1995 Decision, extending it to cover managers, supervisors and staff and workers in corporations.

The crimes of bribery referred to in this paper mainly refer to official bribery. Judicial statistics usually include both corruption and official bribery because both are criminal acts prompted by greed for money. This paper aims only to study the development of legislation against bribery.

Factors Involved in Corruption and Bribery

General Overview

Since the implementation of economic reforms in China, the average annual rate of increase of the gross national product and national income has been about 10 per cent. Along with this rapid economic growth has come a huge increase in crimes of corruption and bribery by state personnel.

From 1983 to 1993, a total of 113,000 crimes of bribery were filed and investigated across the country. In 1994, 36,741 cases of corruption and bribery were filed and investigated, of which 1,827 involved leading officials at or above the level of a department or a county head, a significant increase over 1993.[1] From January to May 1995, the procuratorial organs at all levels filed and investigated 779 cases of crimes of corruption and bribery of cadres at or above the level of a department or a county head.[2]

Characteristics of Crimes of Corruption and Bribery

The rate of crimes of corruption and bribery is high and far-reaching. Statistics suggest crimes of bribery comprise more than 30 per cent of all types of economic criminal cases filed and investigated since 1988, which is second only to that for crimes of corruption. The actual criminal rate is certain to be far higher than indicated by official statistics, however, as bribery is an easily concealed crime, known only to the giver and the accepter. Bribery has penetrated every field of social life, particularly taxation administration, industrial and commercial management, monetary affairs, and estate property.

Crimes of bribery are committed in many different ways, in order to avoid detection. For example, those being bribed can be offered a rent-free property or goods at a nominal price; articles of property can be "borrowed"; money can be intentionally lost to be found by the person being bribed; and "free" tours can be arranged for the purpose of sightseeing or in the name of inspection. Offering "donations" is another form of bribery. This means that no promise is given in return for the bribe, but it still compromises the official's position, and may well influence their judgment in the future.

The number and type of people accepting bribes is expanding. State personnel who have retired or left office may still attempt to extort bribes or simply accept bribes for influencing those currently in office. Some state personnel will not accept bribes personally, but have their family members do it for them. In addition, the size of bribes being offered is increasing rapidly as the economy develops and people experience an increase in living standards.

Reasons for Bribery and Corruption

(a) Reform of the Economic System. China's recent and rapid transformation from a planned economy to a market economy has meant that the new system and rules have been unable to keep pace, and many conflicts between the two systems still need to be resolved. This has resulted in many opportunities for economic crimes to be committed, including the crimes of corruption and bribery.

Under the planned economy, enterprises had no autonomy, with production and sales controlled by the state. Management had nothing to do with the direct personal interests of its staff, and there was no reason to offer bribes to state personnel. With the advent of the new market economy, enterprises must now assume sole responsibility for their profits and losses and operate at their own will. The production of the largest possible profits has now become the main aim.

Although the fundamental principle of the market economy is the reduction of official intervention in economic activities, at this early stage in its development some enterprises are still engaged in bribing state personnel who have the power to influence the workings of the market. This is possible because the functions of state and private enterprise have not yet been completely separated, the system of economic administration still needs to be perfected, and rules and regulations governing the market haven't been established.

An investigation of a wide range of countries by the United Nations Industrial Development Association demonstrates that where the social economic infrastructure is reformed fastest, it is likely that many social problems will occur simultaneously. Corruption was at its worst in Britain in the eighteenth century, and in the U.S. during the nineteenth century, when both countries were undergoing the industrial revolution.

(b) Changes in levels of income. The potential of exchanging power for money has increased rapidly during the transition from the planned economy to market economy, which is a major factor in the increase in crimes of bribery.

Under the planned economy, standard salaries of state personnel were above average, but today they have been substantially reduced. These state personnel still hold the power that others require, however, and this situation has made the giving and accepting of bribes very tempting.

State personnel who accept bribes can "justify" their actions by saying that their salary has not kept pace with China's rapid inflation, so that accepting bribes is merely an issue of self-help. This is supported by the fact that some members of society now receive more and consume more than others as a result of state policy. State personnel may feel that extorting and accepting bribes is a way of rectifying this situation.

(c) The lack of effective internal restrictions and external supervision of those in power.

(d) The flaws which exist in legislation regarding official behaviour. As yet there are no specific regulations on official conduct. If bribery of officials is to be prevented, it is essential to institute a code of conduct for officials.

(e) It is difficult to expose bribery because there is no system of declaration by officials of their properties.

(f) The ineffectiveness of litigation procedures makes it difficult to prosecute crimes of bribery efficiently. In addition, it is often difficult to initiate legal proceedings against government officials with strong powers who are often protected by their social relationships.

(g) Given the vast number of ways in which bribes can be offered and accepted, the criminal justice system is finding it impossible to keep pace with the ever-changing nature of this crime.

Developing a Legal System to Combat Bribery

China's Current Legislation for Dealing with Bribery

Since 1979, a number of laws and regulations regarding the punishment of crimes of bribery of state personnel have been promulgated in China, and a series of judicial explanations have been issued by the Supreme People's Court and the Supreme People's Procuratorate. Chief among these are:

(a) Articles 155 and 185 of the Criminal Law of the People's Republic of China, 1979;
(b) Supplementary Regulations Regarding the Punishment of Crimes of Corruption and Bribery, 1988 (hereafter referred to as "Supplementary Regulations");
(c) Decision Regarding the Severe Punishment of Criminals Who Seriously Undermine the Economy, 1982;
(d) Explanations and Answers of the Supreme People's Court and the Supreme People's Procuratorate Regarding Several Problems Occurring in Concrete Application of Laws During the Handling of Economic Criminal Cases (Trial Implementation); and
(e) Explanations and Answers Regarding Several Problems in Executing Supplementary Regulations Regarding the Punishment of Crimes of Corruption and Bribery (hereafter referred to as "Explanations and Answers").

In addition, the State Council has enacted a series of administrative ordinances and regulations regarding the conduct of state personnel. Chief among these are:

(a) Decision of the State Council Regarding Not Donating and Accepting Gifts in Foreign-Related Activities;
(b) Notice of the General Office of the State Council Regarding the Severe Prohibition of Seeking Unlawful Profits in Social Economic Life;
(c) Provisional Regulations on Administrative Sanctions for Corruption and Bribery by State Personnel of the Administrative Organs; and
(d) Regulations for the Personnel of the State Council.

In addition, various ministries and commissions under the State Council and the People's Bank have also issued a series of rules of conduct intended to improve the honesty and behaviour of state personnel.

What follows is a brief introduction to the laws related to bribery of state personnel in China.

The Concept of Crimes of Accepting Bribes

The Supplementary Regulations introduced in 1988 amended and supplemented article 185 of China's Criminal Law. They stipulate that the definition of accepting a bribe includes all acts of state personnel, personnel of collective economic organizations or other personnel engaged in public service who take advantage of their office to extort another person's property or unlawfully accept other people's property and secure advantages for them. In addition to "violating the regulations of the state regarding economic activities, he shall be punished in accordance with the regulations of crimes of accepting bribes if he accepts service charges and commissions in his own interest".

Those Involved in Accepting Bribes

The Supplementary Regulations stipulate that any natural persons (state personnel and other personnel engaged in public service according to law), or legal persons (state-run enterprises, institutions, state organs, etc.) accepting a bribe are committing a crime. State personnel who have retired or already left office may also be considered to be accepting bribes as stipulated in Explanations and Answers.

The Elements Constituting the Crime of Accepting a Bribe

Although crimes of accepting bribes include both extorting and accepting bribes, they have different elements. A crime is committed if another person's property is extorted, whether it is to gain interest for that person or not. Where another person's property is simply accepted, however, it is necessary for interest to be gained for another person for it to constitute a crime. This is irrespective of whether the interests for another person are legitimate or realized.

Both the Criminal Law and Supplementary Regulations stipulate that "to take advantage of one's office" is an element of the crime of bribery.

The Nature of a Bribe

Bribery is confined to articles of property in Supplementary Regulations. Now, scholars and judicial personnel are proposing this should be expanded to include the profits of property.

Current Legislation for Dealing with Bribery Outside China

Preventing bribery and corruption is an important issue for all governments. Many countries have put a great deal of effort into strengthening legislation against corruption in order to prevent bribery of officials, and have accumulated a great deal of practical experience in this field.

These states have not only instituted punitive measures for bribery under their criminal law, criminal procedure laws and special laws and regulations against bribery, but have also taken preventive measures in the form of a code of conduct for officials that is laid down in public service law, moral law and the law of administrative management. Some states have even established a special organization to fight corruption that is responsible for investigating and prosecuting crimes of accepting bribes by officials.

Punishment of bribery is the most essential part of the legislation, and criminal punishment is considered the most effective deterrent. Most countries stipulate punishment of crimes of accepting bribes in their penal codes, and procedures for investigation and handling in their criminal procedure laws. A few states and regions have also instituted a special law against bribery, such as Hong Kong's Prevention of Bribery Ordinance.

The Concept and Nature of Crimes of Bribery

Crimes of accepting bribes by officials generally refer to officials accepting profits in any form other than their proper pay which is connected with their duties or acts relating to those duties. The laws of many countries stipulate that if an official accepts gifts or holds two or more paid posts concurrently without permission and does not report this to a higher body, he commits a crime of accepting bribes.

Range of Bribable Crimes

Under Japanese Criminal Law, there are seven forms for crimes of accepting bribes:

(a) simple crimes of accepting bribes, meaning that the bribe is not necessarily connected to an official's duties — Under Hong Kong's Prevention of Bribery Ordinance, it is stipulated that just being a government official and accepting a bribe is sufficient to constitute a crime;

(b) normal crimes of accepting bribes, which is to accept bribes in carrying out official duties;

(c) crimes of advance bribery; crimes of subsequent bribery; crimes of bribery for dishonest actions, which is to accept bribes as payment for acts that violate official regulations or duties;

(d) crimes of receiving bribes for exertion of influence, which is to accept bribes to influence another official to act in violation of his duties; and

(e) crimes of bribing a third person.

Under the Criminal Law of the United Germany, two kinds of crimes of accepting bribes are stipulated: one is accepting bribes without violating official duties; the other is accepting bribes for acts which violate official duties. The latter crime is awarded a heavier punishment.

Definition of Bribes

Many countries stipulate that bribes refer not only to articles of property, but also other profits of property, and profits without property. For example, there is a precedent for sexual bribes under Japanese law, and the German criminal code stipulates that bribes refer to "interests", as does Hong Kong's Prevention of Bribery Ordinance.

Removing Limitations on Bribes

All acts of demanding, appointing or accepting bribes in connection with official duties or acts relating to official duties, no matter how large the bribe, are considered crimes. This aims to prevent misdemeanours from becoming felonies and to make the enforcement of criminal law and criminal responsibility more strict. It reflects the concept that public office is not purchasable.

Punishment of Crimes of Accepting Bribes

With the exception of a few countries (such as Thailand), crimes of accepting bribes are not punishable by capital punishment or life imprisonment. In most cases, the punishment is fixed-term of imprisonment.

Official Bribery Versus Business Bribery

Official bribery is generally stipulated under criminal law, while business bribery is stipulated under economic and administrative law, however, both are stipulated under the same law in Hong Kong's Prevention of Bribery Ordinance.

A Proposal to Perfect China's Legislation Against Crimes of Bribery

While the socialist market economy is being established, anti-bribery legislation must be perfected step by step. The best way to do so is through reference to the experience of other countries in this area while taking into consideration current conditions in China.

Altering Policy Considerations in Perfecting the Legislation

The first step in perfecting legislation is changing current thinking on criminal policy from "severe rather than strict" to "strict rather than severe". "Strict" refers to make the criminal law more strict, and "severe" to severe punishment.

"Strict" requires that the amount of money considered to be a bribe under the law should be reduced to be roughly equal to the amounts considered to be crimes of theft and fraud.

In addition, accepting a bribe is currently only a crime when it is accepted for other people's advantages. For "strict", this restriction should be removed, which will mean that officials are committing a crime provided they accept a bribe irrespective of whether it is for other people's advantages. "Strict" also requires that the scope of bribes should be enlarged to include not only articles of property but also other profits of property.

If the law is to be strictly enforced, it will mean that acts of accepting bribes in a disguised form should also be criminalized. This includes crimes of accepting bribes by officials who have left office; crimes of receiving bribes for exertion of influence; and simple crimes of receiving bribes (as in article 3 of Hong Kong's Prevention of Bribery Ordinance). In addition, the crime of owning property that cannot be explained is stipulated in article 10 of Hong Kong's Prevention of Bribery Ordinance, and is a useful legal weapon that has been made use of in China's Supplementary Regulations (article 11), although not as powerfully as in Hong Kong.

Making legislation strict, but "not severe" refers to reducing gradually fixed terms for crimes of bribery and limiting the use of capital punishment. At the same time, better results may be gained from applying heavy fines to criminals who are largely motivated by greed.

Establishing a Code of Conduct

An official code of conduct is important in preventing crimes of accepting bribes. Given the experience of other countries in this area and China's current circumstances, the following stipulations should definitely be included in such a code.

Accepting and Receiving Gifts — Definite norms should be formulated to stipulate the reporting of gifts accepted and received. Those accepting gifts beyond a certain limit without reporting them must be punished. Any gift which may influence public duties should not be accepted, and the practice of dining and drinking with public funds should be checked.

Limitations on Holding Two or More Posts Concurrently — In order to ensure officials are loyal to their duties, they should be prohibited from accepting unlawful or excessive pay and from holding two or more posts concurrently.

Prohibiting Officials from Conducting Business.

Withdrawal from Conflict of Interest Situations — Officials should not employ their relatives as subordinates, and should withdraw from public duties which are directly connected with themselves or their relatives.

Reporting Property of Senior Officials to a Higher Body — The state should stipulate a system for reporting property and a procedure for investigating the reported articles and punishing violators. The circumstances of an official's spouse, children and parents must be also declared. A special institution should be established to receive reports and conduct subsequent investigations, and an investigating and supervising institution should also be set up.

Social security

One of the most fundamental causes of the growth in crimes of bribery is social economics, therefore, it is important to formulate social counter-measures against crimes of bribery.

Separating the Functions of Government and Enterprises — An enterprise can only become truly independent when these functions have been separated. When the government has little power over the administration of enterprises and cannot directly interfere in their affairs, crimes of bribery will certainly be reduced.

Instituting a Strict Administrative System — Reducing government interference in economic activities does not mean totally removing its administrative role. On the contrary, a strict administrative system must be formulated, especially given the new challenges faced during economic reform. The new system must reflect the demands of the market economy in terms of equality and competition. Such a system will help to prevent crimes of bribery, and will be more effective than subsequent punishment.

Increasing the Pay of State Personnel — As previously mentioned, incomes of state personnel have been falling in real terms, and have been a major factor in the increase in bribery. The state should increase their incomes to keep them on a par with their social status. In many other parts of the world, public servants are highly paid, indicating their status in society.

Establishing a Special Institution to Deal With Crimes of Corruption and Bribery — Crimes of corruption and bribery are currently handled by the procuratorial organs at all levels, but these bodies also deal with eight other types of crime. Given that crimes of corruption and bribery are often hidden, many countries have established special institutions to fight this kind of crime. One example is Hong Kong's Independent Commission Against Corruption (ICAC). Although this kind of commission would be impossible in China, the experience of the ICAC should be studied and fully used.

Notes

[1] Zhang Siqing, *Report on Work of the Supreme People's Procuratorates on the National People's Congress*, March 18, 1995.
[2] Telecommunications of Xin Hua News Agency, June 25, 1995.

THE PRESENT AND FUTURE OF CRIMINAL DEFENCE IN CHINA

Dr Fu Hualing

Faculty of Law
City University of Hong Kong

Dr Fu Hualing, *assistant professor at the Faculty of Law, City University of Hong Kong; LL.B. (1983), Southwestern University of Political Science and Law, PRC; M.A. in Criminology (1988), University of Toronto, Canada; D. Jur. (1993), Osgoode Hall Law School, York University, Canada. He is interested in criminal law, criminal justice and human rights.*

This paper is part of a larger study of China's Criminal Procedural Law. Research has relied partly upon interviews with staff from the Legislative Affairs Commission (LAC); the National People's Congress; researchers from both the Supreme People's Court (SPC) and Supreme People's Procuracy (SPP); and judges and lawyers in Beijing, Guangzhou and Zhuhai. The interviews were carried out in 1995.

The author is indebted to Bryan S. Bachner, Arthur Chung, Stephen D. Mau and Richard Cullen for their critical comments on earlier drafts of the manuscript.

Introduction

Justice demands an individual accused of criminal activity has the right to defend himself before the law. The Chinese Constitution (1982) enshrines this principle by stating that "the accused has the right to defence" (article 125). This principle is also repeated in article 26 of the Criminal Procedural Law 1979 (CPL); article 8 of the Organic Law of People's Courts 1983 (OLPC); and article 6 of Interim Rules on Lawyers 1981 (IRL). Article 27 of the CPL further requires the court to appoint a lawyer for the accused if he is deaf, mute or a minor, and for the accused who has not appointed anyone to defend him.[2]

Although the accused in China may invoke the constitutional right to counsel, this right has been substantially limited and grossly distorted by subordinate laws, government regulations and administrative discretion. According to Zhang Sihan (1994:47) from the Supreme People's Court, on average, only 20 per cent to 30 per cent of the defendants were represented by lawyers during the trial; even in cases of serious criminal offences, only 40 per cent of the defendants retained lawyers. Furthermore, the CPL has structured China's criminal process in such a way that a criminal trial and the role of defence attorneys are mere formalities. This paper will argue that the current structure of criminal defence in China is fundamentally flawed. It has to be reformed so as to improve the quality and quantity of legal representation.

The Role of Defence Lawyers in China

Defence Lawyers in Criminal Proceedings

Article 3 of the CPL generally divides criminal proceedings in China into three stages. At the investigation stage, the public security organs (the police) are in charge of investigation, detention and preliminary review of criminal cases; at the prosecution stage, the procuracy approves arrest, conducts procuratorial proceedings and institutes public prosecution; and the court is responsible for adjudicating cases at the trial stage.

A defence lawyer is to "safeguard the lawful rights and interests of the defendants on the basis of facts and the law" (IRL, article 6) and to "prove the innocence of the defendant, the pettiness of his crime and the need for a mitigated punishment or exemption from criminal responsibility" (CPL, article 28).

Determination Before a Trial

Once the procuracy initiates proceedings against an accused and transfers the case to court, the court forms a collegial panel, composed of judges and people's assessors, to try the case.[3] Before the trial, the panel holds meetings to discuss the case, and to make a decision on the nature of the offence as well as on the sentence. In serious cases, decisions are made by the judicial committee, which is the leading body of any court.[4] Where a case is complicated or important, the opinion of the superior court or even the Supreme People's Court may also be sought. It is a normal practice in China that a case is decided before a trial, and those who try a case may not have the power to make the decision.

The court has to try the case unless there is not a "clear and sufficient evidence" to support the prosecution, in which case, the

337

court will remand the case to the procuracy for supplementary investigation (CPL, article 108). The same article also states that the court may ask the prosecution to withdraw its prosecution if no criminal punishment is necessary. When it is necessary to clarify a case, a people's court may initiate its own inquests, examination, search, seizure and expert evaluation. In practice the judicial investigation is mainly limited to reviewing the evidence provided by the police and procuracy. The fundamental characteristic of Chinese criminal trials is that, through the pre-trial investigation, the judges decide on the facts and on the law involved. As a matter of law, no court will open a court session if the collegial panel is not certain about the facts, the offence and the sentence (CPL, article 109).

Judges' involvement in the pre-trial investigation seriously diminishes the role of defence attorneys. The trial judges will necessarily have prejudiced views on the case after they have read through the files and verified the evidence. They have difficulties in accepting alternative views of the parties, especially of the defence. A challenge to the charge is not so much a challenge to the prosecution's case but a direct attack on the court's credibility. Unless there is strong new evidence, an open trial cannot render any assistance to a defendant.[5]

Political Interference of Criminal Defence

When defence attorneys were re-introduced into China's criminal justice system in the early 1980s,[6] the reaction from many governmental departments, including the courts, was hostile. In 1981, there were reports that court regarded defence attorneys as "troublemakers", "burdens" and "hindrances" — the procuracy called them "experts in picking bones from eggs" — who would use loopholes to destroy the prosecution's case (Y. Zhao, 1992:1361). Defence lawyers have complained that the "lawyers' function is not correctly understood and otherwise lawful defences are blatantly interfered with and limited" (Jiang, 1992:1637).

The most blatant interference took place in 1983 when the government launched its war on crime in China. The Ministry of Justice in 1983 issued a notice which severely limited the defence lawyers' authority and eventually made them part of the prosecution team.

This notice required that once the court appointed a defence lawyer to defend an accused, the lawyer was obliged to accept the task. Where there were no defence lawyers, Party and government officers could be "borrowed" temporarily to serve the purpose. Defence lawyers were told that they should not direct their minds to "trivial matters and technicalities" where the main facts were clear; they should not even raise the issue of mitigation if there were no apparent mitigating factors. Furthermore, if defence lawyers found that the main facts of

338

the case were not clear or the application of law was mistaken, they should communicate this with the court or procuracy before a trial. In cases in which the death penalty could be imposed, defence lawyers should first convey their objections, if any, to the local Party committee via the local Bureau of Justice (*ibid.*).

Even though the notice was issued for the purpose of serving the 1983 nationwide war on crime, it continues to have impact today. Jiang (1992:1367) commented in 1985 on incidents involving interference with lawyers' work and harassment of defence lawyers:

> "A few cadres blame defence lawyers for ignoring the larger social interests and blindly following the law during a trial; some departments in charge of lawyers even impose numerous restrictions on the defence. They may forbid lawyers to conduct a serious defence, they may even disallow a not guilty plea. In extreme cases, they even treat lawyers as co-conspirators of the defendants because of their defence, and the lawyers liberty cannot be protected."

For some state owned firms, a reporting system was created to ensure political control over the work of criminal defence. In Nanjing city, for example, "collective decision making is required in serious and complicated cases; for cases where a not guilty plea is proposed or no consensus can be reached in the firm, they will be referred to the Bureau of Justice for a decision" (Tan, 1992:1380).

There has been less political interference in lawyers' defence work in criminal trials during the 1990s. The legal profession in general is gradually becoming more independent, essentially a private enterprise which cannot be tightly controlled by the government (Zhen, 1994:30). One indication of such a development is the frequent use of a not guilty plea. In sensitive cases, such as the *Ming Bao* reporter (Ming Bao Publisher, 1994), where not guilty pleas are seriously argued by the defence.

In addition, the courts are often unsatisfied with the prosecution's case, and use, albeit rarely, a not guilty verdict to assert their independence.[7]

The Rights of Defence Lawyers

Lawyers' Right at Pre-trial Stage

Article 110 of the CPL states:

"After a people's court has decided to open a court session, it shall proceed with the following work:

. . .

(2) to deliver to the defendant a copy of the bill of prosecution of the people's procuracy no later than seven days before the opening of the court session and inform the defendant that he may appoint a defender or, when necessary, designate a defender for himself."

This seven day rule effectively excludes the possibility of any involvement of a defence lawyer at the investigation and prosecution stages of a criminal case. In other words, a defence lawyer has no right in law to enter the police station and the procurator's office to obtain information or meet and correspond with the accused. No legal representation is allowed until a week before the trial.[8]

In the vast majority of the cases there are only one or two days available for a lawyer to prepare a defence. In a complicated case, there may be hundreds of pages of documents. It is impossible for a lawyer to review all the main facts of the case.[9] Defense counsel for a dissident in the 1989 "Tiananmen Turmoil" was only given four days to examine thousands of pages of documents filed by the prosecution (Lawyers Committee for Human Rights, 1994:32). In 30 per cent of the instances, cases are already at trial when the lawyer receives the notice.[10] Without legal representation during the investigation and prosecution stages, the police and procurators may, as happens frequently, force confessions, falsify confessions, or record only those statements favourable to the prosecution's case.[11]

The lack of time to prepare a defence has been recognized officially. A Joint Notice (The Supreme People's Court, etc., 1981) provides that where a case is complicated and time is not sufficient for preparing a defence, the defence lawyer may ask the court to delay the trial. "The court should consider the application if the delay would not affect the trial of the case within the limit provided by law." In practice, however, such extensions are rarely granted (Zhou, 1994).

Even this limited protection was later abolished for some offences. According to a decision of the Standing Committee of the National People's Congress (1983), the seven day time limit "may be overstepped" for defendants "who cause explosions or commit murder, rape, robbery or other crimes seriously endangering public security, and which are punishable by death, where the main facts of the crimes are clear, the evidence is conclusive and the "popular indignation is exceedingly great."

Not only is the time short for lawyers to prepare a defence, but their right to have access to files of the case and to the accused is also limited. At the pre-trial stage, defence lawyers have the right to "consult the file record of the current case, acquaint themselves with the circumstances of the case, and meet and correspond with the defendant in custody" (Article 29 of the CPL). According to the Joint Notice

(Supreme People's Court, etc. 1981), lawyers may go to the court to review the files related to the case, and the court has to provide necessary assistance to defence lawyers, such as providing rooms to review the files and allowing the lawyers to make extracts from the materials. There are two limits in reviewing the court files. First, the minutes of the judicial committee and the collegial panel cannot be reviewed (*ibid.*). This is a serious limitation given the fact that the judicial committee and collegial panel normally make a determination as to the offence and punishment prior to a trial. Second, courts cannot provide satisfactory services for defence attorneys. One study (Fang, 1992:1365) of ten courts and seven law firms in China shed light on the reality of defence rights in reviewing court documents. The author investigated 22 criminal trials at the first instance, and found that lawyers did not have access to the full files in 8 cases (36 per cent). Except for two sets of chairs and tables provided in one court, the other nine courts did not provide any facilities for lawyers to read and extract materials from the files. The main problem, according to the author, is that most of the courts regarded legal representation as a mere formality. They have to produce files to a defence lawyers simply because the CPL requires them to do so. The normal practice is that a defence attorney will be given only what he requested. If he fails to request a specific document, it will not be voluntarily offered by the court. Judges are especially reluctant to share evidence uncovered through their own investigation. They tend to produce that evidence only in court.[12]

Interviewing an accused in police custody is a more difficult matter for lawyers. Police concern over security during the interview has hindered frank communication between lawyers and their clients (Lawyers Committee for Human Rights, 1994). According to the Joint Notice (Supreme People's Court, etc. 1981), the detention centre should provide necessary assistance for a lawyer to interview his client, including the provision of proper premises. The Joint Notice asks the police to strike a balance between security and right to counsel. Though it does not require the guards to be absent during the interview, it requires them to be wary that their presence does not make defendants afraid of talking to their defence attorneys. After the interview, the guards should not question the defendant about the content of their interview.

Pre-trial Disclosure

No exchange of information is required between the defence and the procuracy at the pre-trial stage, and both sides make their first contact in the court room. According to the CPL, the procuracy has to deliver the files of a case, together with the evidence collected, to the court. The defence lawyer has the right to review these files and evidence. In many cases, the family members of the accused retain a lawyer immediately after the detention or arrest, and the lawyer conducts an informal investigation of the case, even though he does not have the right to do so in law. Such an informal investigation may produce new evidence that may not be known to the procuracy and the court. The defence attorney may launch a surprise attack on both the court and the prosecution's case at the trial based on such evidence.

The defence attorney may not want a showdown in a courtroom, however. If the lawyer disagrees with the procurator, it is usually better to convey his disagreement before a trial starts, convincing the procuracy and the court to change their mind, and thus avoiding any serious conflict with the procurators and the judges.

An informal pre-trial conference procedure has developed in China to increase understanding among the parties. Initially used as a measure to expedite criminal trials during the war on crime in the early 1980s, it received positive responses (Wu, 1992:1376). First, it has been argued, especially by defence lawyers, that a pre-trial conference is useful in narrowing down the issues of the case, so that the parties can focus on differences during the trial stage. Secondly, as defence lawyers are only given a brief time in court to put a defence, this short court room exposition may not clearly be understood or accepted by the court and procuracy. If a lawyer can discuss with the judges and procurator beforehand, he has more time to explain his defence. This also allows time for judges to digest the defence argument (*ibid.*).

Finally, perhaps most importantly, courtroom debate is a final showdown, a battle fought in public. A lawyer's defence is perceived to be a direct challenge to the authority of the court and the procuracy. The court especially would not be ready to accept such an open challenge, even if they know they are wrong. As one lawyer comments: "Sometimes a correct defence in court may put the procuracy and court in an embarrassing position and thus damage their dignity" (*ibid.*). Another lawyer from Jiangxi province suggests that: "Once a case is transferred to the court, the case would basically be decided. A public trial is a mere formality. It would be really difficult to ask the judicial organs to withdraw a wrong decision" (Z. Zhang, 1994:6).

Given the fact that a successful defence to a large extent depends upon the good will of the procuracy and judges, it is essential to persuade the court to listen to the defence. A pre-trial meeting gives defence attorneys an opportunity to persuade the judges and procuracy to alter their decision without embarrassing them in court.[13]

There have been strong objections to the pre-trial conference among Chinese lawyers. As a principle, it is said, defence lawyers should be independent from the court and procuracy. If they have to discuss everything with the procurators, it would give the public an impression that the lawyers "wear the same pants and sing the same song" (Guo, 1992:1359).

The pre-trial conference has never been systematized and its existence always depends upon a lawyer's initiative. When properly conducted, it can compensate for a lawyer's disadvantages by providing an informal opportunity for the lawyer to communicate with the judges and procurators.

Right of a Lawyer: During the Trial

Throughout a trial, the judge is the dominant figure. The presiding judge opens the session by announcing the subject-matter of the case and introducing the participants in the trial (CPL, article 113). The public prosecutor then reads out the bill of prosecution, which includes the facts of the case, the law violated and the punishment sought. After the bill of prosecution is read, the judges start to question the defendant. At this stage, the public prosecutor may question the defendant with the permission of the court (CPL, article 114).

After finishing questioning the defendant, the judges and the procurators start to question witnesses, present the records of testimony of witnesses who are not present in court, and read out the conclusions of expert witness and documentary evidence (CPL, article 116).

At this stage, the defence may raise questions. According to article 115, "The parties and the defenders may request the presiding judge to question the witnesses or expert witnesses, or ask the presiding judge's permission to put their own questions directly." The court may stop the questioning of the defence if it considers it irrelevant.

During the trial, the defenders may also call new witnesses and enter new evidence, but the court has discretion in granting such requests (CPL, article 117). For instance, the courts do not allow expert witnesses produced by the defence because there is no provision allowing such witnesses in the CPL (Yang, 1994:8).

When the judicial inquisition is over, the procurator is allowed to make a speech to conclude his case; the victim is also allowed to make a statement. Afterwards, the defence is given an opportunity to make out a defence. Then, a "debate" among the participants follows. When the judge regards the issues of law and fact as fully debated, he may declare the conclusion of the debate and allow the defence to present a final statement (CPL, article 118).

Given the fact that a case is decided before a trial, the trial can only be a morality play, with the parties participating in the ritual, knowing that any new input will be too little and too late. This is not to say that there is nothing a lawyer can say in court. There are occasionally tense debates in court, and sometime names are called and insults are exchanged between procurators and lawyers. As early as 1983, defenders

343

were criticized for using the court room as "a forum of free speech" (Xiao, 1992:1319).

A major difficulty facing a defence attorney is that he cannot directly challenge the procuracy's witnesses, thus he can only argue in the abstract. The problem is not that a defence attorney is not allowed to question the prosecution witnesses. He is normally allowed to raise questions of any prosecution witness who testified.[14] The problem is that there may be nobody to question. Most of the witnesses in China do not testify in the court, normally only a written statement of the witness would be read out.[15] This is tantamount to a trial by affidavits, a practice frowned upon by common law countries.

The other difficulty is that a lawyer's argument will often fall on the deaf ears, because the court will not treat the lawyers' argument seriously. In fact most of the defence lawyers work in the state-owned firms as government employees, but the status of these lawyers is much lower than that of judges and procurators, also government employees. For instance, judges and procurators wear uniforms, lawyers do not; judges and procurators have higher administrative ranks; judges and procurators represent the state, lawyers are associated with criminals. Lawyers are normally overwhelmed in court (Qiao and Sun, 1992:1404).

A judge's background is also relevant. Unlike common law jurisdictions where senior lawyers become judges, a judge and a lawyer belong to two different professions in China.[16] The judges, as procurators, are government bureaucrats who do not appreciate the concept of defence. Asserting the rights of an accused is still as novel an idea today as it was in traditional China (Dutton, 1992).

Some judges openly discourage defendants from hiring lawyers and some regard using a lawyer as a waste of money — "better to spend the money on some good meals" (Tan, 1992:1380).

> "The court treats lawyers' defence argument as they please. They can simply disregard their opinions. You say whatever you prefer, I decide whatever I want ... Some judges openly ask the defendants: what is the use of hiring a lawyer? Don't waste your money. Some even claim that: 'The punishment will be lenient without a lawyer, and will be severe with a lawyer'" (Qiao and Sun, 1992:1404).

The abuse of defence lawyers in criminal hearings was so prevalent that the Supreme People's Court, Supreme People's Procuracy, Ministry of Public Security, and the Ministry of Justice found it necessary to issue a Supplementary Notice (1986) to address the problem. The Notice stipulates that courts should respect a defence attorney's basic rights; courts:

(a) should take a defence lawyer's argument seriously. Written evidence provided by the defence and the statement of defence should be included in the court's files; other materials related to the case should also be included if necessary;

(b) should consider the evidence presented by the defence. The court shall verify the evidence provided by the defence or ask the procuracy to verify such evidence, so that it can be presented during the trial;

(c) may not issue a summons to order a defence attorney to defend an accused in court; and

(d) should pay due respect to a defence attorney in court and should not expel them from court rooms at will.

The Reform

Reforming Legal Representation

China is reforming its criminal procedure. Consultation is already underway, and the reform legislation is expected to be presented to the National People's Congress during its annual session in March 1996.[17] There is a consensus among the key players in the criminal justice system that defence attorneys should be available to an accused at an earlier stage; but opinions differ as to how early it should be, and, coloured by their different institutional interests, the police, procuracy and court have different proposals. The Supreme People's Court holds the most liberal view, proposing that defence attorneys may intervene at the earliest stage of investigation. Through the early intervention of lawyers, the unlawful and deleterious activities of investigators will be brought to the court's attention by the defence attorney.[18]

More importantly, a court's role in supervising the police and procuracy will also be increased. Under the current arrangement, the court's control is limited mainly to the scrutiny of law and fact on the record prepared by the police and procurators. Most of the unlawful and prejudicial activities committed by the police and procuracy do not appear on record and are not evident to the court. The early involvement of defence attorneys may protect the procedural rights of the accused.[19]

The Ministry of Justice, which regulates the legal profession in the country, holds a similar view. The officials state that whenever compulsory measures, such as detention and arrest are imposed on a suspect, or whenever a suspect is summoned, he should be allowed to have legal representation. An earlier legal representation is an interna-

345

tional standard which China should follow; and, through earlier involvement, defence attorneys could supervise the procedural fairness of the investigation.[20]

The Supreme People's Procuracy agrees with the involvement of defence attorneys at the prosecution stage in principle, but argues that the scope of such involvement should be different at different stages of an investigation. In addition, the right and duty of defence lawyers should be clearly stipulated. In particular, a defence lawyer's involvement should not be allowed to "interfere with the normal investigation".[21]

The Ministry of Public Security is the only organization which opposes defence attorneys' involvement in the investigation stage altogether. It argues that investigation is a stage in which the police seek to clarify the facts of the case, to collect evidence and to expose and prove crimes. The investigation would be hampered by defence lawyers. Thus before the police are clear about a case, there should be no legal representation. Furthermore, the incidence of crime will continue to increase in the future, and will be more complex, it argues. Given that the police now bear tremendous responsibilities in criminal investigation, earlier involvement of defence lawyers at the investigation stage will be detrimental to police work.[22]

The debate goes on. It seems that some involvement of defence attorneys at the investigation stage will be unavoidable and the police have to be ready to deal with defence attorneys during police investigations. It is openly and expressly admitted by an official from the Ministry of Justice (Zhang, 1994:40) that the current criminal defence system in China is "inconsistent with article 125 of the Constitution." Lawyers will play a more important role in China's criminal defence, but the extent of the lawyers' involvement, however, has to be resolved through the negotiation and compromise among the key players in the criminal justice system.

In a draft CPL prepared by a law school in Beijing at the invitation of the National People's Congress, it is proposed that, where a suspect is detained or arrested, he should be allowed to contact a lawyer immediately or within 48 hours after his detention or arrest (Li, 1994 a and b).

Attempts to make lawyers accessible during the investigation stage is also made in some local places. In the Lawyers Bill in the Shenzhen Special Economic Zone, for instance, it was provided that in criminal cases lawyers "may be entrusted to provide legal services for citizens or suspects on whom are imposed compulsory measures by the public security organs or the procuracy, or who are summoned by the public security organs or procuracy for the first time".[23] When the Bill was passed by the local legislature these provisions were deleted.[24]

Toward a More Adversarial Criminal Justice in China?

It is commonly held by both academics and decision makers in China that increasing the role of the lawyers will not be sufficient to protect the rights of defendants unless the nature of the criminal trial is changed. It is pointed out that, the pro-active role of the judge and the inquisitorial style of trial are sources of real difficulty. The thrust of the criticism is that when trial judges become investigators, they cannot be fair and neutral in conducting the trial. Serving as both accuser and judge is repugnant to the basic elements of fairness.

The present criminal procedure needs to be modified. It is argued that the inquisitorial system is no longer suitable in China and that a more adversarial system needs to be put in place. The Supreme People's Court supports this notion and proposes that while the presiding judge will continue to play the leading role in criminal trials, the evidence will, be presented directly by prosecution and defence. More importantly, witnesses must testify in court and may be cross-examined.

According to the Supreme People's Court, a more adversarial system has three advantages:

(a) the procurator and defence counsel will be more responsible when each is made to bear the burden of presenting evidence — there have been mounting complaints about the deterioration in the quality of criminal trials in China and a more adversarial model is regarded as a way to improve the situation;

(b) judges would not pre-determine a case and would become neutral adjudicators — a more adversarial system would rectify the phenomena of "convicting before a trial"; and

(c) evidence, when it is presented by the witness directly in court, can be verified according to law.[25]

The main objection to the proposal comes from the Supreme People's Procuracy which insists that, although there are some problems in criminal trials, the present system is satisfactory. China should find its own way to reform the trial procedures, instead of blindly following the "western style" (Lu, 1994:48).

The procuracy objects to reform mainly due to a fear that a more adversarial system would diminish the status of procuracy. Under the current structure, the procuracy plays double roles in court: prosecuting a criminal offence and supervising the court during the trial.[26] The latter role of supervision would be substantially diminished, if not abolished, when the procuracy is to bear all the responsibility of presenting prosecuting evidence and accepting the challenge from the defence. Under a more adversarial system, the prosecution would be a party of the same footing, legally, as the defence, arguing a case to the court (Lu, 1994:47–49).

The procuracy's worry about a more adversarial system is not without merits. Many judges would agree that a more adversarial system means that all the witness would have to testify in court — a goal which cannot be easily achieved in China. Currently, the majority of the witness do not testify in court, only their written statement is presented. This is already difficult because many of the witnesses simply refuse to sign their names on the statement. To demand that witnesses testify in an open court would further aggravate the problems. The lack of civic conscience, hostility toward and fear of testifying in court, and the consequent financial burden of a prolonged trial, all mean that a more adversarial system would face tremendous practical difficulties.[27]

Conclusion

Regardless of which criminal procedure model China chooses for the future, defence attorneys will have to play an increasing role. There is an urgent need for legal representation to protect the rights of the accused, but the current structure seriously limits a defence lawyer's performance. Whether or not the structural defect can be changed would depend upon the direction of a systematic reform of criminal procedure in China. There are optimistic indications which show that things may be better in the future. There is now a nationwide consensus that police power in the investigation stage must be held accountable under law. Sharp criticisms against the police in debating the newly passed Police Law indicates that lawyers will have an important role to play in checking police abuse of power and in protecting the lawful interests of the accused.[28] This will pave the way for a defence lawyer to enter a police station to meet his clients. With an increase in rights consciousness among the public as well as decision makers, defence lawyers will play a more meaningful role in China's criminal justice system.

Notes

[1] There is a small budget in the court system for this purpose. The process of appointing a defence lawyer is as follows: once the prosecution decides to initiate public prosecution, it will transfer the case to a people's court with competent jurisdiction. The court would send the case to a particular firm,

normally a state-run firm, where most of the criminal defence lawyers work. The head of the firm would appoint one of the lawyers in the firm to defend the accused. There are no rules to regulate the process, the firms accept the case as a duty of a state operated firm and, more importantly, to keep a good relationship with the judiciary. In most cases, however, it is the family members of the accused who hire a lawyer on his behalf. Source: Interview with judges and defence lawyers in Guangzhou and Zhuhai, 1995.

The Ministry of Justice is now formulating plans for legal aid in China. Pilot projects have been set up in Beijing and Guangdong. According to Sin Bailu, Head of the Department of Lawyers in the Ministry, China's legal aid will follow international experience and at the same time consider China's actual circumstances. The purpose of the proposed plan is to demonstrate the fairness and justice of the legal profession and force the legal profession to consider not only the economic effect of their profession but also the social impact. Thus the plan is both to serve those unable to afford lawyers and to enhance the lawyers' public conscience and sense of civic responsibility. *Fazhi Ribao* February 22, 1995.

2 Except for minor cases, which can be tried by a single judge, OLPC, art. 10.
3 Art. 11 of the OLPC states that the members of the judicial committee are appointed and removed by the Standing Committee of the People's Congresses at the corresponding levels, upon the recommendation of the presidents of these courts. The task of the judicial committee is to "practice democratic centralism", including summing up judicial experience and discussing important or difficult cases.

As a practice, a judicial committee includes the president of a court, the vice-presidents, and judges in charge of the different divisions (criminal law, administrative law, etc.)
4 In rare cases, a lawyer may be able to persuade the court to change its predetermined verdict. In a recent trial, a trial court was persuaded to accept a not guilty defence after "repeated studies and with permission". It is important to note that the defence lawyer in that case was a well known criminal law professor, Zhao. His personal influence had an effect. (Interview with Professor Zhao Binzhi, July 1995). It is openly conceded by judges and lawyers I interviewed that a "well connected" lawyer will be useful for an accused.
5 The system of lawyers was formally set up in China in January 1956 and abolished in late 1957. Xu (1994:14).
6 Interview with judges in Zhuhai, 1995.
7 Even this seven day rule is violated by provincial legislation. In the Rules on Lawyers in Guangdong province and Anhui province, the notification period is shortened to three days. Art 12, Several Regulations of Anhui Province on the Performance of Duties of Lawyers (1988); Art 8, Several Rules of Guangdong Province on the Performance of Duties of Lawyers (1987).
8 LAC and SPC interviews.
9 LAC interview.
10 LAC and SPC interviews.
11 Interviews with lawyers in Guanzhou and Zhuhai.
12 A lawyer suspected that a defendant in a murder case was a psychiatric patient. He raised the defence of insanity in the pre-trial meeting, but was rejected by the judge. Then the lawyer invited experts to explain the case to the judges. After a pre-trial psychiatric examination participated in by the judge, procurator and lawyer, the procuracy withdrew its charge (Zhao, 1992:1376).
13 Interview with lawyers in Beijing, Guangzhou and Zhuhai.
14 LAC interview.

[15] Although recently more judges are quitting their job to become lawyers, there is no structural linkage between the two occupations.
[16] LAC interview.
[17] LAC and SPC interviews.
[18] LAC interview.
[19] LAC interview.
[20] SPP interview
[21] LAC interview.
[22] Lawyers' Regulations of Shenzhen Special Economic Region, Art. 26 (draft).
[23] Shenzhen Special Economic Zone, Lawyers Regulations of Shenzhen Special Economic Zone (1995).
[24] SPC interview.
[25] Article 15 of the Organic Law of People's Procuracy (1983) provides: "In legal proceedings instituted by a people's procuracy, the chief procurator or a procurator shall attend the court session, in the capacity of state prosecutor, to support the prosecution and exercise supervision over the court proceedings, and to determine whether they conform to the law."
    According to Lu (1994) from the Supreme People's Procuracy, the procuracy has the power to supervise the trial by raising objections whenever "there is something unlawful during the trial", but the objection raised is often ignored by the court. Judges in Zhuhai admit that the procuracy's supervision is not very useful.
[26] LAC and SPP interviews.
[27] LAC interview.

References

Dutton, Michael (1992), *Policing and Punishment in China: From Patriarchy to "the People"*.

Fang, Deming (1992) "Defence Lawyers' Right and Duty in Reviewing Files." In Ministry of Justice (ed.).

Guo, Zhongwu (1992) "The Position of Defence Lawyers in Criminal Litigation." In Ministry of Justice (ed.).

Jiang, Daijing (1992) "Protecting Lawyers' Rights in Criminal Litigation." In Ministry of Justice (ed.).

Li Baoyue (1994a) "On the Question of Lawyers' Participation in Criminal Litigation." 4 *Zhengfa Luntan* (Forum of Politics and Law) 72.

Li Baoyue (1994b) "On the Time When Lawyers Can Participate in Criminal Litigation." 4 *Zhongguo Faxiu* (Chinese Science of Law) 98.

Lu, Fei (1994) "Reforming the Model of Trials." 5 *Zhongguo Faxiu* 48.

Ming Bao Publisher (ed.) (1994) *Xi Yang Dailaile . . .* (What Xi Yang Brings About . . .) Hong Kong: Min Bao Publisher.

Ministry of Justice (1981) Notice on Giving Full Play of Lawyers's Function in Severely Striking on Criminal Offences.

Ministry of Justice (ed.) (1992) *Zhongguo Sifa Xingzheng De Lilun Yu Shijian* (Theory and Practice of Judicial Administration in China).

Qiao Bin and Sun Qikang (1992) "A Preliminary Study of the Psychology of the Criminal Lawyers." In Ministry of Justice (ed.).

Standing Committee of the National People's Congress (1983) Decisions Regarding the Procedure for Prompt Adjudication of Cases Involving Criminals Who Seriously Endanger Public Security.

Supreme People's Court, Supreme People's Procuracy, Ministry of Public Security, and Ministry of Justice, (1981) Joint Notice on Several Concrete Provisions on Lawyers' Participation in Litigation.

Supreme People's Court, Supreme People's Procuracy, Ministry of Public Security, and the Ministry of Justice (1986) Supplementary Regulations on Lawyers' Participation in Litigation.

Tan, Zhen (1992) "On Pre-trial Communication." In Ministry of Justice (ed.).

Wu, Jieming, (1992) "Preliminary Discussion on Pre-trial Communication among Lawyers, Judges and Procurators." In Ministry of Justice (ed.).

Xiao, Shanren (1992) "A Person without Legal Qualification May Not Be a Defender." In Ministry of Justice (ed.).

Xu, Jincun (1994) *Lushi Xiu* (Studies on Lawyers) Chengdu: Sichuan People's Publisher.

Yang Yinche (1994) "Defence Lawyers Should Have Right to Produce Expert Witness." 11 *Zhongguo Lushi* (China Lawyers) 8.

Zhang, Sihan (1994) "Several Proposals on the Reform of the Model of Trial." 5 *Zhongguo Faxiu* 47.

Zhang, Wei (1994) "Several Questions in Lawyers' Participation in Criminal Litigation." 5 *Zhongguo Faxiu* 40.

Zhang, Zhanlin (1994) "Lawyer's Early Involvement Prevents a Wrong Conviction." 9 *Zhongguo Lushi* 6.

Zhao, Binzhi (1995) "Correctly Distinguish a Violation of Financial Disciplines and the Offence of Embezzlement." (1995) 3 *Zhongguo Lushi* 5.

Zhao, Ying (1992) "The Position of Defence Lawyers in Criminal Litigation." In Ministry of Justice (ed.).

Zhao, Zhongqing (1992) "The Necessity of Exchanging Information between Lawyers and Judicial Personnel at Pre-Trial Stage." Ministry of Justice (ed.)

Zhen, Dong (1994) "Lawyers No Longer Officials." 1 *China Law* 30.

Zhou Guojun (1994) "Discussion on the Time when Lawyers' Intervention Is Allowed." 5 *Zhongguo Lushi* 32.

THE PRESENT SITUATION OF CORRUPTION IN CHINA AND ANTI-CORRUPTION COUNTERMEASURES

Zhang Xiaoqin

Department of Law
Peking University

Zhang Xiaoqin, *LL.B., Master of Law (Peking University), is deputy head and associate chief editor of Peking University Publishing House. He has contributed to many books, including* Ten Years of Research on Juvenile Delinquency, Comparative Criminology, *and* Common Crimes in the World.

Corruption can be dated back to ancient times, and corruption occurs all over the world. The situation of corruption in China, however, has recently become so serious that the Chinese Communist Party and the Chinese Government now consider it as a critical issue that can affect the destiny of the country. In recent years, the subject of corruption has been always placed on the top agenda of the National People's Congress and the Political Consultative Conference.

Corruption as a crime indicates illegal activities, connected with political corruption and by which public servants seek illegal economic and other benefits. It has two characteristics: it is related to one's position; and it is an illegal "trade between money and political power". The second feature is the most salient one. The crime refers to not only the illegal activity in non-compliance with the Criminal Law, but also other illegal activities that are against other laws.

The Present Situation of Corruption and Its Characteristics

China is now in a transitional period from the planned economic system to the market economic system. Corruption that occurs during such a period has the following characteristics:

(a) "Trade between political power and money", in which case performance of one's duties is combined with the gain of personal benefits, and abusing of power is related to economic activity, *i.e.* the-conflict-of-interest law is seriously breached. Under these circumstances, the materialization and commercialization of power have reached a substantial degree.

To trade money with political power and crime connected with the performance of one's duties are most typical features of corruption. It means that those with power, directly or indirectly, gain money or other benefits by abusing such power, and meanwhile sacrifice the interests of the country or a collective entity. Bribery is one example; it has become a necessity in some places.

(b) Corruption involves not only the natural person but also the legal person, and occurs in not only the economic branches, but the branches of the law enforcement agencies as well. Bribery and other types of corruptive activities have now become open activities extensively conducted in some places.

Corruption occurs most often in such economic branches such as finance, commerce, construction, railway, foreign trade, real estate, securities and futures. For example, Liang Jianyun, accountant with the Shenzen Futian Branch, People's Construction Bank of China, committed a graft of HK$ 13 million and US$ 800,000, and embezzled HK$ 6 million; Xue Genhe (an accountant with the Dongfeng Office in Haikou, ICBC), together with others, committed a graft of RMB 33.44 million cumulatively during the year of 1992. Such cases involve a tremendous amount of money, and used to be rare since the founding of new China.

Corruption is now penetrating the branches of law-enforcement agencies and judicial departments, such as industrial and commercial bureaux, tax authorities, the customs, public securities, procuratorates, and courts.

The variations of corruption committed by groups and legal persons is now increasing. These types of crime are often committed by those who usually claim that they do something "in the interest of the public". The actual situation is that they gain benefits for individuals and small groups of people by jeopardizing the interests of the country and the collective entity. This category of crime has a variety of types that are difficult to sort out and to deal with.

(c) With the growing amount of corruption, there will be more and more felonies and important cases. Before the 1980s, cases involving several thousands of reminbi, or over RMB10,000 were considered as felonies; and corruption committed by rural government officials was regarded as an important case. During the 1980s, the amount of money increased to tens of thousands of money, and it is not rare for cases involving over RMB 1 million to occur in the 1990s. The case of Wang Baosen, vice-mayor of the Beijing Municipal Government, is strong evidence of the seriousness of corruption in China. Wang caused a total loss of US$ 13 million. His case is the number one felony since the founding of the PRC, and has appalled people both at home and abroad.

(d) The means of committing the crime of corruption are tricky; the purposes vary; and such corruptive activities are usually conducted with covert and deceptive measures. Different from violent crime, the crime of corruption most often, falls into the category of "intelligent crime", therefore, ways used by offenders are usually subtle and hard to be discovered. The great majority of the offenders are Communist Party leaders and government officials, some of whom are senior officials. They use the loopholes in the present laws and regulations, which exist in the transitional period.

The Present Anti-corruption Counter-measures and Thoughts

The anti-corruption mechanism and counter-measures are determined by the following four factors: the proper use of public power and the perfection of the legal system; the qualities of public servants; the supervising and checking mechanism; and the just and proper external environment. The aforesaid factors are connected by law; and are guided, established and safeguarded by law.

(a) Further perfection of the legal system to cope with corruption, and establishment of the legal order under which the market economic mechanism operates against corruption and in favour of clean government.

The market economic system is a legal economic system, therefore, mass movement or administrative orders are not dependable to fight against corruption. Legal measures are the fundamental ones to punish and prevent corruption. Without the improvement of the legal system, the anti-corruption counter-measures will have no effect at all.

First, laws to fight against corruption need to be formulated. At present, a special law to deal with graft and bribery needs to be enacted. They are major forms of corruption. It has become a tendency in the whole world to formulate special laws to deal with them.

Secondly, reform and adjustment are needed in terms of ways of punishing those who commit corruption. Many countries adopt a heavy fine and expel them from the post. China needs to follow suit in respect of such punitive measures.

Thirdly, special institutions need to be set up and perfected as soon as possible to fight against corruption, and their independence and power should be strengthened. Although procuratorates at various levels in China have a branch to deal with graft and bribery, these branches are also in charge of coping with crimes in tax, trade marks, and others. Separation is essential to strengthen the function of the procuratorates. At the same time, independent power needs also to be authorized and strengthened, in which case the procuratorates can meet the need of emergency. Such power include the power to arrest, to search with arms, and to seal up and distrain.

Fourthly, China's ruling party needs to improve its leading method in terms of judiciary matters. Focus should be placed on providing guidelines of policy instead of specific cases. The construction of the judiciary needs to be strengthened, such construction includes offering of training programs. Laws should be strictly enforced.

During the transitional period from the planned economy to the market economy, corruption spreads with China's economic development. To rely solely on legal measures is not enough, and it is necessary to establish the market economic mechanism, which functions against corruption and in favour of clean government.

In terms of the reform of state owned enterprises, focus should be placed on the establishment of the modern enterprise system in which case not only the management team can be prompted to be proactive, but also its day-to-day management shall be placed under effective supervision.

With regard to specific systems, the dual-truck systems concerning price, interest and exchange rate should be gradually abolished so that conditions can be created to establish the systems of equal competition and fair and just market economic system. Under these circumstances, the economic basis for the cause of bribery and other forms of corruption shall be eradicated.

The government's macro-and-micro-control mechanism are also essential to guarantee the aim the market economic system is expected to achieve. Under the market economic system, the government's macro-control and micro-management are also necessary in addition to the spontaneous adjustment of the market, for such duties are performed by individual public servants, of whom some may fail to abide by laws and regulations for personal interests. Government involvement can prevent such cases.

In terms of the distribution of income, a fair and reasonable distribution mechanism needs to be established to guide how the consumption proceeds to be transformed to production funds. The occurrence of corruption is closely related to the unfair distribution of income, which has become a commonplace in the society. A distribution system in conformity with the market economic mechanism needs to be set up to safeguard equal conditions in competition, and in which case different income results from fair competition. At the same time, the tax system needs to be involved in the adjustment of different levels of income.

(b) Government must continue to form, reform and perfect the public servants team to fight against corruption, and to improve their immunity from corruption. The qualities of public servants determine the fate of the fight against corruption. To establish, reform and perfect the system of public service is not only an important aspect of China's political reform, but also key a measure to adapt to the market economic system, and to prevent effectively and control corruption.

To reform the existing public servant's system and establish a strict system concerning the engagement, examination and dismissal of public servants. In terms of selection of public servants, major focus should be placed on the systems of exam and probation, which means that public servants' selection shall be based on examination and that those selected shall be placed on probation. With regard to the dismissal of public servants, the system for public servants to serve for life should be abolished. When found guilty of corruption, those cadres shall be removed from their leading posts.

Strictly enforcing the reporting system of property owned by public servants, and strictly constraining endowments and additional rewards to public servants can put the public servant's property under effective control and graft and bribery from happening.

Government should establish the systems of sidestep and open politics. The system of sidestep means that people from the same family, such as parents and children, husband and wife, brothers, and so on should not hold leading posts in the same organization, and that cadres should not work in their own hometowns. The system of open political affairs means that, except those relations, national defence and state secrets, the government shall publicize the regulations, system, procedures and data concerning activities of public servants. This can increase transparency of the activities conduced by public servants. The present recruitment system based on exemption is an example of such a system.

To improve the compensation package of public servants, and strictly forbid public servants to do business or hold concurrent positions. Improving the public servants' remuneration benefits is an essential measure to prevent and decrease corruption. Efforts also need to be placed on the enactment of relevant laws and regulations to prohibit public servants from doing business and holding concurrent position.

Strengthening the political education and the education of professional virtue for public servants is actually a fine tradition of the Communist Party. Such a measure is especially necessary during the transitional period of the market system.

(c) The lack in the check of power is the cause of abuse of power and corruption. This is a widely accepted viewpoint, which has been proved by both the history and present reality. An inspecting and supervising system needs, therefore, to be established to achieve the effect of checks and balances.

First, the effort to enact the supervising laws needs to be strengthened, and the power of the supervising departments needs to be legalized and formalized. Secondly, the function of supervision should be strengthened to increase the effect of supervision. Thirdly, it is also essential to strengthen the supervising sense of the supervising agency and public servants. Fourthly, the work to widen the supervising channels and perfect the supervising network must be done.

(d) A fine supervising system of public opinion is the key to fighting corruption. It can make up for the imperfection of laws and regulations and their inefficiency; whereas the public reporting system is a legal system used by the procuratorate to encourage and the public to report such corrupt cases as graft, bribery, embezzlement. In 1988, Shenzhen set up a reporting centre for economic criminal cases. In the same year, the Supreme People's Procuratorate made a decision to establish special reporting agencies in the whole country. By the end of 1993, over 3,600 procuratorates had established reporting centres working hours round the clock. According to statistics, around 60 per cent of graft and bribery cases are delected directly following reports made as these centres.

(e) Corruption is a long existing social and historical phenomenon. It exists in different countries with different systems. People have made studies of the causes of corruption, and there have been some theories, such as bureaucracy, the lack in the check of power, the friction of the system during the transitional period, and the lagging behind of the political reform. Yet, further study is still necessary to find a more profound explanation for the occurrence of corruption; then effective countermeasures can be taken.

PART 6

ENVIRONMENTAL AND
CONSUMER PROTECTION

PROTECTING CONSUMERS' RIGHTS TO INFORMATION

Zhang Shouwen

Department of Law
Peking University

Zhang Shouwen, *LL.B., Master of Law (Peking University) was a lecturer at Peking University and became assistant to the dean of the university in 1995.*

Introduction

Information is one of the three pillars of human society, and is particularly important in the smooth functioning of the market economy. Given that consumers are one of the three main participants in the operation of the market, it is very important to enhance legal protection of their rights to information.

When a market economy and an information society are developing simultaneously, all economic activities carried out by consumers are directly related to information. Consumer access to the information they need is directly related to the realization of consumer rights and basic human rights.

In terms of the law, consumer rights to information must be confirmed and effectively protected, in order to protect basic human rights and social public benefits, and maintain the smooth operation of the economy and society.

This paper will, from the point of view of economic law, information law and some other branches of the law, deal with the consumer right to information and its legal protection.

The Consumer Right to Information

The consumer right to information derives from the right to information of all citizens. According to the constitution, all citizens enjoy free rights to information, meaning that they have the right to obtain freely, process, handle, spread and restore information. These information rights can be summarized as the rights of possessing, operating and handling information.

While related to the information rights of all citizens, the consumer right to information focuses on the rights of citizens to information related to the economic role they play as consumers.

The consumer right to information, or the right of knowing and understanding, usually means that consumers have the right to obtain information regarding the goods and services they are purchasing, using or being provided. This right is closely related to basic human rights, and must be given full protection under the law.

Consumer access to information should be protected under economic, civil and commercial law, as well as being the focus of information law. As one of the basic human rights, it should be enjoyed by all consumers, even those not considered citizens.

It is generally thought that the consumer right to information was first articulated by former U.S. President Kennedy. In his famous Special Acts of the President on Protecting Consumer Rights, he pointed out four rights of consumers, including "rights of obtaining correct information on goods".[1]

From then on, these four rights were widely accepted. On this basis, the International Consumers Organizational Association put forward eight rights which consumers should enjoy, including "the right of fully obtaining information materials".[2] As such, the consumer right to information has been widely confirmed as an essential consumer right at both the domestic and international levels.

In addition, many countries and international organizations have extended the consumer right to information to include the consumer right to education, which requires knowledge and teaching. This refers to the fact that, in order to obtain information fully and effectively, consumers must have the right to knowledge regarding consumption and the protection of consumers. In the meantime, governments have a duty to make this knowledge widespread.

There is no doubt that the consumer right to education is a key element in helping consumers to exercise fully and effectively their right to information, and should be included as part of their right to free information.

The Importance of Protecting Consumer Rights to Information

It is very important for consumers to exercise fully and effectively their right to information if they are to have sufficient accurate information regarding goods and services. The following sections serve to analyze the importance of this right from different viewpoints.

The Economic Analysis of Law

From the perspective of the economic analysis of law, it is extremely important to protect the consumer right to information. When the market economy was still in the period of free competition, companies and consumers were equal. Their rights were clearly defined and there was little disparity between them. Consumers could obtain information at little cost, and information and economic activities were carried out according to free contract principles. Consumer rights were not a serious issue.

As the market economy accelerated, however, and monopolies became more common, problems related to consumer rights became more acute. The main reason for this was a situation of information concentration[3] or information asymmetry, a common phenomenon under the market economy.

In fact, information has always been concentrated in the hands of the stronger enterprises or companies, and consumers often have difficulty obtaining sufficient information about the goods and services of these manufacturers. Insufficient information leads to market instability, and increases the cost of obtaining information. This lowers the efficiency of the market system, and results in economic and social problems, particularly where consumers are concerned.

Generally speaking, under the conditions of the market economy, the issue of the concentration of information will always exist. In addition, companies and manufacturers are profit-oriented and will, therefore, tend to use information to infringe on the rights of others to their own benefit.

In order to protect efficiently the rights of consumers and maintain stability, information channels must be kept clear. To achieve this, rules and regulations must be established in law to protect fully the consumer right to information, and ensure that consumers receive sufficient and accurate information.

Information Law Analysis

In the modern information society, there exists a series of contradictions, such as a lack of information versus information overflow. These information contradictions also exist in the relationship between enterprises and consumers.

From the point of view of information law, economic activities between enterprises and consumers involve the exchange of information. Both sides are receiving information, and both have information rights and information obligations. In fact, enterprises do not make enough effective information available to consumers. At the same time, more and more enterprises are producing inaccurate information which makes it difficult for consumers to select information, and pollutes the available information as a whole.

Companies use information to further their interests and to maximize efficiency. Consumers use information to inform their decisions and protect their interests. The two objectives coexist but also contradict each other. In furthering their own interests, companies may ignore the principles of honesty and even legality, resulting in insufficient or inaccurate information regarding goods and services.

In order to maintain the principle of equal exchange, protect consumer rights and safeguard social public benefit, the consumer right to information must be safeguarded and sufficient and accurate information must be provided. This will help to solve the discrepancy in the information available to enterprises and consumers, and promote economic and social development. From the standpoint of information law, therefore, the protection of the consumer right to information is essential.

Strategic Game Analysis

The Strategic Game or Game Theory is an important mathematical theory which is increasingly being used in other areas of scientific research, particularly economics.[4]

Transactions between companies and consumers can be seen as typical components of the strategic game, and are closely related to the bargaining model and the balance of using information and uncertainty for strategic moves. Experts on the strategic game take the common view that information plays a very important role in the strategic game relationship between companies and consumers.

The strategic game theory says that when there is insufficient information, companies and consumers constantly use their own counter-measures in information transmission, and eventually a "Nash Balance" is achieved.[5] Which side will benefit from these counter-measures depends on the information of which they are in possession. Given that consumers often have little knowledge of companies and their goods and services, companies can take advantage of the fact that information is concentrated in their hands to harm consumer interests.

As a result, in order to maintain a balance between the two, consumer rights to information must be protected under the law. Only in this situation can the goal of a perfect balance of countermeasures be achieved that will benefit both sides. The Nash Balance is not beneficial to consumers under the conditions of a standard contract of adhesion.

The above analysis from three different but connected perspectives demonstrates the necessity of protecting consumer rights to information. Only when their rights are protected can consumers obtain sufficient, accurate information. Strictly speaking, the legal definition of consumer rights to information should be that, under the law, consumers have the right to accurate, effective information regarding certain goods and services. In addition, this right should be protected not only in law, but also in practice. This is extremely important in countries where the sale of false or counterfeit goods is prevalent.

The importance of protecting the consumer right to information can be further explained through the historical development of the economy, society and law. As mentioned earlier, when consumers and companies enjoyed relatively equal status under the market economy, issues of consumer rights were not serious, and the relationship between companies and consumers was regulated only by traditional civil and commercial law. In more modern times, however, as monopolies and unfair competition have come to characterize the market economy, the imbalance in the possession of information has become evident, resulting in economic and social problems and a strong consumer rights movement.

Under this movement, consumers demanded sufficient and accurate information about goods in order to protect their rights. They also demanded the establishment of organizations to safeguard these rights. In many countries, this promoted the development of a legal system to protect consumer rights, particularly their right to information. This effectively counteracted the weakness of traditional civil and commercial law in this area.

Legal Protection of the Consumer Right to Information

General Overview

In today's climate of "consumer sovereignty",[6] consumers play a very important role in determining the production and purchasing of companies, because their product choices directly affect commercial success. So, in theory, manufacturers consider consumers as the highest power in the economy. This view, however, is not sufficient to fully protect consumer rights.

Each country has its own policy on protecting consumer rights. In general, however, most countries base their policy on the view that consumers are weak, and work to ensure their rights. Given that consumer rights are both an economic and social issue, most countries have also embodied their policy in law, forming a legal system to protect effectively consumers and their rights to information and other rights.

Under the constitutional law of most countries, the concept of protecting citizens' rights to information is covered under the basic rights of citizens. In the economic realm, this refers to protecting the rights of all natural consumers to information. This concept is evident in all categories of related laws, particularly those with special stipulations aiming at protecting consumer rights.

These special stipulations supplement traditional civil and commercial law, and help to maintain the smooth functioning of the market economy as well as playing an important role in protecting consumer rights. They are largely already existing under economic law, in the form of anti-monopoly legislation which indirectly deals with consumer issues; legislation against unfair competition; and legislation which directly protects consumer rights. Legislation concerning advertising and production quality should also be included, as it is closely related to consumer rights.

Just as domestic legislation to protect consumers has developed, so has legislation at the international level. Principles of Protecting Consumers established by the United Nations, for example, not only establishes goals for protecting consumer rights but also the principles each government must follow. This document provides a guide for developing consumer policy and consumer protection legislation. In addition, The Set of Multilaterally Agreed Equitable Principles and Rules for the Control of RBP[7] adopted by the United Nations General Assembly, also includes some regulations to protect consumers, and is very helpful to the protection of consumer rights at the international level.

Essentially, the consumer right to information should be protected by a number of different branches of law, including civil and commercial, economic, administrative and criminal law. In protecting consumer rights, companies, states and society all have obligations. If these obligations are not fulfilled, they will be responsible under the law. Comprehensive protection under different branches of the law is crucial in ensuring this legal responsibility.

China's Legislation

As mentioned above, a number of different branches of the law play an important part in protecting the consumer right to information. From being non-existent, Chinese legislation in this area has developed very rapidly, and now requires that its stipulations be fine-tuned.

The Law to Protect Consumer Rights

Legislation to protect consumers focuses specifically on protecting consumer rights to information and other rights, and is the key law in this area. In China, the Law of Protection of Consumer Rights stipulates that consumers have the right to know the truth about the goods they purchase or use and the services they receive. Legally, this stipulation ensures consumer rights to information, with some specific stipulations on the subject.

Under these stipulations, in certain circumstances consumers have the right to require firms to provide information about price, production, place, manufacturer, function, performance, standard, main composition, date of production, the term of validity, proof of testing, directions for use, service after sale or the contents of service, standards and charges. These stipulations indicate that consumers should have access to both accurate and sufficent, effective information.

With sufficient and accurate information, consumers can clearly understand the contents of any contract they might make with a company. In one sense, the consumer right to information is a prerequisite for ensuring that rights to security, self selection and equal trade are also protected. Its position relative to other consumer rights is so important that protecting it legally has become the key element in the more general system of consumer protection.

In order for consumers to exercise effectively their rights to information, a number of related laws must come into play. For instance, China's Law of Protection of Consumers' Rights stipulates a number of obligations to be fulfilled by companies, state and society in protecting consumers' rights.

According to these stipulations, firms have the following obligations: to provide accurate information to consumers, and not spread propaganda which will create misunderstandings; to offer accurate and clear warnings regarding goods and services; to give the authentic product name and trade mark; and to ensure the quality of goods and services produced or provided live up to advertising claims.

The Law of Protection of Consumer Rights also stipulates some obligations for state and society. It stresses that legislative, executive and judicial offices of state should protect consumer rights when exercising their powers and functions, and this includes rights to information.

The spirit of these stipulations demonstrates that protecting consumer rights to information is the responsibility of society in general, and should be monitored by society.

This law also carries some regulations regarding the status and function of consumer associations, which are very useful in protecting the right to information. Under the law, if representatives of firms or state bodies breach their obligations to protect the consumer right to information, they will be held legally responsible.

Consistent with the basic principles of the Law to Protect Consumer Rights, some other laws have similar stipulations. The Law Against Unfair Competition, the Law of Advertisement and Production Quality Law all embody the principle of protecting consumer rights and play an important role in protecting the right to information.

The Law Against Unfair Competition

As mentioned above, in cases where there is insufficient information or concentration of information in the market economy, companies can take suspect actions for their own benefit. To deal with these actions, the legislation regarding unfair competition needs to be enhanced. China's Law Against Unfair Competition stipulates 11 categories of unfair competition, such as imitation and producing false propaganda, all of which effectively breach the consumer right to information. This law provides that those involved in unfair competition are legally responsible, and this effectively helps to protect the consumer right to information.

The Law of Advertisement

Closely related to the Law Against Unfair Competition is the Advertising Law which protects consumer rights through regulating advertising. China's Advertising Law provides in its general principles that advertising must be true and legal; it must not have false content or attempt to deceive or confuse consumers.

This law also specifies the principle of advertising: that its contents must help to raise the quality of goods or services and protect consumer rights. In addition, advertisements must have three elements—they must be clear, truthful and distinct. This means the information they contain must be accurate and easy to distinguish from other types of information. There is no doubt that this stipulation is important in protecting the consumer right to information.

In addition to these stipulations, the Law of Advertisement also prohibits certain types of advertising including advertisements which offer attached gifts; advertising of patents; advertising of medicine; and advertising for some other products.

The Law of Advertisement also provides for regulating the management of advertising activities; permitting or prohibiting certain types of advertising; and punishing any infringement of the consumer right to information. All these provisions ensure that the consumer right to information is effectively protected.

Production Quality Law

The Production Quality Law also plays an important part. Given that information on production quality is some of the most important required by consumers, many of the regulations under this law are closely related to the consumer right to information. Much of its content is similar to that of the legislation already mentioned above.

As we have seen, under the market economy, it is essential that the consumer right to information should be protected. China is currently in the process of establishing the legal system required for the smooth operation of a market economy.

The above-mentioned legislation, which serves to protect the consumer right to information, is an important part of this legal system. The problem now is not legislation, but strengthening enforcement and increasing citizens' awareness of their rights as consumers. Only when this has been achieved will the consumer right to information be sufficiently and effectively protected; basic human rights safeguarded; the social system maintained; and the development of the economy and society increased.

Notes

[1] In Special Acts of the President on Protecting Consumers Rights (or White Paper on Protecting Consumer Rights of the President) by President Kennedy in 1962, the following rights are also included: the right of safety in using goods; the right of freely selecting goods; the consumer right to voice opinions.
[2] The consumer rights raised by the International Consumers Organization Association are mainly those of: the right to the necessary materials and services to maintain a living; the right to reasonable prices and selection; the right to security; and the right to education.
[3] In addition to the concentration of information, economic law experts generally take the view that monopolies, public property and other external economies are also important factors in destabilizing the market.
[4] The Nobel Prise winners for economics in 1994 were three experts on the Strategic Game: Mr J. Nash and Mr J. Harsanyi from the U.S. and Mr Reinhard Selten from Germany. They made a significant contribution to explaining economics through the Strategic Game.
[5] The definition of the Nash Balance was put forward by Mr Nash. It basically derives from the theory that no single party participating in the game has the power to determine absolutely the outcome, but that the decisions of all the parties are influenced by the decisions of the others, and it is a combined force which ultimately determines the balance.
[6] The theory of consumer sovereignty is generally considered to be an important theoretical basis for the protection of consumer rights. According to this

theory, consumers have the highest power of deciding what should be produced and in what quantities, because their decisions affect the sale and price of goods. This is much the same as voting in a political election.

[7] The Set of Multilaterally Agreed Equitable Principles and Rules for the Control of RBP was formally adopted at the 35th General Assembly of the United Nations in 1980.

ENVIRONMENTAL TORT AND CIVIL REMEDIES — PROBLEMS IN ENVIRONMENTAL LEGISLATION

Professor Jin Ruilin

Department of Law
Peking University

Professor Jin Ruilin, *LL. B. (Peking University), has been teaching at Peking University since 1959, holding positions as assistant lecturer, lecturer, associate professor and Professor of Law. From 1981 to 1989, he was vice-dean of the law department of Peking University; a member of the board of directors of the China Law Association; deputy director of the China Environmental Economic and Law Management Association; consultant to the Environmental Protection Commission of the State Council; and legal adviser to the State Environmental Protection Bureau. He is the author of numerous books and articles, including* Environmental Law: Protector of the Nature *(1985),* Environmental Protection Law *(1990), and* A Course in Chinese Environmental Protection Law *(1992).*

Introduction

As China's economy grows rapidly, pollution increases and the environment deteriorates,[1] various infringements of rights will occur, and it is expected that environmental torts caused by "public hazards" and civil remedies will become major social issues.

Environmental tort,[2] as a special kind of infringement of rights, differs greatly from the traditional law of tort and remedies set out in legal theory. The traditional law of tort must be amended and developed in order to deal with the special problems caused by public hazards.

Some countries have introduced special laws such as the "Law of Civil Remedies for Public Hazards", "Law of Compensation for Public Hazards" and "Law of Environmental Liability", but there has been little discussion and research on the issue of environmental tort and

371

civil remedies in China. The relevant legislation is not complete, and it is necessary to conduct a systematic study of this issue.

Characteristics of Environmental Tort

Environmental pollution and damage are by-products of the development of the social economy, resources and technology. The cost to human life and property are far greater than under traditional tort. As a special phenomenon of modern society, environmental tort is quite different from traditional tort in terms of its subject, object, activity, severity and scope of damages.

Inequality of the Subjects

The positions of the relevant parties (the injuring party and the injured party) in a tort case are, generally speaking, equal, interchangeable and specific. In the case of environmental tort, the injuring party usually refers to powerful industrial and commercial enterprises. The injured party is usually the general public, which lacks the ability to avoid and counteract the damage. The two parties are not equal.

Wide Scope of the Objects

Tort activity acts directly on the individual property and person of the injured party, so it is easy to identify the injured party. In the case of environmental tort, however, the act of infringement is conducted via the intermediary of the environment on human life and public or private property. The scope of the objects is much wider and more complex.

The Nature of the Infringement

From a legal point of view, tort activity in general is illegal and against social morality. Activities such as failure to pay debt, theft, and physical damage to others are all considered "activities without value". In the case of environmental tort, many of the discharges of pollutants are a by-product of lawful activities conducted by industrial and commercial enterprises except in rare cases of environmental accidents. To a certain extent, these activities are inevitable and possess a certain rationality.

In many cases of tort, tort activity happens only once and does not continue for a long time. In the case of environmental tort, however, the infringement is persistent and usually repeated over a long period of time.

In the case of tort, the tort activity directly affects the interests of the injured party and directly results in the damages, so it is easy for the injured party to recognize the illegality of the tort activity and determine whether it is active negligence. In environmental tort, the causal link between the infringement and the result is not always so obvious and easy to identify. It is often cumulative, potential and compound, making it difficult to identify the injuring party, the time of the infringement, whether it constitutes active negligence, and the causal link between the activity and the damages.

The Wide Scope and Seriousness of the Infringement

In the case of tort, a specific injuring party infringes the individual rights of a specific injured party. In environmental tort, the infringement is usually a combination of the activities of many non-specific discharging sources. These activities constitute a socialized infringement because they affect the interests of a certain social community in a certain geographical area. The scope of the damage to property and human life and health is wider. As a result, precautions against environmental tort must be implemented, and adjustments made with regard to the system and functions of civil remedies.

These specific characteristics of environmental tort are not sufficiently covered by the existing doctrine and legal mechanism of the traditional law of tort. If the law of tort continues to be applied to cases of environmental tort without any amendments, it will be extremely difficult to implement effective remedies. As a result, many countries have focused on establishing a new law of environmental tort and remedies. Under this new legislation, the doctrine of liability for negligence is replaced by the doctrine of liability without fault; the causal link and burden of proof are shifted or reversed; and the principle of instituting precautions and socializing remedies is established.

Attribution — From Liability for Negligence to Liability Without Fault

The doctrine of liability for negligence is an important principle in attribution in civil cases. Together with freedom of contract and unrestricted private ownership, it helps to form the basis of the principles of capitalist civil law. Its original objective was to safeguard the freedom of individuals and ensure free competition. At the same time, it reflects how the law evaluates the illegality of an act and standards of social morality. Under the market economy, it exists in civil law (including Chinese civil law) as a general principle.

When this doctrine is applied in the case of environmental tort, however, several major problems are encountered:

  (a) Environmental tort usually occurs in the normal course of production by enterprises which discharge pollutants. Except in some rare cases of environmental accidents, these normal production activities do not constitute negligence.
  (b) The rapid development of science and technology and the protection of trade and technical secrets make it difficult for the injured party to learn about the technological processes and equipment used by producers, what hazardous pollutants are discharged, and whether this constitutes active negligence.
  (c) A standard for discharges is normally used to measure whether discharges of pollutants are legal or illegal. But where many polluting sources are located close together, individual companies may not be exceeding the standard, but the total amounts being discharged might be enough to exceed the standard and cause serious damage.
  (d) In cases where the injured party has no way to avoid the infringement, if negligence is still used as the basis for the attribution, many infringements will not lead to tort liability. The rights and interests of the injured party will not be protected, constituting a major flaw in the legal justice system.

The question is how to resolve these issues. If liability for negligence came out of the capitalist economic development of the seventeenth century, then liability without fault is the inevitable outcome of modern social, economic and technological development.

The doctrine of liability without fault has evolved over a long period of time from the liability for negligence of the seventeenth century, and the liability of dangerous things of the nineteenth century, to the product liability of this century. In fact, in many countries, the shift from liability for negligence to liability without fault has now become the main focus for legal research and amendments in environmental legislation.

Japan

The doctrine of liability without fault has been established in much of the Japanese legislation related to public hazards. It was first introduced in the Mining Law of 1939. Under this law, if damage is caused to other people during mine excavations, discharge of waste water from mining pits, piling-up or abandoning of ore or slag, or emitting smoke, the owner of the mine will be liable to pay compensation for such damages.[3]

Under the current Air Pollution Prevention Law enacted in 1968, article 25 provides that if factories or enterprises emit substances hazardous to human health (including substances such as smoke and other substances listed by the government), and cause damage to human life or health, the responsible factories or enterprises shall be liable to pay compensation for such damages.[4] The current Water Pollution Prevention Law enacted in 1970 contains similar provisions on liability without fault in civil damages.[5]

Under these laws on public hazards, there are three problems related to liability without fault:

(a) liability without fault only covers mining hazards, air pollution and water pollution, not other public hazards such as noise, vibration, earth subsidence, stench, electromagnetic radiation, etc;

(b) the scope of damages only covers damage to human life and health, but not losses of property, which are governed by the Civil Code of Japan under which liability for negligence still applies; and

(c) the principle of presuming the causal link in the Law on the Punishment of Crimes of Public Hazards Harmful to Human Health shall be applied generally in deciding the elements of liability in the case of public hazards, otherwise the victims will not be able to obtain remedies because of the difficulty in proving a causal link.

Common Law

In countries governed by common law, such as the United Kingdom and the U.S., the law of tort is mainly based on case law rather than on a systematic theoretical framework.

In the United Kingdom, the principle of liability without fault was first established in the well-known case of *Rylands v. Fletcher* (1868) 3. H.L. 330. The judgment in this case imposes liability for any damages caused by "a thing or activity unduly dangerous and inappropriate to the place where it is maintained, in the light of the character of that place and its surroundings". This rule was later applied to all activities which change the normal use of land. Sometimes this rule is referred to as "strict liability" or "absolute liability".

In the U.S., the principle of liability without fault was first applied in cases of product liability. In the well-known case *McForson v. Biek Automobile Co.* (1916),[6] the applicant bought an automobile manufactured by the defendant from an automobile dealer. Defects in the automobile wheels resulted in the applicant being physically injured in an accident. The Supreme Court decided that with regard to things like automobiles, which can be dangerous to human life, although there is no contractual relationship between the manufacturer and the consumer, the manufacturer shall also bear the liability of due care and attention to the consumer.

As a result of the difficulties inherent in applying the law of tort to cases of environmental tort, the federal and many state authorities in the United States have, since the 1970s, been increasingly applying strict liability or absolute liability in legislation on public hazards.

Continental Law

Among the countries governed by continental law, France and Germany are playing an important role in the development of civil law. The legislation and theories of environmental tort and remedies of these countries have recently been reformed.

In France, the law of environmental tort and remedies was originally based on *troubles des voisins*. The problems with this approach are:

(a) it applies only to infringements taking place in geographically adjacent areas, but environmental pollution can affect much wider areas; and

(b) the legal basis of the right to claim damages in the *troubles des voisins* is found in articles 1382 and 1384 of the French Civil Code. These articles are about tort activities provided in chapter 4 of part 3.[7] The right to claim damages is based on *droit real* (property right), and under article 1382, negligence is the basic element in the attribution. The liability of the owner or user, under article 1384, when causing damage to others, is constructive liability, liability for dangerous things, or liability without fault, all of which are very controversial in theory and practice.

As a result, there has been a strong movement in France to reform the traditional law of tort and remedies so that it will be effective in the case of environmental tort. The reform includes two aspects:

(a) The liability for negligence or the constructive negligence of the injuring party is being changed to liability for dangerous things based on the object, the use of the object and the link between the activity and the object; and then gradually being changed to objective liability, liability for dangerous objects and liability without fault. This will replace liability for negligence or constructive liability in the case of environmental tort.

(b) The injured party will be exempt from the burden of proof, so that the procedural rules will be simplified.[8] Liability without fault has already replaced liability for negligence in certain specific legislation. For example, Article 142(2) in the Civil Aviation Law provides that if the aircraft causes damage to human life and property on the ground, the responsible person shall be liable to pay compensation. There is no way to avoid this liability, and no legal ceiling for the compensation. In the Law of Civil Liability for Nuclear Energy, except in cases where an exemption is justified, liability without fault is also applied.

In Germany, environmental tort is referred to as *immission*. In the 1974 Federal Law on Prevention of Public Hazards, *immission* is defined as the causes of air pollution, noise pollution, vibration, light, heat, radiation or other similar damaging phenomenon which affect the lives of humans, animals, plants or other substances.

The legal basis for civil remedies in the case of environmental tort is article 906 of the German Civil Code which was amended in 1960. According to article 906, in the case of *immission*, if no preventive measures can be taken, it is possible to apply for compensation regardless of the negligence of the injuring party.

According to article 14 of the Federal Law on Prevention of Public Hazards, if it is technologically or economically impossible or difficult to prevent public hazards, the injured party may claim damages.

In 1991, Germany also enacted the Law of Environmental Liability. This law not only provides for strict liability for damages caused by facilities listed in the Federal Law on Prevention of Public Hazards, but also extends the scope of compensation to cover damage to the ecosystem as well as damage to human health and property losses.

The Causal Link Construction and the Shift of the Burden of Proof

The Causal Link

The causal link between the infringement, the damaging result and the burden of proof on the side of the applicant are traditional elements of the law of tort. If applied to cases of environmental tort, however, a number of difficulties arise:

377

(a) The cause of environmental tort is often the discharge of various kinds of pollutants. Much about the nature of such discharges is still unknown, such as their levels of toxicity, and the patterns of their movement, diffusion and transformation.
(b) The effect of pollutants on the environment is usually potential and accumulative. It often takes months or years for the damage to become obvious, making a definite causal link very difficult to establish.
(c) A great deal of the harm caused by pollution is the compound result of a number of factors. For example, there are many causes of diseases such as asthma, including pollution and cigarette smoking.

If the strict and direct causal link continues to be applied in the case of environmental tort, it is likely to result in scientific uncertainty and controversial judgments, and victims will not receive the remedies they deserve. As a result, certain changes in theory and legislation are required. Japan, in particular, has made some progress in this area.

The first approach to reform is to apply the doctrine of "probability" when the causal link is to be proved. This means that if it can be proved that the result wouldn't have occurred without the activity, there is probably a causal link between the activity and the result.

The second approach is to apply the doctrine of epidemiology in proving the causal link. This means the method of collective statistics used in epidemiology is applied, *i.e.* the common causes and the most likely causes of certain diseases. In this analysis, four factors must be taken into account:

(a) the effect of factors prior to the disease;
(b) the more obvious the degree of the factor, the higher the ratio of the patients;
(c) the lower the effect of the factor, the lower the ratio or degree of the patients; and
(d) the conclusion regarding the cause of the disease is not contrary to the theories of biology.[9]

In fact, this is a doctrine of causal link construction which is widely accepted in legal theory in Japan. It is considered to be the main approach in judicial practice, and has been applied in many well-known cases of public hazards.

The Japanese Law on the Punishment of Crimes of Public Hazards Harmful to Human Health (enacted in 1970, implemented in 1971) also provides that if a person, in managing a factory or enterprise, discharges substances that are likely to cause serious damage to public health, and the volume of these discharges has already reached the level of damaging public health, it may be presumed that the damage is caused by the discharges. In other countries such as Germany and France, it is also possible to presume the existence of a constructive causal link.

The Burden of Proof

Another relevant aspect is the shift of burden of proof. For similar reasons, the burden of proof on the side of the applicant should also be changed. That is to say the burden of proof on the applicant should be lightened or shifted to the defendant — a reversed burden of proof.

The Environmental Protection Law of Michigan has adopted this approach. Article 3 of this law provides that, if the applicant can prove that the defendant has caused the pollution with simple evidence, the case will be accepted. If the defendant denies his liability, he bears the burden of proving that he has not caused or not possibly caused such pollution. In Germany, the reversed burden of proof is also applied in the law of tort in the area of liability for dangerous things, such as product liability and *immission*.

Civil Remedies in Environmental Tort

The remedy system is one way in which the law works to protect rights and eventually achieve fairness and justice. The trend is for remedies to be both preventive and socialized; that there should be equal focus on eliminating the infringement and the payment of damages; that a balance of interests should be maintained; and that the fair share of the losses caused by public hazards and the remedies for public hazards should be socialized.

The Equal Importance of Preventive Elimination of the Infringement and Payment of Damages

Damages are paid once an infringement has been committed. Eliminating an infringement means either removing a current infringement or preventing an infringement from occuring. In traditional tort activity, a specific injuring party usually commits a single infringement against an injured party, so the normal method of compensation is to pay damages. This remedy is the most common and widely used method of compensation in much civil law.

The situation with regard to environmental tort is quite different, however, because the object of the infringement is social rights and interests. The infringement is often accumulative and potential, occurring over a period of years, which makes it difficult to prevent. The resulting damage is usually very serious, being continuous, repetitive and non-recoverable.

If the traditional payment of damages is applied to such cases, it will represent only a kind of passive remedy, which cannot help to eliminate or prevent infringements. As a result, the establishment of a preventive remedy system which puts equal emphasis on eliminating infringements and payment of damages is essential.

The Balance of Interests

Public hazards which are widespread and severe will often result in a complex situation of conflicting social interests:

(a) From a national perspective, environmental policy and strategies to prevent public hazards will affect the country's economic development, social stability, public security and public health. This can sometimes result in serious conflicts of interest.

(b) In the utilization and disposition of environmental resources, it is essential to consider the needs of the next generation. Current excessive damage to and use of resources means we are expending the environmental assets of the next generation. If this is continued by every generation, the eventual result will be a loss of the basic requirements for survival.

(c) Most public hazards originate in industrial activities which are both socially necessary and useful. At our current stage of social, economic and technical development it would be impossible to prevent these activities, which would be required for total elimination of public hazards. There is an obvious conflict between the cause of public hazards and their social usefulness.

(d) From the point of view of the interests of the two parties, if public hazards are to be tolerated, the rights and interests of the public will not be sufficiently protected. The justice and rational function of law will be lost, and widespread environmental infringements could result in social instability. If too much emphasis is placed on eliminating and preventing public hazards, however, social and economic development will be hampered, which is also not good for social stability.

These factors demonstrate that the potential conflicts of interest which could occur in the case of environmental tort are much more complex than in the case of traditional tort. As a result, it is necessary to represent a balance of various interests in the remedy system for environmental tort. In general terms, the balance of interests should take into account the relative and efficient use of environmental resources under the national environmental policy, economic costs and benefits, and the fairness and justice of law. In more concrete terms, it should take into account the nature and seriousness of the infringement, its rationality, the possibility of eliminating it, and the damages it has caused. It should also take into account the nature and content of the injured interests,[10] and finally, the scope of the interests to be protected and the forms of remedies.

Generally speaking, in the case of damages already caused for which no exemption exists under law, payment of compensation should serve as the remedy. The major problem with this remedy is the allocation of the liability and the calculation of the damages. In the case of continuous, repetitive and non-recoverable damages, it is also necessary to adopt preventive remedies in order to eliminate the infringement.

The compulsory and absolute elimination of the infringement, such as the shut-down or merging of factories and changes in production activities, will seriously affect industrial and commercial activities, so the balance of interests should be considered in reaching a final decision.

In the case of *Boomer v. Atlantic Cement Co.*,[11] residents living near the cement factory were affected by the dust, noise and vibration it produced, and applied to a New York court for an injunction to shut the factory down and seek payment of damages. The court confirmed an infringement by the factory, but found that the defendant had invested more than US $45 million in the factory and employed over 300 workers, while damages claimed by the applicants were only about US $185,000. The economic interests were not in balance, so the court refused to order the shut-down of the plant, instead ordering the defendant to pay compensation.

In this case, the court put the emphasis on the balance of the economic interests of the two parties. In the U.S., in the case of "public hazards of enterprises", there is a policy of balancing the equities. This means that only after an evaluation of the economic results of a decision is carried out, can a decision be made on whether to eliminate completely the infringement. This is sometimes referred to as "double balance".

Over time, the doctrines and systems of partial injunction and damages in lieu of injunction have emerged. Partial injunction can be widely applied to a range of situations, including:

(a) installing facilities for pollution prevention and treatment in order to lessen the environmental infringement;

381

(b) reducing the time period of the operation in order to reduce the volume of discharges;

(c) prohibiting factories from discharging waste gases or polluted water for a certain period of time; and

(d) establishing working times for noisy airports, construction sites, etc.

An example of damages in lieu of injunction is provided in Germany's Federal Law for the Prevention of Public Hazards. Article 14 provides that for facilities with a specific permit, one cannot rely only on the right to apply for elimination of the *immission* without having a specific right in private law to stop the operation of the facilities. It can only apply to the adoption of preventive measures against public hazards. If this is technically impossible or economically difficult, only compensation may be applied for.

The use of damages in lieu of injunction is applied in cases of serious infringement, where the infringement exceeds what the average person can tolerate and it is not economically or technically feasible to install facilities to prevent or treat the public hazard.[12]

Socialization of Remedies for Public Hazards

In some countries, the remedy system considers that the losses caused by public hazards are socially shared, and the liability for them is socialized.

Public hazards are a social infringement, which are often caused by situations which are a certain social usefulness and are in the public interest. Some serious pollution accidents, such as the Chernobyl, Bhopal and Three-Mile Island incidents,[13] have affected large areas and caused great human suffering. Under these circumstances remedies for public hazards no longer concern an injuring party and an injured party. They are social problems which require a socialized remedy system. A socialized remedy system means the infringement of environmental tort is considered a socialized infringement whose losses are shared by society. The focus is on remedies for the victims, rather than on punishment.

Under the Japanese Law of Health Recovery from Public Hazards, a recovery fund is established in order to pay compensation to the victims of public hazards. In the U.S., France and the Netherlands, various kinds of environmental recovery funds are established in order to provide compensation to victims. In some countries, the remedy system is connected to the social insurance system. This effectively socializes the remedy system by using insurance to divert and disperse the risk of damages.

Civil Remedies for Environmental Tort in China

\

In China, provisions on environmental tort and civil remedies are contained in the General Principles of Civil Law, the Environmental Protection Law and other separate laws on prevention of marine, air and water pollution.

All this legislation contains certain provisions on the questions of attribution, exemption clauses and forms of remedies, but it is not complete and neglects many important issues. It also lacks coherence, simply repeating the provisions contained in other legislation, and some of the provisions actually contradict each other. In general, a systematic, coherent and co-ordinated legislative system has not yet to be established.

In the Chapter on Civil Liability of the General Principles of the Civil Law, article 106 provides for liability without fault. Article 124 specifically provides for civil liability in the case of environmental pollution, but the prerequisite for this liability is "infringement of the relevant provisions on environmental protection and pollution prevention of the country". This is interpreted by some academics to mean:

"The civil liability arising from an infringement of environmental pollution is only applied when the relevant provisions on environmental protection and pollution prevention of the country are infringed. That is to say, the responsible party will only be liable if the discharges of pollutants exceed the discharging standards of the country."[14]

This type of provision and interpretation probably represents a flaw in the legislation, at least, it is inconsistent with reality. It is also in conflict with the relevant provisions in the environmental protection laws. In Chinese civil law, the General Principles of Civil Law are used to provide some general principles for various types of infringement, including environmental tort. More detailed and specific provisions should be contained in specific laws, and the principles contained in the two should not contradict each other.

The first provision for liability without fault in Chinese environmental protection law occurs in article 42 of the Marine Environmental Protection Law (1982). Article 43 of this law provides force majeure and the intention of the third party as the exemption according to international customs. Articles 41 and 42 of the Water Pollution Prevention Law (1984) then established the legislative formula for liability without fault in the case of remedies for public hazards in China. These Articles also provide an exemption clause if the damage is caused by the injured party itself. The revised Environmental Protection Law (1989) almost repeats what is provided in the Water Pollution

Prevention Law, although natural disasters are considered the only exception.

The Environmental Protection Law is a special law and is also the basic law in the framework of environmental protection legislation. With regard to environmental tort and remedies, the provisions in the Environmental Protection Law should be consistent with the General Principles of Civil Law, while making more detailed stipulations. It should provide a comprehensive framework for the questions of attribution, exemption, forms and elements of remedies in the case of environmental tort.

In current Chinese legislation, there are no explicit provisions on the questions of causal link and burden of proof in environmental infringements. Only article 74 of the Supreme People's Court's Opinion on the Application of the Civil Procedural Law of the People's Republic of China provides some guidelines. In the case of damages caused by environmental pollution, this article provides that the shift of burden of proof should be interpreted as follows: "If the defendant denies the infringement provided by the applicant, the defendant bears the burden of proof."

The question of causal link and burden of proof are crucial in environmental infringement proceedings and protecting the interests of the injured party. They should be explicitly outlined in both procedural laws and special environmental protection laws. With regard to the equal importance of preventive elimination of infringements and the remedy system, the interests should be balanced.

All these relevant questions, such as complete elimination or partial elimination of the infringement, damages in lieu of injunction, and the socialization of compensation and social insurance, should be considered in the light of China's social climate. Thorough research and analysis on the subject is required before relevant provisions are incorporated in China's environmental legislation.

Notes

[1] See the *Chinese Journal of the Environment*, 1993 and 1994.
[2] "Nuisance" is referred to differently in the laws of different countries: in Japanese law, it is referred to as "public nuisance"; in German law, it is "immission"; in common law, it is "nuisance"; in French law, it is *"troubles des voisins"*.
[3] See Article 109 of the "Mining Law" of Japan.
[4] See the Japanese Air Pollution Prevention Law, in "Selected Documents of Foreign Environmental Protection Laws" (Chinese), Chinese Social Science Publication, 1979, p.154.
[5] Article 19 of the Water Pollution Prevention Law of Japan.

[6] The original reference in English is not available, so this is a translation from Chinese.

[7] *French Civil Code*, Commercial Publication, in Chinese, 1979, p.189.

[8] Ke Ze-Dong, *On Environmental Law*, Taiwan National University, 1988, pp.136–138.

[9] See Nomura Yoshihiro, *Guide to the Japanese Law of Public Hazards*, Chinese, Chinese Society of Environmental Management, Economy and Law, 1982.

[10] The right to life and health is a right that shall be absolutely protected in law. Strictly speaking, the balance of interests does not affect this much. If it is interpreted more widely, it may affect the limitation of life, damage to environmental interests and mental damage. The balance of interests mainly applies in the case of loss of property.

[11] *Boomer v. Atlantic Cement Co. Inc.* N.Y. 2nd, 219.

[12] See Qiu Cong-Zhi, *Principles of Law of Public Hazards*, revised ed. 1987, pp.183–184.

[13] The reference in English is not available.

[14] See Zheng Li and Wang Zuo-Tang eds. *Civil Law*, Peking University Press, 1995, p.689. Other works such as Li You-Yi ed. *Civil Law* and Tong Rou ed. *Chinese Civil Law* contain similar interpretations.

WILL THE BALANCE BETWEEN ECONOMIC DEVELOPMENT AND ENVIRONMENTAL PROTECTION BE TIPPED TO THE LATTER?— AN EXAMINATION OF THE 1995 AMENDMENTS TO THE LAW OF THE PRC ON PREVENTION AND CONTROL OF ATMOSPHERIC POLLUTION

Lin Feng

Faculty of Law
City University of Hong Kong

Lin Feng, *LL. B. (Fudan University), LL. M. (Victoria University of Wellington), Ph.D. candidate (Peking University), is an assistant professor of law at the Faculty of Law, City University of Hong Kong. He is interested in comparative research on environmental law, labour law and administrative law.*

Introduction

After the opening up to the outside world since 1978, China's economy has developed rapidly and is regarded as the hope of the twenty-first century, however, rapid development has caused serious environmental pollution. In many areas of China, air is getting darker, dust is getting heavier and acid rain pollution caused by emission of sulphur dioxide (SO$_2$) is spreading rapidly in south China. In order to curb the deterioration of air quality, amendments have been made recently by the Standing Committee of the National People's Congress to the Law of the People's Republic of China (PRC) on the Prevention and Control of Atmospheric Pollution (hereinafter "1995 Amendments").[1] This paper intends to examine what progress has been made under the 1995 Amendments compared with previous air pollution legislation, and whether the 1995 Amendments can achieve the objective of curbing further deterioration of air quality. In order to do so, examination of the relationship between economic development and environmental protection, which has been debated for years,[2] will be conducted in order to reveal how the issue has been dealt with in China's air pollution legislation.

This paper will first present a picture of the current status of air pollution in China and then examine briefly the 1987 Law of the PRC on the Prevention and Control of Atmospheric Pollution (hereinafter "1987 Air Pollution Law"). The overview will show that under 1987 Air Pollution Law balance was required between environmental protection and economic development and was tipped both in legislation and practice towards economic development. That is possibly why the 1987 Air Pollution Law failed to curb further deterioration of air pollution and hence reveal the necessity for the 1995 Amendments. It will then scrutinize the contents of EPB Proposals and the arguments for and against those original proposals suggested by the Central Environmental Protection Bureau (hereinafter "EPB Proposals"). Comparison between the 1995 Amendments and EPB Proposals will be made to identify the differences between the two. The comparison will tell that the 1995 Amendments are quite different from the EPB Proposals and the former is a much watered down version of the latter. The fundamental difference between them comes down to the issue of how to balance economic development and environmental protection. This paper will examine how the issue has been dealt with in China's air pollution legislation. It then goes on to evaluate whether or not the 1995 Amendments can achieve the objective of curbing the deterioration of air quality. The 1995 Amendments have not changed the purpose of the 1987 Air Pollution Law as laid down in article 1, which put as one objective the promotion of the development of socialist modernization.[3] The decision-makers and enforcement agencies have to consider the issue of balance in setting air quality standards and pollutant emission standards, and also at almost every stage of implementation of the legislation. The paper argues that the 1995 Amendments, together with 1987 legislation, are bound to fail to be effective in controlling air pollution because of this fundamental problem. Moreover, the 1995 Amendments have only proposed some changes with the intention addressing several specific pollutants. They have not provided for any specific implementation schedules or specific environmental targets to be achieved. The future does not seem to be that optimistic. This paper does not, however, try to argue that no consideration should be given to economic development in environmental legislation, which does not seem realistic as far as China is concerned. Nevertheless, the paper maintains that once balance is acquired, the relevant legislation should also provide guidance with regard to how the balance should be achieved, which is exactly what is lacking in China's air pollution legislation *per se*, and environmental legislation as a whole. That has led to the situation where the balance of implementation and enforcement of air pollution legislation has tipped to economic development ever since the enactment of the 1987 Air Pollution Law. It concludes by pointing out that the legal mechanisms proposed under 1995 Amendments are, even though they may have incorporated some effective ones, overall still insufficient to prevent the deterioration of air quality. Only after appropriate guidance for balance is provided can the air quality in China be stopped from deteriorating.

Current Status of China's Air Pollution

The 1987 Air Pollution Law is the first comprehensive national legislation enacted to prevent and control atmospheric pollution.[4] While acknowledging that it has contributed to the prevention and control of air pollution and the fact that the air pollution situation may even be worse without that piece of legislation, it doesn't seem that the 1987 Air Pollution Law has achieved the stated legislative objective completely. In fact, eight years after the adoption of the 1987 Air Pollution Law, the air quality in China, especially in cities, is worse than it used to be.[5]

According to the information from the central EPB, the central and local governments in China have made great efforts since 1973 to reduce air pollution. Millions of dollars have been spent on the renovation of industrial furnaces and the installation of equipment to reduce flying ash and dust from industrial furnaces. All those measures have contributed to dust reduction and energy saving. However, the rapid economic development, increased consumption of fuel, out-of-date technologies of fuel use, unreasonable energy structure, insufficient funding for environmental protection, unsatisfactory environmental management and incomprehensive legal provisions have all contributed to the worsening of air pollution.[6]

The main air pollution source in China is coal burning, which produces both SO_2 and fly ash (or suspended particulates). The situation is getting worse owing to various reasons. Among those mentioned in the last paragraph, one, which needs to be emphasized is the lack of strict legal requirements for the emission of SO_2 from coal burning. According to the statistics from the central EPB, the cities where SO_2 level exceeds national standard are increasing. In 48 out of

73 cities where measurement was carried out national SO_2 standard is exceeded.[6] The whole picture of China is even more worrying. The current emission in China has reached more than 20 million tons per year and is still increasing because of the increased consumption of standard coal.[8] As a result, acid rain pollution caused by emission of SO_2 is worsening, which has affected many parts of China and the affected area has increased to cover most of southern China.[9]

Another major problem is pollution caused by suspended particulates. In all those 73 cities chosen for sampling, the density of total suspended particulates (TSP) exceeds China's national standard.[10] The same report also reveals that the TSP density in five metropolitan cities in China which participated in global atmospheric supervision in 1992 exceeded the standard set by International Health Organization by three to nine times. They were among the top ten most polluted cities in the world, though their air pollution is far from the worst in China.[11]

The air pollution has caused enormous economic and ecological losses. It is reported that annual economic loss caused by air pollution in the four provinces of Sichuan, Guizhou, Guangdong and Guangxi has exceeded 14 billion Renminbi (Chinese yuan)(RMB).[12] The amount for the whole country will be much bigger. Furthermore, air pollution has also caused health problems in many polluted areas. The investigation conducted in 20 cities in China showed that there were more than 1.6 million people who fell ill because of air pollution every year.[13]

The above information has shown clearly that the air quality has further deteriorated since the promulgation of the 1987 Air Pollution Law and has resulted in serious side effects. Under such circumstances, the central EPB proposed to amend the 1987 Air Pollution Law to stop further deterioration of air quality in China. The paper moves on to examine the 1987 Air Pollution Law as it is important to find out the reasons why it has failed to achieve its legislative objective as outlined clearly in article 1. Only in so doing can we properly evaluate the EPB Proposals and the effect of the 1995 Amendments.

Examination of the 1987 Air Pollution Law

Apart from the legislative objective(s), the fundamental issue in any environmental legislation is the setting of environmental quality standards and then their strict enforcement. As pointed out by one American scholar, environmental quality standards begin with a political decision as to how clean the environment should be.[14] In order to set the standards properly, it has to be decided whether or not the standards should be based strictly on one concern such as public health or on the balance of several concerns, including economic, technological, ecological and human health, etc. If the latter approach is adopted, an economic and environmental benefit-cost analysis needs to be conducted in order to produce the maximum overall benefit to society.[15] In fact, environmental legislation in many countries is often amended "according to the shifting winds of political sentiment and perceived needs of the body politic".[16] That is to say, different approaches may be adopted for environmental legislation at different stages of historical development.

Based on this basic thesis, let us move on to review the 1987 Air Pollution Law. It has six chapters, including 41 articles. The long title of the 1987 Air Pollution Law says that it is the law to prevent and control atmospheric pollution. However, article 1 lists several other purposes, *i.e.* to protect and improve people's and ecological environment, to safeguard human health and to promote the development of socialist modernization.[17] It seems to suggest that at least three factors should be taken into account in setting air quality standards, *i.e.* people's and ecological environment, human health, and economic development. It may be reasonable to argue that China does not want to sacrifice its economic development for environmental protection. Otherwise, it is not necessary to incorporate economic development into an environmental protection legislation, which is also a bit unusual compared with air pollution legislation in other countries.[18] Since article 1 states the objective of the whole legislation, it has in fact set limitation upon the effectiveness of the 1987 Air Pollution Law because of the requirement that the issue of balance will always need to be taken into account when the 1987 Air Pollution Law is implemented.

As far as the procedure for achieving the legislative objective in article 1 is concerned, the first step is to set environmental quality standards. Under the 1987 Air Pollution Law, the central EPB shall establish national standards for air quality while local people's governments may establish their local standards for items not specified in the national standards for air quality and report to the central EPB for record.[19] Though the 1987 Air Pollution Law did not say what considerations should be taken into account in setting both national and local air quality standards, it is generally agreed that air quality standards should be set to ensure public health.[20] Once air quality standards are set, the central EPB shall set national emission standards in accordance with national air quality standards and "the country's economic and technological conditions".[21] Local people's governments may then set their local emission standards for items not specified in the national standards for emission. If the pollutants are already specified in the national emission standards, they may set local emission standards which are more stringent than the national emission standards and report to the central EPB for record.[22]

Logically speaking, air quality standards and emission standards for air pollutants are closely related. The latter should be set at a level to ensure the achievement of air quality standards. That is the case with the Clean Air Act of the U.S.[23] Under the 1987 Air Pollution Law, however, the central EPB or local governments have to take into account economic and technological conditions in setting emission standards. That is to say, economic and technological conditions may have equal or even more weight as the achievement of air quality standards. That means that a statutory requirement exists on the consideration of the balance between economic development and environmental protection.

Whether or not balance is necessary is a political decision of the law-makers and, therefore, determined by public will in the country. A review of the legislative history of the 1970 Amendments to the Clean Air Act in the United States shows that the debate in both the House and the Senate was quite heated on the issue of whether or not technological feasibility and economic factors should be taken into account in setting standards. At the end the necessity of ensuring public health welfare attracted more support. The amendments adopted in 1970 contained no explicit provision for considering economic and technological feasibility in setting or achieving the standards.[24]

In the case of China, it will be determined by the National People's Congress or its Standing Committee. It is clear from the methods how the emission standards are set in China that air quality standards are not something which must and can actually be achieved when the emission standards are met. At most, air quality standards are only an important objective but not the only objective the 1987 Air Pollution Law intends to achieve. In fact, when a government is required to make a choice, it would not seem unreasonable for the government to set its national emission standards at the level at which the reduced risks to society just equal the costs of control or even at a lower level. That argument supports the position adopted by Chinese Government in the 1987 Air Pollution Law.

Once it is determined that balance is needed in setting standards, the next issue is how to balance different factors. One scholar has argued that all elements to be taken into account, such as public health and economic cost, etc. should be made explicit rather than being hidden behind something. In doing so, public welfare can be best served.[25] In fact, when all relevant factors are made explicit, a cost and benefit analysis can be conducted to ensure that the benefit can be maximized. The 1987 Air Pollution Law does not, however, provide any guidance with regard to how the balance should be achieved. It is, therefore, not surprising that balance between environmental protection and economic development has tipped towards the latter and air quality could not be guaranteed under the 1987 Air Pollution Law.

Given that economic and technological considerations have at least equal weight as air quality, it is not surprising either that the provisions on enforcement in the 1987 Air Pollution Law are also very weak. The first requirement is to report. It is provided that polluters that discharge air pollutants must, pursuant to the provisions of the central EPB, report to the local EPB their existing discharge and treatment facilities for pollutants and the categories, quantities and concentrations of pollutants discharged under normal operation conditions. The polluters are required to submit to the same local EPB the relevant technical data concerning the prevention and control of air pollution.[26] If the discharge of pollutants exceeds the prescribed standards, the polluters need to take effective measures to control the pollution and pay a fee for excessive discharge according to state provisions. It may be argued that the polluters can still discharge pollutants even if the standards are exceeded provided that they pay the required fees. Only if an enterprise or institution causes severe atmospheric pollution, shall it be ordered to eliminate and control the pollution within a certain period of time,[27] but the term of serious pollution is not defined in the 1987 Air Pollution Law. That will make the enforcement of this provision extremely difficult and it is very likely not to be enforced effectively.[28] It may, therefore, be argued that discharge of pollutants is always allowed.

As to specific measures for combatting air pollution, the 1987 Air Pollution Law, together with the detailed rules for its implementation passed by the State Council in 1991, has few such provisions. One measure adopted under the 1987 Air Pollution Law is about soot discharged from boilers and industrial kilns. The focus is on technical requirements. It is provided that the department concerned shall, according to soot discharge standards, stipulate corresponding requirements in boiler quality standards. Those boilers which do not meet the prescribed requirements shall not be permitted to be manufactured, sold or imported.[29] This statutory requirement is only targeted at newly-built or newly-installed industrial kilns and boilers. As far as existing ones are concerned, there are no effective provisions at all. It is only mentioned that various measures should be taken by the relevant departments under the State Council and the local people's governments to improve the urban fuel structure, gas supply and the production and utilization of shaped coal.[30] Those provisions do not have much teeth.

As far as air pollution caused by sulphur is concerned, the 1987 Air Pollution Law did mention the installation of desulphurization equipment though that requirement is limited to units which refine petroleum, produce synthetic ammonia or coal gas, coke fuel coal and smelt non-ferrous metal.[31] It also promoted the use of shaped coal as a principle though no detailed plan was outlined in the 1987 Air Pollution Law as to how the principle should be implemented.[32]

Apart from those, the 1987 Air Pollution Law is mainly silent on other aspects of pollution caused by coal burning. No other measures were incorporated in the legislation to control air pollution such as the quality of coal, *i.e.* whether the density of sulphur should be reduced from coal excavated in certain regions or whether its consumption should be discouraged, coal washing, the adoption of a permit system, pollution charge for discharge of any air pollutants and so on.

It is, therefore, fair to draw the conclusion that the political decision in 1987 was not strong enough to stop the deterioration of air pollution in China. Benefit-cost analysis was required by the 1987 Air Pollution Law to ensure that economic development would not be hindered even at the price of decrease in air quality. The weakness of the 1987 Air Pollution Law has been realized by the central EPB. That has led to the EPB Proposals and finally the 1995 Amendments. The next part of the paper will examine both of them and a comparison of the two will be made to see whether or not the EPB Proposals or the 1995 Amendments may stop the trend of air quality deterioration.

Analysis and Comparison of the EPB Proposals with the 1995 Amendments

Being aware of the deteriorating air quality situation and lack of effective measures in the 1987 Air Pollution Law, the central EPB proposed many changes to the 1987 Air Pollution Law by suggesting about 20 new articles and amendments to many existing ones. The major changes include provisions on coal washing and processing, production and utilization of shaped coal, the installation of desulphurization equipments, the adoption of a permit system, pollution fee charge system, and control of automobile pollution.[33] All had proven to be controversial throughout the legislative process, and each of them, together with the reasons for such a proposal and its pros and cons, will be examined in the following paragraphs.

Coal Washing and Processing

As mentioned before, coal burning is the major source of air pollution, releasing soot and SO_2 pollution, and SO_2 pollution is getting so desperate that it has to be dealt with.[34] China has rich coal resources, however. China's Agenda 21, the blueprint for environmental protection into the twenty-first century, states clearly coal will continue to be China's main source of energy for a long time in the future, and both the output of coal and the sulphur content in coal resources will increase.[35] Under such circumstances, one measure which may reduce soot and SO_2 pollution is coal washing. It may help decrease the contents of fly ash and sulphur in the coal and eventually their emission into air.

The current picture is that it has been China's state policy since the early 1980s to encourage coal washing and processing[36] and several regulations have been adopted.[37] At present, however, only about 18 per cent of the coal produced in China is actually washed, which could merely meet the need to refine coke coal. It has been estimated that to increase the percentage of washed coal to 35 per cent will require investment of RMB 14 billion. At the moment, neither the state government nor the enterprises are willing to make that investment. It is because environmental protection is still not regarded as a priority. In fact, most of the coal used by power plants, about 800 million tons, is still raw coal. The central EPB has strongly argued for coal washing. Its report argues that about 20 per cent of coal produced in China has high sulphur content (where sulphur exceeds 3 per cent), and sulphur in majority of the coal with high sulphur content is in an inorganic form which can be removed through a washing process.[38] It is, therefore, feasible to plan coal washing and processing for that 20 per cent as a priority. If that can be done, SO_2 emission will be dramatically reduced. The equipments and technologies for coal washing process has matured and been commercialized in China. Moreover, coal washing will also bring apparent economic benefits.[39] Based on these considerations, the Central EPB proposed to add the following article:[40]

"The state encourages the development of coal washing process, the reduction of fly ash and sulphur contents of coal, and the restriction on the extraction of coal with high content of fly ash and sulphur. After the adoption of these amendments, the newly built coal mines which produce coal of which the fly ash and sulphur contents exceed national standards must install necessary accessary coal washing equipments to reduce the fly ash and sulphur contents in the coal so as to reach the national standard.

For those coal mines which are already in existence before the promulgation of the amendments, the environmental protection bureau of local government should set a time limit for the installation of coal washing equipments. For the coal which cannot meet the standards after washing, the relevant local government should restrict its excavation or set a time limit for the closure of the excavation."

Various counter arguments against the proposed article were raised by the State Council, local governments and enterprises. They can be summarized as follows.[41] First, it is argued that organic sulphur in coal cannot be removed through washing. There does not exist any feasible technology in China which is also reasonable economically to remove organic sulphur in coal.⁴² Secondly, there still exist technological problems. In some places, the sulphur content in coal is still as high as three or four per cent even after washing.⁴² Thirdly, use of washed coal leads to another problem, *i.e.* the adjustment of existing furnaces because existing furnaces are designed to use raw coal. Changes may have to be made in order to use washed coal, which need large amounts of investment. Those enterprises concerned would not be able to bear such cost if the state government does not provide funding. Fourthly, the coal with high sulphur content is mainly produced in southwest China, *e.g.* Guizhou Province, where it is very hilly. Even drinking water supply is very difficult to guarantee, let alone the supply of sufficient water for coal washing. Fifthly, the production cost for one ton of washed coal will increase by 15 to 20 yuan, which is about 25 to 40 per cent increase of the price for one ton of raw coal. That may make it difficult to sell washed coal as the supply of coal in Guizhou is mainly for the use of local enterprises and families, which normally opt for cheap fuel. Sixthly, about half of the coal produced in Guizhou Province is from small township coal mines, which is more or less the same throughout the country. Now it is even difficult for state-owned large coal mines to install coal washing equipment. It is bound to be more difficult to require small coal mines to install washing equipment. To do so may simply force them to close down. Finally, coal washing will produce coal soil. It may become a new kind of solid waste as it cannot be utilized and is also very difficult to dry.

The EPB proposal says that the excavation of coal should be limited or stopped if the national standards for sulphur content can not be reached after washing. That means those mines have to be closed down, which will cause a series of problems such as the employment issue, *i.e.* resettlement of the redundant employees, and social problems and so on. Without a satisfactory system of social insurance, it is unlikely that the Chinese Government will make such a radical decision for the sake of environmental protection.

Despite the existence of opposition, the 1995 Amendments have incorporated the coal washing requirements and the provisions are rather similar to those proposed by the Central EPB.⁴³ There are, however, two main changes. The first is that the standards for newly-built mines are different. The Central EPB proposes the compliance with the national standards while the 1995 Amendments state that "the prescribed standards" have to be met. Here "the prescribed standards" will be set by the State Council which has to balance different kinds of interests in setting the standards for sulphur content. The second difference is for existing coal mines. Under the EPB Proposals, the Central EPB has the authority to set the schedule for the implementation of coal washing and processing, but the 1995 Amendments provide that the schedule, still to be made by the EPB, has to be approved by the State Council. It would not be surprising if economic consideration is taken into account in setting the schedule for implementation. It is quite obvious that the two changes in essence have shifted the final decision-making authority from the Central EPB to the State Council. The State Council is in charge of all ministries. Apart from environmental protection, economic development is its most important task. It is, therefore, quite natural that the need for environmental protection will be compromised by the need for economic development.

Use of Shaped Coal

The Central EPB has also proposed to replace raw coal with shaped coal in order to reduce fly ash and SO_2 emission. Under the EPB Proposals, domestic kitchen ranges in urban areas are required to use shaped coal or other clean fuel. Use of raw coal will be directly prohibited. Similarly, industrial furnaces and kilns are also required to use shaped coal or other clean fuel.[45]

Many different opinions were expressed during the legislative process. In summary,[46] the general feeling is that the EPB proposal is very difficult to implement because there are some thorny issues which need to be tackled for the use of shaped coal. The first issue relates to the improvement of existing industrial furnaces and kilns which need technology and money, neither of them may be available.[47] Secondly, the price for shaped coal will be RMB 10 higher than raw coal per ton, which is difficult for enterprises to bear. Thirdly, the supply of shaped coal at present may not be guaranteed. It has been pointed out by several power plants that they are not using shaped coal and do not know whether or not there would be sufficient supply of shaped coal if they are all going to change to use shaped coal.[48] Moreover, even if the supply of shaped coal can be guaranteed, another more important issue is whether high quality steel can be produced with shaped coal. It is very unlikely for them to change to shaped coal if the answer is unsatisfactory. As far as the use for domestic kitchen ranges is concerned, raw coal is the main source of energy supply because the supply of shaped coal is still not available in many remote cities and townships due to insufficient funding, transportation problems and increased cost. Therefore, it is difficult for urban districts to stop using coal of which the sulphur content exceeds state standards as required by the proposed amendments.

The 1995 Amendments have nevertheless incorporated a provision on the use of shaped coal, but its scope of application is extremely limited.[49] First, the use of shaped coal is only applicable in cities of large or medium size; secondly, it is limited to domestic kitchen ranges, not industrial furnaces and kilns; thirdly, even for kitchen ranges, it is a gradual phasing out rather than strict prohibition as suggested by the EPB proposal.

Installation of Desulphurization Equipments

Of the pollution caused by coal burning, SO_2 is the most serious. It leads to acid rain, causing various health problems and huge economic losses. At present, about one-third of SO_2 emission comes from power plants.[50] In order to reduce SO_2 pollution, the EPB proposed that the EPB should be empowered to designate acid rain control zones. Power plants and other enterprises of large or medium size within the designated zones should, according to the requirements of local EPB, set up desulphurization equipment or adopt other measures to control SO_2 emission.[51] The installation of desulphurization equipment is no doubt the trend of development for power plants and enterprises of large and medium size, especially in the areas which have been designated as acid rain control zones or where SO_2 pollution is very serious. It has been pointed out that there are practical difficulties with regard to installation of desulphurization equipment as required. The current scenario is that most power plants have not installed such equipment. If they are required to do so, a large amount of investment will be required. The estimated figure is about five billion. Such a financial burden can hardly be born by the enterprises, of which most are not even profit-making.[52] It has been maintained that strict enforcement of the proposed requirements will not only hinder the development of the energy sector but even force many existing power plants out of business.[53] Furthermore, the desulphurization technology in China is still not that satisfactory and the installation of state-of-the-art desulphurization equipment will need a piece of land even larger than that which the main plant occupies. That will raise a series of issues such as the availability of land, the acquisition of land, the funding for the acquisition of land and so on.[54] The solution to all those issues will finally come down to the issue of funding, *i.e.* where the money will come from.

While incorporating the requirement to install desulphurization equipment, the 1995 Amendments have made a few changes to the EPB Proposals. The first is that designation of acid control zones needs the approval of State Council. The second is about the installation of desulphurization equipment. The 1995 Amendments only provide that installation of desulphurization equipment is compulsory for newly built plants. As far as existing ones are concerned, the 1995 Amendments are much more lenient and only require them to adopt control measures and encourage them to adopt advanced technology.[55] Such provisions are flexible and unlikely to have any impact upon existing enterprises.

Implementation of Permit System and Pollution Fee

Though the emission permit system was not incorporated in the 1987 Air Pollution Law, it has been used on trial basis for air pollution control since 1987.[56] It was also discussed in 1989 when the Environmental Protection Law was made final.[57] The EPB Proposal argues that its statistics have shown that permit system has proved to be effective. One example given by the Central EPB is that one city has actually shown a reduction in SO_2 density by 32.5 per cent after the emission permit system had been in force for one year.[58]

The essence of the permit system is to control the total amount of pollutant emitted into the environment. The ideal scenario is that the total amount of pollutants emitted into the environment is within the self-purification capacity of the air. It is impossible for China to achieve that target at the moment though that is the objective. What China is doing now is to set the target amount according to economic conditions or feasibility, not purely according to the self-purification capacity of air or the need for public health.[59] Once the target amount is set, quota will then be allocated to enterprises.[60] The Central EPB believes it is feasible to adopt a permit system for air pollution and provides in its proposals that polluters must, according to stipulations, apply to the relevant local EPB for a permit in order to emit air pollutants and emit pollutants according to the stipulated kinds, amount, density, method and time as specified in the permit.[61]

That proposal met opposition.[62] The main reasons are as follows. Firstly, it is argued that such a provision in law is meaningless if it cannot be implemented in practice. For example, the Guiyang power plant was allowed to emit three tons of SO_2 in 1993, but it actually emitted five tons.[63] There were two ways for it to achieve the target of three tons. One was to improve the out-of-date technology. As the power plant is a state-owned enterprise, it means that investment has to come from the government, but the government was not willing to make that investment. The other was to reduce the production of electricity, which would affect local economic development and, therefore, was not allowed by the local government. That is to say, such a provision on a permit is very unlikely to be enforced strictly owing to the two reasons mentioned above. Moreover, facilities in most township enterprises, which are the backbone of China's economic development, are quite rudimentary and it is difficult for them to meet the emission standards. Hence, if the requirements under the permit will be strictly enforced, local economy will be seriously affected.[64] That is not something local governments are willing to do.

The second argument is that ancillary measures for the implementation of a permit system are not satisfactory. It is because the basis of a permit system is total amount control which is determined by the self-purification capacity of air, but it is difficult to evaluate exactly the capacity of air. That is to say, the total amount of pollutant which may be allowed to be emitted cannot be figured out scientifically. If that is the case, it will be difficult to provide for emission quota for enterprises concerned. Moreover, the technologies to measure the density and various kinds of air pollutants are not available, and China is still in the transitional period from control of the density of pollutants to control of total amount of pollutants. Under such a situation, the adoption of permit system may still need time.[65] Thirdly, it may also duplicate other mechanisms such as environmental impact assessment and the reporting system, and increase the burden of enterprises.[66] These opposing arguments must have influenced the final decision of the Standing Committee of the NPC because the permit system proposed by the EPB was dropped from the 1995 Amendments.

As far as payment of pollution fee is concerned, the 1987 Air Pollution Law provided that a fee would only need to be paid for discharged pollutants exceeding the prescribed standards.[67] The Central EPB argues that such a provision is no longer adequate to curb air quality deterioration because the amount of pollutants emitted within the prescribed standards far exceeds the amount emitted exceeding the standards,[68] therefore, it proposes to levy fees for any air pollutants emitted regardless of whether they are within or outside the prescribed standards. It has been argued that such suggestions have in fact been tried in certain areas and proved to be effective. It is also maintained that payment of fees for any pollutant emitted is an important measure to ensure the harmonious development of environment and economy.[69]

The EPB proposal has not won the support of those with vested interests. The first counter argument is that the proposal has broadened the scope for levying pollution fees and will increase dramatically the burden on the enterprises concerned.[70] The second argument is that such a charge will not have any positive effect on the motivation of enterprises to control pollution as they have to pay fees anyway. As a result, such a change may discourage enterprise to take positive measures to control pollution. Moreover, it is also unreasonable to levy a pollution charge if the emission standards have already been achieved. It is because of this the setting of emission standards will become meaningless.

These arguments seem to have merits in them for two reasons. The first is that one is very likely to be more motivated to reduce emission of pollutants so as to remain within the standards if one knows that no fee needs to be paid once one keeps emission within the standards. The second one is that there does seem to exist alternatives to levying fees for emission of any pollutants regardless of whether they are within or outside prescribed standards. For example, to increase the standards accordingly can achieve the same objective.

Pollution from Mobile Sources

The main mobile source of pollution is emission from automobiles. Currently, there are about nine million vehicles in China. Most of them exceed the emission standards. Even for newly manufactured vehicles, only about 40 per cent of them reach the emission standards. As new vehicles are increasing annually at the rate of 1.1 million, it is not surprising that air pollution caused by emission from automobiles is getting worse and worse. In fact, it has been realized that emission from automobiles has caused serious air pollution in cities such as Beijing, Shanghai, Guangzhou, Shenzhen and many other cities.[70]

It happens not because of lack of legal provisions. In fact, article 30 of the 1987 Air Pollution Law provides that:

> "Motorized vehicles and vessels shall not be permitted to discharge atmospheric pollutants in excess of the prescribed discharge standards; measures shall be taken to deal with motorized vehicles and vessels that discharge atmospheric pollutants in excess of the prescribed discharge standards. Automobiles that discharge pollutants in excess of the national discharge standards shall not be permitted to be manufactured, sold or imported. Specific measures for supervision and management shall be formulated by the State Council."

Shortly after that, new emission standards were set for vehicles in 1989. One year later, a regulation was promulgated by the EPB, together with some other relevant departments, on supervision and management of pollution emitted from vehicles (1990 Regulation). At that time, only 50 per cent of vehicles in China met the prescribed standards, but reduction of the emission of pollutants from automobiles was not considered as a priority by relevant government departments and enterprises. As a result, no measures had been taken to improve the technology in order to reduce the emission of pollutants from automobiles. Even worse, it has been reported that when technologies are imported for automobile manufacturing, those on emission reduction were deliberately not imported.[72] When the time came to draft amendments to the 1987 Air Pollution Law in 1994, still only 50 per cent of newly manufactured vehicles met emission standards.

The EPB Proposals have merely incorporated the similar provisions from the 1990 Regulation and inspection should be made with regard to all vehicles. For new ones, if standards are not met, they should not be manufactured or sold. For those in use, they should no longer be used if standards are not met. The Central EPB believes its proposal is feasible. China's emission standards are 20 years behind developed countries where technology is available for the reduction of pollutant emission from automobiles. Furthermore, Beijing has been cited by the Central EPB as an example to show that emission from automobiles can be controlled effectively in a short period of time.[73]

The proposal met strong opposition from manufacturers of vehicles. It is argued that the main reason for the emission in excess of standards is due to the old-fashioned engines used for the vehicles manufactured in China. The innovation of engines needs a large amount of investment and time. Even in developed countries, the improvement of one kind of technology normally needs four to five years. It will be impractical to stop manufacturing or selling of vehicles as suggested by the Central EPB immediately after the promulgation of the 1995 Amendments.[74]

The EPB request to tighten the requirements on emissions from automobiles is not incorporated into the 1995 Amendments. That seems to have gone to another extreme. Nevertheless, the 1995 Amendments do have one provision aiming at reduction of pollution from automobiles, *i.e.* the provision on the elimination of leaded petrol. The added provision stipulates that the State encourages and supports the production and use of high grade unleaded petrol, and restricts the production and use of leaded petrol. The relevant department in charge under State Council should plan to reduce gradually the production of leaded petrol and eventually stop the production and use of leaded petrol.[75] Such a provision will certainly help, but cannot solve the problem of worsening of air pollution in cities caused by emission from vehicles.

Adoption of Effective Technology

Another main amendment to the 1987 Air Pollution Law is the provision on the adoption of energy-effective and clean facilities and technological processes, including several detailed requirements.[76] The first requirement is for enterprises to adopt as a priority energy-effective and clean technological processes which emit fewer pollutants. The second requirement is that the State shall adopt an elimination system for out-of-date facilities and technological processes which seriously pollute the environment. The third requirement is that a list of facilities and technological processes, which seriously pollute air and will be prohibited or a time limit will be set for their prohibition, will be promulgated by the department in charge of the economy together with other relevant departments under the State Council. The fourth requirement is that all producers, sellers and

401

importers of those facilities or technological processes should stop producing, selling or importing within the prescribed time limit. The fifth requirement is that those phased-out facilities or technological processes are not allowed to be transferred to any third parties. If anybody breaches any of those requirements, he will be ordered to rectify the situation or temporarily stop business or close down completely depending on the seriousness of the breach. Compared with the EPB proposal, several changes are made. The 1995 Amendments delete the requirement of the use of lower energy consumption technology. It replaces complete restriction with gradual elimination of out-of-date facilities or technological processes on the list which cause serious air pollution.

Conclusion

After lengthy discussion of the original proposals of the EPB and their comparison with the 1995 Amendments, the following conclusion can be drawn. The analysis of the 1987 Air Pollution Law shows that that piece of legislation failed to curb air quality deterioration for two main reasons. One is the lack of specific or effective measures to control air pollutants. The other is more fundamental, *i.e.* the inherent necessity to balance environmental protection with economic development. The lack of guidance in the 1987 Air Pollution Law as to how the balance should be struck has tipped the balance to economic development for years.

The examination and comparison of the EPB Proposals with the 1995 Amendments shows that the Central EPB did propose some specific measures targeting the two most serious sources of air pollution, *i.e.* coal burning and emissions from automobiles. Some proposed measures are, mainly due to the problems of technological feasibility and economic affordability, dropped out of the 1995 Amendments. Others, such as coal washing and adoption of clean facilities, etc. have been incorporated into the 1995 Amendments. The comparison reveals clearly that those measures adopted in the 1995 Amendments appear in a much watered-down version. The outstanding feature is that State Council has been given the authority under some provisions to make the final decision. That means the final balance between environmental protection and economic development will be made by the State Council in carrying out those specific measures. It would not be surprising if its decision will be tipped to economic development given that its attitude was clearly leaning towards economic development during the legislative process of the 1995 Amendments as exposed through the above analysis.

Despite the changes adopted by the 1995 Amendments, *i.e.* those specific measures, the 1995 Amendments did not make any change to article 1 of the 1987 Air Pollution Law which sets the bottom line of the whole legislation — the balance among several factors, especially economic development and environmental protection, is required. Even if balance between environmental protection and economic development had not been required under those specific measures incorporated in the 1995 Amendments, the implementation of those specific measures is nevertheless governed by article 1. That means balance still needs to be considered.

Whether or not the 1995 Amendments will be effective really depends on how the balance will be struck as it is required in the implementation of those adopted measures and under article 1. This paper argues, therefore, that the 1995 Amendments are still fundamentally flawed, the same as the 1987 Air Pollution Law, because it did not address at all the issue as to how the balance between environmental protection and economic development should be struck and no guidance is provided in the 1995 Amendments. This paper does not try to argue against the necessity of balance. Instead, it is the author's belief that it would be unrealistic for a developing country like China to enact environmental legislation solely on public health considerations while millions of people still do not have enough food to feed themselves. But clear guidance as to how the balance should be achieved needs to be provided in such a basic legislation as Air Pollution Law or its amendments. Otherwise, the implementation of the 1995 Amendments may well fall into the old trap as under the 1987 Air Pollution Law whenever the balance is required.

Notes

[1] See newspaper report, "There Will Be Major Amendments to Air Pollution Law", People's Daily (overseas edition), p.3, 2 September 1995.
[2] In international environmental law, scholars started to debate the relationship between economic development and environmental protection at least from the Stockholm Conference in 1972 when the concept of sustainable development was raised, and the debate had attracted worldwide attention by 1991 when the Earth Summit was held in Rio de Janeiro on Environment and Development.
[3] See article 1 of 1987 Air Pollution Law.
[4] Apart from this objective, it also has several other objectives such as protecting and improving people's environment and the ecological environment, safeguarding human health, and promoting the development of socialist modernization. See article 1 of 1987 Air Pollution Law.
[5] For details, see the EPB submitted report to the NPC on "the Air Pollution Situation in China and Some Proposals on the Amendments to the Air Pollution Law.
[6] For detailed description, see above n.5.

[7] See above n.5, p.2.
[8] According to China's Agenda 21, this situation in China is unlikely to change in the near future as China has rich resource in coal and will definitely rely on it for the foreseeable future. See China's Agenda 21 (English Version), published by China Environmental Science Press, 1994, Beijing, paragraph 13.38 & 13.39, p.130.
[9] See above n.5, p.2.
[10] *ibid.*
[11] The five cities are Beijing, Shenyang, Xian, Shanghai and Guangzhou. See above n.5, p.2.
[12] See above n.5, p.2.
[13] *ibid.*
[14] See Bonine and McGarity, *The Law of Environmental Protection*, (2nd ed.), West Publisher, p.377.
[15] See above n.14, pp.379–380.
[16] *ibid.*
[17] Socialist modernization includes four modernization, one of which is economic modernization meaning economic development.
[18] Air pollution legislation in the U.S. is one of the examples.
[19] See article 6 of 1987 Air Pollution Law.
[20] See Professor Jin Ruilin, Environmental Law, chapter 8, Peking University Press, 1990.
[21] See paragraph 1 of article 7 of 1987 Air Pollution Law.
[22] See paragraph 2 of article 7 of 1987 Air Pollution Law.
[23] In the U.S., a different concept is used, *i.e.* ambient air quality standards instead of emission standards. How they should be set is clearly expressed in s. 50.2 of the Clean Air Act:

> "(b) National primary ambient air quality standards define levels of air quality which the Administrator judges are necessary, with an adequate margin of safety, to protect the public health. National secondary ambient air quality standards define levels of air quality which the Administrator judges necessary to protect the public welfare from any known or anticipated adverse effects of a pollutant. Such standards are subject to revision, and additional primary and secondary standards may be promulgated as the Administrator deems necessary to protect the public health and welfare.
> (c) the promulgation of national primary and secondary ambient air quality standards shall not be considered in any manner to allow significant deterioration of existing air quality in any portion of any State."

[24] One witness even argued that technological feasibility should be the sole basis of emission standards. Whereas Senator Muskie said that:

> "It seems to me that we may have to force uneconomic policies or close down industries in particular locations that don't have a technological answer to the problem. . . . [I]t seems to me that to tie ourselves purely and simply to the idea of moving only as fast as somebody judges economically and technologically feasible is not going to get us the results we need in terms of the public health."

For details, see above n.14, pp.379–381.
[25] See Thompson, *Margin of Safety as a Risk Management Concept in Environmental Legislation*, 6 Columbia Journal of Environmental Law, 1, 22 (1979), p.26.

404

26 See article 10 of 1987 Air Pollution Law.
27 See article 11 of 1987 Air Pollution Law.
28 Amendments have been suggested by the central EPB in this aspect.
29 See article 17 of 1987 Air Pollution Law.
30 See article 20 of the 1987 Air Pollution Law.
31 See article 24 of 1987 Air Pollution Law.
32 See article 20 of 1987 Air Pollution Law and article 17 of the detailed rules for its implementation.
33 For details, please refer to "The Comparative Chart of the articles of the Law on Prevention and Control of Atmospheric Pollution before and after the Proposed Amendments". It is a comparative study prepared by the Legislative Affairs Commission of the National People's Congress.
34 Please refer to section two of this paper on air pollution situation in China.
35 China's Agenda 21 is made with the intention of implementing the Agenda 21 adopted at the 1991 United Nations Conference on Environment and Development for the protection of international environment. For details, see China's Agenda 21 (English version), p.130.
36 See above n.5, p.3.
37 Those regulations include: 1982 Instruction from State Council on Saving Coal Use from Industrial Furnaces, 1984 Provisions from State Council on the Policy on Technology relating to Control and Prevention of Pollution Caused by Coal, and so on.
38 This point is argued by the central EPB. But it is not mentioned in No.79 Report on Legal Work prepared by the LAC of NPC, entitled "Main Opinions on Amendments to Air Pollution Law from Local Governments, Departments and Enterprises". The soundness of this argument needs further investigation.
39 See above n.5, p.4.
40 See above n.34.
41 These are the parties who are concerned more about economic development than environmental protection.
42 It is not clear what is the percentage of organic sulphur in coal compared with inorganic sulphur and further investigation needs to be carried out.
43 See above n.5, p.4.
44 The incorporated provision is as follows:

> "The State promotes coal washing and processing, the reduction of fly ash and sulphur contents of coal, and the restriction on excavation of coal with high content of fly ash and sulphur. Newly-built coal mines which produce coal of high contents of fly ash and sulphur must install necessary accessary coal washing equipments to ensure that prescribed standards are met.
>
> Those mines already built, which produce coal of high content of fly ash and sulphur, should, according to the schedule approved by the State Council, install necessary accessary coal washing equipments with limited time."

45 See article 32 of the EPB Proposals, above n.34.
46 See comment made on article 32 in Comparison, above no.34; see also above n.39, pp.5–7.
47 See above n.5, pp.5–7.
48 They need about one-third of national coal production, see above n.5.
49 The added article provides that:

> "People's Governments in cities of large and medium sizes shall make plans to set a time limit to realize the use of shaped coal or other clean

fuel by domestic kitchen ranges in urban areas and gradually replace direct use of raw coal."

[50] See above n.5, p.5.
[51] See paragraph 2 of article 35 of EPB Proposal, above n.34.
[52] *E.g* the Guiyang power plant.
[53] See above n.5, pp.7–8.
[54] See above n.5, pp.7–9.
[55] See article 27 of the amended Air Pollution Law.
[56] The trial of the permit system started with 18 cities and two provinces in 1987 with water pollution, and 16 cities with emission of air pollutants. Up to now, 192 have established permit system for emission of pollutants.
[57] Before 1989, the Environmental Protection Law was on trial and was made final after two years of trial. At that time, the general feeling was that more experience was needed before the incorporation of a permit system into legislation.
[58] See above n.5, p.8.
[59] *ibid.*
[60] *ibid.*
[61] See article 15 of EPB Proposals, above n.34.
[62] It is mainly opposed by the State Council, local government, relevant governmental departments and enterprises, all which have vested interests.
[63] See above n.5, p.11.
[64] See above n.5, p.12.
[65] See above n.5, p.13.
[66] *ibid.*
[67] See article 11 of 1987 Air Pollution Law.
[68] On the other hand, it may well prove to be the case that the prescribed standards are too low. The increase of the standards may be an alternative.
[69] See above n.5, p.9.
[70] See above n.5, p.14.
[71] See above n.5, p.6.
[72] *ibid.*
[73] It is stated by the EPB that in Beijing, the owners of vehicles are first required to report the emission of their vehicles. Statistics showed that only 50 per cent of vehicles met the emission standards; then a regulation was passed saying that vehicles exceeding emission standards are not allowed to be sold in Beijing. As a result, the statistics in 1994 showed that 90% of vehicles reported met the standards. The credibility of this statistics remains doubtful. See above n.5, p.7.
[74] See above n.5, p.9.
[75] See article 28 of the Amended Air Pollution Law.
[76] See article 15 of the Amended Air Pollution Law.

COMMON LAW, COMMON SENSE
AND THE ENVIRONMENT
IN HONG KONG

Bryan Bachner

Faculty of Law
City University of Hong Kong

Bryan Bachner *is a graduate of Tufts University and the Washington College of Law at The American University. He is an assistant professor of law at the City University of Hong Kong and the chairman of the Hong Kong Environmental Law Association. He is the Managing Editor of the Asia Pacific Law Review. His principal research interests are environmental law and comparative environmental law.*

Due to the state's implementation of a laissez-faire economic policy with little concern for the considerable pollution costs that have resulted, the deterioration of Hong Kong's environment has become serious. In response to this ecological problem, the current government has committed considerable human and financial resources to attempt to manage the social costs associated with the economic by-product of pollution.[1] In particular the government has, despite its avowed policy of "passive non-interventionism", established an extensive public regulatory regime that sets out environmental legal standards and the enforcement mechanisms to ensure that these standards are met.

Whilst public law remedies remain the primary tool for implementing environmental standards in the territory, they are not the only ones. In addition to the regulatory framework of pollution control, private law remedies arising out of the common law are also available. In light of the grim nature of the environmental problem in Hong Kong, it seems all the more necessary to explore all realistic legal alternatives to *supplement* the public legal system. Regrettably, analysis and application of the common law approaches to environmental protection in Hong Kong has been inadequate.

The purpose of this paper is to try to begin to come to terms with why the common law measures concerning environmental protection have not been considered and applied satisfactorily in Hong Kong. In the first part of the paper I will set out a basic framework of the common law system of Hong Kong in order to provide background to understand how private law remedies to pollution control may be more effectively used. In the second part I will survey the common law approaches to environmental protection. In the third part I will explore why these legal measures have been insufficiently applied in Hong Kong.

Evolution of the Common Law in Hong Kong

In this section I will comment upon the present and future constitutional underpinning for the common law in Hong Kong, especially in light of 1997. I will also discuss the judicial structure, whose role it is to interpret and apply the common law.

Constitutional Basis

In light of 1997 and the transition from a British-oriented form of governance to a Chinese form of governance, which promises to maintain a "free market" system in Hong Kong, an appreciation of Hong Kong's common law origins becomes all the more relevant to help understand the present and future application of that law.

Great Britain acquired the island of Hong Kong through the Treaty of Nanking, which, according to British law, is a treaty of cession. It was signed on August 29, 1842. According to British principles of constitutional law, when the government takes power over a territory via a treaty of cession, the authority to administer the territory vests in the executive arm of the British Government unless Parliament had promulgated a law specifically designating a different form of government over the territory.[2] As no act of Parliament had been passed with the intention of forming a special government in Hong Kong, the monarch necessarily became responsible for organizing the government. In accordance with the prerogative powers retained by the British monarch under British constitutional law, the Queen provided the constitutional guidance on how Hong Kong's government was to operate. This guidance was summarized in two documents, namely the Letters Patent and the Royal Instructions.

In addition to establishing the constitutional framework of Hong Kong through the Letters Patent and the Royal Instructions, Great Britain decided that the English legal system, in particular the common law would be imported into the territory. This transference of law was legitimized through the the enactment of section 5 of Hong Kong's

Supreme Court Ordinance 1873. It stated that all English law which existed on April 5, 1843 would be incorporated into Hong Kong's legal system. In other words the Ordinance excluded all Acts of Parliament passed after April 5, 1843 from implementation in Hong Kong, unless the British Act specifically stated that it should apply to Hong Kong. An alternative approach to the importation of English law into Hong Kong would arise if Hong Kong legislation expressly stipulated that a British Act is applicable in Hong Kong. In consideration of the fundamental legal and economic differences between Great Britain and Hong Kong, the law stated that all English law considered inappropriate for the circumstances of Hong Kong or its inhabitants would not be applicable in Hong Kong's jurisdiction.

Although the application of the British legislation to Hong Kong was restricted by a specific date, the implementation of the common law, by virtue of its legal nature, could not be. The common law could not be restricted by an artificial date because the common law, through the interpretation of the judges, reveals that law that already exists; in other words exclusion of the common law based on time would be logically impossible because the role of the courts is to report the common law that has always existed but had yet been expressed. Some rules restricting the application of common law, nevertheless, were used by the Hong Kong courts. For instance, the general rule followed by the courts was that the common law decisions could be applied in Hong Kong unless specific local circumstances restricted the application.

While this process did allow Hong Kong to enjoy the advantage of the use of the common law that was specifically relevant to local circumstances, the law itself became tangled in the inconsistencies arising from its own rules of application. The difficulties stemmed specifically from the designation of the artificial cut-off date of April 5, 1843. For instance the Hong Kong courts could find it problematic to apply a post-1843 common law decision from the courts of England which considered British legislation that was enacted prior to 1843 (which would make the common law applicable to Hong Kong) but had, since 1843, been repealed by Parliament. The difficulty for the Hong Kong courts was determining whether that common law should have authority in Hong Kong even if it were based on a piece of legislation that had been abolished in Britain.

In order to try to clarify this murky situation, section 3(1) of the Application of the English Law Ordinance 1966 was enacted. It stated that English common law and the rules of equity shall apply in Hong Kong if they are relevant to the local context or modified as necessary. The situation, however, was still unsatisfactory as changes in the common law that had not accounted for the Hong Kong situation could still technically be imposed upon Hong Kong.[3] As a result the Application of the English Law Ordinance was amended again in order to prevent the occurrence of the imposition of English common law based on British legislation that had no authority in Hong Kong. As mentioned, courts, generally, will not apply English common law if its application would cause injustice or oppression.[4] It is to the structure of these courts that we will now turn our attention.

Judicial Structure[5]

The judiciary have the responsibility of applying the common law. In order to understand the application of the common law system in this court structure, it will be helpful to discuss the framework of the judiciary.

The judicial system of Hong Kong, by virtue of its common law foundations, is largely independent from other branches of government. The reason that this type of system is so important is that it assures that a judge may exercise his discretion impartially without undue influence from any party. The judge's autonomy is not explicitly protected by any regulation; indeed the court's independence has been assured only through convention and the recognition by the executive and legislative branch that the court *should* be treated independently. Additional factors such as reasonably permanent appointments, personal immunity and a substantial salary have all contributed to the maintenance of judicial independence in the territory.

In Hong Kong there are four primary levels of judges including the Magistracy, the District Court, the Supreme Court and the Privy Council.[6] At the first instance of the Hong Kong judicial system is the Magistrates Court.[7] The magistrates, for all intents and purposes, handle criminal cases, unlike the English system, where magistrates have substantial civil jurisdiction. The magistrates, nevertheless, handle many environmental cases. The magistrate sits alone and acts as judge and jury. Some cases can only be dealt with by the magistrate summarily[8] while other cases can only be dealt with on indictment. The maximum fine that a magistrate may impose is HK$10,000 and the maximum sentence two years.

An appeal from a decision by a magistrate will be heard by the High Court before only one judge. In Hong Kong, the High Court and the Court of Appeal are both situated in what is known as the Supreme Court. These appeals are not re-hearings but are a review of the case record and the magistrate's rationale for conviction. After due consideration a single High Court judge has the discretion to refer the appeal to the Court of Appeal if it is felt that the case raises important jurisprudential matters.

The High Court deals only with the most serious cases.[9] Trial is based on an indictment before a judge and jury. The jury is normally composed of seven but may include up to nine persons. Normally the jury is required to arrive at a unanimous decision, however, there is provision for a majority decision. Appeals from the High Court go directly to the Court of Appeal. The Crown cannot appeal an acquittal by jury but has the right to apply to the Court of Appeal to review a High Court sentence. Such appeals are normally based on questions of law.

The Court of Appeal only has appellate jurisdiction in criminal cases. Three judges will usually hear the cases. Decisions are based on majority views with dissenting opinions permitted. The Court of Appeal adopts the English system which involves an examination of the trial of the lower court, rather then an inquiry into guilt or innocence. Appeals from the Court of Appeal will go to the Privy Council in London until this power of appeal is transferred to a Final Court of Appeal to be based in Hong Kong. Either side may appeal a decision of the Court of Appeal but leave or permission is needed either by the Court of Appeal or by the Privy Council for the appeal to be heard by the Privy Council. Very few appeals reach the Privy Council.

In a legal status between the Supreme Court and the Magistracy sits the District Court. In the District Court the judge sits alone without a jury.[10] The District Court has the authority to imprison for up to seven years. The District Court is a court of first instance without appeal jurisdiction for a magistrate's decision. Prosecutions in the District Court are conducted by crown counsel or private barristers. Appeals from the District Court go to the Court of Appeals. Appeals normally are based on a question of law, or may with permission of the Court of Appeal, deal with an issue of fact or a mixture of law and fact.

Constitutional Nature, Post-1997

The Basic Law is the mini-constitution agreed upon by the United Kingdom and the People's Republic of China. It is the constitutional blueprint that will govern Hong Kong after 1997. For now it will be helpful to introduce some basic issues concerning how the *Basic Law* may impact upon the application of the common law in Hong Kong.

The common law has been recognized within the mini-constitution as an integral element to the Hong Kong system. According to article 2, the Basic Law promises to provide a "high degree of autonomy" to the Special Administrative Region and to allow the SAR government to "enjoy executive, legislative and independent judicial power". Also the Basic Law contains provisions for the protection of the common law tradition. Article 8 of the *Basic Law* provides that:

"The laws previously in force in Hong Kong, that is, the common law, rules of equity, ordinances, subordinate legislation and customary law shall be maintained, except for any that contravene this Law, and subject to any amendment by the legislature of the Hong Kong Special Administrative Region."[11]

Articles 80 to 96 specify the judicial structure. Article 82 establishes the replacement of the Privy Council by a Court of Final Appeal for the region, "which may as required invite judges from other common law jurisdictions to sit on the Court of Final Appeal".[12] According to article 84 the courts of the Hong Kong Special Administrative Region shall decide cases according to applicable laws and "may refer to precedents of other common law jurisdictions".[13]

The implementation of the Basic Law and its impact upon the common law, however, have not been free from controversy. The extent to which the Court of Final Appeal will maintain authority over constitutional affairs in Hong Kong and the extent to which the Standing Committee of the National People's Congress , the ultimate authority for interpretation of the national constitution, will exercise its authority over Hong Kong's constitution remains unsettled.[14] Part of the controversy stems from the unclear meaning of some of the words in the Basic Law. For instance, Article 19 of the Basic Law states that:

> "The courts of the Hong Kong Special Administrative Region shall have no jurisdiction over acts of state such as defence and foreign affairs. The courts of the Region shall obtain a certificate from the Chief Executive on questions of fact concerning acts of state such as defence and foreign affairs whenever such questions arise in the adjudication of cases."[15]

Clause 4, paragraph 4 of the Hong Kong Court of Final Appeal Ordinance 1995 adds that "before issuing such a certificate the Governor shall obtain a certifying document from the Government of the United Kingdom of Great Britain and Northern Ireland."[16]

The definition of an "act of state" is unclear and some are concerned that this ambiguity and others may be used to impose the National People's Congress's constitutional viewpoints arbitrarily on Hong Kong.[17] The Chief Justice of Hong Kong, however, remains sanguine. He states that:

> "While Article 158 vests power of interpretation of the Basic Law in the Standing Committee of the National People's Congress, the same article provides that the Standing Committee shall authorize the courts of the Hong Kong Special Administrative Region to interpret on their own, in adjudicating cases, the provisions of the Basic Law which are within the limits of the autonomy of the region."[18]

The Common Law and the Environment

The previous discussion of the constitutional background of the common law in Hong Kong and the nature of the judicial structure responsible for applying the common law provides a useful context for understanding the structure of the common law. This section will further explain how the common law itself relates to environmental protection.

On the whole, the common law concerning the environment involves private law actions. A private law action is distinguishable from a public law action in that public law actions usually arise from violation of specific legislation and standards which are enforced by public officials. Alternatively a private law action arises when an individual is harmed as a consequence of the defendant's action and the victim, or plaintiff, decides to sue the injurer for the harm he or she caused. In addition to private law actions, the common law to be discussed will involve the mechanisms available to hold authorities accountable for the decisions they are empowered to make through legislation relating to the environment.

Private Law Actions

Private Nuisance

Private nuisance is a wrong designed to protect a person's use or enjoyment of land from being adversely affected by the activities of his or her neighbours.[19] A claim for nuisance is founded upon a balancing of interests related to reasonableness. As the common law states:

> "The court must consider whether the defendant is using his property reasonably or not. If he is using it reasonably, there is nothing which at law can be considered a nuisance; but if he is not using it reasonably . . . then the plaintiff is entitled to relief."[20]

In determining whether a use is reasonable the court must consider three factors: the locality of the nuisance, the duration of the nuisance and any hypersensitivity on the part of the plaintiff.

Locality Doctrine — The locality doctrine obliges a judge to take into consideration the local conditions before determining whether a nuisance actually exists. As the common law states:

> "It does not follow that because I live, say, in the manufacturing part of Sheffield I cannot complain if a steam-hammer is introduced next door, and so worked as to render sleep at night almost impossible, although previously to its introduction my house was

a reasonably comfortable abode, having regard to the local standard; and it would be no answer to say that the steam hammer is of the most modern approved pattern and is reasonably worked. In short, if a substantial addition is found as a fact in any particular case, it is no answer to say that the neighbourhood is noisy and that the defendant's machinery is of first class character."[21]

The locality doctrine has been interpreted by the courts in two different ways. The first interpretation states that where there is any interference with property rights that is not trivial then there should be a right of action in private nuisance to prevent such interference with these rights.[22] The second interpretation states that the courts must balance the social utility of the action complained with the environmental harm caused by action before determining whether a private nuisance arises.[23]

Sensibility — Another factor that the judge must take into account when determining whether a nuisance has arisen is whether the nuisance can actually be *sensed*. Nuisance actions cannot be brought without proof of damage. Proof exists if it can be shown that nuisance can be sensed by reasonable members of the community.[24]

Duration of the Nuisance — Nuisance actions will be heard if it can be proven that the nuisance will last for more then just a temporary period of time.[25] The common law has determined that nuisances of a impermanent duration must largely be tolerated.

The hypersensitive plaintiff — The common law rule is that if a potential plaintiff is particularly sensitive to one type of nuisance then the nuisance will not be actionable. A nuisance will not arise unless it would have affected a "reasonable person".[26]

Trespass

The rule concerning trespass states that any unauthorized interference with a person's property is unlawful.[27] The interference with the right must be direct rather then consequential. Further, an act of trespass must be intentional or negligent. The difficult part about proving trespass is that a causal link between the directness of the act and the inevitability of its consequences must be proven.[28]

Whereas trespass may once have looked like an attractive remedy against water or air pollution, the House of Lords has since reduced the effectiveness of trespass actions against polluters. It was held by the House of Lords that oil dumped from a ship which landed on a downstream beach could not be trespass because, although the water flowed downstream, there was no "inevitability" about the deposit of oil onto the shore, a prerequisite for trespass, as the deposit itself depended on the action of wind, waves and tide.[29]

The Rule of Rylands v. Fletcher

The rule of *Rylands v. Fletcher*[30] is intended to prevent a person situated outside particular premises from being injured by the activities of an individual occupying those premises.[31] It originates in a case concerning the construction of a reservoir on the defendant's land. The contractor did not block off mines shafts below the land with the result that when the reservoir was flooded, the mine shafts filled up and flooded the mine belonging to the plaintiff. The principle established in this case was that:

> "The person who for his own purposes brings onto his land and collects and keeps there anything likely to do mischief if it escapes, must keep it in at his peril, and, if he does not do so, is prima facie answerable for all the damage which is the natural consequence of its escape."

This rule establishes a form of strict liability for the person responsible for allowing anything to escape from his or her own property. The application of strict liability to pollution control cases may serve as an effective deterrent to polluters because it means that liability will arise regardless of the state of mind of the defendant. It is advantageous from the government's viewpoint because the difficult-to-prove subjective standards of carefulness or the extent of the defendant's awareness need not be dealt with. The basic rule is whoever is shown to have caused the pollution shall be liable for the related injury.[32]

Although the law has been successful in prosecuting individuals responsible for allowing transboundary pollution, a recent House of Lords decisions suggests that the use of the rule may not be as effective in the future.[33] It is worthwhile here to digress briefly from the strict discussion of the rule of *Rylands v. Fletcher* to consider the potential impact of this case. In *Cambridge Water Company v. Eastern Counties Leather*,[34] a factory was found to have dumped chemicals into the ground which had seeped through an underground waterway into a water source, poisoning the source and rendering it undrinkable by the community. The water authority that had, at considerable expense, attempted to extract water from the source for use by the community sued the factory for its damages.

The court found that the factory ought not be held responsible for the financial damage suffered by the water authority on the grounds that the factory could not have reasonably foreseen that the dumping of the chemicals would result in the damage caused. In fact it was shown that the chemicals had taken several years to flow to the location of the water source. Also it was found that the quality standards of drinkability had altered drastically over the years. Indeed, if the water quality at the time of the legal action had been measured taking into account the quality standards that had existed at the time that the chemicals had been originally dumped the water would have been deemed drinkable.

Generally speaking it is believed that this decision will to some extent limit the applicability of *Rylands v. Fletcher* to transboundary pollution control cases.[35] Ogus states that

> "... to reach this outcome by reference to a general principle that reasonable foreseeability of interference is a necessary condition of liability in all cases of private nuisance and *Rylands v. Fletcher* is, to say the least, controversial. Such a 'softening' of traditional notions of strict liability may create unnecessary obstacles to the enforcement of private property rights in circumstances in which such rights are more certain than those asserted in the *Cambridge Water* case."[36]

Non-Natural User — With specific regard to the application of the rule of *Rylands v. Fletcher*, the most important restriction on its use arises where a substance is kept on land by means of a non-natural user. Originally "non-natural" was interpreted to mean artificial but later it was defined as "abnormal". This interpretation was based on a description of non-natural as "some special use bringing with it increased danger to others and must not merely be the ordinary use of the land or such a use as is proper for the general benefit of the community."[37] It is now common for a court to find that an ordinary industrial use is a natural use if it is sited with due care and consideration. This view stems from a case where a judge decided not to find a defendant liable for an injury resulting from an explosion at the defendant's manufacturing plant for high explosives. The court asserted that:

> "Every activity in which a man engages is fraught with some possible element of danger to others. Experience shows that even from acts apparently innocuous, injury to others may result. The more dangerous the act the greater is the care that must be taken in performing it ... those who engage in obviously dangerous operations must be taken to know that if he does not take special precautions, injury to others may very well result. In my opinion it would be impracticable to frame a legal classification of things as things dangerous and things not dangerous, attaching absolute liability in the case of the former but not in the case of the latter ... accordingly I am unable to accept the proposition that in law the manufacturer of high explosive shells is a dangerous operation which imposes on the manufacturer an absolute liability."[38]

No personal liability — It is generally accepted that as the *Rylands v. Fletcher* rule applies to landowners, no personal liability will subsist from actions concerning the escape of things from a non-natural user of land. Negligence is the realm of personal liability.

Negligence

Under the rule of negligence, an action may be brought against a polluter if it can be shown that the polluter has not used reasonable care during the activity that caused the pollution and the injury. Negligence actions are not common in pollution control cases,[39] how-ever, its principles are often discussed in the context of other pollution control private law actions.[40] The reasons are two-fold. First a negli-gence action requires the finding of fault in the defendant, a difficult standard to meet. Negligence, therefore, would only be applied if trespass and nuisance were unavailable.[41] Furthermore the proof of negligence largely depends upon the state of technology and the tech-nological standards required by state regulation; as a consequence where an alleged polluter meets the legislated standards or the general standards required of other firms, the alleged polluter will not be found negligent.[42]

Although pollution control cases regarding negligence and private firms have been infrequent, more and more cases concerning potential negligence of the state have arisen. It would be most useful, therefore, if this discussion pursued the question of whether a government may be held negligent for pollution created as a result of governmental activity. The general principle is that a negligence action arises if a person, which may include the state, has caused injury as a result of action or omission when he or she should have reasonably foreseen the kind of injury that did occur.[43] The case of *Wycheron District Council v. National River Authority* concerned pollution of a river that re-sulted from the responsible council's alleged failure to prevent medical effluent from flowing into it.[44] Although the case was brought under a violation of the English Water Act, *obiter dicta* from the court's deci-sion urges that where facts suggest that the inactivity by the council amounted to possible negligence an action may arise. It should be noted, nevertheless, that it is a recognized principle that a public authority will not normally be held responsible for damages resulting from the authority's non-feasance. If the authority may be found at fault for its actions, however, liability may arise.[45]

Remedies for Private Law Actions

The remedies for common law actions that have been established include compensatory remedies, preventative remedies and abatement.

417

The goal of awarding damages at common law is to place the plaintiff in the position he or she would have been in had the wrongful act not occurred. There are two ways that this may be determined: either to figure out the clean up costs or to determine the difference in the value of the property after the effect of the pollution in comparison to its value prior to the pollution.

The order of an injunction is an equitable remedy. It prohibits a defendant from performing an activity which is causing pollution. An injunction will not be granted if the activity complained of is of insufficient gravity or duration to rationalize the prohibition of the defendant's activities.

An abatement refers to the elimination of a nuisance without seeking legal recourse.

Environmental Accountability and the Common Law

As mentioned above, the common law also provides legal measures to hold the government liable for acting outside the scope of its authority. This type of action is particularly relevant to environmental concerns where authorities may take decisions that show a bias against legitimate and legal environmental interests.[46]

Judicial Review

Environmental enforcement bureaucracies are public bodies responsible for enforcing laws designated by the legislature as stipulated in particular ordinances and regulations. They are not permitted to disobey the regulations, come to decisions unfairly or overstep the limitations of their power. Judicial review of a particular governmental decision may be brought if an enforcement authority can be shown to have exercised his or her power irresponsibly. There are three grounds for judicial review.

Authority to Decide — Judicial review may be brought where it is thought that a particular enforcement authority has gone beyond the authority designated to it by the legislation.

Discretion — The improper exercise of discretion may give rise to a judicial review. It includes taking into account irrelevant considerations, failing to take into account relevant considerations, and acting so irrationally that the decision taken could only be taken in bad faith.

Procedural Integrity — Procedural unfairness may also give rise to judicial review. It usually includes the notion that everyone is entitled to a fair hearing and that there should be no bias in a decision making process.

Remedies — An order of certiorari is used to quash an illegal administrative decision. If the possibility exists that a regulation will be implemented in an illegal way, then a prohibition is ordered to forbid this threat. An order of mandamus forces a statutory body to carry out its statutory requirements.

Commissioner for Administrative Complaints

Another form of administrative review concerns the office of the Commissioner for Administrative Complaints (CAC) and the Commissioner for Administrative Complaints Ordinance (Cap 397) 1988. The purpose of the CAC is to consider any administrative action by government where a person, who claims to have been injured by the unjust administrative action taken by the government, brings the complaint.[47] Maladministration includes inefficient, bad or improper administration, unreasonable conduct such as delay or discourtesy, and abuse of power such as the implementation of oppressive or discriminatory decisions.

Recently the office of the CAC was involved in a administrative action that directly related to the environmental protection policy of the Government. The case concerned the government approval of a golf course in the location of one of Hong Kong's country parks. The complainants involved the office of the CAC even though the case was being brought before the High Court. In the end the CAC agreed with the High Court Justice who issued an injunction upon the decision that the wrong section of the Country Parks Ordinance was used to approve a golf course. His overall recommendations were that there be improved public consultation, regular review of development applications, better decision making with regard to conservation and that further decisions with regard to development in parks should have an environmental impact assessment.[48]

Bill of Rights

Additionally the recently enacted Bill of Rights Ordinance has been considered as a tool to evaluate the fairness of the application of certain aspects of environmental legislation. It has been argued that recent amendments to the Air Pollution Control Ordinance (Cap 311) may fail to meet guarantees of substantive and procedural standards embodied in the Bill of Rights.[49] The Air Pollution Control Ordinance applies strict liability in the determination of an offence.[50] The amendments have increased the fines under the law and added possible prison terms. It has been asserted that the amendments may violate articles 11(1)[51] and 5(1)[52] of the Bill of Rights Ordinance because it is unfair to receive such a heavy "criminal" punishment without proving that the alleged malfeasor knew or should have known that the crime had been committed.

Other Forms of Civil Liability

Statutory Nuisance

Statutory nuisance represents a bridge between the common law and regulations. Statutory nuisance was created to allow for a speedy and efficient way to abate nuisances without resorting to the complex litigation of common law principles.
Noise Control Ordinance (Cap 400) — According to the Noise Control Ordinance, section 4(1):

> "Any person who between the hours of 11 pm and 7 am, or at any time on a general holiday in any domestic premises or public place makes or causes to be made any noise which is a source of annoyance to any person commits an offence."

An annoyance according to the ordinance means an annoyance that would not be tolerated by a reasonable person.
Air Pollution Control Ordinance (Cap 311) — According to Part III, section 9, when the authority determines that an air pollution nuisance exists or is imminent, the authority may issue an abatement notice to force the polluter to reduce the pollution.
Summary Offenses Ordinance (Cap 228) — The Summary Offenses Ordinance provides the legal mechanism to regulate "nuisances committed in public places".
Public Cleansing and Prevention of Nuisances (Cap 132) — This law restricts the nuisances including the dumping of litter.

Public Nuisance

Although public nuisance and private nuisance are similar, their primary difference is that a public nuisance is a nuisance that affects a wide class of individuals whereas private nuisance arises when individuals are adversely affected. Lord Denning M.R. tried to describe a public nuisance in the following way:

> "I prefer to look to the reason of the thing and to say that a public nuisance is a nuisance which is so widespread in its range or so indiscriminate in its effect that it would not be reasonable to expect one person to take proceedings on his own responsibility to

put a stop to it, but that it should be taken on the responsibility of the community at large."[53]

A public nuisance is a criminal offence which normally will be heard in the magistrate's court. Usually only the Attorney General will bring the actions on behalf of the public. A private citizen may bring an action in public nuisance by way of a "relator action".[54]

Restrictive Covenants

Although a restrictive covenant is not part of tort law, it is worthwhile to bring up here as its use effects the control of pollution through the control of the use of land. A restrictive covenant is used in Hong Kong in lease conditions to regulate the activities that are carried out on land.[55]

Problems with the Application of the Common Law of Environmental Protection

Despite the extensive array of legal measures available, the use of common law approaches to control pollution in Hong Kong is negligible. There are probably two explanations. The first concerns the costs involved in bringing the action. The second concerns the difficulty of proving a case based on common law principles.

The primary reason why more private law actions concerning environmental protection are not brought concerns the issue of expense. Generally speaking in pollution control cases, plaintiffs are individual citizens and defendants are larger industrial concerns, usually with access to a greater financial and legal resources than the plaintiff. The plaintiffs who are often harmed by pollution, normally cannot afford to bring private law actions to remedy the wrongful act. Accordingly this leads to the argument that the government ought to protect the interests of the weaker elements of our community through the promulgation and enforcement of effective pollution control laws.

Some scholars have misunderstood the economics of the situation and argued that more public regulation and more involvement of the government in the activities of the marketplace will only lead to greater and greater inefficiencies and waste.[56] They suggest that the government should not interfere in the marketplace, especially in the field of environmental protection, because the government does not have an incentive to behave in an efficient manner and therefore will only serve to distort the efficiency of the marketplace. Generously they agree that the marketplace does, at times, fail to serve the interests of the community, *e.g.* pollution, and that law is necessary to remedy the problem. Rather than advocate public action, they argue that private law actions would be the most effective means to correct the wrongs that arise as a result of the pollution. Regrettably they fail to appreciate the circularity of their argument; namely that the necessity of effective public law measures stems from the fact that individual plaintiffs cannot pursue litigation to deal with their pollution problems.

Another reason why common law approaches to pollution control are so infrequently used may be the lack of clarity and precision traditionally attributed to the application of the common law.[57] An analysis of the common law form of private nuisance reveals the ambiguity. As previously mentioned, private nuisance is an unreasonable interference with the reasonable use and enjoyment of one's own land. This definition, however, is vague and merely serves to raise a number of other questions such as: What is a reasonable use? What would be unreasonable?

Additionally, an interpretation of the locality doctrine, a notion meant to assist in the determination of whether a nuisance exists, provides further insight into why the application of the common law to environmental protection is problematic. The locality doctrine, as embodied in *St Helens Smelting Co v. Tipping* basically states that those who live in the town or close to factories have to expect a dirtier environment then those who live in the countryside. The bias of the doctrine seems to be in favour of the defendant. According to one commentator "what is a nuisance on the peak would not necessarily be a nuisance in Mongkok . . . If the standard of amenity is low, then the factory noise or smell or smoke will blend in with other noises, smells or smoke, and there will be no nuisance."[58]

The problem of proof is another considerable problem in common law actions. Proof that the common law has been breached is difficult to achieve because there needs to be evidence showing a link between the origins of pollution and the damage. For example, the nature of particulates emitted into the air is to travel along with the windstream, sometimes miles away from the source of the pollution. It is likely that the particulates may mix with other forms of pollution emitted by other factories. Proving which pollution caused the injury at the site of harm would likely prove extremely difficult.

Assessing reasonableness with regard to the dumping of pollutants is also extremely subjective. What may be acceptable to one party may not be acceptable to another. An issue which must be decided is which party's view of reasonableness needs to be given more weight, the polluter whose work is contributing to the economy of the area or the victim, whose health ought be protected by society. While it may be difficult to assign meaning to reasonableness, it is arguable that the difficulty in and of itself ought not to be ground for not bringing an action.

A final problem with private law controls are that they are reactive and compensatory rather than preventative. Anticipatory injunctions are rarely issued to prohibit potentially environmentally harmful practice. Private legal actions cannot permanently monitor a situation, leading to further potential environmental deterioration. Usually procedural reasons prohibit actions from being brought until the harm has arisen. It ought be noted, nevertheless, that the *realistic* possibility of private legal action may deter potential polluters from polluting.

Conclusion

Certainly the problem of pollution is today so serious that the government cannot neglect its responsibility to act; the point is especially compelling in the densely populated environs of Hong Kong. One possible approach to overcome the problem of litigation costs and uncertainty in private law actions would be for the government to provide some sort of a legal aid scheme for the environment. In this way not only will injured parties have their day in court but the courts will be forced to clarify the legal uncertainties which hinder the application of a just and sound environmental protection policy. In fact this approach would assist in the establishment of a more effective marketplace as wrongdoers would be suitably punished for environmental transgressions and victims of such transgressions would receive appropriate compensation.

One nevertheless must be realistic in the pursuit of environmental justice. It would be helpful to keep in mind the thoughts of the third Report of the Royal Commission on the Pollution of Rivers in 1867 in their consideration of private law actions:

> "It is an expensive remedy. For the same money which is spent over a hard fought litigation against a single manufacturer, a Conservancy Board armed with proper powers, might for years keep safe from all abuse, a long extensive river with hundreds of manufacturers situated on the banks."[59]

The most effective way to deal with the pollution problem is to strike a balance between the application of private law and public law actions. The alternative is no approach at all.

Notes

1 See Bachner, "Sweep Before Your Own Door: The Legal Concept of Environmentalism in the Pearl River Delta" in *Hong Kong, China and 1997: Essays in Legal Theory* (Hong Kong: Hong Kong University Press, 1993) 229–260. See also Bachner, "Coming Home to Roost: Pollution, Law and Economics in the People's Republic of China", V, 3, *Georgetown International Environmental Law Review* (Summer 1993) 635–650. See further Bachner, "No Law, No Sky: Economic Development and Environment in the Fifth Dragon", *Development in Southern China* (Hong Kong: Longman, 1995) 186–199. See also, Bachner, "The Quest for Environmental Justice in the People's Republic of China", *Colorado Journal of International Environmental Law and Policy* (Summer, 1996).
2 P. Wesley Smith, *An Introduction to the Hong Kong Legal System* (Hong Kong: Oxford University Press, 1993) 32–38 & 65–73. See also P. Wesley-Smith, *Constitutional and Administrative Law in Hong Kong*, (Hong Kong: Hong Kong and China Legal Studies, 1994).
3 *Gensberger v. Gensberger* [1968] *HKLR* 403.
4 P. Wesley Smith at 38. For examples of how Hong Kong judges have varied the English law to take into account local circumstances, see *Chan Hing-cheung v. R. Full Court*, Crim App. No 579 of 1974. See also 15 *Hong Kong Law Journal* (1974) 302.
5 I am grateful to Mr Anthony Upham for bringing to my attention material for this section.
6 There are also a set of courts with special jurisdiction that deal with legal areas including small claims, labour, land disputes, immigration, air transport licences, planning appeals and obscene articles among others.
7 Magistrates Ordinance, Cap 227.
8 See Summary Offenses Ordinance Cap 228.
9 Supreme Court Ordinance Cap 4.
10 District Court Ordinance Cap 336.
11 Bureau of Legislative Affairs of the State Council of the People's Republic of China, "The Laws and Regulations of the People's Republic of China Governing Foreign-Related Matters" (Beijing: The China Legal System Publishing Press, 1991) p.362.
12 *ibid.* p.372.
13 *ibid.*
14 See Wang Guiguo, "A Comparative Study on the Act of State Doctrine" in this book.
15 Bureau of Legislative Affairs of the State Council of the People's Republic of China, "The Laws and Regulations of the People's Republic of China Governing Foreign-Related Matters" (Beijing: The China Legal System Publishing House, 1991) p.364.
16 *Court of Final Appeal Ordinance* 1995.
17 For example, see Byron Weng, "The Hong Kong Model of 'One Country, Two Systems': Promises and Problems" in *The Basic Law and Hong Kong's Future* (Hong Kong: Butterworths, 1988) pp.67–84.
18 *South China Morning Post*, December 5, 1995, p.1.
19 R. Kidner, *Casebook on Torts* (London: Blackstone Press Ltd, 1994) 3rd ed, p.336. See also Bachner, Hong Kong Tort Law (Hong Kong: Hong Kong and China Legal Studies, 1996), p.80, [hereinafter cited as *Tort Law*].
20 *Saunders Clark v. Grosvenor Mansion Company Limited & D'Alles-Sandry* [1900] 2 Ch 373.

21 *Rushmer v. Polsue and Alfieri* [1906] Ch 234.
22 *Bellow v. Cement Company* [1948] Ir.R. 61.
23 *St Helens Smelting Co. v. Tipping.*
24 *Attorney General v. Gastonia Coaches Limited* [1977] RTR 219.
25 *Harrison v. Southwork and Vauxhall Water Co.* [1891] 2 Ch. 409.
26 *Robinson v. Kilvert* (1889) 41 Ch.D. 88.
27 M. Jones, *Textbook on Torts* (London: Blackstone Press Ltd., 1994) 4th ed., p.325. See also *Tort Law* at p.62.
28 *Jones v. Llanrwst UDC* [1908] All E.R. 922.
29 *Esso v. Southport Corporation* [1956] A.C. 218.
30 *Rylands v. Fletcher* (1865) H.&C. 774. See *Tort Law* at p.97.
31 R. Martin, *Law of Tort in Hong Kong* (Hong Kong: China and Hong Kong Law Studies, 1987) p.185.
32 Compare with Bill of Rights section below.
33 But see Glofcheski R., "Reasonable Foreseeability, Pollution and the Rule in *Rylands v. Fletcher*", 24, 2 *Hong Kong Law Journal* 189 (1994).
34 *Cambridge Water Company v. Eastern Counties Leather* [1994] 1 All E.R. 53.
35 See D Wilkinson, "*Cambridge Water Company v. Eastern Counties Leather plc*: Diluting Liability for Continuing Escapes", 57 *Modern Law Review* 799 (September 1994).
36 A Ogus, "Water Rights Diluted", 6, 1 *Journal of Environmental Law* 156 (1994).
37 *Rickards v. Lothian* [1913] A.C. 263.
38 *Read v. Lyons* [1947] A.C. 156.
39 See S Ball & S Bell, *Environmental Law: The Law and Policy Relating to the Protection of the Environment* (London: Blackstone Press, 1995) 3rd ed., p.185.
40 See *supra* endnotes 33–36 and accompanying text. See *Tort Law* at p.1.
41 See Ball & Bell, *supra* endnote 39.
42 *ibid.*
43 See Baillie, "Public and Private Remedies" in *Environmental Law in Hong Kong: Problems and Prospects* (Hong Kong: Hong Kong University Faculty of Law, 1993) 31–32.
44 See *Times*, September 17, 1992 as cited in Baillie.
45 *East Suffolk Catchment Board v. Kent* [1941] A.C. 74.
46 Compare with section on negligence *ante.*
47 P Wesley Smith, *Constitutional and Administrative Law in Hong Kong* (Hong Kong: China and Hong Kong Law Studies, 1994) p.126.
48 Hong Kong Environmental Law Association Newsletter, Volume I, Number 1, June 1994.
49 E. Epstein, "Air Pollution Control in Hong Kong: Where to Next?" 23 *Hong Kong Law Journal* 448, 456.
50 See also Water Pollution Control Ordinance (Cap 358), section 10. It states that it shall not be necessary for the prosecution to prove that the "acts or omissions in question, were accompanied by an intention, knowledge or negligence on the part of the defendant as to any element of the offence".
51 Section 11(1) of the Bill of Rights states that "everyone charged with a criminal offence shall have the right to be presumed innocent until proved guilty according to law".
52 Section 5(1) of the Bill of Rights Ordinance states that "everyone has the right to liberty and security of person. No one shall be subjected to arbitrary arrest or detention. No one shall be deprived of his liberty except on such grounds and in accordance with such procedures as are established by law.

⁵³ *Attorney General v. PYA Quarries Ltd* [1957] 1 All E.R. 894.
⁵⁴ Baillie, "Public and Private Remedies" p.21.
⁵⁵ See *The Attorney General v. Melhado Investments Ltd* [1983] *HKLR* 327 (holding that restrictive covenants restricting the land for agricultural purposes could not prohibit the leaseholder from using the land to store steel girders). See generally A Cooray, "Enforcement of Planning Control in Rural Hong Kong: Reflections on Recent Legislative Reforms", 1, 1 *Asia Pacific Law Review* 108 (1992).
⁵⁶ A Mitchell Polinsky, *An Introduction to Law and Economics* (Boston: Little, Brown & Co, 1983) pp.90–91. This specious argument has even been made for Hong Kong. See Kwong J., *Market Environmentalism: Lessons for Hong Kong* (Hong Kong: The Chinese University Press, 1990). *Cf. supra* endnote 1.
⁵⁷ For a comprehensive discussion of the problem, see Ball and Bell, *Environmental Law* (London: Blackstone Press Ltd, 1995) 3d ed., pp.167–201.
⁵⁸ Martin, *Law of Tort in Hong Kong* (Hong Kong: China and Hong Kong Law Studies, 1987) p.182.
⁵⁹ As cited in Ball and Bell at p.182.